LEGENDARY SPORTING RIFLES

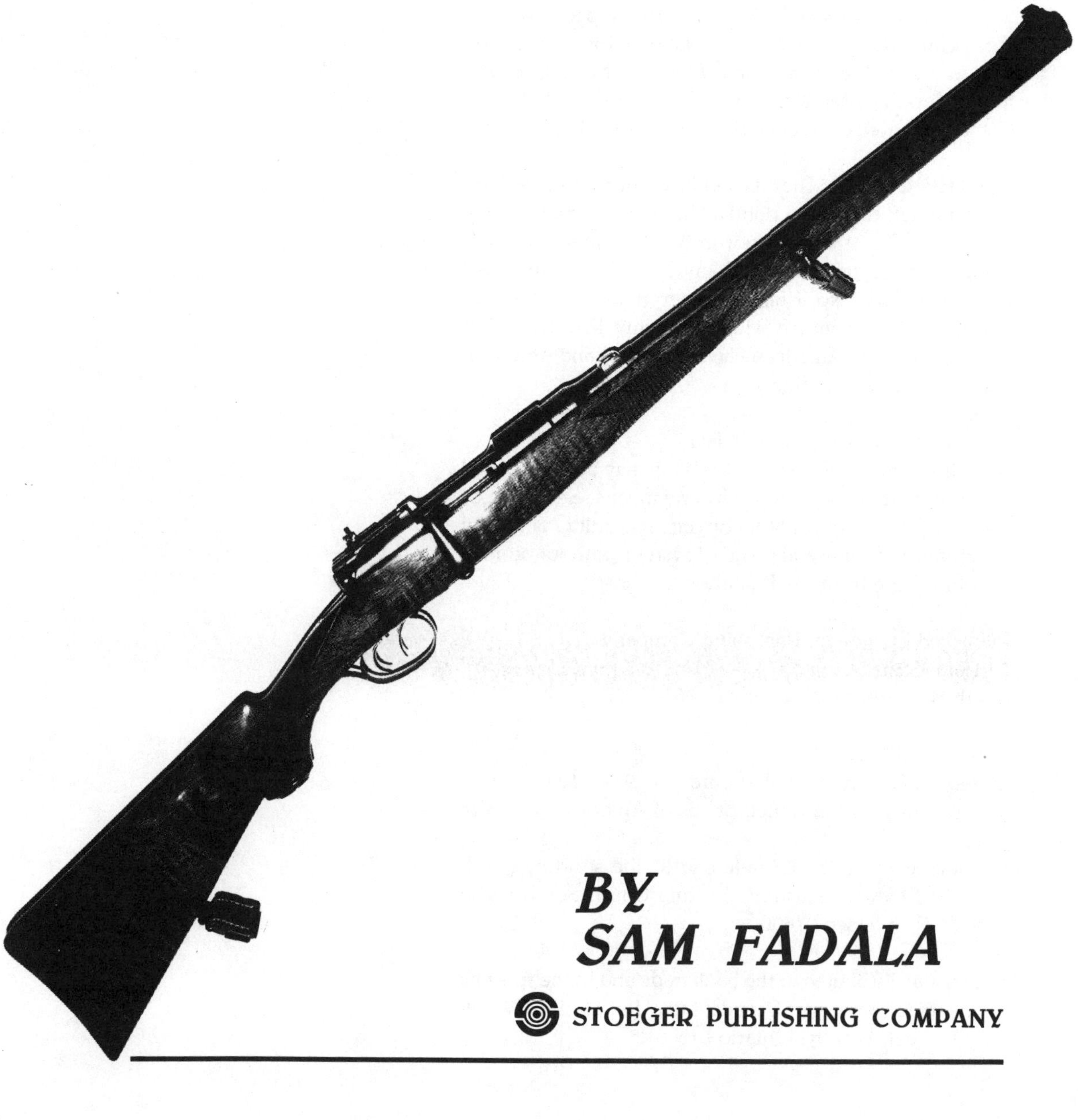

**BY
SAM FADALA**

⊙ STOEGER PUBLISHING COMPANY

COVER PHOTO and DESIGN: Ray Wells
BOOK DESIGN: Cat Alfano
EDITOR: Charlene Cruson Step
RESEARCH: Nancy Fadala

PHOTO/ILLUSTRATION CREDITS: pages 7, 76, 78, 80, 81, 82 (top), 168, 169, 177, 186–*Remington Arms in American History*, by Alden Hatch (Revised Edition) © 1972 by Remington Arms Co., Inc., courtesy Remington Arms; pages 11, 40–Cat Alfano; page 14–Nancy Fadala; pages 31, 35, 36–courtesy U.S. Repeating Arms; page 34–from *American Rifleman*, courtesy the National Rifle Assn.; 212, 215, 216, 217, 218–from *Marlin Firearms*, by Lt. Col. William S. Brophy, used with permission of Stackpole Books, Cameron & Kelker Streets, Harrisburg, PA 17103.

ON THE COVER: The "Legendary" rifles pictured are (from top left to bottom right) a Flintlock Kentucky Longrifle; Ruger No. 1 Creedmoor in 45-70 caliber with half-octagon barrel, engraved by John E. Wallace with raised gold inlay; Ruger No. 1 Light Sporter in 30-06 caliber, engraved by Paul Lantuch with Old Army Revolver 1816 Calvary saber and American flag on one side and American Eagle on the reverse side.

Copyright © 1992 by Sam Fadala
All rights reserved. No part of this book may be reproduced or transmitted in any form or by any means, electronic or mechanical, including photocopying, recording, or by any information storage and retrieval system, without permission in writing from the Publisher.

Published by Stoeger Publishing Company
55 Ruta Court
South Hackensack, New Jersey 07606

ISBN: 0-88317-167-8
Library of Congress Catalog Card No.: 91-67406
Manufactured in the United States of America

Distributed to the book trade and to the sporting goods trade by Stoeger Industries, 55 Ruta Court, South Hackensack, New Jersey 07606

In Canada, distributed to the book trade and to the sporting goods trade by Stoeger Canada, Ltd., Unit 16, 1801 Wentworth Street, Whitby, Ontario L1N 8R6

PREFACE

John Rivers turned the old gun over and over in his calloused hands, inspecting every inch of it. "My dad bought this little rifle in Texas before I was born; he never did know who owned it before him," the ranchman said. "I wish it could talk. What a story it could tell." He traced a finger over a long scar etched into the wood, wondering how it got there. Three neat notches were cut near the toe of the stock—more mystery. Rivers looked at the front sight, obviously bent at one time by accident, then bent back again on purpose to straighten it. The buttplate was chipped. Scratches coursed through the wood, matching the weathered lines of the old cowboy's face. I was wishing the lever-action 44-40 Winchester could talk, too, as I watched firelight play over its speckled receiver. The idea for this book was born that night on the ranch as my friend and I meandered through his collection of firearms.

Rivers admired the sporting arm I had brought with me to hunt whitetails along the creekbottom. A Mannlicher 9×56mm Model of 1906 that left the factory in 1921, the rifle was sitting in unfired condition when I found it in a gunshop in Wyoming. I swapped for it. The carbine had no personal story to tell, since it had never been in the field until I owned it, but its lineage was fascinating. The Mannlicher was the favorite rifle of many famous sportsmen of the early 20th century. I realized that night on the ranch that all successful sporting rifles offered the same interesting history—a biography—if you will allow the loose application of the word. When was the rifle developed? Who designed it? And for what specific sporting purpose? How many different styles or variations did it boast? How well did the public of sport shooters receive it? What cartridge(s) was the rifle chambered for and with what ballistics? These are some of the questions I asked myself. The answers to them have created the stories that unfold in this book.

ABOUT THE AUTHOR

Sam Fadala is Technical Editor for *Handloader/Rifle* magazines, Feature Editor for *Muzzleloader Magazine*, and Special Projects Editor for *Guns Magazine*. A freelance writer since 1969, Fadala is featured nationally in such magazines as *Gun World, Outdoor Life, Sports Afield* and *Bow and Arrow Hunter*. He has written 15 books at last count, including *The Book of the Twenty-Two: The All-American Caliber* (1989) and *Great Shooters of the World* (1990), both Stoeger publications (see below). An avid shooter with muzzleloader, 22-caliber rifle or bow, Fadala has stalked most of the western U.S., Canada, Alaska and part of Africa. He lives in Casper, Wyoming, where he and his family (four children) thrive on the outdoor life. Sam's wife Nancy assists with the writing projects by doing some of the research and working the bugs out of the computer.

OTHER STOEGER BOOKS by SAM FADALA

Great Shooters of the World (1990)
Fascinating stories of the big game hunters, marksmen, trick shooters, barrel-makers, arms authors and others who devoted much of their lives to the world of shooting. From Selous, the ivory hunter, to Jack O'Connor, the writer and hunter, to Annie Oakley, Harry Pope and Teddy Roosevelt—every chapter is filled with shooting information, biographical tidbits and entertaining anecdotes. Fully illustrated.

The Book of the Twenty-Two (1989)
From the 22 BB Cap through the powerful and unique 226 Barnes centerfire big game cartridge, this book is about the All-American 22 caliber, its ballistics, histories, cartridge developments, accuracy and more. Fully illustrated.

CONTENTS

1. THE KENTUCKY LONGRIFLE—*Early American Accuracy* 7
2. THE PLAINS RIFLE—*King of the Western Frontier* 19
3. HUNT, JENNINGS AND VOLCANIC RIFLES—*Rapid Fire, Rockets and Repeaters* 31
4. THE HENRY RIFLE—*Arm and Ammo Succeed* 39
5. WINCHESTER'S 1866—*The Popular "Yellow Boy"* 47
6. MODEL 1885 WINCHESTER—*The Single-Shot Excels* 55
7. THE SHARPS SINGLE-SHOT—*Bison-Hunting Breechloader* 65
8. REMINGTON'S ROLLING BLOCK—*Buffalo Runner's Friend* 75
9. THE 1873 WINCHESTER—*Centerfire Success* 85
10. WINCHESTER'S 1886—*A Repeating Powerhouse* 95
11. THE WINCHESTER '92—*Short, Slick and Versatile* 105
12. WINCHESTER'S MODEL 94—*The Sportsman's "Old Faithful"* 115
13. THE 1895 WINCHESTER—*First Box Magazine Lever-Action* 125
14. THE MAGICAL MANNLICHER—*Big Game Superiority* 135
15. MODEL 70 WINCHESTER—*The Rifleman's Rifle* 147
16. WINCHESTER MODEL 71—*Modernized Lever-Action* 157
17. REMINGTON AUTOLOADERS—*Firepower With Fingertip Control* 167
18. REMINGTON'S MODEL 700—*A High-Power, Bolt-Action* 175
19. THE REMINGTON PUMPS—*Reliable and Trail-Ready* 185
20. SAVAGE MODEL 99—*Action So Smooth* 193
21. MARLIN'S MODEL 1894—*Side-Ejecting Safety* 203
22. THE 1895 MARLIN—*Punch with Repeatability* 211
23. THE MARLIN MODEL 336—*Long Lasting, No Nonsense* 221
24. SPRINGFIELD SPORTERS—*A "Best" in Customizing* 231
25. SPORTING MAUSERS—*Potent and Accurate* 241
26. RUGER'S SINGLE-SHOT—*The No. 1 That's No. 1* 253
27. WEATHERBY RIFLES—*High-Tech, Tall Quality* 261
28. SAKO SPORTING RIFLES—*Precision Nonpareil* 273
Index 284

THE KENTUCKY LONGRIFLE
EARLY AMERICAN ACCURACY

1

Early American longrifles were individual in nature. Skillfully crafted one at a time, they reflected the spirit and virtues of the first settlers—they were rugged, honest and diverse. Hundreds of variations existed, right down to repeating flintlocks and halfstock models. So a look at original rifles of Early America reveals many different types. With only a little license, however, and even less imagination, it's possible to project a picture of a truly American long arm: the "Kentucky Rifle." More properly called a Pennsylvania/Kentucky rifle, this unique product was crafted by the keen minds and gifted hands of many Pennsylvania gunmakers who settled in from various parts of central Europe. Schools developed and were named by

Original Kentucky-style flintlock made by E. Remington, circa 1816–1846.

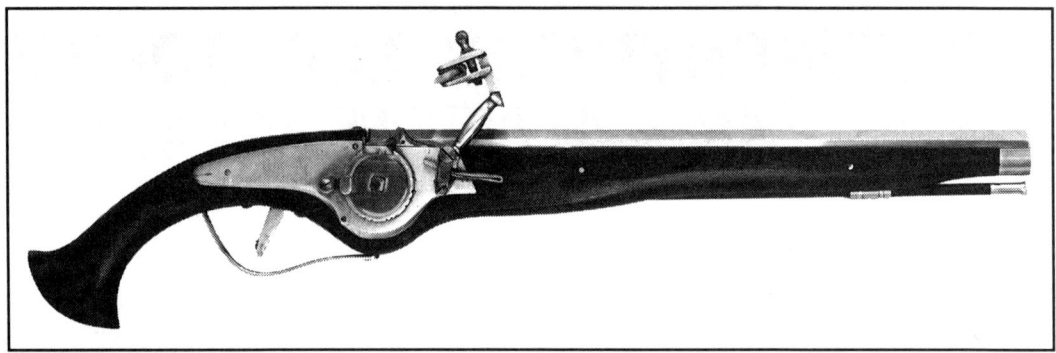

A look at a wheellock, the precursor to the flintlock used in the American longrifle, reveals the circular lock with its wheel of pyrites.

style and by the counties in Pennsylvania from which the guns originated. The early gunmakers of Pennsylvania and their artwork continue to be separated by counties. An expert gun collector or student of firearms often recognizes a rifle from the Pennsylvania county of its origin: Bedford, Lancaster, Clarion, Jefferson, Elk and others.

We call these long guns Kentucky rifles to this day because the name just stuck. Even in 1848, a gunmaker from Pittsburgh, Pennsylvania, advertised his handmade firearms as Kentucky rifles, even though not one of them came from, or followed the design of any arm built in, that state. Possibly, the term "Kentucky Rifle" caught on because of a ballad that became popular after the Battle of New Orleans. Of all battles for American independence, this one stands out in the minds of riflemen because of the sharpshooters from Kentucky and Tennessee. Their keen eye was brought to bear upon the British in a most decisive way, with only a handful of Americans killed or wounded while hundreds of the enemy were dropped. The ballad applauded these men and their rifles, especially the rifles of Kentucky. Daniel Boone's exploits into the unknown region of bluegrass fame no doubt added impetus to the rifle's name as well.

Although most shooters know what a Kentucky rifle is, generally speaking, the experts are much more careful to place each American longrifle in its proper niche whenever possible. And such isolation is possible quite often. Students such as Colonel Russell Harriger of Harriger Hollow near Brookville (PA) have dedicated years of careful research to the clarification and pigeon-holing of the various American longrifles. This precise study has revealed the names, locations, shops, exact rifles, even price sheets and business records of many handcrafters of America's first recognizably unique firearm. Harriger, for example, studied and wrote about gunmakers from only three Pennsylvania counties in his book *Longrifles of Pennsylvania, Volume 1, Jefferson, Clarion and Elk Counties*, a title printed in the George Shumway Publisher's Longrifle Series in 1984. Colonel Harriger devoted his search to exactly 46 gunsmiths: 23 from Jefferson County, 15 from Clarion County and 8 from Elk County.

Of course, it is not geography that truly delineates American longrifles. It is the hand of the gunmaker. But regionally isolated longrifle types are recognizable. Study is so keen that many experts can categorize various American longrifles by virtue of their specific features. For example, researchers discovered that longrifles made in New England often had stocks built of walnut wood, as opposed to maple, cherry or other stock materials of the era. New York guncrafters used different designs when they carved a gunstock as compared with the designs of Pennsylvania gunmakers. And if a rifle carried an extreme amount of ornate silver inlay work, chances are that piece was handmade by a smith living in Ohio. The study is ongoing. It will never die because interest in America's first rifle designs will persist as long as shooters and shooting endure in this country.

INSPIRATION FROM ABROAD

Although American pride may compel us to believe that our forebears invented many major firearm refinements leading to the Kentucky rifle, the fact is, this is not true. Most of the major developments that made the Kentucky rifle great arose on other soils. So did shooting developments that did not directly affect the Kentucky rifle, but had much to do with arms that followed it. Good black powder was born abroad. Smokeless powder also came from across the sea. The envelope bullet (or jacketed bullet) was born in Europe, too, so long ago in fact that these projectiles preceded the wide use of smokeless powder. Although jacketed bullets and smokeless powder had nothing to do directly with the American longrifle, rifling and patched round balls did, and were paramount to the long-range accuracy of the Kentucky rifle. Rifling was around long before there was an America, and while our early gunmakers are credited with the patched ball, the truth is, patched projectiles were mentioned in writings long before the Pilgrims saw Plymouth Rock. To understand the development of the Kentucky rifle, let's travel back across the vast ocean to the Old Country, where the original masters lived and worked before they immigrated to America.

The rifle of the central European region that predated gunmaker immigration to America was the Jaeger. As with American arms, no one specific rifle model was popular in any given period. However, the Jaeger (which means "hunter" or "sportsman" in German) was a rather short-barreled piece in comparison to the pole vault length of some guns. The Jaeger barrel measured 30 to 36 inches (a few were 40 inches long). Considering that the Jaeger was not used against pachyderms or dangerous game, calibers were quite large, 60s and 70s being common. Yet, these rifles were rather light in weight. I handled an original Jaeger in 70 caliber that weighed

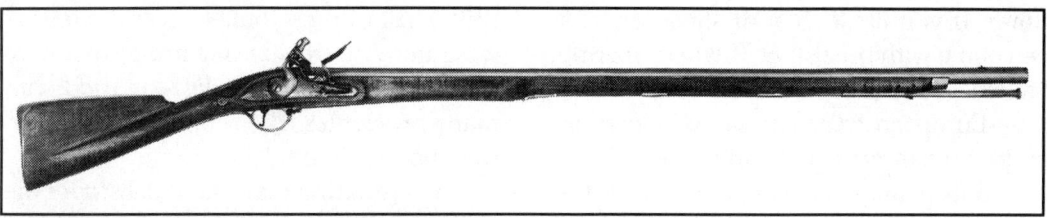

Students of the American longrifle often compare it to the British Brown Bess musket, a smoothbore flintlock of roughly 75 caliber. Rifling made the American longrifle far more accurate than the Brown Bess.

under 8 pounds.

A product of the late 18th century, the Jaeger was a flintlock. Wheellocks were reliable. The quickly revolving wheel of this design generated a good shower of sparks for powder ignition. But, wheellocks were comparatively expensive to make. Flintlocks were not, in all regards, as reliable as the wheellocks that preceded them. But they were cheaper to manufacture and did not have to be wound up with a key as the wheellocks; they were simpler, smaller and well-liked by sportsmen as well as soldiers.

Of high importance was the stock design. The Jaeger was made to fire comfortably from the shoulder, which offered far greater control of the piece and consequently better accuracy than previous arms that were held primarily in the hands. The Jaeger stock allowed the shoulder to absorb recoil rather than the hands taking on all of the rifle's kick. The octagonal barrel of the Jaeger was rifled, not smooth, which produced sufficient accuracy for all big game hunting in European forests. Barrels were often swamped; that is, they started large at the breech end, tapered inward at the middle of the barrel, and then flared out again toward the muzzle. This was a cosmetic touch, for swamping did nothing to enhance performance.

Mentally hold the Jaeger in your hands and explore it carefully. It's built around a smallish lock of flintlock ignition with a nicely designed wooden stock for the times. If you lift it to your shoulder, you can aim it with precision. This was the rifle known to the early gunmakers of America—European transplants—who were to build the famous American longrifle.

But—while the Jaeger was fine for hunters abroad—it wasn't suited to the needs of the New World. The caliber was overly large for the eastern seaboard where deer, wild turkeys and self-protection against human threats were the major uses of a shoulder gun. The Jaeger was well-steadied at the shoulder, but wouldn't it have been better for offhand shooting if it had carried more weight up front? So bore size shrank and barrel length stretched. Depending upon which expert you choose to believe, the average size of the Kentucky rifle's bore is said to run from 38 to 45 caliber. Caliber 38 is often mentioned, but visits to museums and gun collections show many 45s.

The Kentucky longrifle fired a good many bullet types. One was a round ball with a deep indentation (groove) all the way around its circumference. The value of the impression in this lead projectile, if ever there was any, escapes the mind of the modern ballistician. Another grooved missile appeared as two pointed shankless bullets stuck together end to end—ballistic value doubtful. A different Kentucky projectile almost defies verbal description. It appeared as two round balls connected by a shank, with a groove all the way around the shank as well as a groove around each round ball—three grooves in all. Still another bullet looked like the pointed end of a lead bullet, only with no shank and a deep recess in the base. Inside of that recess or cavity was a pellet, the idea being that the force of gas behind the pellet would drive it forward into the cavity, thus spreading the bullet out to fully engage the rifling. All of these bullets, sources reveal, were under bore size, each one requiring a patch. So the Kentucky was tried with many projectiles. The round ball, however, was the most popular.

Considering that round balls were the type of bullets fired most often (bullet referring to all projectiles, not only elongated missiles), caliber 45 is not too large because a 45-caliber round ball runs undersized so that it can be rammed downbore wrapped in a patch (made of cloth or leather which would take up the space or "windage" in the bore). A .440-inch round ball fired in a 45-caliber American longrifle weighs only 128 grains. That is not much lead. However, the Kentucky rifle's barrel was large enough across the flats (width of the octagonal barrel) that reasonable powder charges could be installed downbore without risk of damage to the breech. Therefore, velocity was comparatively high. The rather small powder charges used in the big-bore Jaeger rifles provided only modest muzzle velocity, so trajectory was looping. This made the Jaeger a short-range firearm. The Kentucky, by comparison, was capable of shooting its round ball in the neighborhood of 2000 feet per second at the muzzle, offering what was then, fairly flat trajectory.

The small ball provided another important benefit: a lot of ammo could be carried. When American armed forces went from the 30-06 Springfield cartridge to the 308 Winchester cartridge, military experts immediately listed ammo portability as a big plus. Same for the old Kentucky rifle. A single .690-inch round ball for a 70-caliber Jaeger rifle weighs 494 grains. As already noted, a 45-caliber .440-inch ball only weighs 128 grains. Carry only fifteen 70-caliber round balls and you're packing about a pound of weight. In 45 caliber, that same pound amounts to about 55 bullets.

Not all Kentucky rifles were of smaller bore size, however. Bores ran from 35 to 60 caliber, but the big ones were rare. Because bore sizes were primarily small, most

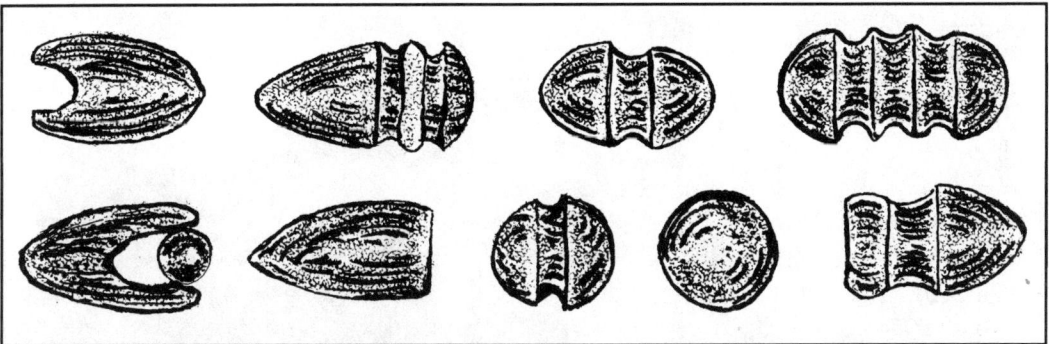

Although the Kentucky longrifle was capable of shooting bullets of diverse shapes, the round ball was by far the most popular. All the designs shown above were loaded with cloth patches and not lubricated in the grooves.

Kentucky rifles shot accurately with rifling twists of around one turn in 40 inches (1:40). As the lead sphere grows in diameter, it gains in mass far out of proportion, as clearly seen above with 45- and 70-caliber round bullets. The heavier the missile, the less RPS—revolutions per second—required to stabilize it in flight. The English gunmaker seemed to understand this better than his American counterpart. British rifles shooting heavy round balls often carried very slow rates of twist. An example is a 70-caliber English sporting rifle that had a 1:90 rate of twist, one revolution of the round ball in 90 inches, which provided ample RPS to spin that big globe of lead on its axis all the way from muzzle to target.

The flintlock American longrifle was a firearm of outstanding accuracy and served many an early settler. Here the author uses a pan powder dispenser to trickle a small amount of FFFFg black powder into the pan of a flintlock rifle.

Rifling was normally cut with six to eight grooves, incidentally.

In addition to the advantages discussed above, the Kentucky Rifle had a few other pluses. The smaller caliber, even with a decent powder charge downbore, delivered light and highly manageable recoil. The long barrel offered a lot of up-front weight and also a long sight radius—distance between front sight and back sight—for a clear sight picture. The drop of the buttstock brought the sight picture clearly to the eye of the shooter from the offhand stance. This meant high accuracy in the hands of a skilled marksman. Today this fact is easily proved when original Kentucky longrifles are benchtested. Groups made with iron sights (no scopes used) are on a par with groups provided by modern big game rifles also using iron sights. In theory, the human eye is not supposed to be discerning enough to provide groups of much better than four inches at 100 yards—in theory, remember. In actual practice, a good rifleman with a properly loaded American longrifle can make groups about half that size—if not regularly, at least often enough to prove that the capability of the rifle, accuracy-wise, is there.

Add it all up. The American longrifle was unique and special: modest caliber;

light recoil; long sight radius; in fact quite well balanced; easy to hold steady in the offhand shooting posture; accurate (due to a carefully rifled bore); powerful enough for self-protection and for the game normally hunted in the region. Accuracy and good rifle management promoted excellent bullet placement, so what was lost due to the lightweight bullet was at least in part regained because the missile could be put right on target.

The Kentucky rifle offered even more. It also had a good trigger system and good sights. Triggers of the multiple-lever (double-set) system were common. The rear trigger was the "set"; the front trigger, the "hair." Pulling the rear trigger back set the front trigger so that it could be touched off with only ounces, not pounds, of pressure. These fine triggers were in part responsible for the delivered accuracy of the Kentucky rifle. Instead of the sights and line of bore being forced away from their respective aimpoints by the working of a "hard" trigger pull, the Kentucky's trigger pull did not disturb aim. When the sights were properly lined up, the shooter maintained control of his rifle and "touched her off." The multiple-lever trigger system promoted bullet placement, in short.

The iron sights were of the open variety, with a simple blade-type front and an equally simple rear notch. These sights were far more refined than modern shooters might think. A "fine bead" could be taken that did not visually obliterate the target. "Barking a squirrel," whereby the hunter shoots the ball beneath the squirrel and into the limb of the tree that the squirrel is standing on, rather than hitting the edible target directly, was possible with such good sights. Debris lifted from the limb dispatched the little game animal. Of course, peep sights (aperture-type) could be found on a Kentucky rifle. Peeps were certainly nothing new to early American gunsmiths. The peep sight had been used on Chinese and Roman crossbows long before gunpowder was an influence in warfare.

THE TOUCHY FLINTLOCK IGNITION

The biggest disadvantage of the Kentucky Rifle was its flintlock ignition system. It was not entirely surefire, of course, although it was far more reliable than modern gunwriters often suggest. Had flintlocks been as primitive in function as some writers say, the early settler would have been driven into the Atlantic by hostile native Indians or eaten by bears. On the other hand, the flintlock rifle was slow-loading and getting off that fast second shot was difficult at best. Some of the same marksmen who whipped the British at the Battle of New Orleans during the War of 1812 were themselves defeated by Indians who quickly shot arrow after arrow, while the riflemen laboriously tried to reload their arms. The result was success for the archers.

To prepare the gun for shooting, the rifleman would drop an appropriate charge of black powder downbore, followed by a patched ball introduced to the breech by the ramrod. Then fine powder was installed in the pan, the pan cover closed and the trigger pulled. Things could go wrong. For starters, the channel (touchhole) leading from the pan to the main charge of powder in the breech of the rifle could be clogged. Some original shooting bags were found to have a feather in them, the quill of which was squashed down in a perfectly cylindrical shape. Some arms experts believed that the tip of the feather was forced into the touchhole to block it during the loading process. This would prevent powder from the breech from clogging the touchhole. It makes sense and in fact has been shown to aid flintlock ignition integrity today. After the powder was downbore and packed solid by the force of the patched ball, only then was the quill withdrawn, leaving a clear path for the flame from the pan to detonate the charge in the breech.

The frizzen, also called a frizzle, had to be clean and oil-free. The flint held in the jaws of the hammer (also called a cock) fell forward against the face of the frizzen, thereby scraping hot curls of metal away from the surface of the frizzen. The ignited metal bits fell into the pan and its cargo of fine-grain powder, thereby creating a flash.

A "flash in the pan" was not enough, and that term referred to nothing more than the pan powder going off without ignition of the main charge. This was a misfire. The rifle did not go off at all. There could also be a hangfire, whereby the flame from the pan did its work, but not right away. So the rifle went off like this: Fttttt! — Boom! That lag can be disconcerting to a shooter's concentration. But the best flintlock marksmen of yesterday—and today—have great control over their rifles. They have learned to maintain the sight picture right on target *after* the trigger is pulled, so that if there is a lag before the rifle goes off, the sights will still be aligned.

Black powder made the Kentucky rifle

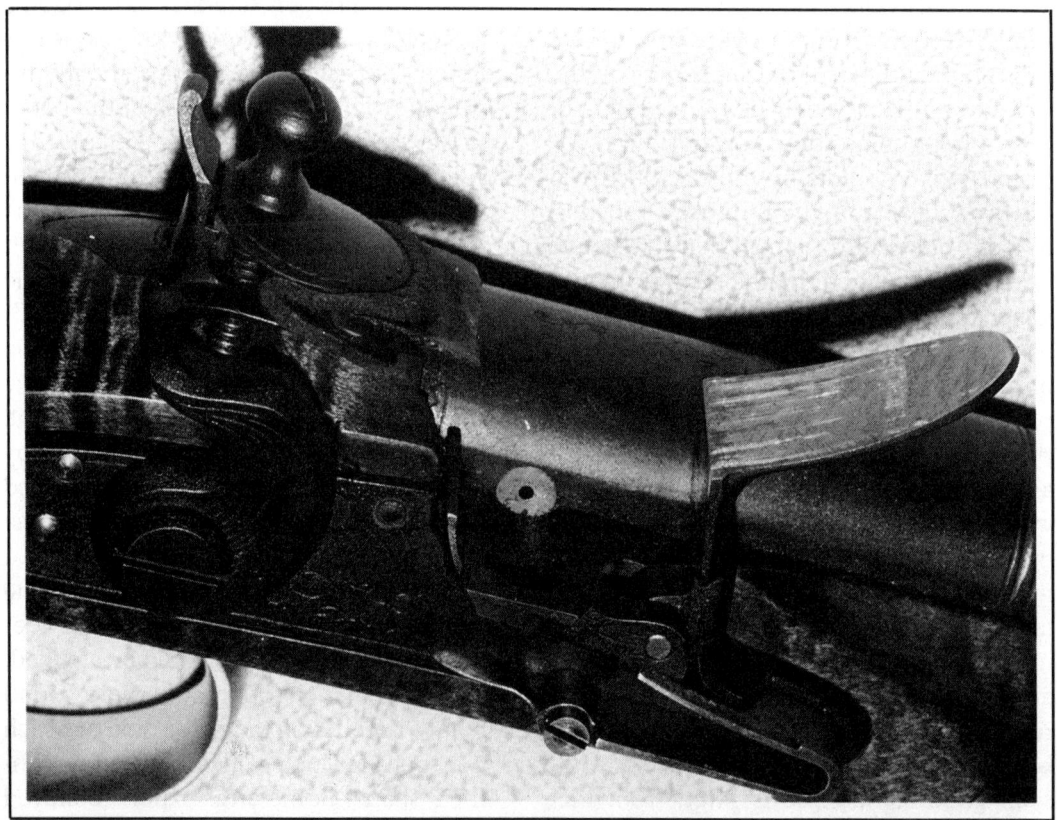

This original flintlock rifle displays proper touchhole positioning, rather high on the barrel flat so pan powder will not invade the touchhole, thereby creating a fuse and slowing down ignition.

all the more difficult to master. A mechanical mixture of saltpeter, charcoal and sulfur, it is hygroscopic, meaning it tends to attract moisture. "Keep your powder dry" was imperative advice. Furthermore, black powder is corrosive. It does not etch metal "on sight," but it does cake up and foul the bore of the firearm, as well as the touchhole of the flintlock. This means that the muzzleloader has to be cleaned after a shooting session, and also during shooting. If it's not cleaned during repeated shooting, pretty soon it will be impossible to ram a patched ball home. Even though shooting a flintlock could be tricky, many thousands of marksmen mastered it.

Kentucky rifles by the thousands underwent change around the middle of the 19th century. The percussion cap had been invented. The idea of cap 'n' ball shooting did not catch on overnight and many marksmen stayed with the flintlock system. But as with other imposing inventions, the percussion style of ignition finally took over. When it did, thousands of Kentucky rifles were destined for obsolescence, unless they could be updated. And of course they could be. Rifles had already been returned to gunshops everywhere for "freshing out," which meant to cut a new larger bore, effectively eliminating the old pitted bore. Certain rather odd calibers found in some original rifles probably resulted from freshing out, whereby a 45-caliber rifle bore was enlarged to 48 caliber, for example. So returning a rifle to the gunsmith to give it a new lease on life was nothing new for 19th-century shooters.

After the percussion cap caught on, the flintlock was transformed into a caplock rifle. By enlarging the touchhole and inserting a small drum and nipple assembly, the flintlock effectively became a percussion firearm. The drum part of the unit is

The drum and nipple was an ingenious device used to turn a flintlock into a percussion rifle. The threaded portion was screwed into the side flat of the rifle where the touchhole used to be and a nipple was installed in the top of the drum as shown here.

a metal cylinder with its own flash channel. The nipple is seated on this metal cylinder and a percussion cap is placed on the cone of the nipple. When the percussion cap is struck by the hammer and detonated, the resulting spark travels through the channel in the drum into the main charge of powder in the breech, very much the same as the flame from the pan once traveled through the touchhole. This conversion process is important to know about because it explains why we can find examples of percussion Kentucky longrifles today that were originally flintlocks.

THE GUNMAKER'S CRAFT

In general, the overall style of the Kentucky or American longrifle is clearly evident, with its long octagonal barrel, slender full-length stock (a few half-stock models were made, though), flintlock ignition system and graceful appointments. The venerable patchbox of the Jaeger was retained on many American longrifles, although not every example has one. Consisting of a metal hinged cover that revealed a recess in the buttstock, the patchbox was a perfect place to store extra patches as well as small tools and whatever else the individual marksman could fit into the cavity. The metal furniture, often of brass and custom-fitted to the rifle, included ramrod thimbles, toe plates, buttplates, lock plates, upper and lower tangs and other parts as well as inlay embellishments.

The barrel, usually 40 to 48 inches in length (rarely over 44 inches), was forged of steel and might be tapered. One example of an original Kentucky rifle has a breech $1\,{}^{1}/_{8}$ inches across the flats, the barrel tapering down to 1 inch across the flats at the muzzle. Most barrels were finished in a plum brown color, accomplished by a rusting process. The exterior of the barrel was chemically rusted until the desired effect was achieved, then it was doused with oil to retard further rusting. The end result was a soft pleasing hue.

The stock, sometimes made of ordinary walnut, cherry, maple or other woods, might also be crafted of beautiful curly maple or other highly figured fancy wood. A hand-rubbed oil finish offered protection for the wood as well as soft luster that accentuated the grain. Along with metal inlays, thin wire inlays might also be carefully recessed in the wood, a handsome touch. Many Kentucky rifle stocks carried additional carving, which lent beauty as well as individuality to the piece.

Who was the gunmaker that combined metal and wood to create this functional work of art? How did he work? And where? Most often the Kentucky longrifles, as well as the attending accouterments (tools), were crafted in a one-man gunshop. It is impossible at this late date, in spite of existing records, to know exactly how these shops were run. We do know that they were not always one-man operations. Apprentices were very much a part of the program, with young men given over to the care, tutoring and personal management of a master gunmaker.

The master gunmaker was multi-talented. In addition to making the obvious barrel and stock, he handcrafted numerous gun parts, usually exclusive of the lock, which he tried to purchase from a lockmaker, thereafter tuning and fitting the lock to the rifle. The gunmaker was also responsible for creating the proper powder charge load for a specific rifle, as well as a correct mould to cast the round bullet (as well as other shapes). Special moulds, powder measures and other accouterments remain in collections to this day.

Because sights were of the "fixed" variety, the riflesmith probably sighted in his creation for its future owner, rather than the hunter/shooter sighting the piece in for himself. Sights had to be manipulated by filing or drifting either front or rear sight in its respective dovetail notches in order to put the group on target. For example, a taller front sight would be installed to make the next bullet hit lower on the target, in contrast to filing down the front sight to make the next bullet hit higher. The front sight could be drifted left in its dovetail notch to make the next bullet strike to the right on the target, or drifted right to make the next projectile hit to the left. The rear sight, in contrast, is moved in the same direction the shooter wants the next shot to go. Such undertakings may seem primitive to modern shooters who are used to adjustable sights that require minimal

Muzzleloaders, then and now, carried numerous attending tools, among them the powder horn and powder flask. Making powder horns, often with exquisite carving, became an art in itself.

movement with a screwdriver in order to affect a change in point of impact on the target. But in fact these fixed sights were quite good. Plus, once calibrated, they tended to stay in line permanently.

Accouterments had to be made by someone, of course, and that task fell upon the gunmaker or his apprentice, too. Shooters also made some of their own hardware and software. There were and still are so many attending tools for muzzleloaders. And once the caplock became widely used, the gunmaker was soon in the business of supplying parts for both percussion and flintlock firearms simultaneously. Nipples (also known as "tubes") were handmade, as were worms, screws, jags, vent or touchhole picks, loading blocks, short starters, nipple wrenches and other small gadgets. They were fitted into shooting bags, also known as hunting bags and erroneously referred to nowadays as "possibles bags," which they are not. Ornate or simple, the bags were generally fitted with a strap for easy carrying on the shooter's shoulder.

Powder horn handcrafting became an art of its own. The powder horn was not a hangover from ancient times that was used simply for its historical interest. It had distinct merits. Horn in and of itself is hard and strong, and on the trail could take quite a beating without cracking. The powder horn was non-sparking; its cargo of black powder could not be ignited when the horn scraped against an object, an important

> ### THE KENTUCKY LONGRIFLE AT A GLANCE
>
> **Period of Manufacture:** Flintlocks from the early 1700s to the mid-1820s, when the percussion system took hold; percussion versions were made until the late 1850s. Most originated in Pennsylvania, but others were made elsewhere.
>
> **Calibers:** 38 to 45 average, but full range was from 35 to 60 (rare). Ammunition was black powder with various-shaped patched bullets, although the round lead ball was most popular.
>
> **Ignition:** Flintlock, later converted to percussion
>
> **Barrel:** Single. 40" to 48" in length, later models shortened to 34" to 36"; octagon, may be tapered. Rifling twist 1:40
>
> **Sights:** Iron; fixed; open blade front; simple notch rear; occasional peep sights
>
> **Triggers:** Double-set or multiple-lever
>
> **Stock:** Full stock of walnut, cherry, maple or other wood; patchbox in rear; hand-rubbed oil finish
>
> **Furniture:** Of brass, most often incl. ramrod thimbles, toe plate, buttplate, lock plate, upper and lower tangs, inlays
>
> **Variations:** Many, depending on origin. Later rifles enjoy ornate embellishments and fancier grade wood.

consideration. The powder horn was so-shaped as to provide a natural funneling effect so that powder could be poured with minimal spillage. It was also light in weight and easy to carry. Inexpensive and easily obtainable, horns varied in size, so a shooter could own many powder horns of different sizes. In addition, a horn could be shaped by softening it in boiling water and bending it. It could also be scraped thin so that the shooter could see how much powder he had left. Finally, the horn took well to carving and many a blackpowder hunter carved his with maps, symbols, sayings and other personal adornments.

Our first national rifle of recognition still lives on today. Originals abound. On a visit to a collector in New Jersey, I saw several dozen original Kentucky rifles for sale, some of them at modest prices because they were simple working arms with minimal collector value. Furthermore, the longrifle replica is popular all over the country, some made in factories, others handcrafted very much like the American longrifle of old. Dennis Mulford, modern custom armsmaker, built a Lancaster-style rifle for me about a decade and a half ago. He copied the rifle after a piece found in a museum. The barrel had been shortened to 34 inches and freshed out to a larger caliber. A drum and nipple switched the old rifle from flint to percussion ignition. Mulford loosely copied the rifle with a handsome handmade model of his own design. Since that time, I've carried the custom piece in the woods, on plains and mountains, successfully harvesting game with the patched round ball, the same ammunition fired from the early longrifles.

Graceful and beautiful, with classic lines, the American longrifle served its owner well with accuracy and reliability. No wonder that it is still taken into the hunting field, collected and replicated to this day.

THE PLAINS RIFLE
KING OF THE WESTERN FRONTIER

2

The Hawken brothers, Samuel and Jacob, built the most definitive Plains Rifle. The Hawken rifle held such sway over the world of riflemen that the style exists to this day, not only in collected originals, but also in custom and factory replicas (almost exact copies of original Hawkens) and in the name itself. Many muzzleloaders that no more replicate the Hawken than a buzzard looks like a sparrow carry the name, too. These are, for the most part, well-made highly serviceable muzzleloaders that shoot with accuracy and dependability. However, although they are called Hawkens, they are not copies of originals.

The Hawken is a "Plains Rifle." But not all plains rifles are Hawkens. A plains rifle, generically speaking, is a stout, rather

A fine example of the Plains-type rifle is Ithaca's Hawken model.

plain (versus ornate), large-caliber caplock (percussion system) muzzleloader of 19th-century America. There was no better firearm at the time for the work that the plains rifle was invented to do. It was king of the western frontier. The Hawken fit into a special chronological and historical niche. The word "if" surrounds its inception. *If* percussion-sensitive detonating mixtures had not been invented, the Hawken and its plains rifle brothers would have been flintlocks, as some of them were. And *if* Thomas Jefferson had not decided on the importance of the Far West, there may never have been a plains rifle at all.

Jefferson had made up his mind that there should be an American presence west of the Mississippi River in the vast region known as the Far West. Most of the area was unmapped and virtually unknown in the early 1800s. Furthermore, many leaders felt that the wide open spaces of the West were not worth the bother. Jefferson disagreed. French travelers were looking over the region and had been for quite some time. English trappers and explorers were also in the area, a number of them filtering down from Canada to take advantage of beaver streams rich with pelts. Jefferson, according to historical reference,

The bison, the largest four-footed mammal in North America, was the impetus for making the sturdy, large-caliber plains rifle that helped tame the West.

wanted to keep the western half of America for Americans. He developed a plan that included exploration. Lewis and Clark were chosen to spearhead a westward trek, and their famous expedition lasted two years, from 1804 to 1806. Many stories about the Far West winged their way eastward to fall upon "civilized" ears.

"Lies," most Americans said. The explorers, especially John Colter, who remained in the Far West after leaving the Lewis & Clark party, were considered fabricators of wild stories. Colter told about a place where smoke billowed up out of the ground and a jet of hot water shot up into the air on a regular basis. He talked about bubbling pools so hot they could ignite a stick of wood thrown into them. "Colter's Hell," it was jokingly called by disbelievers; Colter died, unjustly branded as a liar. Today, millions of people visit Yellowstone Park firsthand and marvel at its wonders.

But the people back East did believe in one widely told story: that beavers filled the wild streams of the West. And beaver pelts meant money. The English top hat was best made of felt procured from the pelt of the beaver, and top hats were the rage for quite some time. General William Ashley decided to turn beaver pelts into cash. The idea followed the basic tenets of business enterprise: form a company; have your workers do the labor; give them a reasonable profit and skim the cream off the top of the money pot for yourself. Ashley put an advertisement in a St. Louis, Missouri, newspaper calling for stout-hearted men to join him in a westward fur-trapping venture. St. Louis became the jumping-off point for these and many other trappers. That's how mountain men were born. They helped secure the West for Americans and staked out the lands that now represent our western states. The creation of the fur trappers themselves, which we call mountain men to this day, prompted another development--the plains rifle.

A POTION AND A PERCUSSION CAP PAVE THE WAY

But first, two major events that preceded Lewis and Clark's exploration paved the way for a new kind of rifle. The first was the invention of a percussion-sensitive material. Typically, this innovation was claimed as the brainchild of many intrepid souls, but the man who ended up with his name attached to the development was the Reverend Alexander John Forsyth, a clergyman from Scotland. In 1807 Forsyth was granted an English patent for fulminate of mercury. An explosive compound, fulminate of mercury is essentially made by treating mercuric nitrate with alcohol to produce a substance that will detonate by friction, heat or percussion. In short, the stuff will blow up if it's struck hard enough. The Forsyth patent was legally protested by others who claimed previous knowledge of fulminates, but Forsyth won out.

He succeeded most likely because the base of his concoction was mercury. As far back as November 11, 1663, *Pepys' Diary* notes a fulminate of gold that detonated violently. Iron fulminate was also mentioned. And silver fulminate decidedly preceded Forsyth's mercury recipe. There was another big difference: others who wrote of fulminates did not necessarily apply them to anything. Forsyth did. He said that fulminates could be used to discharge firearms. Somewhere around 1810–1811, Forsyth took his invention one step further. He started a rifle company called the Forsyth & Co. Patent Gun Makers located at 10 Piccadilly in London. The manufacturing company was dedicated to building ri-

The percussion system eventually overtook the flintlock. It consisted of a percussion cap, as shown here on a nipple, that was detonated by a blow from the hammer above.

fles predicated on Forsyth's special priming system. How far away could a percussion cap be? Inventive minds had but one step to take from priming tapes and other ways of using fulminate of mercury to a unit that permanently held the substance in place, a device that could be whacked with the hammer of a gun and detonated to create a hot spark that would travel into the breech of the firearm just as the flame from black powder in the pan of the flintlock rifle had done.

The second event was of course the invention of a good percussion cap, which Joshua Shaw came up with in 1813. An English artist, Shaw settled in Philadelphia and applied for a United States patent in 1814, but he was turned down because he was not an American citizen at the time. Shaw came out with an iron percussion cap at first, which could be reused by filling it with fulminate of mercury after detonation. This was impractical at best. Caps were easily lost after use anyway and saving them was a problem. By 1815 Shaw had a disposable pewter cap that made more sense. And by 1825 he really hit the jackpot when he replaced the pewter cap body with a copper unit. The U.S. Army and the Navy both adopted its use. Although Shaw never actually received a patent, he was eventually awarded a sum of $25,000 by an act of Congress on February 20, 1847 as full compensation for the use of his cap by the U.S. Government. The $25,000 paid for all past use of the cap and all future use of the same invention. Shaw, at that point, was over 70 years old.

Now the stage was set for the invention of a new firearm that some would call the Rocky Mountain Rifle. All the players were ready to act: a detonating element, a percussion cap, exploration of the Far West by Lewis & Clark's party a couple of decades earlier, acceptance of the fact that beaver pelts were ready to be pulled like wet dollars from cold streams in the West, a consequent fur trade era and a new adventurer—the mountain man—to carry it all out.

As wonderful as the American longrifle was for the East, that beautiful firearm was not entirely right for work in the West. Conditions were different. Since the mountain man often traveled on the back of a horse over great distances, a rifle with a barrel like a church steeple was not ideal under these circumstances. The Pennsylvania/Kentucky longarm was tough enough for the East, but long western trails beat the handsome rifles without mercy. If something went wrong with your longrifle near Boston, you could find a gunsmith to fix it. The only gunsmiths in the West were the trappers themselves.

The fauna were different in the West, too. Bison were not unknown to eastern hunters, but the brutes ranged all over the western prairies. Here was the largest four-footed animal in North America, a herd bull weighing a ton, with real heavyweights tipping the scale at close to 3,000 pounds. (A herd bull recently weighed near Gillette, Wyoming, went just shy of a ton and a half.) Pop a bull "buffalo," as the animal was and still is popularly called, in the neck with a 45-caliber round ball and the huge animal might just walk off. You could also find Shiras moose, another big boy, mule deer, white-tailed deer, and of course pronghorn antelope. Antelope were small, but often taken from longer-than-usual distances, where a larger ball would create better effect than a smaller one. There was no doubt about it—the Kentucky rifle had to undergo change. In a few respects, the new arm reverted to the Jaeger of old that had predated the American longrifle.

THE HAWKEN BROTHERS HELP TAME THE WEST

Jacob Hawken found his way to St. Louis in 1807, coincidentally the same year that Reverend Forsyth patented his detonating material. Jake opened his gunshop in 1815. His brother Sam followed from Ohio in 1822, a time when the gun business was humming. The Hawken plains rifle was born. It was a firearm of necessity. But it was also in every way a sporting rifle. The major use of the Hawken was, for years, hunting big game. Certainly, the Hawken and other plains rifles were significant tools in taming the West. But the point cannot be forgotten that all of these rifles were hunting implements foremost. They were rugged, practical, sufficiently accurate and dependable. In a sense, the Hawken and its cousins were the high-tech hardware of the hour. Of course, the plains rifle would fall by the wayside in time, but for now it was king of all hunting shoulder arms.

But what specifically was the Hawken rifle like? What was its style? How did it function?

In certain ways, the Hawken was the antithesis of the Kentucky rifle, which was too long and too cumbersome to suit western trail life, somewhat too fragile, and too ineffectual in caliber. Hawken rifles were

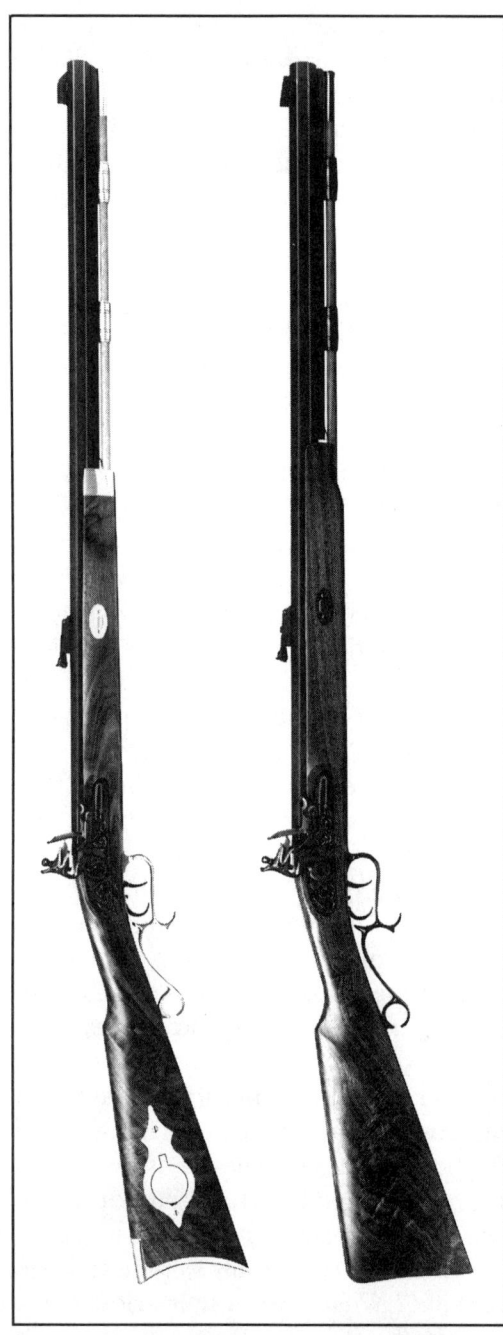

The Hawken rifle, with its halfstock design and plain furniture, is the epitome of the plains rifle. The non-replica Hawken remains the most popular blackpowder rifle of the present time, here represented by Thompson/Center's Hawken (left) and Renegade flintlock models.

shorter overall than the American longrifle, due to decreased barrel length. Since the Hawken was a handmade implement, there are no standard dimensions, including barrel length. Generally, though, the "average" barrel measured about 34 inches. One museum piece shows a barrel length of 34¾ inches, for example. Several proved to be 34 inches on the nose. Another is 36 inches. A special rifle built for General Ashley and called the "Super Rifle" had a barrel 42 inches long. But something in the domain of three feet is commonplace. Barrels could be tapered or straight. One original shows a breadth of 1⅛ inches across the flats all the way. Another barrel was tapered from 1⅛ inches at the breech down to an inch across the flats at the muzzle. The weight of the Hawken varied from 9 pounds to 12½ pounds, but something in the area of 10 pounds, roughly speaking, can be considered an average weight.

While calibers varied, too, the Hawken was decidedly of big-bore persuasion. A fictional work on the life of John Johnston (Jeremiah Johnson) noted a Hawken of 30 caliber. Such would have been built by Sam or Jake for fun only--never for sale to a mountain man. The notation of the 30-caliber Hawken was probably a misprint that should have read "50 caliber." The special Super Rifle for Ashley, mentioned above, was 68 caliber, larger than usual for a Hawken. (Another source shows 66 caliber.) Each of its round bullets weighed about an ounce, a one-ounce projectile weighing 437.5 grains. There were 52-caliber Hawkens, 55s and 58s. Some students of the Hawken list 53 caliber. The Harpers Ferry rifle carried by some men in the Lewis & Clark group were 53 caliber. Perhaps that size was considered a good one by the Hawken brothers. It is prudent to say that most Hawken rifles fell into the 50–55 caliber range.

Largely because of its stock, the Hawken proved a rather compact hunting rifle. The stock was made sturdy for two reasons: first to achieve the intended ruggedness needed of a plains rifle and second to match the heavy steel barrel. Stocks were usually made of maple wood with plain and simple lines. While fullstock Hawkens did exist, halfstock models were more prevalent. Today, the plains rifle is epitomized by halfstock versions. A few carried patch boxes, but these are not a major feature of the Hawken. Some Hawken stocks bore false. Hawkens balanced just fine. Custom and factory replicas of Hawkens prove that. Handling and shooting originals (yes, some originals have been fired by collectors) also proves the fact that Hawkens handle well. These rifles settle in the offhand shooting posture quite well and they are stable.

The Hawken wears good sights, too. Most were of the plain and simple fixed variety not terribly unlike the open sights found on the Kentucky rifle. However, some Hawkens had adjustable rear sights. Using elevator bars, these rear sights could be adjusted for elevation. Drifting front or rear sight in its dovetail notch will change

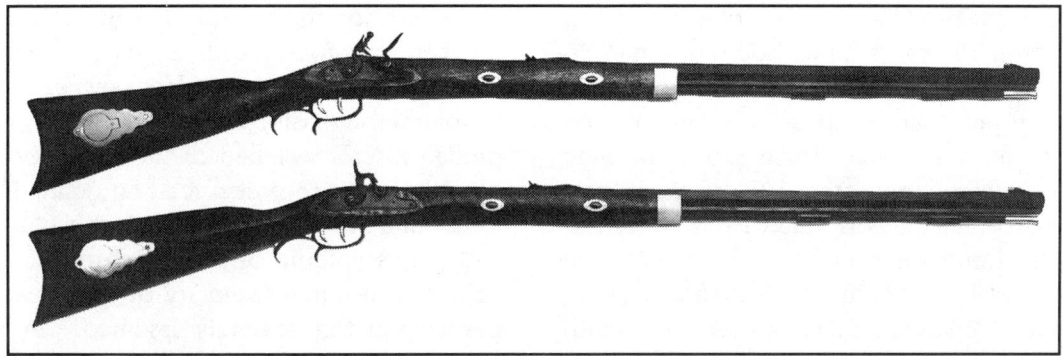

The double-set triggers on the CVA Mountain Rifle are typical of the trigger system used on many plains rifles of the 19th century. These non-replica rifles represent the most popular Hawken-type blackpowder firearm of the day.

carving and others had brass tacks embedded in the wood to "dress them up." Allegedly, the models with tacks were owned by Indians, but that cannot be substantiated; mountain men also dressed up their Hawkens with brass tack patterns. A few metal inlays were used. Some Hawkens had engraved silver plates embedded in the cheekpiece area of the buttstock.

All in all, the furniture of the Hawken and other plains rifles was of iron. Here again, ruggedness and practicality took precedence over decoration. However, the idea that Hawken rifles were "clubby" is point of bullet impact on the horizontal (windage). The front sight is drifted to the left to put the next bullet to the right on target and to the right to force the next shot to the left, while the rear sight is drifted in the direction desired for the bullet to strike. Other sights can be found on Hawkens. There were many Hawken conversions and some of the sights you may see on originals were placed there not by Sam or Jake, but by someone else. This certainly pertains to a few original Hawkens that were found wearing scopes!

Triggers on the Hawken share the

same general design as those on the Kentucky rifle. They are double-set or multiple-lever in function with the rear trigger pulled back to sensitize the front or hair trigger. Modern versions of the Hawken, including most non-replicas as well as replicas, carry this trigger configuration.

Accuracy? The inherent accuracy of the Hawken remains an open question. Some have been tested. However, shooting original Hawkens is not always a good idea because using them may erode their collector value. So a large body of data concerning Hawken accuracy does not exist. It's safe to say that accuracy was adequate for the purpose—big game hunting within reasonable blackpowder ranges—up to about 150 yards for a good marksman. In one test, an original was found to be less accurate than a replica rifle benchtested at the same time, which proves nothing one way or the other. All Hawkens supposedly had a twist rate of 1:48, a turn of the round ball in 48 inches. That single rate of twist was produced by the brothers because it was the only rate they were set up to make. Every student of firearms knows that no single rate of twist is correct for all calibers and bullet styles, and that fact attends the Hawken as it does all firearms.

A 50-caliber or larger round ball requires very little RPS (revolutions per second) to stabilize it on its axis. There is ample proof that a turn in 66 inches, for example, will do the job, keeping the ball spinning well beyond normal hunting ranges. Remember that forward velocity is lost far more rapidly than rotational velocity. In other words, once a projectile is put into rotational motion, the spinning of that bullet is retained to a high degree, and when a missile is well-stabilized at short range, it tends to remain stabilized at longer ranges. Naturally, there is a point downrange where spin may drop off to a point where the bullet no longer flies true. It loses its aerodynamic ability and tumbles in the air. The 1:48 obviously worked for even the larger caliber Hawken rifles. But to call it the wisest choice or the best choice is folly. Calibers in the half-inch range could have done very well with 1:66 or similar rates of twist. Calibers over 50 could have faired well with even slower rates of twist.

Remember that the ammo used in the Hawken was the round bullet held in place downbore via a patch. Ballistics were good considering the era. The stout Hawken barrel of rather soft steel could withstand a fair charge of black powder, which was good fuel for the times. One 50-caliber Hawken was found with a charger that threw about 120 grains of black powder on a volumetric basis. The powder charge probably scale-weighed in the neighborhood of 110–115 grains for FFg granulation. For a 50-caliber round ball with 100–120 grains volume of FFg black powder behind it, a muzzle velocity of 1900 feet per second can be safely assumed. Considering the weight of the ball at 180 grains, muzzle energy would have run around 1400 foot-pounds for that muzzle velocity. The ball would have slowed down to something under 900 feet per second at 100 yards and about 325 foot-pounds. Energy-wise, these figures are not much. The often-stated remark that mountain men shot at game out to 150 yards may be true, for a number of historians seem to think so. On the other hand, in light of raw ballistic figures, a Hawken was more of a 75-yard rifle with the round ball when it came to big game such as elk, bison, moose and the like and 100 to 125 yards for deer-sized animals.

Historians also note that one of the attributes of the Hawken plains rifle was

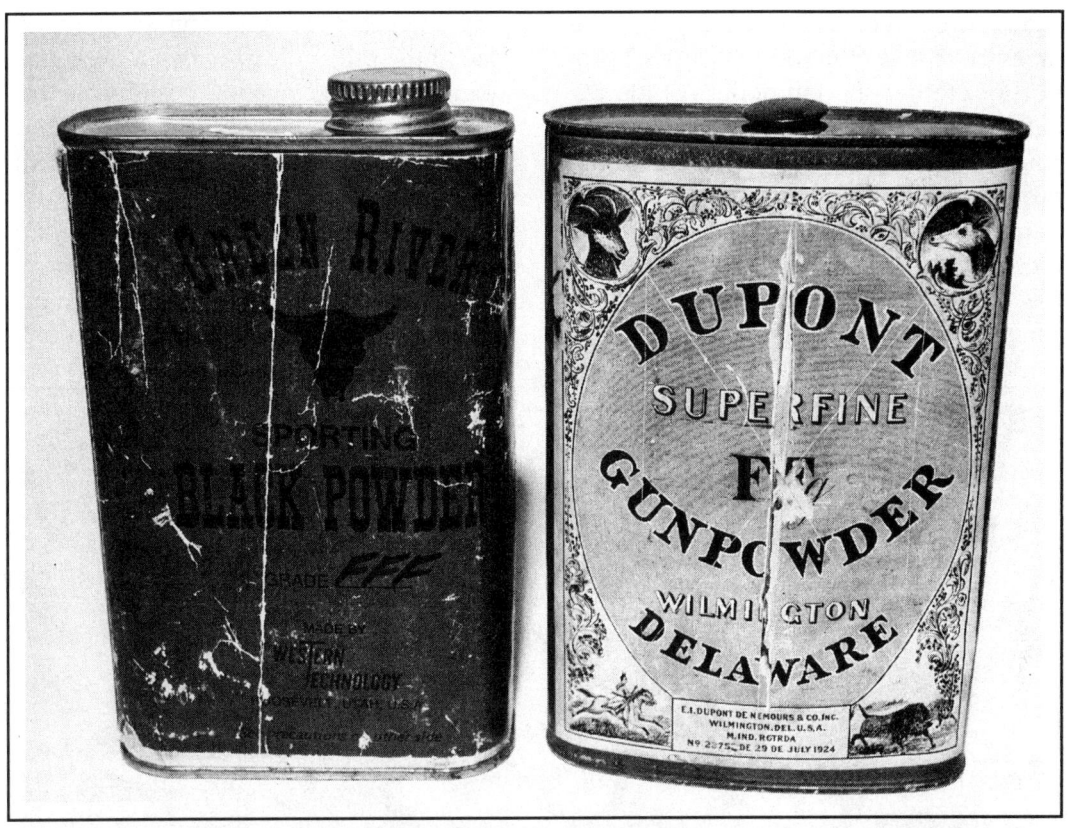

Black powder was the heart of all shooting well into the 20th century, with the first smokeless powder rounds showing up in the late 1800s. The plains rifle was fueled by black powder such as found in cans like these from the "old days."

its flat trajectory. "It shot flat to 150 yards," they say. But no cartridge known to man shoots a bullet flat to 150 yards, including the 220 Swift. Bullets begin to drop when they leave the muzzle of the gun due mainly to bucking the atmosphere and in part because of gravity. A round ball, even a large one, loses speed rapidly and has a rainbow trajectory. A 50-caliber Hawken, well-loaded and sighted dead on the bull's-eye at 75 yards, would enjoy a 125-yard effective range for most big game hunting because the round ball would drop about a half-foot at that distance. Bullet placement beyond 125 yards would quickly become a matter of "Arkansas elevation," whereby the shooter raises his sights above the target and fires with the hope of dropping the projectile back into the zone of effectiveness at long range.

General Ashley's Super Rifle with its one-ounce ball was a bear gun. Some writers say that every major camp had such a rifle for grizzlies. The major wild animal threat in the Far West, grizzly bears accounted for the deaths of a number of fur trappers. Supposedly, the big rifle was kept loaded and at the ready. If news of a nearby bear came in, or indeed if the Bruin invaded the camp area, this big gun was brought to bear on the brute. A one-ounce round might achieve an actual muzzle velocity of around 1600 feet per second with anything like a normal load. As the bore grows ever larger, efficiency drops off. It takes more and more powder, out of proportion, to get the job done. A little 32-caliber squirrel rifle can scoot its 45-grain round ball at 2000 feet per second with around 40 grains of black powder, depending on length of barrel. But a 50-caliber ball requires more like 110 grains of black powder to achieve that velocity range. And Ashley's big bore would have

up at after exiting a game animal. The sheer size of the projectile provided a fairly pronounced wound channel. Since the ball was of lead (i.e., mainly free of tin, antimony or other ingredients to harden it), the "pure" lead bullet had high molecular cohesion, which means it "sticks together" rather than fragmenting. Penetration is improved because of this integrity. A missile that breaks apart loses some of its abil-

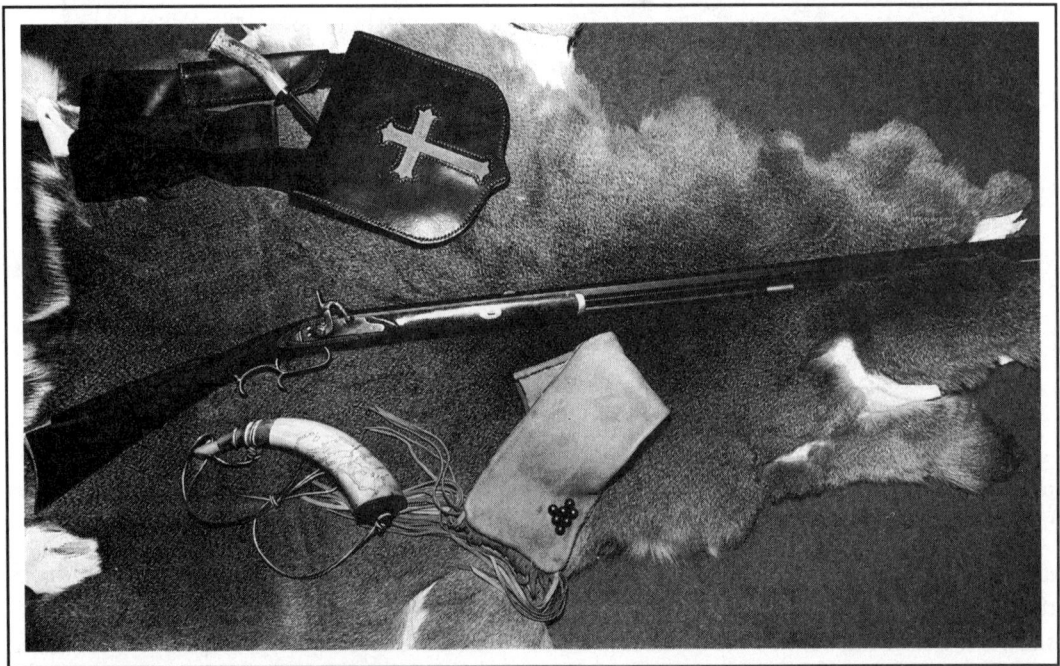

The Ozark Mountain Arms Muskrat rifle, no longer made, is typical of a fine halfstock longarm that a modern mountain man might carry. Note all the accouterments.

demanded a huge powder charge to generate any sort of reasonable muzzle velocity. Of course, a lead pill of around 438 grains at 1600 feet per second would generate almost 2500 foot-pounds of energy.

By modern standards, Hawken energies were nothing to crow about. But let's look at caliber for its own sake and the potential of an all-lead bullet. The big-bore ball from a Hawken started out larger in diameter than many modern bullets end

ity to punch a long wound channel. Modern shooters who hunt with muzzleloaders are often amazed at how effective the round ball is at modest ranges. It's not uncommon for a 50-caliber lead ball to travel the total breadth of a deer's chest cavity, for example. Part of the reason for such performance is the lead bullet on the usual "soft-skinned" game of this continent.

One of the marks of a plains rifle is its percussion ignition system. True, some

Shooting the Hawken rifle is not a thing of only the past. Today expert "buckskinners," like Jim "Bear Claw" O'Meara, emulate the life and dress of the early mountain man.

Hawkens were created on flintlocks. But the norm was a percussion-style lock with a nipple of some sort. The nipple, also called a tube in fur trade days, was and remains no more than a metal insert with a cone-like shape. The nipple has a vent in it or channel. A percussion cap is placed on the topmost part of the nipple's cone.

PLAINS RIFLE 29

The Plains Rifle at a Glance

Period of Manufacture: About 1815 through 1849, made primarily by the Hawken brothers of St. Louis; other makers west of the Mississippi River are known (rare).

Calibers: 50 to 55 average, but also 58, 60, 68. Ammunition was black powder with patched round lead ball.

Effective Shooting Range: 75 to 125 yards, depending on caliber

Ignition: Percussion cap usually

Barrel: Single, 34" average, but some as long as 42; octagonal, may be tapered or straight. Rifling twist 1:48

Weight: 10 pounds average, but ranged from 9 to 14 pounds

Sights: Fixed; some had adjustable rear

Triggers: Double-set or multiple-lever

Stock: Simple design usually of maple wood; half stock more common than full stock; brass tacks used to dress up the rifle; occasional metal inlays and engraved silver plates (rare)

Furniture: Of brass, most often incl. ramrod thimbles, toe plate, buttplate, lock plate, upper and lower tangs, inlays

---

When the hammer falls forward, it whacks the percussion cap with a strong blow, detonating the chemical contents of the cap, which provides a flame that darts through the vent of the nipple and into the main charge of powder in the breech. The rifle goes off. While flintlocks were far more trustworthy than a lot of us may think, the caplock or percussion system was more foolproof. And more convenient. In Chapter 1, conversions from flint to percussion were noted. Similar conversions were made on some plains rifles.

In addition to the drum and nipple, here are two other methods of converting flintlocks to percussions: The flashhole of the flintlock was replaced with a threaded plug, thus entirely closing off this avenue of gas escape from the breech of the rifle. A new threaded channel was introduced from the top of the barrel. Into this threaded receptacle a nipple was screwed firmly in place. The pertinent parts of the flintlock were removed and replaced by a hammer that would fall directly upon the new nipple. Thus, a caplock or percussion rifle was the result. Another method was to cut off the breech of the flintlock and attach a new breech plug with a bolster arrangement housing a nipple seat. A nipple was screwed in place, thus making the flinter a percussion model.

While there tend to be more students of the Kentucky rifle than the Hawken or other plains rifles, the latter longarms enjoy plenty of followers, too. Unfortunately, fewer original plains rifles remain for study compared to the American longrifle. However, original Hawkens belonging to famous mountain men are still housed in museums and collections to be studied, including Kit Carson's rifle and Jim Bridger's, as well as Mario Modena's and others. Furthermore, the Hawken devotee has an abundance of accouterments to absorb his attention.

The Hawken rifle and similar Rocky Mountain models helped to open up the West, not as "army guns," but as hunting rifles in the hands of intrepid adventurers. We are fortunate to have original and replica examples to admire today.

HUNT, JENNINGS AND VOLCANIC RIFLES
RAPID FIRE, ROCKETS AND REPEATERS

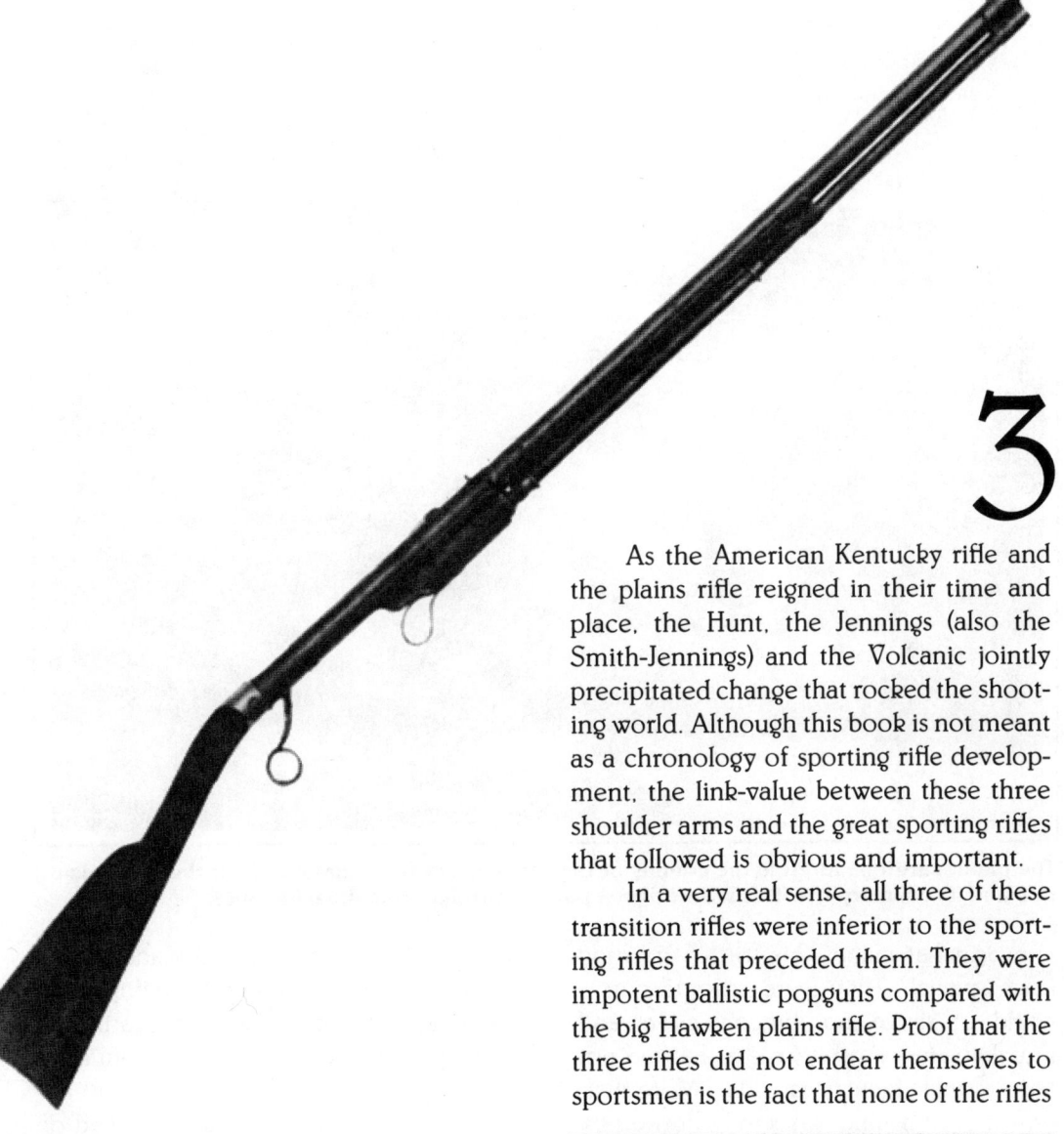

3

As the American Kentucky rifle and the plains rifle reigned in their time and place, the Hunt, the Jennings (also the Smith-Jennings) and the Volcanic jointly precipitated change that rocked the shooting world. Although this book is not meant as a chronology of sporting rifle development, the link-value between these three shoulder arms and the great sporting rifles that followed is obvious and important.

In a very real sense, all three of these transition rifles were inferior to the sporting rifles that preceded them. They were impotent ballistic popguns compared with the big Hawken plains rifle. Proof that the three rifles did not endear themselves to sportsmen is the fact that none of the rifles

The Hunt Repeater with ring lever action used the first self-contained ammo.

endured very long in the hunting/shooting field and that single-shot rifles were chosen by many hunters during the lives of these three repeaters. If a modern big game hunter had to choose between a Hunt, Jennings or Volcanic versus a Sharps single-shot, he'd be wise to take the Sharps for its much greater power and accuracy.

Hunters wanted shoot-again guns, too. So did explorers and adventurers. Repeaters date back to flintlock times, of course, but the Hunt, Jennings and Volcanic rifles were on track for another highly desirable improvement: self-contained ammunition, although not true cartridges. The paper cartridge was workable in the muzzleloader

The paper cartridge foretold the coming of the cartridge, as did ammunition for the Volcanic rifle and its counterparts. This is an original paper cartridge from the mid-1800s.

So what makes this trio of sporting rifles special? They were repeaters in a world of single-shot breechloaders and muzzleloaders. And in an era that did not have a single factory cartridge! More than one shot at a time was sorely desired by military men—firepower that could beat down an attack or spearhead a charge.

and in single-shot breechloaders. But wouldn't it be convenient if two important shooting attributes—reliable repeating capability plus dependable self-contained ammo — could be melded together? Everyone and his distant cousin worked on the problem. A fortune could be made by the inventor who could bring about these desirable goals. And an even greater reward could be realized by the company that marketed them successfully.

Walter Hunt was an imaginative man. The safety pin, a dandy item, was his creation. He's also noted by the great researcher, George Madis, as inventor of a special fountain pen and a lockstitch needle. In the ammo arena, rapid fire preoccupied Hunt's mind. He was the first to get a patent on what we today would call "caseless ammo." To this hour, researchers are working toward a self-propelled bullet, as it were, whereby the powder charge and the bullet are one, without a cartridge case to get in the way. The Daisy company had such ammo on the market at one time, but it did not make it. Further work on a rocket-like bullet ensues, especially by military researchers. A good caseless projectile would streak its way to the target by virtue of a propellant attached to the base of the bullet, or perhaps within the body of the projectile. It isn't impossible that this rocket bullet would not burn all its powder within the bore with no further energy imparted to the bullet. A rocket bullet might enjoy continued thrust in flight. The rocket bullet is currently a pencil-and-paper idea only, with no plans for manufacture in the near or distant future. But rocket bullets certainly got things started in the 1800s.

Hunt was definitely thinking along the lines of a rocket when he titled his patent of 1848 "Rocket Balls." In his type of rocket ball or bullet, the interior of the missile was hollow. Inside this cavity rested a powder charge. A wad made of cork covered the base of the bullet to hold the powder in place. An avenue for ignition flame to reach the powder charge contained within the bullet was provided by a hole through the center of the cork wad. Over the hole was a thin paper to contain the powder. A jet of flame instantly burned through the powder to ignite the charge that was held within the body of the bullet. (There were variations in materials used, but the above was one means of making the rocket bullet work.) It wasn't a bad idea, except for the fact that black powder was entirely the wrong fuel because of its inefficiency. It takes a lot of ebony granules to do a credible ballistic job and Hunt's bullet obviously held only a little fuel. Some of today's explosives and propellants are capable of getting a great deal of work done with a tiny volume of fuel. Hunt of course had no access to such chemicals.

When Hunt was granted U.S. Patent No. 6663 in 1848, the inventor already had a rifle for his special ammo. His 54-caliber longarm used a tubular magazine underneath the barrel to contain the Rocket Balls. Hunt called it his "Volition Repeater." A lever (finger loop) at the back end of the magazine within easy reach of the shooter's hand worked each bullet into place for feeding into the receiver of the rifle. The Volition was not entirely reliable, and its manufacture included some very delicate parts. Priming pellets, fed into place automatically, were used to detonate the charge of powder contained within each bullet. Although Hunt's rifle never saw manufacture, plenty of inventors saw Hunt's rifle. It stirred interest, and that interest turned into further repeating sporting rifle developments.

JENNINGS IMPROVES THE HUNT

George Arrowsmith, whose New York company made engines, acquired manufacturing rights for the Hunt repeater. Arrowsmith put Lewis Jennings to work improving Hunt's idea. The changes engineered by Jennings were sufficient to earn a new patent granted in December of 1849.

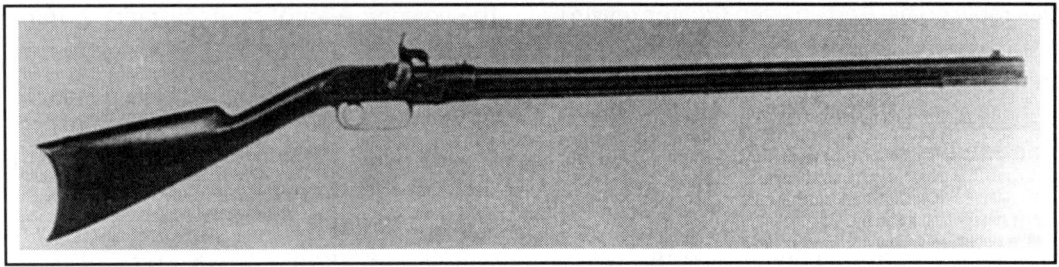

Lewis Jennings improved on Hunt's repeater by using a single ring trigger (with or without trigger guard) that performed the loading functions with a simple back and forth stroke. Note the large ring (above) in this Jennings 54-caliber percussion breechloader.

There was only one pertinent change—a single lever (a ring trigger in this case) that performed all necessary loading functions with a simple forward-rearward stroke. That alteration rocked the world of shooters and was eventually seen on later lever-action rifles. Jennings retained Hunt's Rocket Balls and pill-lock primers, but the Jennings conversion worked better than the original Hunt design. Still, the rifle had serious faults. Jennings felt that everything possible had been done to improve Hunt's original concept. Arrowsmith was business-smart. When Jennings told him that the Hunt repeater could be refined no further, he searched around for a buyer of this Brooklyn Bridge of rifles. And he found one.

Courtlandt C. Palmer not only bought the rights to the Jennings rifle design, he also got ready to build it through the Robbins and Lawrence manufacturing company of Vermont. Palmer gave the go-ahead for 5,000 rifles. Manufacturing problems got in the way immediately. Many Jennings repeaters turned out to be single-shots because Robbins and Lawrence found that they could leave out the complicated repeating feature and produce the rifle as a one-shot breechloader, retaining the automatic priming feature.

Palmer tried to salvage his investment by hiring another engineer, Horace Smith. Smith set to work to see if he could improve upon Jennings' work. Probably the most important aspect of Smith going to work on the Jennings/Hunt rifle was an upcoming alliance with Daniel Baird Wesson and Benjamin Tyler Henry. Henry was also involved in building the Jennings' version of the repeating rifle. Every shooter knows about Smith & Wesson, and Henry would eventually become so important to Winchester that an "H" was stamped upon the head of 22 Winchester rimfire ammo for decades after Henry's passing.

Smith & Wesson, in 1855, bought manufacturing rights for revolvers and they also teamed up with Palmer to form the "Volcanic Repeating Arms Company." The Volcanic company would last only from 1855 to 1857, but the enterprise claimed a very important stockholder named Oliver F. Winchester who took part in the new operation. Manufacture was in full operation in 1856. Winchester ended up president of the company that year because Volcanic's first president, Nelson B. Gaston, died. The new company had been moved to New Haven, Connecticut, in 1855 and B. Tyler Henry acted as Superintendent of the operation known as the Volcanic shops. Anyone who takes a look at one of the Volcanic firearms will see immediately that here is the forerunner of the Henry rifle, which in turn led to the famous Winchester sporting rifle.

THE VOLCANIC—FORERUNNER OF THE HENRY RIFLE

The Volcanic's lines were good. An under-lever loop served the functions of the rifle with a separate trigger enclosed by a trigger guard integral to that loop. But one huge problem plagued the Volcanic— the lack of a true cartridge. The 38-caliber Volcanic "cartridge," the original hollow lead bullet with powder, rendered a muzzle energy of only 56 foot-pounds, less than a current 22 Short rimfire round. The Volcanic cartridge would be supplanted by a real cartridge later on, the 44 Henry. The 44-caliber Henry, incidentally, even though weaker than a newborn kitten, was a giant step ahead of "bullets with powder in them." And it used a metallic cartridge case that could affect a good seal. The fact that a metallic cartridge sealed the bore led to the success of later smokeless loads.

Smith & Wesson, however, had a rimfire round before Henry. That cartridge— for it was a cartridge with a metallic case— worked by virtue of a wet fulminate introduced into the rim of the round, where it dried in place. When the rim was struck by a blow, the fulminate detonated, igniting

The Rocket Ball ammunition used in the Volcanic Carbine had exterior grease grooves and an internal cavity for the powder charge. As far as ballistics are concerned, it was a pretty anemic round.

the powder charge within the cartridge case. By now engineers had figured out that putting a dab of powder inside a bullet cavity created only a ballistic toy. The 1857 Smith & Wesson cartridge was what we would call a 22-rimfire Short. Modern shooters are used to thinking of the 22 Short as a recreational cartridge with modest small game capability; however, the round was originally intended for self-

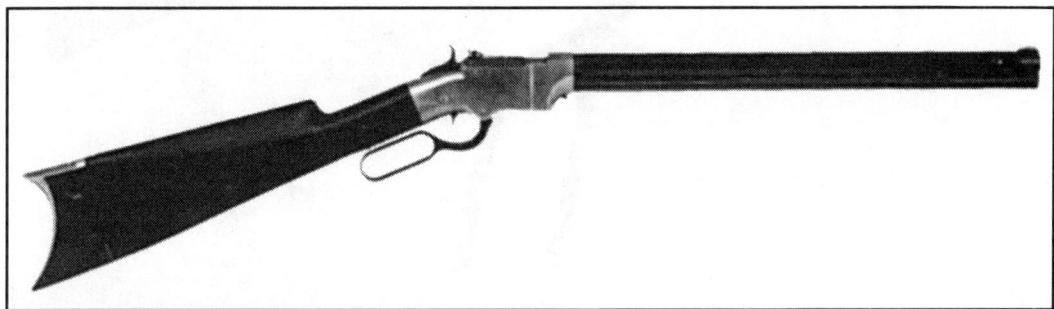

The brass-framed lever-action Volcanic was another step in progress toward a reliable repeating arm with self-contained ammunition.

defense. The little Short grandfathered hundreds of rimfire rounds, large and small. Moreover, it was the rimfire cartridge that put the skids under the 31- and 41- caliber self-contained "powder bullets" used in the Volcanic and its predecessors.

The Hunt, Jennings and Volcanic rifles were attempts toward reliable repeating firearms. And the rocket ball each used was an attempt to come up with self-contained ammo. Henry worked with all of the rifles and their ammo, resulting in his historical 44 rimfire round, in effect an overgrown Smith & Wesson Short. Therefore, it's difficult to call Henry the inventor of a totally new cartridge. The 44 Flat, although it was better ballistically than the self-contained ammo of Volcanic days, was no earth-shaker.

So why did rifles chambered for this and other rather anemic rimfire rounds fare so well? Obviously, the ability to shoot again and again without reloading, especially without having to ram a bullet downbore on top of a powder charge one shot at a time. The repeater changed American hunting forever. Some might say that it took away from the sport. After all, a hunter with a single-shot rifle had to be extra careful. He had to count on that one shot to deliver the goods—meat for the table. But if you missed with a repeater, you cranked in another round and fired again. Furthermore, while a 200-grain chunk of lead, even at low velocity, is formidable especially on deer-sized game at close range, here was a real pipsqueak up against big quadrupeds such as the bison, elk or moose of the West. So bullet placement was of utmost importance—even

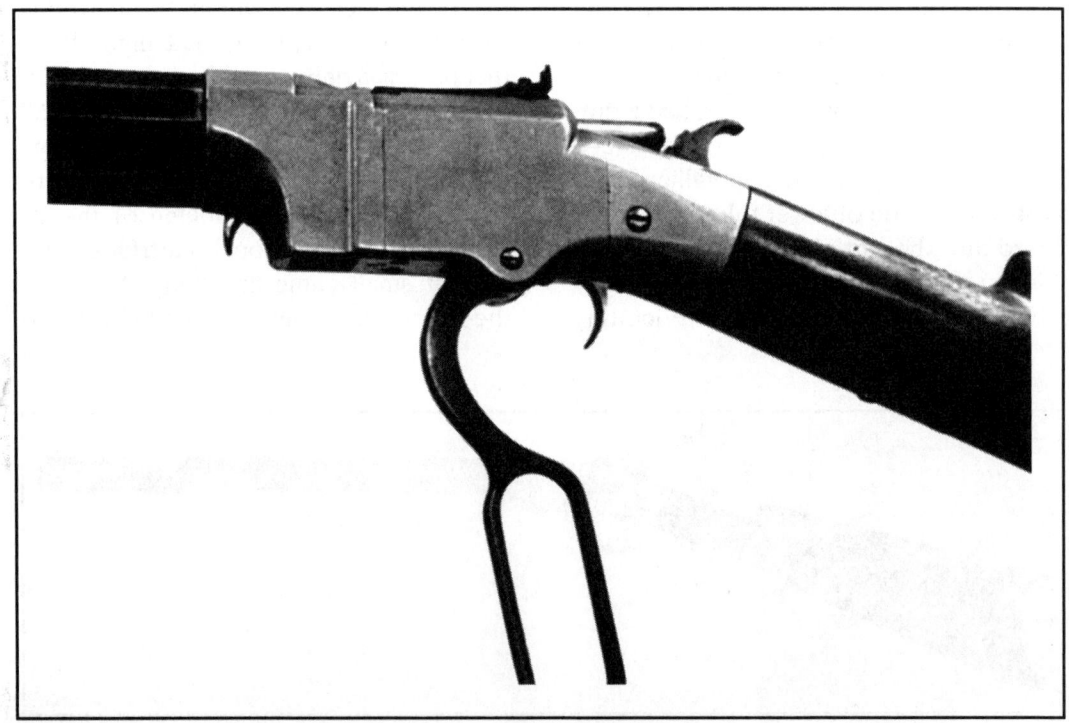

Close-up of the brass receiver on a late-model Volcanic Carbine. Note the tab in front of the receiver, which is a magazine follower that moves the full length of the magazine tube.

> ## THE HUNT, JENNINGS AND VOLCANIC RIFLES AT A GLANCE
>
> **THE HUNT REPEATER:** A 54-caliber ring lever-action designed by Walter Hunt and made circa 1848. Considered the first "Winchester," Hunt called it his "Volition Repeater." He invented the first self-contained ammo, the "Rocket Ball" cartridge, to be used in the rifle. The rounds were fed into the rifle through a tubular magazine underneath the barrel; priming pellets, fed into place automatically, were used to detonate the charge of powder contained within each bullet.
>
> **THE JENNINGS REPEATER:** A 54-caliber percussion breechloader, an improved version of the Hunt repeater. Design change by Lewis Jennings included a single ring trigger with simple back-and-forth motion that performed all the necessary loading functions. Jennings retained Hunt's Rocket Balls and pill-lock primers. Manufactured by Robbins and Lawrence of Windsor, Vermont, circa 1850.
>
> **THE VOLCANIC REPEATER:** Ring lever-action carbine in 38 caliber with separate trigger, patented by Horace Smith and Daniel Wesson in 1854. Basically an improved Jennings repeater, manufactured by the Volcanic Repeating Arms Co. (1855-1857), run by Smith & Wesson, and by the New Haven Arms Co. (1857-1860). Had integral magazine underneath the barrel and self-contained cartridges. Later models eliminated the ring lever. All had brass frames and crescent-shaped buttplates. Barrel found in 16½-, 21- and 25-inch lengths.

more so than with a big-bore round ball rifle.

Take the Volcanic. It was impotent on truly big game with anything but perfect bullet placement and only then from close range. And it was expensive. What the company called a carbine, although it had a 25-inch barrel, cost about $40. A look into any of the gun catalogues of the day reveals that 40 American greenbacks for one low-powered rifle was no bargain. The only price bonus was that a purchaser of the rifle could have embellishments, including top-grade engraving, added for very little extra cash outlay. But the basic 40-dollar ticket was still too high for the product. Also, because the priming charge was attached to the base of the "caseless" bullet cartridge, there was potential for the ammo to be detonated in the magazine by a jarring of the rifle. While the problem was more latent than real, it was still there. Hardly a praiseworthy advertisement for a hunting rifle. Furthermore, the Volcanic and its brothers all experienced gas leakage at the breech. This was not so much a design fault of the rifle as it was a product of using caseless ammunition. The repeating action did not lock up quite as snugly as a rolling block or falling block single-shot. In addition, the caseless ammunition jetted gas backwards into the breech as well as upward into the bore of the rifle. That gas looked for an escape in the mechanism and found what it was looking for. So the owner of a Volcanic might get a jet of gas coming his way. Again, not exactly a strong ownership feature.

The Volcanic plant went down financially. The company was declared insolvent on February 18, 1857, even though it is arguable that what were essentially Volcanic rifles were turned out until 1860. Winchester was the only member of the business venture who stayed with the company. Palmer left. So did Smith and Wesson. On April 25, 1857, Oliver Winchester created a new gun business called the New Haven Arms Company. B. Tyler Henry played a prominent role from the start. The copper-cased 44 Henry round, the 44 Flat and other examples of real cartridges were clearly going to change the world of sport shooting and riflemaking. Winchester knew it.

Winchester also knew he had inherited a solid base of operation and knowledge from his association with Smith and Wesson, as well as others in the gun industry. The one-time shirtmaker was now, and would be for the rest of his life, a gunmaker. Smith and Wesson had left behind a prototype of a lever-action rifle that Winchester planned to build. The Smith-and-Wesson jointly designed lever-action rifle of 1854 might be quite workable with a true cartridge. The New Haven Arms Company was underway. Now the world of sport shooting was truly in for a big change. Winchester's name would become so associated with the lever-action repeater that the dictionary would later describe "a Winchester" as a generic type of rifle, just as "Kodak" is synonymous with "camera."

THE HENRY RIFLE
ARM AND AMMO SUCCEED

4

The Rocket Ball employed in the Volcanic and earlier rifles was not totally the brain-child of Walter Hunt. The idea had been known abroad long before Hunt's patent. Voss, superintendent of the Royal Danish Arsenal, made a version of a rocket ball, possibly the first of the breed. Patented in 1834, Voss' self-contained bullet/powder unit was used by the Dutch Army for a while. Experimenters in Germany worked on self-contained ammo in the 1840s. In 1847, Fusnot of Belgium perfected an improved rocket ball with a completely sealed base loaded with fulminate plus an extra charge of powder within the cavity of the projectile. That small powder charge was guncotton. That's right. Here was an early use of smokeless

The iron-frame Henry with 24-inch octagonal barrel, a replica from the Navy Arms Co.

gunpowder! The Balle Fusnot, as it was called, could be categorized as smokeless powder ammo. But none of these self-contained bullet/powder packages, not even the comparatively modern products of World War II Germany, lasted very long. They were practical in terms of offering a self-contained missile/powder charge unit, but not sufficiently powerful to compete with the true cartridge.

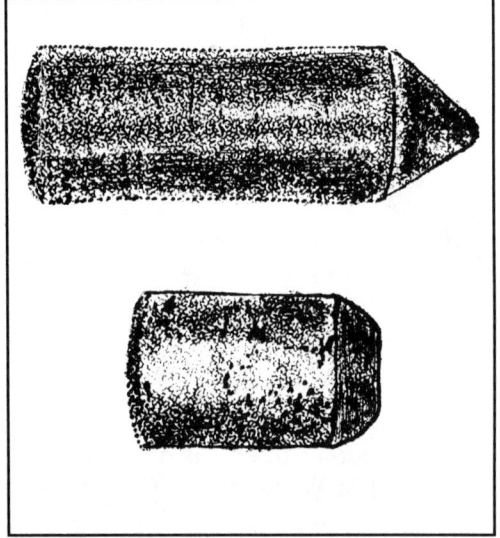

Forerunner of the Hunt and Henry cartridges was the Voss rocket cartridge. Voss, superintendent of the Royal Danish Arsenal, patented his version in 1834. The top illustration is Voss' self-contained rocket cartridge; the bottom is the Voss breechloader for separate ignition.

B. Tyler Henry was granted a patent for a lever-action rifle based on the Volcanic on October 16 in 1860, the year production of the Volcanic ended. The new rifle had an improved and decidedly heavier and stronger action. More important, however, was the ammo the rifle fired, the 44 Henry cartridge. This was a true cartridge, a rimfire round with a copper case. The big advantage was the cartridge case, which acted as a breech seal. Gas leakage behind the cartridge was minimal and certainly not the problem posed by the Volcanic's self-contained bullet/powder load.

B. Tyler Henry's assignment from Oliver Winchester had been clear: develop ammo with a lot more power than the puny self-contained bullets provided. The result was small peanuts for power, too. But Henry's rimfire was a 44-caliber round that fired a pointed lead bullet. Over the black-powder charge, it was loaded with a wad, on top of which was a lubrication disc. The lube in the disc could leak into the powder charge on a hot day, causing a misfire.

The important 44 Henry rimfire was altered in many ways during its tenure. Using a flat-nosed bullet, it was called the 44 Flat or 44 Henry Flat. There are discrepancies in load data for many of these old-time rimfire rounds, plus numerous variations in loads. However, a bullet of 216 grains was probably the missile loaded in the 44 Flat rimfire round. Behind that lead bullet was a charge of 26 grains of black powder. Later on bullet weight was reduced to 200 grains, but the powder charge was retained at 26 grains. The bullet was lubricated, which aided repeated fire. After all, the whole idea of the repeater was reliable firepower. It is doubtful that a velocity much higher than the speed of sound was achieved by the 44-caliber rimfire round. A figure of 1200 feet per second is more than a fair assessment. That velocity would give the 44 Flat a muzzle energy of about 640 foot-pounds—a lot better than the hollow-body rocket bullet—but not ahead of either the old American longrifle or the plains rifle. A 45-caliber Kentucky rifle shooting a .440-inch round ball at around 2,000 feet per second muzzle velocity churned up around 1137 foot-pounds. And a Hawken tossing a 225-grain ball at about the same muzzle velocity was worth close to a long ton of muzzle energy.

Large-caliber rimfire ammo actually had been offered as early as 1858, but there was a lag of two years before 44 Henry ammo was readily available. This caused no problem because the Henry rifle did not see widespread use until 1862. Between 1858 and 1867, three popular rimfire rounds were available: the 44 Pointed, 44 Flat Short Case and the 46 Carbine, the latter appearing more as an overgrown 22 Long Rifle cartridge than a big 22 Short round. There were so many different designations, as well as truly unique rimfire cartridges, that it's no wonder confusion remains to this day concerning names and actual loads. As late as 1916, the Winchester catalogue listed many large-bore rimfire rounds, including a 44 Flat (not called a 44 Henry, but noted as adapted for the Henry rifle as well as the Winchester Model 1866 rifle), a 44 Short and a 44 Pointed. The 44 Flat fired a 200-grain flat-nosed bullet, while the 44 Pointed used a sharply pointed projectile. The 44 Flat case carried 28 grains of black powder in this particular load noted in the 1916 catalogue, while the 44 Pointed case held 26 grains of black powder. Meanwhile, the 44 Short, also with a 200-grain bullet, was loaded with 21 grains of black powder.

The ammunition is important to understanding the Henry rifle because without the new cartridge, the Henry would never have been as well-received as it was. The 44 Henry Flat was so popular that it was used until 1934. So B. Tyler Henry's powerful influence on sporting rifles came with his updated Volcanic rifle *and* his new rimfire cartridge with its copper case.

The Henry rifle was built from 1860 into 1866 in a quantity of about 13,000—not a huge number. However, the Henry impacted sport-shooting like colliding planets. While the Henry rifle was not in the hands of every sportsman, no one would ever know it by looking at ammo sales for the 44 Henry cartridge. In late 1862, for example, records show that 10,000 rounds of 44-rimfire fodder flowed out of the factory every day, loaded and ready to stuff into a rifle magazine somewhere. By 1865 that figure doubled to 20,000 rounds per working factory day. Improvements in the 44 Henry cartridge were in part responsible for its continued success. The lubrication products that often melted on warm days were bettered by a tallow mixture with a higher melting point.

B. Tyler Henry's rimfire cartridge, the 44 Henry Flat, was so popular that it was used until 1934. Loaded with a 200- to 216-grain bullet, it let go a muzzle velocity of between 1100 and 1200 fps.

This made the ammunition more reliable.

Of even greater merit was that in 1865, the 44-rimfire ammo was redesigned to eliminate the internal wads and make crimping possible. By machine, the neck of each cartridge case was neatly crimped into the lead bullet. This held the bullet firmly in place, highly important when cartridges were carried in tubular magazines. The rounds lined up one after the other, with the head of one cartridge case bumped up against the nose of the bullet behind it. During recoil, even the modest recoil created by the rather puny 44-rimfire round, there was always a possibility that the bullet would be shoved back into the case. The concern was not great, actually, because the 44-rimfire case was full, or nearly so, with black powder, which meant no internal air space for the bullet to occupy. Nonetheless, a loose projectile was no good. Crimping remedied that problem forever. In 1865, the U.S. Government purchased 2,085,000 rounds of the newly crimped 46-rimfire ammo. Any shooter can see what was happening. The Henry and its cartridge were paving the way toward truly viable repeaters worthy of sportsmen everywhere.

After B. Tyler Henry received the 1860 patent for his rifle and cartridge, tooling up began. This was the real beginning of the Winchester dynasty. A good supply of Henry rifles hit the streets in the summer of 1862, touted as "The Most Effective Weapon in the World." A brash advertising claim, perhaps, but Oliver Winchester asserted that a marksman could get off "sixty shots per minute" with the new rifle, and that "For a house or sporting arm, it has no equal." Moreover, "A resolute man, armed with one of these rifles, particularly if on horseback, cannot be captured." The Indian Wars were ongoing, and the whole idea behind Winchester's claim was that a determined horseman, armed with a Henry, was well-protected.

While the Henry was not a military rifle, the Civil War was a reality. And in fact the Government did order Henry rifles for the conflict, records showing about 1900 Government-issue Henry rifles. Furthermore, soldiers who used the Henry rifles liked them for their firepower. So although the rifle was positioned as a hunting piece, Oliver Winchester never forgot to enlarge upon its possible military capability. He wrote: "It is very powerful for its size and because of the rapidity with which it can be loaded and fired ten men armed with them are a match for 50 armed with any other gun." When asked if he could supply a Henry rifle with a bayonet mount, Winchester replied, "No bayonets on the Henry. Doesn't need bayonets. No one could get within 40 rods [220 yards], if one is armed with the Henry."

In fact, numerous Civil War reports—Union and Confederate—confirm the reliability and rapidity with which the Henry could be dispatched. Major William Ludlow, for example, in his account of the Battle of Allatoona Pass stated: "What saved us... was the fact that we had a number of Henry rifles... These were new guns in those days ... held in reserve [by] an Illinois Regiment ... until a final assault should be made. When the artillery reopened ... this company of 16-shooters sprang to the parapet and poured out such a multiplied, rapid, and deadly fire that no men could stay in front of it, and no serious effort was thereafter made to take the fort by assault."

The Volcanic-like Henry with its stronger action retained a tubular magazine that was loaded from the front (there was of course no loading gate cut into the action). Fifteen rounds, the literature says, could be stuffed into the Henry. The stubby 44-rimfire round made that possible via the long tube resting beneath the 24-inch octagonal barrel. That made the rifle a 16-shot repeater, taking into account the round in the chamber. Each cartridge was of small potency, but a lot better than previous Volcanic self-contained bullet-ammo. A pointed or flat-nosed bullet of 200 to 216 grains in front of 26 to 28 grains of black powder was stout enough for close-range deer-sized game, and packed enough ballistic oomph to discourage an intruder from walking away with the family cookie jar.

In spite of all these wonders, however,

newspaper accounts, no doubt prompted by the manufacturer, were highly exaggerated. The papers reported that many orders were rolling in—an overstatement, to be kind. Furthermore, according to Winchester, the Henry was a whale of a long-range rifle with great effectiveness way out yonder, with 1,000-yard dispatching capability. In truth, what could the little Henry 44 rimfire knock off at 1,000 yards? Grasshoppers? It also possessed stupendous accuracy, its excited maker preached. There were a number of testimonials, most of which came from sea captains who apparently admired the Henry for on-shipboard service. These seafaring men claimed the Henry was impervious to the ravages of salt air, that the rifle did not rust or fail to function in any way. It was, in a word, weatherproof. Furthermore, for sea duty or offshore work, a Henry had plenty of power to accomplish close-range work, where firepower (the number of shots gotten off per minute) was more important than one smashing blow followed by laborious reloading for a second shot. Alas, the claims were mainly smoke without fire. The Henry was a lousy long-range rifle. Single-shot rifles, such as the Sharps, chambered for true powerhouse black-powder cartridges, proved at long range to accomplish in fact what the Henry got done only in fiction. As for accuracy, a good handmade Kentucky/Pennsylvania longrifle easily produced tighter groups than the average Henry rifle.

THE SIMPLE, RUGGED DESIGN IS WELL-RECEIVED

The design of the Henry was utterly simple and made for a fairly rugged arm. The plain walnut stock was stained and oil-finished. It had no cheekpiece and no pistol grip. Plenty of drop at comb offered good balance and fit for the off-hand stance shooting. A crescent-shaped, or "rifle-style," buttplate also aided off-hand shooting. Today, most rifles are provided with a "shotgun-style" buttplate—flat. The straight grip was well-suited to the single loop lever underneath it. It's easy to see why the Henry rifle ranks as so important among sporting arms. It's essentially the Volcanic, an already workable model, with sufficient refinements to make it a handy rifle in the field.

The receiver on the Henry was made of brass, which was easy to work with and quite machinable. Tools that cut brass lasted longer than tools that cut iron. The brass receiver was strong enough to contain the little 44-rimfire low-pressure round. So brass was a good choice. To be sure, some iron-frame Henrys were offered in time, but the rifle made its reputation essentially with its brass receiver.

Various sights adorned the blued steel Henry barrel, a front blade of German silver, also known as electrum, albata and nickel silver (a white alloy of copper, nickel and zinc), being most popular. Brass was also used for some of the simple blade front sights. These were matched with an open notch rear sight called a sporting adjustable model. Fixed sights could be special-ordered, but customizing was discouraged primarily because of the war. Oliver Winchester wrote in a customer letter, "We intend to make both globe and telescope sights for our rifles." However, few factory Henrys appeared with such sights. One particular Henry rifle in a collection wears a Malcolm telescopic sight. Malcolm, of Syracuse, New York, was known for his special scope sights very early in American glass sight manufacture. The Winchester company would have its own brand of telescopic sight as well. And imported scopes from Germany were hardly unknown. The Malcolm scope sight found on the Henry rifle could have been factory-installed, of course. But the normal sight setup on the Henry was the adjustable rear sight matched with a blade front sight. A "ladder" rear sight for the Henry is now replicated by the Navy Arms Company to such close original tolerances that it will fit an original Henry rifle. In later years, not only Henry rifles, but old-time arms of every company were remodeled in various ways, including sights. The attachment of a tang peep sight, for example, would pose no special problem on a Henry.

In keeping with its policy of discouraging special orders, the New Haven Arms Company did not invite customers to order engraving on the Henrys. However, engraved Henry rifles did leave the factory, some of them beautifully appointed. It is not difficult to understand why certain buyers wanted their rifles engraved. The Henry begged for embellishment due to its large flat receiver. Full scroll work, along with personalizing with name of owner, covered the majority of the action on a few Henry examples. Engravers from "the Old Country" were often hired to do the work. Even though they did not receive high pay, they were artists of the top order. They produced eagles, dogs, flowers, American flags with eagles, vines, leaves, grapes, deer and other figures. If engraving was rare, high-grade wood was even more scarce on the Henry. A few samples were fitted with fancy-grain walnut stocks, however. The Henry rifle already cost 40 American dollars. While engraving made the purchase a real bargain, enough of it could raise the cost of the piece by 25 percent for the average buyer. Presentation models were always worth the effort, though, for their aesthetic appeal as well as their subtle influence on prominent people of the day. Exquisitely engraved and custom-fitted with rosewood stocks, a few singular rifles were presented to President Lincoln, Secretary of War Edwin Stanton and Secretary of the Navy Gideon Welles.

A hunter could order sling swivels on his Henry, fitted to the side of the buttstock and to the side of the barrel/magazine tube. This made sense, since the rifle was "slab-sided," i.e., without a projecting bolt or other fixture. With a sling so arranged the rifle was easily carried in the field. With no forend, a right-handed marksman simply grasped the barrel/magazine tube in his left hand; a left-handed marksman used his right hand. The absence of a forend was not appreciated by everyone, as evidenced by the fact that when rifles emerged from the future Winchester plant, they wore fore arms of wood.

Some Henry rifles had lever catches that secured the lever in position. Others did not. Some had half-cock capability. Others did not. The lack of a half-cock setting may seem a trespass against safety. However, the idea was to carry the Henry on an empty chamber. By snapping the lever down-up rapidly, a round was carried from the tubular magazine into the chamber in a split second and the rifle was ready for action. Future Winchester products carried the half-cock hammer.

The Henry single trigger functioned entirely differently than the refined multiple-lever triggers of Kentucky or Hawken rifles. Considering the fact that it operated with a different sear arrangement, the Henry trigger was good enough. Pull was measured in pounds, not ounces. But that's not a black mark. After all, weight of pull is measured on today's best hunting rifles in pounds and not ounces unless they are special, double-set or single-set triggers. Twin firing pins ensured that the rim of the Henry cartridge received sufficient force to explode the fulminate therein. This feature helped make the Henry a reliable rifle.

Of course, the Henry had its shortcomings, too. In addition to the absence of a forend, loading the magazine from the front was not ideal. Numerous experiments were performed on the Henry, including various barrel lengths and magazine capacities, magazines with detachable tubes, and various stock style improvements.

The impact of the Henry rifle is still felt today—in private collections, in museums and in the response that contemporary shooters have shown to modern replicas. Today a hunter can take a Henry

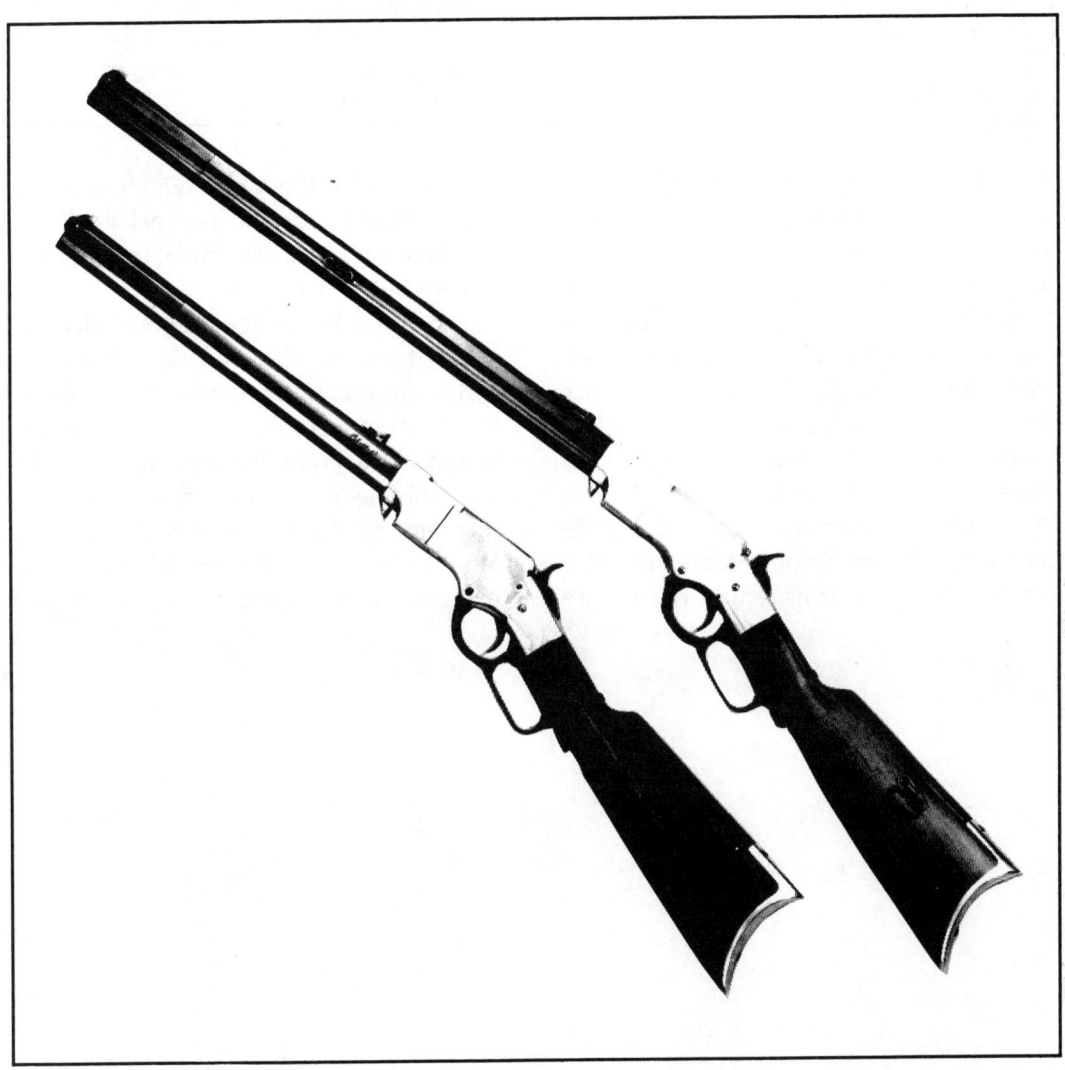

Although not a military arm, some Civil War soldiers were lucky enough to have been able to use the Military Henry. Shown at right in replica (Navy Arms Co.), this brass-framed Henry had a 24-inch octagonal barrel and bar swivels on the barrel and stock. The Henry Trapper (left) is a modern replica for sporting use with 16½-inch carbine barrel.

> ### THE HENRY RIFLE AT A GLANCE
>
> **Period of Manufacture:** 1860 to 1866 by the New Haven Arms Co.
> **Calibers:** 44 Henry Rimfire, Flat or Pointed; 15 rounds plus 1 in the chamber
> **Action:** Lever-action repeater loaded from the muzzle end of the magazine (integral with barrel)
> **Barrel:** Of steel, blued, 24-inch octagonal, usually
> **Triggers:** Single
> **Safety:** Some had half-cock hammer
> **Sights:** Blade front of German silver or brass; adjustable (open notch) rear; few variations
> **Stock:** Straight-grip stock of walnut, oil-finished; no forend or cheekpiece; crescent-shaped or rounded buttstock
> **Furniture:** Brass receiver and crescent-shaped buttplate; some iron-frame models made with rounded buttplate
> **Variations:** Little customizing done because of the Civil War, although some embellished with engraving, etc.; sling swivels on military model

look-alike into the field after big game wherever the cartridge is allowed by conservation law. The Navy Arms Company, for example, provides several well-made Henry replicas for today's shooters, including iron-frame and brass-frame models with 24-inch barrels. The Henry Military Rifle, weighing 9¼ pounds, also sports a 24-inch barrel as well as sling swivels on the side of the rifle, as the original had. A 22-inch barrel Henry Carbine and a 16½-inch barrel Henry Trapper Model are also offered. All Navy Arms replica Henrys are chambered for the 44-40 Winchester centerfire round (not the original 44 Henry rimfire round) and are available with three levels of engraving.

B. Tyler Henry took a good idea and made it better. The rifle named for him and its ammunition provided a springboard for other developers to leap to greater heights of accomplishment in the design and building of sporting rifles. A direct descendant of the Henry was Winchester's Model 1866, the first rifle to bear Oliver's name—and the subject of the next chapter.

WINCHESTER'S 1866
THE POPULAR "YELLOW BOY"

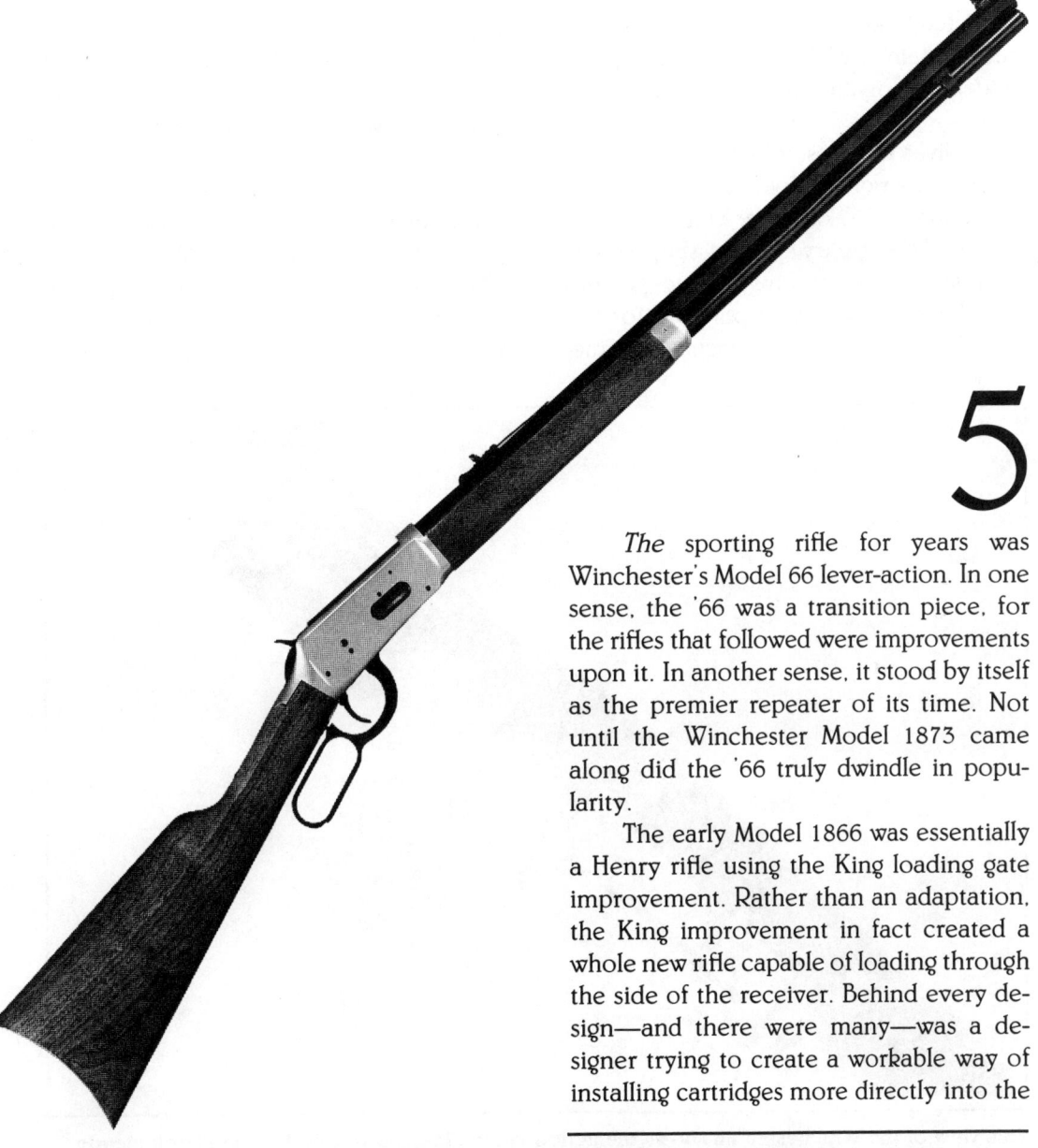

5

The sporting rifle for years was Winchester's Model 66 lever-action. In one sense, the '66 was a transition piece, for the rifles that followed were improvements upon it. In another sense, it stood by itself as the premier repeater of its time. Not until the Winchester Model 1873 came along did the '66 truly dwindle in popularity.

The early Model 1866 was essentially a Henry rifle using the King loading gate improvement. Rather than an adaptation, the King improvement in fact created a whole new rifle capable of loading through the side of the receiver. Behind every design—and there were many—was a designer trying to create a workable way of installing cartridges more directly into the

Winchester's Commemorative Model 1866 Rifle with brass receiver.

magazine of the repeating lever-action rifle, rather than dropping them down the front of the tube, as was required of the Henry rifle. For example, James D. Smith had a fine hinged loading gate patented in 1866. Nelson King's was just one more way of accomplishing the task. However, to show how successful King's idea was, his perfected loading gate (or port) of spring steel remains viable in the ever-popular Model 94 Winchester lever-action "deer rifle."

Oliver Winchester had a penchant for drawing the right people to him, and Nelson King was one of them. King had taken over B. Tyler Henry's job as shop superintendent. Because of his loading-gate design, he was partially responsible for the first rifle ever to bear the Winchester name, the Model 1866. Oliver Winchester, in 1865, had decided to steer the company in a new direction and the state of Connecticut that year granted a new charter for the "Henry Repeating Rifle Company." The following year, however, a special act changed the name to "The Winchester Repeating Arms Company," abbreviated for years as "WRA." The enterprise moved to Bridgeport, Connecticut, where the first '66s were made, and by March of 1867 the operation was in full swing building firearms.

Gunmaking was transpiring between towns, as it were, and Oliver wanted that changed. By August of 1870, the entire Winchester operation was under one roof in New Haven, Conn. Within a few months, Winchester rifles were smoothly flowing

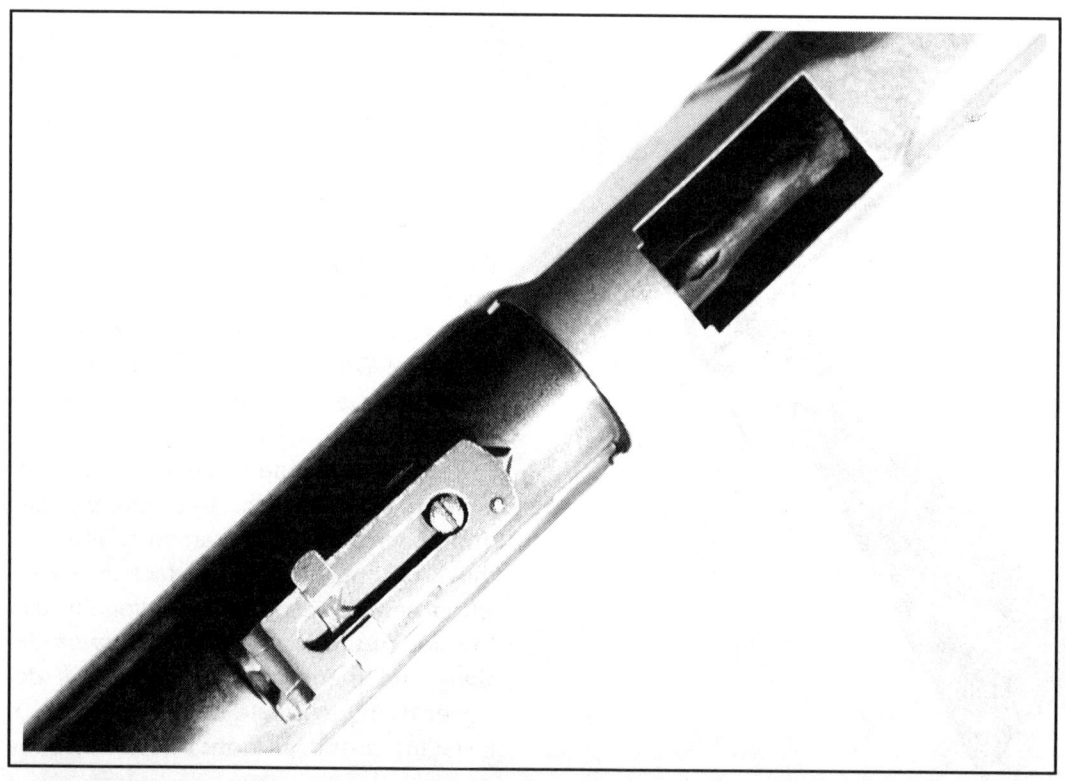

This view of the Winchester '66 shows the action in the closed position. The small bolt clearly reveals the lack of strength in an action of this type, but it was entirely adequate for mild black-powder rounds. Note the adjustable rear sight.

from the factory at a good clip. The Model '66 paved the way for great company success. King's development took less manufacturing effort, while functioning better than the Henry magazine. Over 150,000 were made, with the first '66 serial numbered 12476 in 1866. The reason for the advanced serial number, rather than No. 1, was the fact that the early '66 was indeed a take-off of the Henry rifle. Manufacture continued into 1884. However, the last Winchester Model 1866 did not leave the plant until 1898 because the company built a number of '66s from spare parts left over from the '66 boom years. The very last Model 1866 Winchester was No. 170,101.

The Winchester Model 1866 rifle was important to sportsmen everywhere because it was primarily a sound, reliable repeating firearm. The anemic—by our standards—44 Flat demanded good bullet placement, of course, but there was a fast second shot coming up, and another, and another, to provide firepower where ballistic force was lacking. Against a foe, this brand of firepower was more important than extra bullet energy, for it kept an antagonist at bay. In the heyday of the '66 the outdoorsman enjoyed his hunting. He reveled in putting meat on the table with his rifle. But he had to think, too, of saving his own skin if the situation arose. And the situation did arise in a land where "the law" was yet to filter into all parts of the territory.

The Model '66 was popular in foreign countries as well as in America. Since old records are lost, it is impossible to know exactly how many '66s were sold out of the U.S., but between 70,000 and 100,000 would be reasonable. Turkey bought a good many of the slick-operating lever-action rifles. Mexico, Chile, Peru and Argentina were other purchasers. The Model 1866 became a benchmark hunting rifle. All the same, Oliver Winchester was initially disappointed. He had had other plans for the '66 at the onset—big sales to the U.S. Government. But those sales never materialized because the testing procedures used by the Army included operation with sand in the action and rust. The single-shot Springfield Trap Door Service rifle kept the job.

Oliver Winchester had too much vision to linger long on the trail of tears over failure. He himself was bent on invention. He believed in his company, his men and himself. His inventive efforts earned Winchester some patents, including a refined loading tube and an auxiliary percussion chamber, a device that was inserted into the repeating rifle in order to turn it into a single-shot muzzleloading rifle. Why a muzzleloader from a repeater? There were probably load efficiency reasons. Winchester's ideas, good enough to earn patents, were, however, not outrageously successful.

THE '66 HAD STYLE, FUNCTION

The Model 1866 Winchester had the same brass receiver as found on its predecessors. In fact, the material is better-called "gunmetal." Yellow in color, this particular brass is composed of bronze, copper and zinc, whereas usual brass is copper and zinc. Because of its color, the Indians allegedly called it the "Yellow Boy." This unique metal was amply strong to hold the pressures of the same 44 Henry cartridge that served the Henry rifle. All '66s were chambered for this rimfire cartridge, in both Flat and Pointed versions. Confusion arises on this point because it is quite possible to encounter Winchester Model 1866s with centerfire chamberings. While it is true that 1,020 centerfire '66s were sent to Brazil in 1891, these had been converted from rimfire to centerfire and were not originally built as centerfire chamberings. Furthermore, gunowners could have had their personal '66s rechambered to shoot other cartridges or converted from rimfire to centerfire. This is an important point, for it clearly shows that certain sportsmen were thinking along the right lines when they wanted to improve the Winchester Model 1866 rifle by getting away from the 44 Henry rimfire round, a condition that was eventually satisfied by the Winchester company itself.

The '66 rifle carried a standard octagonal 24-inch barrel, while the carbine had a 20-inch round barrel. Barrels of up to 36 inches long were available through special order, with all sizes in between. One sample rifle, for example, had a barrel 28 inches long. The 1866 Musket carried a round 27-inch barrel, no doubt an attempt to interest the military-minded. The '66 remained, for the most part, a sporter, however. The steel barrel was usually blued and barrels could be ordered partially round/partially octagonal and browned. Early '66 barrel muzzles wore a flat crown with no recess at the muzzle. Later Winchester '66s had the standard recessed muzzle crown.

The longer barreled models had commensurately long magazine tubes. An 1866 loaded with the 44 Henry Flat cartridge carried 17 rounds, 13 for the carbine version. The earlier round-nosed version of the 44 Henry rimfire cartridge cut these

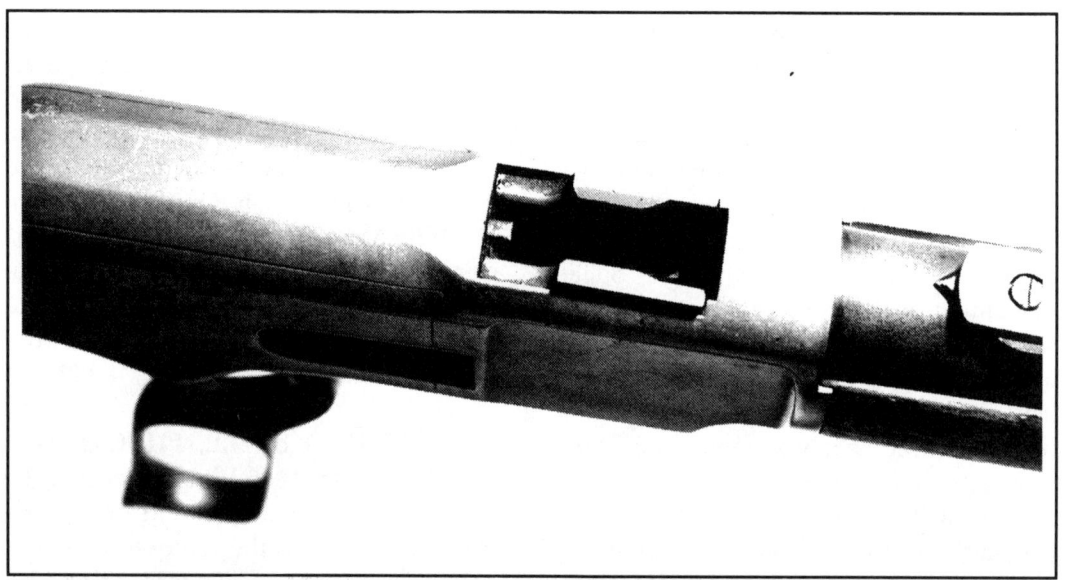

Here the '66 is shown with the action open, indicating why the design was not strong enough for cartridges of higher pressures. It clearly shows why Winchester went with a stronger action for smokeless powder.

figures down by two rounds. If a shooter didn't need so many shots, he could opt, after 1871, for a half-magazine Model '66.

The carbine version of the '66 weighed $7^3/_4$ pounds, the octagon barreled rifle went $9^1/_2$ pounds, and the musket '66 weighed in at $8^1/_4$ pounds, according to Winchester advertisements.

The finger levers were provided with a latch, the idea being to secure the lever from falling or being pulled downward out of the battery position, rendering the rifle incapable of firing. Of course, when the latch was in place, it demanded moving it aside before the action could be worked. The action was open up top to all sorts of elements—rain, snow, sleet, bits of branches broken off by horse or man in motion, dirt, dust, whatever. That is why a sliding port cover was built in. In place, the cover prevented any foreign elements from entering the workings of the action. Some models had loading port covers as well, a perhaps overly concerned reaction to thwart entry to the magazine of the same foreign elements that might invade the top of the action. Double firing pins were retained. These had worked well on the Henry rifle and it was felt that the sometimes tough copper rimfire case might be best served with two firing pins to ensure positive ignition.

The '66 was considered a safe rifle. And it was—at least as safe as the shooter behind the hammer. Speaking of the hammer, early models had no half-cock safety setting. There was plenty of pro and con argument for this sort of hammer. A great many customers felt that the half-cock setting was less safe than the hammer without this notch. But after about 23,000 models were made, the half-cock hammer became the norm.

The trigger that tripped the hammer of the Model 1866 was a single-stage type. Trigger pull was acceptable. Once again, the standard trigger offered on the lever-action repeating rifle simply could not match those special triggers so often provided on the longrifles and plains rifles of old. However, they served the function of the rifle quite well enough for most applications.

The stock of the Model 1866 Winchester was as plain as a pane of clear glass. To be sure, the wood was good, being for the most part select straight-grain American black walnut. Special order fancy-grain walnut (burl) was very rare. The dimensions of the stock were standard. Straight grip. Special (personal) dimensions, including length of pull and drop at comb, could be purchased on special order. This model, however, had a forend. The shooter of a '66 had a wooden handle up front, rather than the cold barrel/magazine of the Henry rifle that had no forend of wood. Both forestock and buttstock were oil-finished; varnish wood finish was available at extra cost. The standard buttplate of the stock was made of brass. For the rifle and carbine, the buttplate was "rifle style" or crescent-shaped. On the musket, it was a modified shotgun style. Steel buttplates were found on later Model '66s.

The Model 1866 shows up with an incredible array of variations. This is an important fact, because it highlights the trend started in very early American riflemaking—customizing a piece for a specific buyer. Modifications on the wood, stock and barrel dimensions, as well as options for checkering and gold-plating the receiver, or plating it in silver or nickel, were available. Nickel was the most popular option, while gold the least. Engravings were possible in any imaginable configuration. Artists in metal, such as C.F. Ulrich, created beautiful work on the ample metal canvas of the '66, including animals such as buffalo, deer, elk and others. The ordinary blued-steel rifle barrel could be ordered in a plum brown finish, very much the same stain as found on early rifles of muzzleloader genre.

The saddle ring was popular, and somewhat practical. The ring was useful for retaining the rifle in its boot on horseback. Tie a leather thong through the ring and

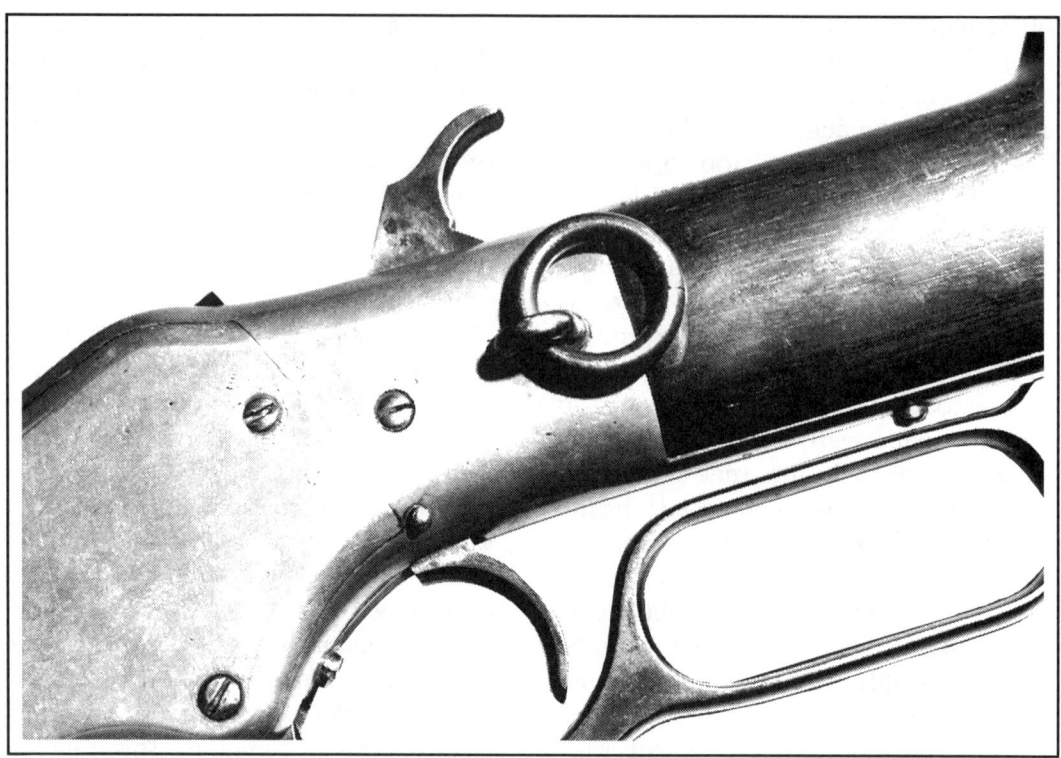
Close-up of the saddle ring attached to brass receiver on the Model 1866 Winchester.

onto the saddle and the rifle would stay put in its scabbard. A bayonet lug was available for the musket model, again in keeping with the idea that the '66 would make a good army rifle. Some of the later models had sliding trapdoors in their steel buttplates. Other models had hinged trapdoors made of brass. These opened to recesses in the buttstock. Cleaning rods with brass tips were first offered, later to be replaced by those with steel tips.

By 1872 a customer could order a Model 1866 with a recoil pad. The pad was probably useful for preventing slippage on the shoulder and preventing the rifle from falling over if it were rested in a corner. Certainly, no recoil pad was needed for shoulder comfort. The '66 with its low-yield cartridge did not develop enough kick to push a mouse over.

Sights were the typical open variety of the day. Again, the variations were numerous and bountiful. Carbines might have non-adjustable leaf rear sights with standard post or blade front sights. Muskets had adjustable leaf rear sights, but could be purchased with fixed sights as well as sporting open rear sights. These, too, were combined with rather simple front sights. By serial number 166,000 there was a standard adjustable rear sight for the carbine. Again, the front sight was plain, but could be of one-piece steel. Tang sights were not popular, but these peep sights did fit well on the Winchester Model '66. The sights of the '66 were put to the task of hitting a target by shooters well-versed in the art of sending bullets downrange. Modern marksmen who practice with the sights of the "old guns" are very often surprised at

52   LEGENDARY SPORTING RIFLES

how effective practice makes these seemingly crude devices. Certainly, there is challenge in taking a clean sight picture through the notch of an open rear sight and optically aligning that aimpoint on target. But it was done once with credit. And it's done all the time today by experts who have not forgotten how.

In its 1884 catalogue, the E.C. Meacham Arms Company of St. Louis presents Winchester Model 1866 rifles for sale. The carbine, its weight noted as 7¼ pounds with a 13-shot magazine (no barrel length noted), sold for $20. A Sporting Rifle, weight 8¾ pounds with 24-inch or under round barrel and 17 shots, sold for $22. Another Sporting Rifle with octagonal barrel and 9-pound weight, also $22. All three rifles were chambered of course for the 44 rimfire, listed as the 44 Flat with a 200-grain lead bullet and 28 grains of powder. In 1895, Montgomery Ward offered discounted Model 1866 Winchesters for only $12.83—a bargain in any era. Of course, the same store sold the then brand-new Winchester Model 1894 lever-action repeater for only $10.94 in the round barrel version.

A hunter, outdoorsman or adventurer could hardly do better in the 1860s and

The Model 1866 Carbine had the same "Yellow Boy" brass receiver as the rifle version, but the shorter 20-inch round barrel. A popular sporter for years, it held 13 rounds of 44 rimfire ammo and weighed about 7¾ pounds.

> ### THE MODEL 1866 WINCHESTER AT A GLANCE
>
> **Period of Manufacture:** 1866 to 1898
> **Calibers:** 44 Henry Rimfire Flat or Pointed; 13 to 17 rounds; later conversions to centerfire chamberings
> **Action:** Lever-action repeater w/sliding port cover to prevent foreign elements from entering the action
> **Barrel:** Of steel, blued or browned. Rifle, 24-inch octagonal; Carbine, 20-inch round; Musket, 27 inches. May be part round/part octagonal, up to 36 inches
> **Weight (approx.):** Rifle, 9 1/2 lbs.; Carbine, 7 3/4 lbs.; Musket, 8 1/4 lbs.
> **Triggers:** Single-stage type
> **Safety:** Half-cock hammer
> **Sights:** Open; carbine offered with post or blade front, non-adjustable leaf rear; a number of variations
> **Stock:** Straight-grip plain stock of American black walnut; a few special order fancy-grain walnut; wooden forend; oil-finished, a few varnished
> **Furniture:** Brass receiver of yellow gunmetal from which "Yellow Boy" got its name; brass rifle-style (crescent-shaped) buttplate; steel buttplates on later models
> **Variations:** An incredible array, including engraved models; saddle rings attached to some receivers; sliding or hinged trapdoors in buttplates; recoil pads; etc.

1870s than the Winchester Model '66 for medium-sized game and for protection. But there was another repeating rifle on the horizon that would eclipse the great little rifle. It would work as well—and better—than the '66, with an even stronger action and a much improved cartridge. That rifle, the famous Model 1873 Winchester, is the subject of Chapter 9. But before that, let's look at three single-shots that provided big-time power, long-range accuracy and immense overall effectiveness in the hands of riflemen: the reliable Winchester Hi-Wall, the great Sharps "Buffalo Rifle" and Remington's strong-actioned Rolling Block.

MODEL 1885 WINCHESTER
THE SINGLE-SHOT EXCELS

6

Firearms development is a game of leap ahead—jump back. If this were not so, the excellent Winchester Single Shot rifle would never have been developed, let alone manufactured. After all, by the year 1885, Winchester had a number of fine lever-action repeaters on the market, as did the Marlin company. In 1886, Winchester's dependable Model '86 would emerge—not only as a repeater, but as a powerful big-bore rifle of high power chambered for cartridges of the 45-70 Government class. No matter. The single-shot rifle was to be offered from the company known for repeaters. Perhaps that's what makes the rifle so interesting. How good would it have to be to compete with its own company's models? And would

The Winchester Model 1885 Single Shot (high wall), as currently made by Sharps Arms.

anyone buy a single-shot when repeaters were commonplace and highly admired? Looking back, a modern firearms enthusiast has to wonder if Winchester leaders didn't sit around the conference table asking the same questions. Perhaps. They may have decided on the Browning invention only as an expediency. Here is why.

Without malice, John Moses Browning had violated a Winchester patent. T.G. Bennett, vice president and manager of Winchester, went to Utah to discuss patent infringement with the Browning brothers on May 17, 1883. The problem was with a reloading tool. Winchester held a patent for the King 1880 model reloading tool and the Browning brothers had been making a version too similar to the King device. Perhaps Winchester managers felt that going after the Brownings for monetary compensation would not be as fruitful as striking a bargain with the brothers. John Browning had developed a rifle that Winchester could be interested in manufacturing.

Browning's first rifle of consequence was built by the gun genius in his 22nd year. (*See* the story of John Browning in *Great Shooters of the World*, Stoeger Publishing, 1990.) Supposedly, John had studied an overly complicated single-shot design that he knew he could improve upon. And he did. The improvement earned Browning his first patent, No. 220271, applied for May 12, 1879, and granted the following October 7. The Browning boys are supposed to have built about 600 examples of their single-shot ri-

Close-up view of the Single Shot action. This is the high-wall version of the Model 1885 currently built by the Sharps Arms Company of Big Timber, Montana.

fle, named the "Model Single Shot." This figure is arrived at, in part, through serial numbers. The lowest number Model Single Shot in collection (per my latest information) is No. 118. The highest is No. 488. But no one knows if Browning production began with a No. 1 or a No. 100, or if indeed any models beyond No. 488 were ever built. Students of the Browning single-shot say that 600 is too high. They reason that John and his brothers, having only hand-powered tools and machines at the time (reportedly), would not likely build 600 rifles in a few years. They also conclude that if 600 were built, more Browning single-shots would have survived. Instead, they are very rare.

Winchester bought Browning's patent, *plus* any remaining stock of Model Single Shot Browning-manufactured rifles for $8,000. Nobody knows, nor do any records show, how many finished Browning single-shots Winchester acquired. The company called its version of the Browning rifle the Model 1885. It was also known as the Winchester Single Shot.

The company had to make a few changes in design to facilitate factory production, but the Browning invention remained quite close to its original concept. The earlier suggestion that Winchester leaders may have had reservations about producing a single-shot rifle during the era of the repeater is somewhat overshadowed by the fact that the Sharps single-shot rifle had not been at all forgotten by hunters in the year 1885 when Winchester offered its version of a single-shot big game rifle. Sharps had closed its doors in 1881, but unlike so many good products that for one reason or another fall by the wayside, the Sharps rifle was warmly remembered and sought after.

Winchester wanted to capitalize on that fact. Expert hunters had always done well with a single-shot rifle. The theory was that "It's the first shot that counts," and that a successful outdoorsman needn't make up for poor shot placement with a fast second opportunity. The Winchester Model 1885 offered another plus: accuracy. Without the least reservation, it can be said that the Model 1885 was more accurate "out of the box" than any of its lever-action contemporaries. American shooters always were, and always will be, interested in top-grade accuracy. So it came to pass that the Winchester single-shot was destined for success, although in no way did it seriously cut into the sales of repeaters.

The Great Western Gun Works company carried the Winchester advertisement for the new 1885 Single Shot. Great Western called the rifle "The Winchester Single Shot" and the ad reads, "This gun has the old reliable Sharp's model breech-block and lever, and it is as safe as that arm." An immediate reference to the Sharps supports the idea that Winchester wanted to take advantage of the image created by that superb rifle. (Incidentally, Winchester's notice is in error concerning "Sharp's." The name was Christian Sharps and the company was called the "Sharps Rifle Mfg. Co.") The ad continues: "The firing pin is automatically withdrawn at the first opening movement of the gun, and held back until the gun is closed." This is in reference to the fact that the firing pin could not be damaged or sheared off during the working of the rifle's action. "The hammer is centrally hung," the notice states, "but drops down with the breech-block when the gun is opened and is cocked by the closing movement. It can also be cocked by hand. This arrangement allows the barrel to be wiped and examined from the breech." These words are vital in understanding one of the outstanding reasons for the success of the Winchester Single Shot.

Why the concern for being able to wipe the bore out easily? Because 1885 represents blackpowder days. It would be 1895 before Winchester would have its Model 1894 sporting rifle chambered for a smokeless cartridge. (*See* Chapter 12.) The single-shot could be cleaned quickly and easily, with blackpowder fouling removed without concern for soot encumbering the workings of a magazine, or the feeding of cartridges into the chamber area. The advertisement closes, "In outline, everything has been done to make the gun pleasing to the eye. It can be furnished with or without set trigger, with barrels of all ordinary lengths and weights, and for all standard cartridges; also with rifle and shot gun butt, plain or fancy wood, or with pistol grip. The rifle has elevating rear sight." The part about the sleek lines is understatement. Handling a Winchester Single Shot original, or the current Browning replica, is sweet. The rifle feels slender in the hand, but fits snugly to the shoulder for easy management.

THE RICHNESS OF VARIETY

Students of the Winchester Single Shot are faced with a tremendous challenge in trying to enumerate two things about the Model 1885: extras and chamberings. Nobody knows exactly how many special appointments were built into various Model 1885 rifles. Certainly it is impractical, if not impossible, to list all the cartridges chambered in the 1885. The price list accompanying the ad notes that "These guns are adapted to all standard sizes of cartridges, both rim and center fire." Rimfires carried barrels of 24-inch length. All other cartridges got 26-inch barrels. The new rifle, with octagon or partly round/partly octagon barrel, ran about $11. A round barrel Model 1885 was $10.50. Except. The word "except" runs rampant concerning the 1885, and this "except" extends to numerous special orders and dozens of sub-models. So accept the remarks on barrel length as marginally accurate.

Here are a few extras offered in the early days of the Model 1885, which give the gun a special flavor. It's clear that Winchester meant to entice the hunter with a myriad of special-order refinements. For example, choose, if you like:

- Longer barrel at $1/inch
- Full nickel plating, $4
- Nickel trim, $2.50
- Silver trim, $4
- Gold trim, $8
- Set trigger, $3
- Fancy walnut stocks, $4
- Checkering, $4
- Casehardening, $1
- Pistol-grip, extra fancy checkered walnut stocks, $12

There were finish options, swivels, carrying straps, canvas gun cases, leather cases and woven cartridge belts. Actually, the extras advertised for the Winchester 1885 rifle by the 19th-century Pittsburgh gun house were just the beginning of those currently available from Winchester.

The strong Winchester Model 1885 single-shot action is familiar to us as the falling-block style. Because of this action, Winchester was able to make the accurate claim that the Model 1885 was like the Sharps single-shot. The breech block lowers by working the lever, which includes the trigger guard on this model. Winchester suggested that the 1885 was even more Sharps-like than it was. As noted above, the company called the action "the old reliable Sharp's model breech-block." Re-

The single-shot rifle has never gone entirely out of vogue. This single-shot with Monte Carlo stock and scope is typical of the breed. The marksman who believes in the adage, "Make the first shot count," does not feel handicapped with a one-shot rifle.

member that the original Browning single-shot was different from the factory Winchester model of 1885. The frame of the Browning is flat-sided and shorter than Winchester's; on many Winchesters, the frame flares out where wood and metal join. Browning's upper and lower tangs are of the same length and integral to the action; Winchester's Single Shot has longer tangs, plus the lower tang detaches from the action. Making statements of 100% validity concerning all these points is difficult because of the many variations in the field; however, these points are fairly solid. And, for our purposes, it's fair to say that the Browning single-shot and the Winchester Model 1885 are basically alike, and that only minor differences, some of them associated with factory production, separate the two.

The Browning company was ever trying to improve its single-shot when the brothers had control of its manufacture. Winchester was no different and upgraded versions abound. While most variations are subtle, one alteration is definitely outstanding—the exact configuration of the action housing proper or what we know as the "High Wall" and "Low Wall" actions of the 1885. When this feature is left unexplained, the reader sometimes turns to his imagination for an answer. However, the High Wall/Low Wall models are so distinct that their names are often capitalized as proper nouns describing what one would assume are entirely different firearms, which they are not. All of Browning's single-shots were of the high-wall style, where the sides of the receiver come up around the hammer with just part of the hammer showing from the side. After about 5,000 Winchester Single Shots were manufactured, the company offered a low-wall version, where the sides of the action do not come up as high, thereby visually exposing the hammer spur as well as much of the hammer. The advantage of a low-wall frame meant greater access to the breech of the rifle, making loading and unloading more convenient. A high wall was not deemed necessary for modest-pressure cartridges, so there was no danger of action failure for the low-wall design.

The high-wall model was favored by gunsmiths who built special rifles for special uses. Harry Pope, one of the world's most gifted barrelmakers, built his famous Schuetzen-style rifles on the high-wall action. These were used mostly for offhand shooting and many were chambered for the 32-40 Winchester cartridge or the 38-55 round, both known for their accuracy. These rifles could be muzzleloaded, even though they were breechloaders. The shooter inserted a primed but empty cartridge case into the action and closed it. Then powder was poured downbore to settle into the cartridge case. Or the case could be inserted with powder already in it. Either way, the bullet was run home with a ramrod. Great care was made to ensure that the projectile was seated the same way each time. The value of running the bullet home separate from the cartridge case was an alleviation of cartridge caseneck pressure (neck friction) on the bullet. Harvey Donaldson, a contemporary of Pope's and a great marksman of his time, explained how to "frontload" the Schuetzen rifle to his audience of readers. (Both Pope and Donaldson are featured in *Great Shooters of the World*.)

There were also thin-side models and thick-side models. Thickness or thinness again refers to the walls of the action housing proper. Many low-wall models were of thick-side design. Also, when Winchester built Express Single Shots, these had thick sides. Express referred to cartridges carrying heavy loads. Thin-side models were slightly flared. But once again, trying to completely define and isolate special features of the 1885 is awesome. The special features were not necessarily cosmetic, ei-

Special 32-40 ammunition was available from Winchester for a while. Many marksmen still consider the 32-40 one of the more accurate cartridges of all time and a number of fine single-shot rifles of the Model 1885 type were chambered for this cartridge.

ther, for in many cases they were mechanical. For example, a shooter could order, for one dollar extra, a "fly" or detent in the action that left the hammer at half-cock instead of full-cock at the opening and closing of the action. This could be considered a special safety measure. Of course there was a takedown model that appeared in 1909. Takedowns were popular in the 19th and early 20th centuries.

A KALEIDOSCOPE OF CALIBERS

Chamberings for the Winchester Single Shot we know were wildly broad. Some experts say that no other Winchester rifle has been chambered for so many different cartridges. The rounds run the gamut from 22 rimfire through 50 caliber, and there are notations of a "577 English cartridge" chambered in the Winchester Single Shot. Winchester's Express calibers in 38, 40 and 45 were chambered in the 1885. These rounds were made for the Single Shot using a case 3¼ inches long, much like the 45-120 Sharps, which, by the way, was also factory-chambered in the Single Shot. The 35 WCF was a Model 1885 offering, as was the 405 Winchester. So were the smokeless powder 30-30 and 30-40 Krag rounds. Don't forget that the Model 1885 action was used to build a 20-gauge single-shot shotgun with full choke bore, modified or cylinder, also available on special order.

The 1895 catalogue of Montgomery Ward & Co. of Chicago illustrated the Winchester Single Shot with open action, to show its function clearly. The advertisement noted that "Although this rifle is a recent production, it has become almost as famous as the 'Winchester Repeater' and stands in the 'front rank' with the very best target rifles of this and other countries." Wards individually listed several Single Shots in their advertisement, to include:

Rifle of many cartridges, the Single Shot was chambered for the 22 WRF (Winchester Rimfire) cartridge with 45-grain lead bullet at about 1200-1350 feet per second.

22 rimfire BB Cap, 22 Short or 22 Long from a 24-inch barrel or 26-inch barrel; 32 caliber rimfire Extra Short, Short and Long, 26-inch barrel; 22 caliber centerfire also in a 26-inch barrel. The latter no doubt influenced "hotshot" 22 centerfires later on. Wards also listed 25 and 32 caliber centerfires. The 32-40 was listed with a 30-inch barrel. More cartridges were offered: 38-40, 38-55, 40-60 Winchester, 40-65, 40-70, 40-82 Winchester, 40-90, 45-70, 45-90, and the 30 US, which was the 30-40 Krag smokeless powder round.

Ward's list is long, but hardly complete. It doesn't show the 30-30 or a 44-40, or 45-120 Sharps, or 50-95 Express or 50-110 Express. Shoverling, Daly & Gales of New York in its catalogue of 1903 also presented the Winchester Single Shot (they do not call the rifle a Model 1885). Listed are calibers 22 Short, Long and Long Rifle, 22 WRF (Winchester Rim Fire), 25 Stevens, 32 Short and Long, 38 Express 40-70 Straight, 40-70 Ballard, 40-90 Ballard, 40-90 Sharps, 40 Express, 40-60 WCF, 40-65, 45-60, 45-75, 45 Express, 50-95 Express, and 50-110 Express. The 30-40 Krag is also in the lineup, along with the 22 WCF, 25-20, 30 US Army, 32 WCF (32-20), 32-40, 38 WCF, 38-55, 38-56, 40-82 and the 44-

40 WCF. Just when you think you have a handle on the calibers, remember that the rifle was first chambered in the 45 Ely, which is seldom included in lists. That's right, Serial No. 1 was a 45 Ely.

Furthermore, what about all those special order rifles? We know of these: 236 Rimmed, 236 Rimless (6mm Navy), 7mm Mauser, 30-06 Springfield, 7.65mm (no further designation), 8mm Mauser, 9mm Mauser, 401 WCF, 43 Spanish, 44 Comblain, 45 Sharps (with a case 2.4 inches long), 45 Sharps (with a case 2.6 inches long, 45 Sharps (with a case $2^{7}/_{8}$ inches long), the 45 Sharps (with $3^{1}/_{4}$-inch case)

Another cartridge used in the Single Shot was the 38-40 Winchester, a round for which many fine old rifles were chambered.

considered a special order by Winchester during part of the Single Shot's history, the 50-90 Sharps (with $2^{1}/_{2}$-inch case), a $50 \times 3^{1}/_{4}$ cartridge and the 577 Ely, which is no doubt the "English 577" referred to earlier.

Of the variations, individual styles and special order surprises, one of the more interesting is the Musket. In a sense, the Musket defies the very principle underlying the '85—graceful lines, neatness, compactness. The musket is, at least to my eye, uglier than a truckload of tarantulas. The Musket, by the way, was noted as "trim" by at least one observer in the early 20th century, so my comment must be taken as opinion, if not prejudice. While the Musket version of the Single Shot may not have been as pretty as the standard version of the rifle, at least to this pair of eyes, it was however accurate. The Musket was brought out in 1905 with a high-wall receiver in solid frame, in caliber 22 Long Rifle, with long forend, almost full-length of the barrel, and two stout military-like barrel bands plus military sights. The musket was called a "Winder" model, named after Colonel Charles B. Winder. One of the finest marksmen of his day, Winder enlisted in the Ohio Infantry in 1897 and served in the Spanish-American War. He won the Leech Cup match of 1903 and received a gold medal for the National Trophy Individual Rifle Match in 1905. He won many other trophies as well.

Winder became a captain and with that rank held the position of Inspector of Small Arms Practice of the Ohio National Guard. He introduced indoor rifle practice to his men. He also made a number of significant alterations in existing arms to promote their accuracy and use as target-shooting guns. Winder received patents for sights, special targets, firearm parts and ammunition. He developed a tube sight for target shooting that ended up on the Springfield service rifle of 1903. Winder was in part responsible for alterations in the Single Shot. Said Winder, "After a correspondence covering several months I succeeded in interesting the Winchester people and they made up a .22 caliber musket for me." Therefore, the "Winder Musket" was named in his honor.

Accurate and inexpensive, the Musket was also chambered in 45-70 Government and other calibers, so it was not a 22 rimfire only. Some muskets were chambered for the 22 Long Rifle, while others were chambered for the 22 Short, the latter being more popular at the time. There was also a 25-20 Musket, but more interesting were muskets in 25-35 Winchester, 30-30, 32 Winchester Special, 303 British, 33 Winchester, 35 Winchester and 405 Winchester.

In the late 19th century, a Schuetzen Single Shot appeared. The German style of offhand target shooting and a search for supremely accurate rifles and cartridges to serve this competition prompted the Schuetzen Winchester Single Shot. They were expensive rifles and not greatly in demand, so only a comparative few were made. But these rifles did qualify for the Schuetzen code of accuracy and style, with spur finger levers, the Schuetzen buttplate with its "horns" above and below for control during offhand shooting, double set triggers and other traits.

An existing Schuetzen Winchester Single Shot in 30-30 supports the fact that the 30-30 cartridge was always capable of fine accuracy from the correct rifle. Another Schuetzen rifle with scope and palm grip, looking like a rifle designed for 200-meter competition, turns out to be cham-

SOME CHAMBERINGS FOR THE 1885 WINCHESTER SINGLE-SHOT

Rimfires

22 BB Cap	22 WRF	32 Extra Long
22 Short	22 Winchester Auto	38 Short
22 Long	25 Stevens	38 Long
22 Extra Long	32 Short	38 Extra Long
22 Long Rifle	32 Long	44 Flat

Centerfires

22 Extra Long	35 WCF	40 Express
22 WCF	38 WCF	40-60 WCF
22 Winchester Single Shot	38 Short	40-65 WCF
25-20 Single Shot	38 Long	40-82 WCF
(not 25-20 WCF)	38 Extra Long	405 Winchester
25 WCF	38-40	44 WCF
25-35 Winchester	38-55 Winchester	44-40
30 WCF (30-30)	38-56 Winchester	45 Ely
30 Army (30-40 Krag)	38-72 WCF	45-60 WCF
303 British	38 Express	45-70 Government
32 Short	40-50 Straight	45-75 WCF
32 Long	40-60	45-90 WCF
32 Extra Long	40-65	45 Express
32 WCF	40-70 Straight	45-120 Sharps
32 Winchester Special	40-70 Ballard	50-95 Express
32 Ideal	40-82	50-100 Express
32-40 Winchester	40-90 Ballard	50-110 Express
33 WCF	40-90 Sharps	577 English

The chart above shows some of the chamber offerings in the 1885 Single Shot, as compiled by George Madis in his title, *The Winchester Book* (1971), and augmented from subsequent research.

> ### The 1885 Winchester Single Shot at a Glance
>
> **Period of Manufacture:** circa 1885 to 1920
> **Calibers:** An incredible array, from the 22 rimfire to large centerfire rounds (*see* separate chart)
> **Action:** Single shot
> **Barrel:** Of steel, blued; usually between 24" and 30", depending on type and customizing
> **Triggers:** With or without set trigger
> **Sights:** Elevating rear sight
> **Stock:** Straight-grip or pistol-grip plain stock of American walnut; graceful forend; oil-finished usually
> **Furniture:** Casehardened receiver; buttplate, if desired
> **Variations:** Numerous. Made in high-wall and low-wall versions, Musket, Carbine, Schuetzen, etc. Extensive customizing of every possible feature

bered for the 22 Short cartridge. Of course, the 32-40 was represented, being a round well-liked by Pope, Zischang, Schalk and many other premier Schuetzen riflemen and gunmakers.

Almost the antithesis of the Schuetzen Single Shot was the carbine, or "Baby Carbine," as it was called. While at least one Single Shot had a 36-inch barrel, the carbine carried a truncated barrel of only 15-inch length and might wear a saddle ring. And it came in standard chamberings for the 32-20, 38-40, and 44-40 rounds. Low-wall receivers were used for carbines in lighter calibers, but high walls were employed on carbines that were chambered for larger rounds. Carbines were also available with 16-, 18- and 20-inch barrels, but the 15-inch barrel was the standard length.

The Single Shot was made from 1885 to about 1920, according to Norm Flayderman, and stamped from No. 1 onward, but this is no guarantee of an accounting of precisely how many 1885s were made by Winchester—well over 130,000.

The rifle has withstood a certain test of time that has been applied to the other firearms in this book. Would a particular rifle be viable today under modern shooting conditions? The answer for the 1885 is a resounding—Yes! It would be. So much so that the 1885 is still manufactured. Now called the "Browning Model 1885 Single Shot Rifle," it is a replica of John Moses Browning's high-wall falling-block rifle. It has a 28-inch octagonal barrel, weighs about 8½ pounds and comes in calibers 223, 22-250, 270, 30-06, 7mm Remington Magnum and 45-70. Some rifles just live forever.

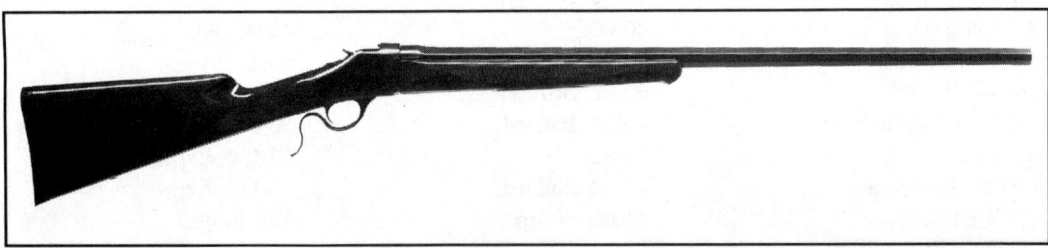

The Browning version of the Model 1885 Single Shot is chambered for several excellent modern cartridges, including the 223, 22-250, 270, 30-06, 7mm Remington Magnum and 45-70. Note the handsome octagonal barrel.

THE SHARPS SINGLE-SHOT
BISON-HUNTING BREECHLOADER

7

The Sharps cartridge rifle was so efficient in its day that a modern marksman or hunter armed with a Sharps in any one of its better original blackpowder chamberings could today successfully hunt all big game in North America. And he could do so loading the cartridges with black powder. In short, the rifle is so good that it can compete with today's fine arms in the field.

Essentially, there are two Sharps rifles: The first is an ingenious, if not perfectly designed, percussion breechloading firearm. The second, and of greater importance to the theme of this work, is the single-shot cartridge breechloader famous for its role during the buffalo days of the 19th century. The enduring myth that a handful

The 1874 Sharps, one of the greats of its time. This by the present C. Sharps Co.

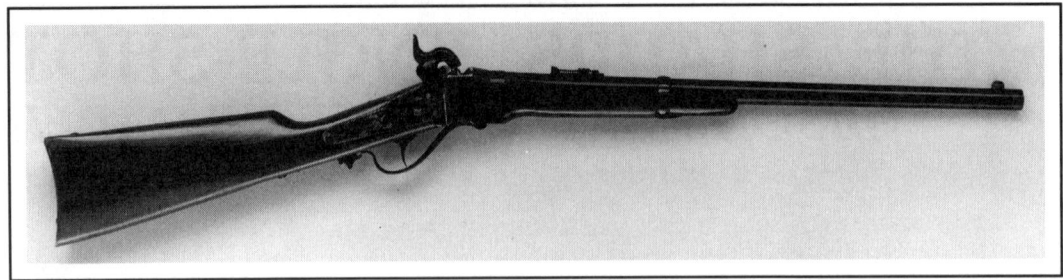

The earlier Sharps blackpowder carbine (1863-1869 type) laid the groundwork for some fine Sharps breechloaders to come. Barrel bands were usually found on the military types.

of hunters traveling in mule-drawn wagons and shooting single-shot rifles wiped out between six and 12 million bison is just that—a story. No such thing happened, any more than that a few fellows with butterfly nets could capture all of the English sparrows in New York state in only a few years.

In spite of the fact that there was a vicious and low-thinking attempt to eliminate the bison with the very rifles spoken of here, there were too many animals covering far too much area for "hunters" to do the whole job. Figuring into the slaughter were so-called sportsmen who blasted shaggies from trains and wagons and many others who wantonly destroyed one of America's greatest wild animals. However, the birth rate added at least two or three million animals per year to the vast herds that covered a region so immense it is difficult to see all of it in a motor vehicle, let alone by animal-powered wagon. It took disease to drop the gigantic bison. The herds disappeared rapidly after the introduction of domestic cattle to the range. Anyone who thinks guns are more powerful than germs must remember that after World War I, Spanish influenza killed more people in less time than in all the battles put together.

This particular view of the bison's demise is important when considering the Sharps rifle and the famous Remington Rolling Block rifle as well, for it has been believed and continually reported that it was the efficiency of these cartridge-shooting guns that brought down millions of bison in a few years. The Sharps and its Remington brother were great rifles, but not that good. However, it was the bison slaughter that promoted the fame of the Sharps firearm. The Congress of 1870 considered giving up on the Far West. The Plains Indian remained a formidable fighter, well-entrenched and mobile. Rooting him out would be almost impossible considering the expanse of his territory and the warrior's ability to roam at will and live off the land. A plan was formulated: get at the Indian through the bison. Army wagons hauled free ammo onto the plains. Salted buffalo tongues alone were worth an American dollar each. Hides brought more cash. Later, even the bones of the unfortunate beasts were sold.

The plan worked only indirectly. The bison were reduced to a scant few. Unbridled shooting caused great inroads on herd numbers, but disease finished the job. The Sharps was not invented as a buffalo rifle. But certain models served so well on the prairie that the rifle's fame was sealed forever because of the high praise afforded by the "buffalo runners."

Piecing together a truly accurate picture of the Sharps saga is like building a thousand-part puzzle without all the segments. However, it's fairly safe to say that the fame of the Sharps began with the military rifle, a boxlock model. It had a percussion hammer affixed to the lockplate and was therefore known as a boxlock action rifle. Furthermore, it had a fine-working automatic priming tape feeder. Comparing the firepower of a muzzleloader to the percussion Sharps is pointless. The latter could be shot at a rate of about 10 rounds a minute—a soldier's delight. The percussion breechloading Sharps rifle was one of the most important stepping stones toward the powerful cartridge-shooting single-shot breechloader.

The priming device of the Sharps percussion is important to any study of the rifle. The original priming unit was engineered by Dr. Edward Maynard, a dentist from Washington, D.C. It was somewhat like our toy cap rolls of today. Each time the hammer of the Sharps was cocked, the priming tape advanced from its container to an in-line position with the hammer's nose cup and a fulminate priming pellet was ready to detonate and send a spark of ignition toward the chamber. Patent No. 5,763 for a "sliding breech" action granted on September 12, 1848, began the Sharps story. Christian Sharps knew he had a good idea. His blackpowder rifle was a breechloader, not a muzzleloader. His first guns, made around 1850 by the Nippes manufacturing company, seriously leaked gas from the breech. The firm was not capable of making parts to the close tolerances demanded of the C. Sharps design.

Sharps decided to look for a new manufacturer and contracted with the Robbins & Lawrence Company of Vermont to build his rifle. Sharps was retained as a consultant and received one dollar for each rifle produced. In 1851, a plant named the Sharps Rifle Co. was opened in Hartford, Conn., and a major goal was a government contract. Robbins & Lawrence spent $100,000 early in the venture. In January

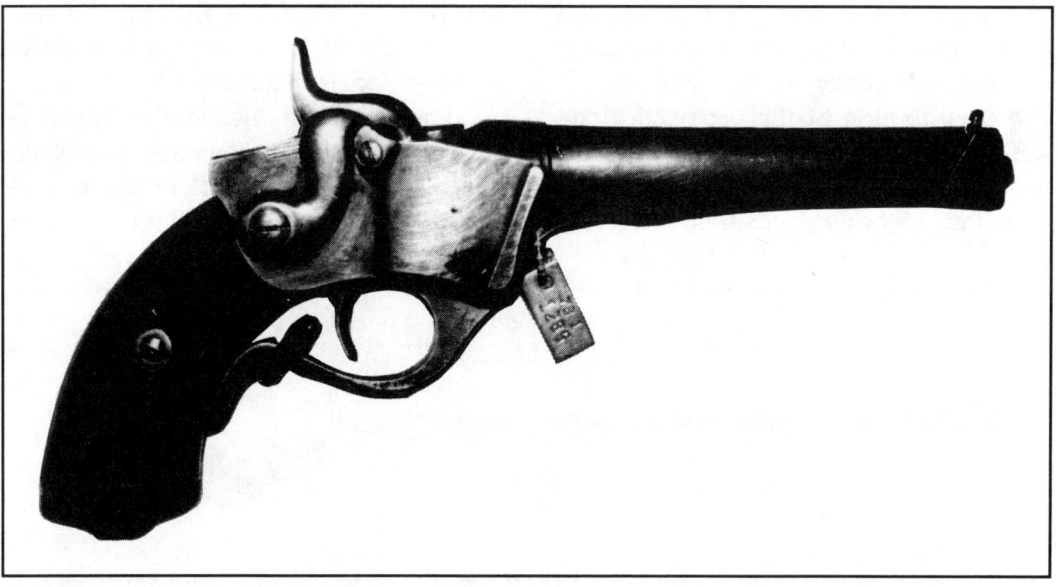

A student of Sharps rifles knows that Christian Sharps was also a builder of pistols. This is a 32-caliber Sharps percussion pistol from the mid-1800s.

of 1852, the government kicked in with an order for Sharps rifles, buying 200 Maynard-primed 52-caliber samples.

Robbins & Lawrence turned out many Sharps sporting rifles as well. The history of these is clouded because the company offered custom-built models. Therefore, no single prototype of sporting rifle was outstanding. Many were caliber 44, but Sharps sporters were chambered in calibers 52 and 36 as well, and there were also smoothbores used as shotguns (marked "S.G." for shotgun). Heavy octagonal barrels were the rule, but round barrels were known too. Robbins & Lawrence worked on the Maynard priming system and bettered the idea with a Sharps disk primer. A slant-breech action was also designed.

BASIC, STRONG, EFFICIENT, FAST

The reliable and simple function of the Sharps led to its initial fame. When the trigger guard was flicked forward, it caused the breech block at the rear of the barrel to drop downward, exposing the breech and chamber. This type of action is called a "falling block." A paper or linen cartridge was inserted directly into the open breech. The back portion of the paper cartridge was cleanly sheared off when the action was closed (by pulling the trigger guard back into its original position). The rifle was basic, strong, efficient and fast.

At the Marine Barracks on February 6, 1860, the Sharps was tested against a military muzzleloading musket used by the Marines. From 100 yards, 30 shots were fired with the musket. Thirteen hits were recorded. Of 40 rounds fired, the Sharps rifle delivered 35 hits. At the close of the test, which included 200- and 300-yard shooting, a regulation musket was placed "in the hands of a recruit who had never loaded a musket" and the soldier was ordered to commence firing. In two minutes, the soldier shot four times, hitting the target once. The same soldier fired the Sharps rifle nine times in two minutes, scoring eight hits.

Report followed report of the Sharps' telling effect in war. Sharps himself stated: "In April 1858, Col. Suasue, at the head of 1,000 men of Vidsuri's force, armed with Sharps' carbines, attacked Governor Manero, in command of 3,000 men of the government forces at San Luis, in Mexico, and achieved a most signal victory, killing upward of 600 men, taking the city, and making prisoners of Governor Manero and three of his colonels, with slight loss." Later a modified Sharps, dubbed the Model of 1863, was sold by the company as a military piece. Called the Sharps BL Percussion Military Rifle, it was chambered for the caliber

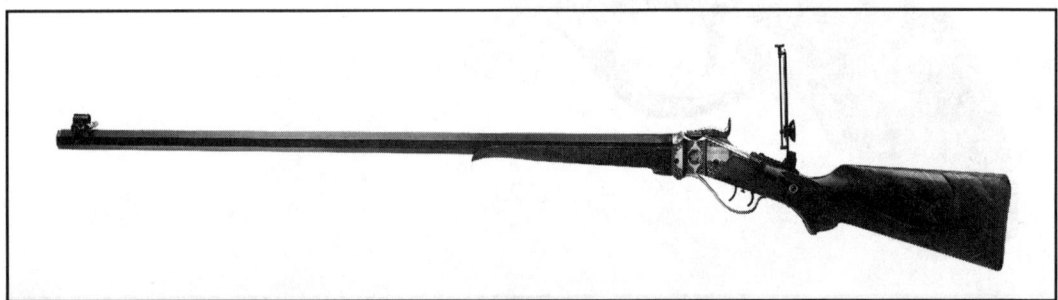

The 1874 Sharps was perfect for the buffalo runner's task. This modern long-range target version, made by the C. Sharps Company of Montana, is a custom-grade arm.

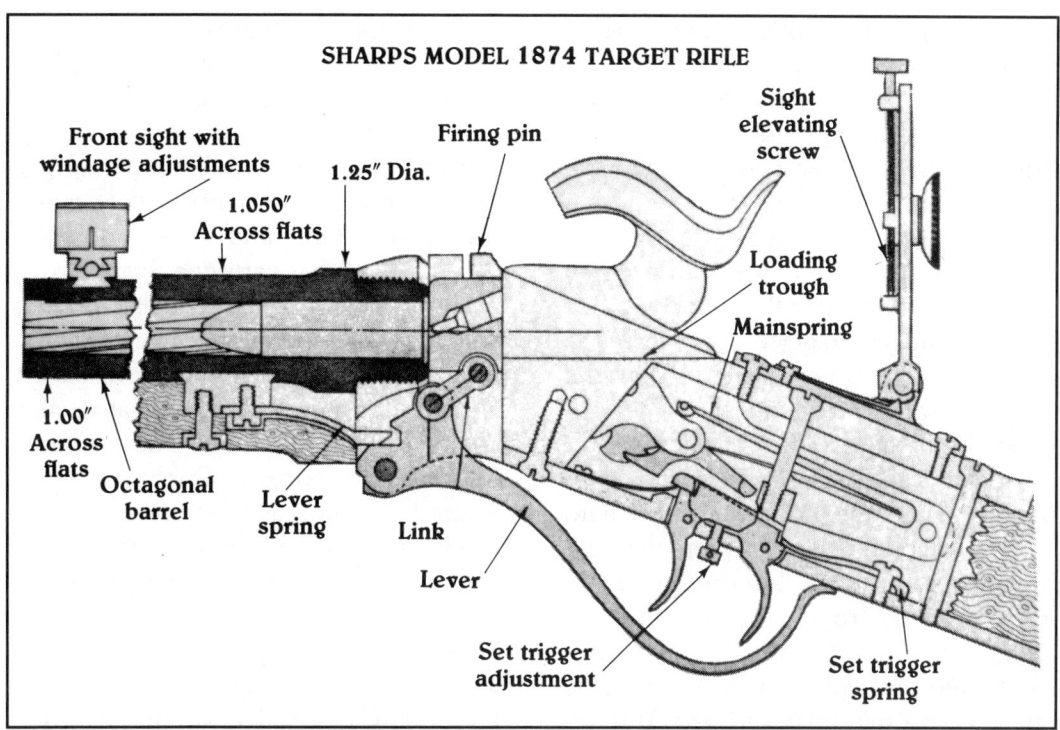

Close-up of the workings of the 1874 Sharps Target Rifle. This is a multiple-lever trigger rifle with set trigger and adjustment screw in between the set and hair triggers.

52 Sharps Linen cartridge only and weighed 8.75 pounds. About 6,000 of these rifles were supplied to the U.S. War Department in the spring of 1865, but were not in time to see heavy action in the Civil War.

The paper cartridges used in this and other percussion models are as interesting as the rifle itself and certainly the forerunners of metallic cartridges. Also called "skin" cartridges, these rounds functioned as follows: Pull or tug at the tail end of the paper cartridge to loosen the package a little. Shove the paper cartridge into the open breech of the Sharps rifle. Close the action. The face plate now automatically slices away the latter portion of the cartridge, thereby exposing the powder for ignition. The paper cartridge could be flat on the end without the "tail" section, but it worked the same way, with the latter portion sheared off to expose its cargo of black powder.

The percussion Sharps could be loaded as a muzzleloader as well as a breechloader by pouring powder directly down the barrel followed by a bullet; however, in actual practice this was not a good idea, at least with certain models. One shooter who tried this method of loading found that the loose powder tended to invade the action. Fouling problems caused the action to lock up. So the breechloading of the paper cartridge was and still is preferred.

The making of the paper cartridge is an art in itself. Shooters vary in their materials and methods. Here is one method: Procure a wooden dowel sized to match the chamber diameter of the rifle. Get a supply of paper or linen for the body of

SHARPS SINGLE-SHOT 69

the cartridge (photocopy machine paper is good for its strength and specific thickness). Cut paper to size depending upon the caliber of the rifle. Roll a paper tube using the dowel. Wrap twice for a double thickness of paper. Glue the edge with standard paper glue. Slide the paper cylinder away from the dowel. Cut a paper disc and seal one end of the paper cartridge by gluing the disc in place. This will be the back end of the paper cartridge. Pour the proper powder charge into the paper cylinder. Hold the powder in place with a cardboard wad forced down snugly upon the powder charge. Do not push too hard or the cardboard wad will rupture the walls of the paper cartridge. The cardboard wad absorbs grease from the projectile, protecting the powder charge. Seat the projectile into the tube with the base of the bullet against the cardboard wad. This, remember, is only one way of making the paper cartridge. The paper or linen can be treated with a nitrate to promote incineration of the paper cartridge body itself, which promotes ease in loading the next round.

THE FAMOUS BUFFALO SHARPS

The Sharps percussion rifle and its paper cartridge foretold of a better Sharps rifle to come and a metallic round to go with it. As important as the percussion Sharps was, the famed "Buffalo Sharps" was an altogether different breed of firearm. This is the rifle referred to earlier as capable of taking North American big game under today's hunting conditions. The percussion Sharps had, as noted, a leakage problem at the action. Gas escaped because there was no cartridge case to prevent it. The Sharps model of 1863 was improved in this respect via a sliding faceplate, which R.S. Lawrence used in 1859 to upgrade the Sharps. A "sliding ring" was also invented, by H. Conant. But the details of these devices are not important here. Keep in mind the 1863 percussion model—with its pellet priming magazine containing 50 Sharps pellet primers, instead of a tape, and its sliding plate—because the great cartridge Sharps would need no sliding plate, no pellet primers, and would leak no appreciable gas.

Records were penned in invisible ink, it seems, for there is confusion as to when the first Sharps cartridge rifle appeared. Known as the Sharps BL Cartridge Carbine, it used the percussion frame and was chambered for the Sharps 52-caliber centerfire (not rimfire) cartridge. Improved cartridge rifles followed in many versions. One of the more important rifles on the way to the model that would become known as Old Reliable was the Sharps BL Sporting Rifle of 1868. It was chambered for the 40-50 Sharps bottleneck cartridge and the Sharps 40-70 bottleneck, another excellent round. A fine 44-77 cartridge followed. Then the rifle was chambered for the 50-70 Government. Sharps cartridge rifles with falling-block actions were noted as safe, accurate, durable and amenable to easy parts exchange. They were single-shot, breechloading cartridge rifles with iron sights offered in many different chamberings. Sportsmen loved them. The Sharps rifle won many shooting matches, especially long-range competitions. Hunters found these reliable firearms amazingly effective in the field.

The Sharps company intelligently continued to upgrade cartridge performance. These were blackpowder rounds, remember. Therefore, the best way to gain more power was to increase case capacity for bigger powder charges and caliber dimension for the use of heavier bullets. High velocity was out of the question without smokeless powder, so a big bullet was the ticket to success on large game. Model after model was brought out.

It is impossible to declare with total reliability that one certain Sharps rifle was the best of the clan. However, it is certain that the Model 1874 was one of the greats of its time or any other era in terms of a fine hunting tool. Be prepared to read that the Model 1874 made its fame because of the 45-120-3¼-inch Sharps cartridge. Also be prepared to disbelieve that statement. John Schoffstall, president of the current C. Sharps Arms Company of Big Timber, Montana, and one of the country's leading

caliber bullet in front of a charge of up to 120 grains of black powder and has a case length of 3¼ inches. Another unit of measure often attached to these cartridges is the bullet weight. It is common to see a Sharps round printed as 45-120-550 for 45 caliber, 120 grains of black powder and a 550-grain bullet. Regardless of the fact that the rifle lacked the now famous 45-120 Sharps chambering, the Model of 1874 gathered a staunch following among plainsmen in general, hunters of big game, "Indian fighters," as the term was coined, and many of the buffalo runners.

The rifle sold for about $150 when it first came out, but later witnessed a real

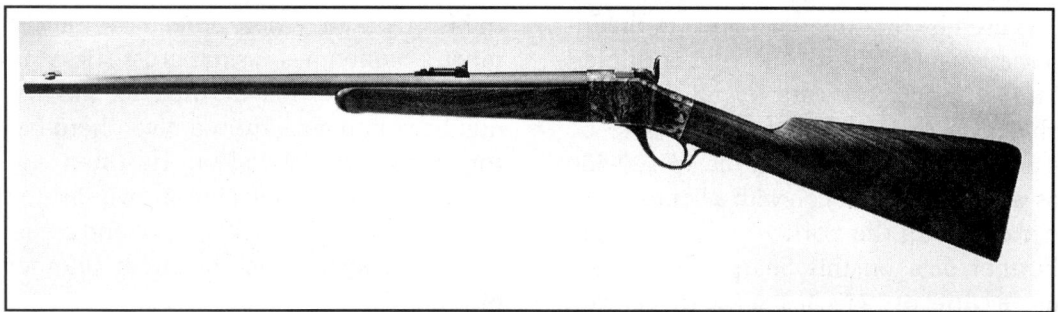

This is the Sharps Model 1875 Carbine, manufactured today by the new C. Sharps Company.

Sharps experts, states in *The New Sharps Cartridge Loading Manual*: "The 45-110-2⅞ Sharps was the largest 45-caliber cartridge originally chambered in the Model 1874 Sharps. It was developed to satisfy the needs of the buffalo hunters for more power and range. This cartridge made its debut for the 1876-1877 winter buffalo hunting season." As for the marvelous 45-120-3¼ Sharps cartridge and the Model 1874 rifle, Schoffstall says: "Although never offered in the original Sharps rifles, the 45-120-3¼ Sharps is the big 45 caliber of the New Sharps line."

Incidentally, the nomenclature "45-120-3¼" means that the round fires a 45-

see-saw of prices. The Homer Fisher Company of New York, for example, listed a "Sharp's" Long Range Rifle, style of 1878, in a "new calibre" (exact cartridge not stated) for $90, while the E.C. Meacham Arms Company of St. Louis, catalogue of 1884, showed a "Sharps Saddle Rifle" in caliber 40-70 straight (straight-walled case) selling for $12.50. The same rifle chambered for the 40-70 BN (bottle neck case) sold for $11.25. The Meacham catalogue also presented a Sharps Sporting Rifle Model of 1875 Hammerless for $22. However, the same catalogue showed a "Sharp's New Long Range Creedmoor Rifle" with a list price of $125 and a net price

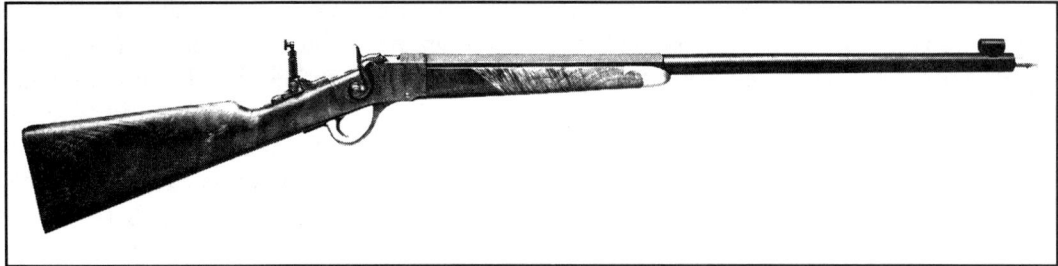

This handsome version of the C. Sharps Co.'s New Model 1875 Sporting Rifle boasts fancy-grain walnut, tang aperture sight and Hartford nosecap.

of $35. The latter seems a preposterous reduction in price for a new Sharps; however, it is quoted exactly as shown here. Perhaps the price was made up for in ammunition, which was presented at $60 per thousand rounds. This Creedmoor was advertised "As used by the American team in the International Matches." The rifle is offered in 45-100-550, but case length is not included in the information and it's to be assumed that this is exactly the 45-120-550 as we know it, although with a lighter powder charge in this particular factory load. Further data on this Sharps Creedmoor are: a barrel of 32 inches, single trigger with 3-pound pull, weight "just under 10 lbs.," a "hand-made pistol grip," with rear peep sight with Vernier scale "giving elevation for 1300 yards." There is also a wind gauge "with one each pinball and aperture, interchangeable disks, spirit level." Used Sharps were later sold for only a few dollars each as the rifle was replaced by repeaters.

Colonel Frank Mayer, a buffalo hunter who lived in Denver during his last days, was a living source of information concerning the era of the buffalo slaughter on the western plains. Mayer said, "I was a buffalo hunter, or 'buffalo runner' as we men in the game preferred to call ourselves, for nine years; longer, I think, than any other man." Mayer hunted buffalo in a typical manner for the times. He had a wagon and hired skinners. He could only shoot so many bison per day because if he shot more, his skinners could never get the hides off, and they were worth two to three dollars each. The idea was to find a herd first. Easy? Yes and no. There were millions of bison, but they were spread over a vast range. Sometimes using cross-sticks to steady his rifle, Mayer tried to shoot a number of animals from a given herd before the beasts moved on. He often collected his lead bullet from within the shaggy so he could melt it down and recast it into another bullet to shoot another bison.

Mayer used several Sharps rifles. The first he bought from Colonel Dodge for $125. It had a 32-inch barrel and weighed 11 pounds. Chambered for the 40-90 Sharps cartridge, it wore a full-length telescopic riflesight, which allowed Mayer to place his bullet just right. He used stadia wires (an extra horizontal crosshair in the scope) to judge the distance of his shot. The system was quite accurate if you practiced a lot. "I could kill any buffalo that walked, up to 400, 500, or 600 yards; kill it with one shot provided I hit in neck or heart." Mayers reported that "Meanwhile, the Sharps Company had listened to the echoes from buffalo land for more power." The old hunter related that a new rifle was brought out, the 45-120. "But this rifle was never in common use," said Mayer, because, "They came out too late." Colonel Mayer also pointed out that the new 45-120 rifles were very expensive. He paid $237.60 for his, but it was provided with a German telescopic sight. Consider how much money that was in the 1800s!

While it's difficult to uphold one specific Sharps rifle as a prototype that includes all of the attributes of the breed, here is a sample rifle that shows the reader what one Sharps rifle was like, exactly. The rifle, stamped "Sharps Rifle Co., Hartford, Conn.," was chambered for the 50-90 Sharps cartridge. The rifle was stamped "Cal. 50." and "C. Sharps Patent, Sept. 12th, 1848," serial number, C54074. It probably left the Sharps factory in 1874 or 1875. The rifle wore a full octagon 30-inch barrel that tapered from 1 1/4 inches across the flats at the breech to 1 1/8 inches at the muzzle. Rifling consisted of six wide grooves and six narrow lands, the narrowness intended to mar the projectile as little as possible. The twist was right-hand, one turn in 24 inches (1:24). Groove depth proved to be about .05 inch. The rear sight was a folding tang (peep); the front sight, a German silver blade.

The rifle had a single trigger, but pull was noted as crisp and clean. This particular original Sharps shot accurately with 88 grains of Fg black powder combined with what was noted as a "small charge" of DuPont Bulk Shotgun Powder next to the primer. This duplex load, a few grains weight of smokeless powder behind the full charge of black powder, is considered safe in Sharps cartridge rifles in perfect condition. Of course appropriate charges of smokeless powder are allowed in the current Sharps rifle, but the load must consist of only that smokeless powder and charge approved by the company.

This Sharps rifle was tested with open sights and an Ideal No. 51542 cast bullet "sized" (swaged down) to .512-inch diameter. The bullet weighed 525 grains and was cast from an alloy of lead, tin and antimony. Groups of 3.5 inches at 100 meters were recorded, in presumably five-shot groups.

The story of the great Sharps sporting rifle cannot be told without mentioning the Sharps cartridge line. The 50-90 cartridge cited above is a perfect example of the big power afforded by the single-shot Sharps rifle, far more oomph than the little 44 Henry or similar cartridges. The round was introduced in 1872 for buffalo hunters with a case 2 1/2 inches long. Truly, this is the "Big 50 Sharps." Often, the 50-140-3 1/4 cartridge is called "The Big 50 Sharps," but it was not a traditional Sharps chambering.

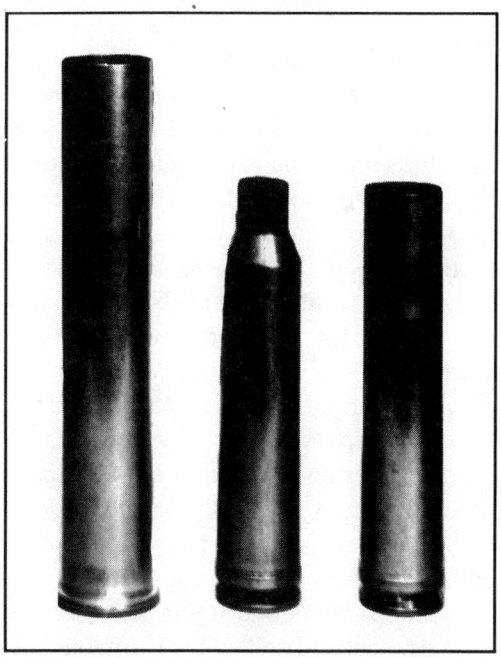

This comparison illustrates the huge size of the 50 Sharps cartridge (far left). The 7mm Remington Magnum stands in the center, flanked by the 458 Winchester Magnum on the right.

> ### THE SHARPS SINGLE SHOT (1874) AT A GLANCE
>
> **Period of Manufacture:** 1871 to 1881*
> **Calibers:** 40-70 BN, 40-90, 44-77, 45-110-2⁷⁄₈, 50-70, 50-90
> **Action:** Falling-block, single-shot breechloader
> **Barrel:** Of steel, blued; 22″ to 32″, depending on whether it was a carbine, sporting rifle, military arm, etc.; full octagon or part round/part octagon
> **Triggers:** Single-stage type or double-set
> **Sights:** Open; some iron; some had German silver blade front, rear tang aperture with Vernier scale; variations
> **Stock:** Straight-grip plain stock of walnut; a few special order fancy-grain walnut, crescent-shaped buttstock; wooden forend; oil-finished or varnished
> **Furniture:** Casehardened receiver, buttplate, trigger and lever; blued barrel bands on military models
> **Variations:** Numerous combinations of features in barrel length, finishes, weight, etc.
> *Name "Model 1874" not applied until after 1871

The 50-140 was brought out in 1884, three years after the Sharps company stopped manufacturing rifles.

The 45-120-550 remains a popular chambering in current Sharps rifles. The modern chronograph shows this cartridge developing as high as 1550 feet per second with a 500-grain bullet for a muzzle energy approaching 2700 foot-pounds. We're talking about a thumb-sized hunk of lead that starts out larger in diameter than some modern bullets expand to. Therein lies its force: a large-caliber bullet traveling at modest speed. The 50-90 Sharps could launch a 600-grain bullet at about 1300 feet per second for an energy of 2250 foot-pounds, again not impressive on paper, but powerful enough for all big game. And the 50-140 Sharps, which is now available on special order chambered in a newly manufactured Sharps rifle, shoots a 600-grain bullet at about 1400 feet per second for an energy of around 2600 foot-pounds.

Sharps rifles live today, not only in their original and collectible form, but also in replication. The percussion Sharps has been copied successfully in a well-made unit, but the cartridge rifle has truly come to the fore in several fine models offered by Montana Armory, Inc., 100 Centennial Drive, P.O. Box 885, Big Timber, MT 59011. There are both target and sporting models. The New Model 1875 is especially excellent. It's chambered for many cartridges from the 22 rimfire through the 50-70, 50-90 and even the 50-140 rounds. A New Model 1875 Carbine with 24-inch barrel and a Business Rifle are also available. Numerous sight options are offered.

The Sharps made-in-America rifle allows the modern shooter to enjoy a famous sporting rifle that would otherwise be relegated to a case in a gun museum. Ned Roberts, famed for his connection with the 257 Roberts cartridge, said it all in a *Hunting and Fishing* magazine article printed in 1944. "Having used practically all the various models and calibres of American made rifles produced since 1874 as well as the majority of our present 'wild cat' calibres and the 300 H.& H. Magnum rifles, I know that if I were placed in a position where my life depended on JUST ONE SHOT—*the first one*—at any range including 1000 yards, I would choose the Sharps .45-120/550 calibre buffalo rifle instead of any modern high power rifle now made." What more can you say?

REMINGTON'S ROLLING BLOCK
BUFFALO RUNNER'S FRIEND

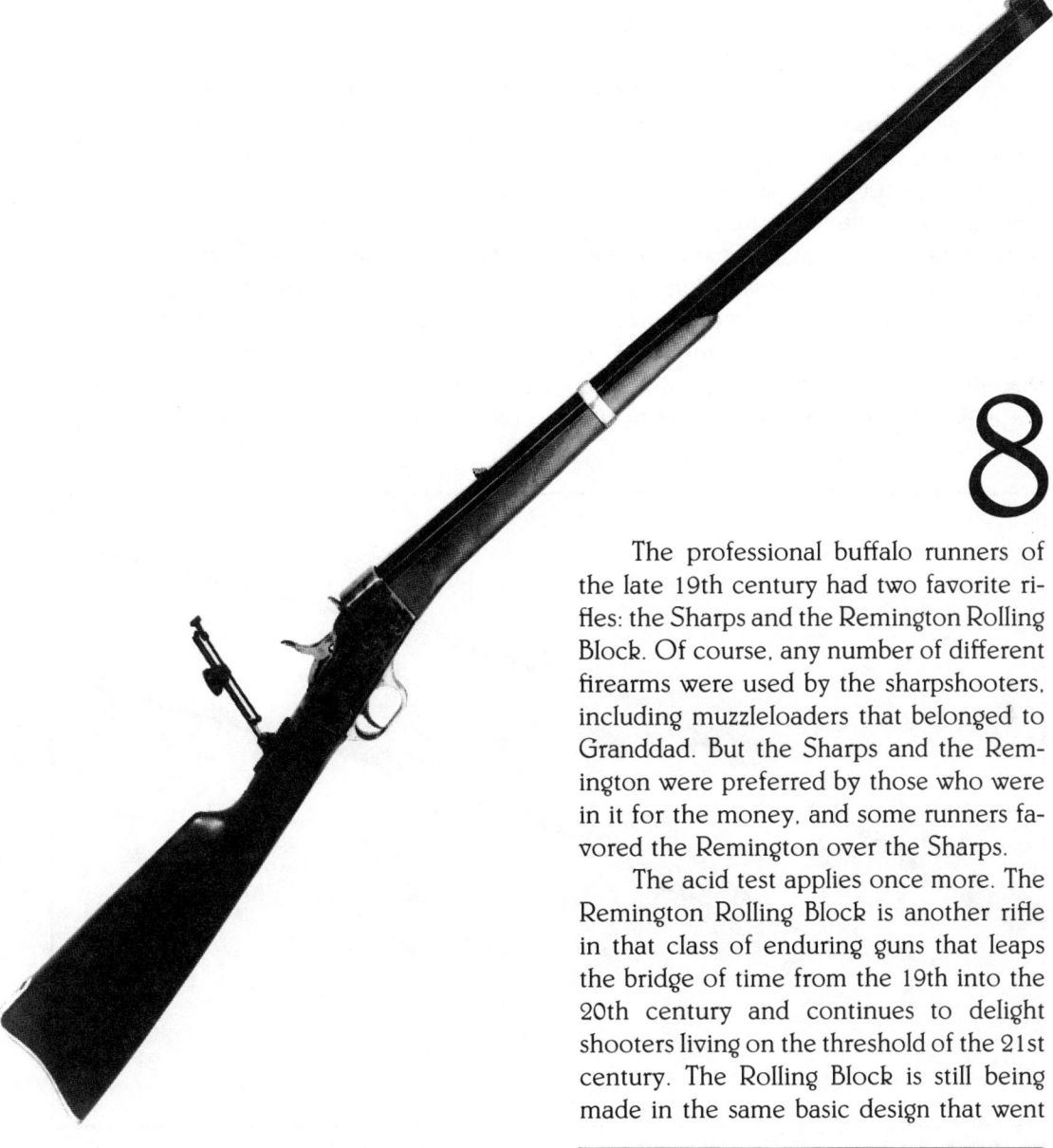

8

The professional buffalo runners of the late 19th century had two favorite rifles: the Sharps and the Remington Rolling Block. Of course, any number of different firearms were used by the sharpshooters, including muzzleloaders that belonged to Granddad. But the Sharps and the Remington were preferred by those who were in it for the money, and some runners favored the Remington over the Sharps.

The acid test applies once more. The Remington Rolling Block is another rifle in that class of enduring guns that leaps the bridge of time from the 19th into the 20th century and continues to delight shooters living on the threshold of the 21st century. The Rolling Block is still being made in the same basic design that went

Long Range Remington Rolling Block rifle by the Navy Arms Company.

unchanged for years. For a while, the rifle fell into a period of general disuse, but it resurfaced as a replica to delight shooters of the space age.

What made the Remington Rolling Block so famous, so beloved that it survives to this hour? Rugged dependability probably sums it up—and utter simplicity through genius of design. The rifle is not now, nor was it ever, beautiful. Of the various action sizes, the petite actions did make it into fine-handling pieces, and of course the action was used in all sizes to build custom single-shot arms in a boatload of cartridge chamberings. It's another single-shot, developed from the Remington-Geiger split-breech system, historians say. In 1866, Joseph Rider, an employee of Remington, improved the basic design of the action and it's common today to see the rifle referred to as the Remington-Rider Rolling Block. It's also known as a falling-block action, although the name applies better to the Sharps design and to the Browning/Winchester Single Shot. The early rolling-block rifles did see action in the Civil War and their application as soldiers' weapons continued from there. Muskets in 58 caliber were converted during the Civil War using rolling-block actions; they were cut in half at the lock and the two halves were joined by the rolling-block action.

The rifle leapt from blackpowder days into the smokeless era because the action was so inherently strong, it required little alteration to render it worthy of high-pressure smokeless powder ammo. This is not to say that anyone should pick up an old Remington Rolling Block built for a

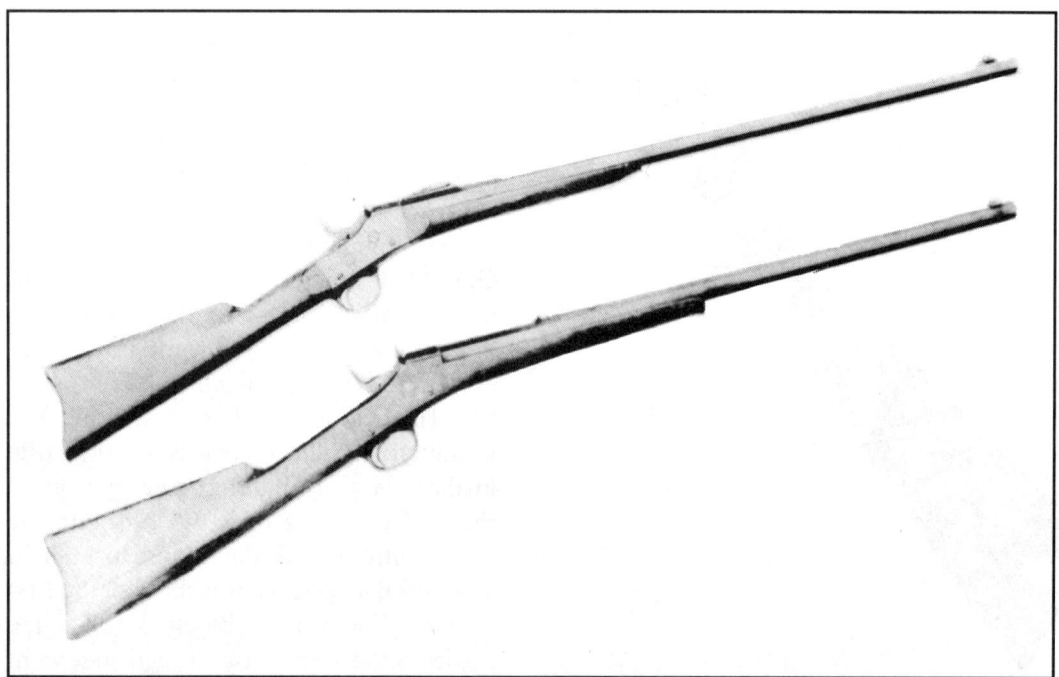

The Remington No. 1 (top photo) and No. 1½ were both built on the No. 1 rolling-block action. Chambered in a large array of rimfire and centerfire calibers, they were popular with hunters, buffalo runners and military personnel alike.

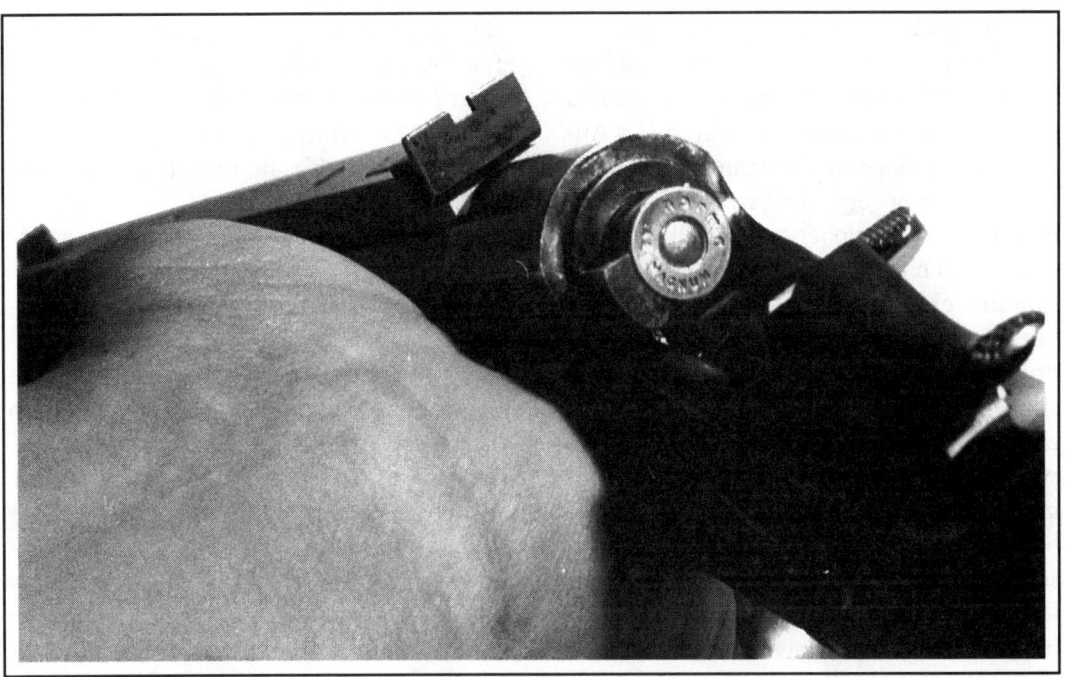

This is the rolling-block action showing a round fitted into the chamber. The extractor, engaged with the rim of the cartridge here, is easy to see on the left-hand side of the cartridge head.

blackpowder cartridge and load the round with smokeless powder. However, the fact remains that the rolling block was so tough as an action that many larger-action military models were stripped of barrel and stock, with the action alone serving as the heart of a rifle chambered for a high-intensity cartridge; this included some of the hotshot 22 centerfire rounds that developed relatively high breech pressures.

In its lifetime, the rifle was chambered for blackpowder and smokeless cartridges as well as calibers 22 through 58. It was popular with hunters, revered by the military, and well over a million Rolling Blocks in its various configurations were produced over an extended period of time. For our purposes, the beginning of mass manufacturing of the Remington Rolling Block is around 1866. Manufacture was discontinued in 1933 as far as sporting small arms was concerned; rolling-block actions were used to build military rifles at the beginning of World War I and continued to thrive for a couple more decades. The rifle was reborn later in the 20th century in replica form.

Two original Remington Rolling Block rifles that linger in my memory book are telling examples of the model. The first is a Model 4, owned by the father of a friend. The tiny single-shot was his means of procuring small game, from bullfrogs to rabbits. He used only 22 Shorts in the rifle and he made every shot count. The single-shot aspect no doubt helped to promote such careful shooting, although a second shot could be gotten off fairly rapidly. The rifle was accurate. I got to shoot it both on paper and in the game field. I remember that little Rolling Block fondly.

The second one in my life is an old

military piece. I lived in Yuma, Arizona, where mail order arms were commonplace in the mid-1950s. A check for $16.95 brought the rifle from Winfield in Los Angeles to my door in the arms of the postman. It was an ugly longarm with a two-man-necessary trigger pull. Caliber 7mm Mauser. The bore looked a lot like the inside of a chimney after a long cold winter, but the rifle was highly accurate. I won 20 dollars with it one afternoon at an informal shooting range out of town. "Hey, boy," the man called out, "What is that thing you've got there? A Civil War gun?" I didn't know at the time that a Rolling Block had been used in the war between the states, so I answered politely that it was a 7mm Remington Rolling Block. The fellow and his partner couldn't leave the issue alone. They thought the rifle looked pretty funny, which it probably did. The gentleman had with him a Winchester semiauto rifle in 401 Winchester. The man wanted to show me what his rifle could do and what mine

five times at a large tomato can about a hundred yards off. He missed. One shot later I pocketed his 20 dollar bill. The can had a neat 7mm hole through it. Later I got two deer with the rifle, then gave it to a friend.

Obviously, the action is what made the Rolling Block reliable and popular. There is none other exactly like it. The Rolling Block looks like it wears two hammers, but it doesn't. There is one exterior hammer, all right, but the other projection is an "ear" that is pulled back toward the shooter in order to operate the action. Both the breechblock and the hammer pivot on individual, heavily polished metal cross-pins. The block is initially unlocked when the hammer is cocked back. With the hammer cocked back, the unlocked block is free to roll back and down, which is accomplished as noted by pulling the ear toward the shooter. Now the chamber is clearly accessible. A cartridge is pushed into the cleared chamber. The breechblock

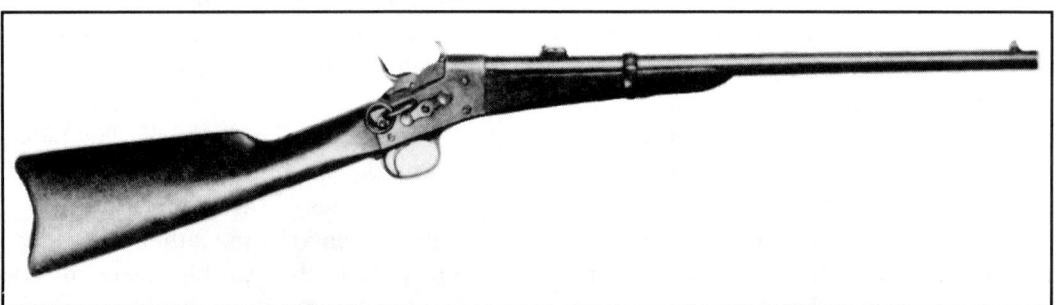

The Remington "Baby Carbine," or Light Carbine, built on the No. 1 rolling-block action, weighed a mere 5³/₄ pounds. Note the saddle ring and single barrel band.

couldn't. "Bet you 20 bucks this little rifle can outshoot the blunderbuss," he said, or words like those. A high school kid working in a grocery store didn't have 20 bucks. The bet ended up his 20 bucks against what I had on me, about five dollars. He shot

is rolled back into place with a forward push on the ear. The action is now in the closed position; however, it is not locked. It is secured or held by spring-action, but it can be easily flipped open again, withdrawing the loaded round, by once more pulling back on the ear.

That's what makes the Rolling Block so interesting. The hammer remains at full cock if the rifleman is going to shoot, or it can be clicked into a half-cock mode. In order to fire the rifle, the hammer is of course returned to full cock position and the trigger is pulled. As the hammer falls forward to strike the firing pin, it locks the action first. The nose of the hammer secures the breechblock. So the hammer ends up being the locking device for the action. The hammer engages just before it strikes the firing pin, which in turn dimples the primer of the cartridge. The action style itself is workable for any cartridge size. Of course, it made no sense to offer a 22 rimfire Remington Rolling Block rifle using the same size action necessary to contain a 7mm Mauser cartridge. So it is that numerous action sizes were built.

LOTS OF ACTION WITH THE ACTIONS

At least five basic actions were developed to accommodate the vast selection of calibers and chamberings that the Rolling Blocks enjoyed. The Remington No. 1 Sporting Rifle was the first, introduced about 1867. This rolling-block model was a sporter with a small frame, chambered for a number of rimfire rounds, including the 22 Long (not the Long Rifle, which was unavailable at the time). It was a blackpowder action until 1890. No lightweight, the gun weighed 8 pounds, up to $9^{1}/_{2}$, depending upon caliber and barrel length. In caliber 32 Long (rimfire), the octagonal barrel was 26 inches with optional 24-, 28- and 30-inch tubes. It was also chambered for the 32 Extra Long, as good a close-range wild turkey cartridge as one could want. Later, the No. 1 was made into a centerfire rifle chambered for the 32-20 Winchester and the 32-40 Remington Straight. Remington was not finished with rimfires in this model, for rimfires in 38 Short, 38 Long and 38 Extra Long were also made.

In the 1889–1890 Great Western Gun Works catalogue, the J.H. Johnston company of Pittsburgh, PA, listed a Remington No. 1 as the Remington Breech-Loading Target and Gallery Rifle, No. 1 Rifle. It was shown with sporter stock, which is no more than an exceedingly plain straight-grip walnut stock with rifle-style buttplate and ordinary forend; available in calibers 22, 32, 38 and 44 rimfire or calibers 32, 38, 40, 44 and 45 centerfire. No further data was given to clarify the exact cartridges, but the information above explains that fairly well. Barrel lengths listed by Johnston include 24, 26, and 28 inches in caliber 22, with all of these 30 inches plus in the other calibers. The most expensive model listed—a 32 caliber with 30-inch barrel and open sights—sold for $13.75 in this catalogue.

Remington was not finished with cartridge offerings, however, for this Rolling Block. The company brought out a 38-40 Winchester chambering and then a special cartridge called the 38-40 Remington centerfire—quite different in dimensions from Winchester's 38-40. And a 38-50 Remington, another entirely different cartridge from rounds with similar blackpowder names; a 40-50 Sharps, the 40-70 Bottleneck, the 40-65 Remington, 40-45 Remington Straight, 44 Short rimfire, 44 Long centerfire, 44 American centerfire, 44-70 Sharps Bottleneck, 44-40 Winchester, 45-70 Government, 46 Long rimfire, 57 Government rimfire and 50-70 Government centerfire. The No. 1 was also chambered for the 45 Peabody centerfire, and in this chambering was called the Adirondack.

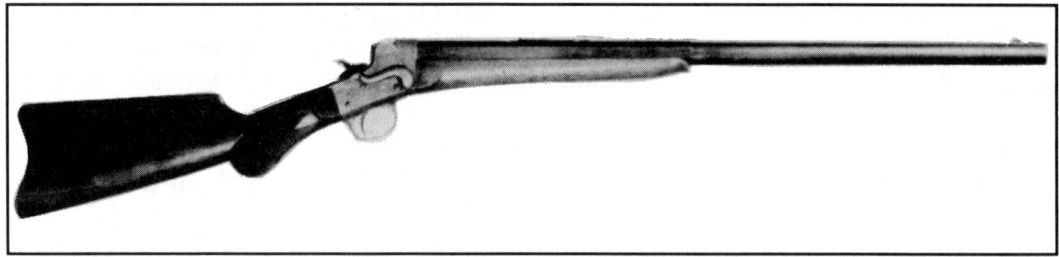
The Remington-Hepburn No. 3, another famous sporter in the series, was technically a falling-block action rifle, designed by Lewis Hepburn.

The Remington Deer Rifle was a No. 1 chambered for the 46 Long rimfire round. It was an 1872 announcement. The Remington Buffalo Rifle of 1872 lasted in the lineup until 1890. It, too, was a No. 1 rolling block, chambered for the 50-70 Government cartridge, the 40-50 Sharps Bottleneck and the 40-70 Sharps Bottleneck. The difference between the Buffalo Remington and other No. 1 rifles was the 30-inch barrel and special sights for long-range shooting. The rifle was intended for use by professional buffalo runners.

Another No. 1 was called the Black Hills Rifle for sale starting in 1877 and taken off the list about 1882. It was chambered for the 45-60 round supposedly, but experts don't think so. Students of the Rolling Block think that information passed down on the Black Hills Rifle is wrong. Not one collector has shown up with a Black Hills Rifle in 45-60. But collectors do have Black Hills Rifles in 45-70 Government chambering.

The first Long Range "Creedmoor" rifle was a No. 1 Rolling Block. A superb Remington arm, it was produced from about 1873 to 1890. It carried the long-range Vernier rear sight and a globe front sight. With some checkering on its subtle pistol grip and fancy grain wood, it was a prettier sight than some of the other No. 1 variations. One particular Creedmoor rifle sold through E. Remington & Sons of Ilion, NY, in 1880, beckons to anyone interested in fine firearms. Remington took advantage of the fact that a number of well-known marksmen had used this particular rifle with pronounced success. Remington's advertisement read: "The Remington Breech-Loading Rifle used by Dakin, Fulton, Bodine, Hepburn, Coleman, Farwell, Canfield, Hyde, Rathbone, Crouch, Sanford, Weber and many others." Variations of the model were listed and priced in the notice, including a Pistol Grip version with Vernier and Wind Gauge sights at a price of $100 even. That's a lot of money for 1880. The same rifle with plain stock cost $75. And essentially the same rifle with military stock was priced at only $55. Colonel John Bodine endorsed the rifle in a letter written on March 28, 1876. The last line capsulizes his feelings about rolling-block rifles: "Their accuracy and power at long range, up to twelve hundred yards, is astonishing, even to those familiar with their use."

Another sporter that carried the No. 1 action was the Remington Baby Carbine, or Light Carbine. It was highly regarded, according to record, by sportsmen, police and horsemen alike. Manufactured between about 1892 and 1902 in a quantity of barely 3500, the Baby Carbine was chambered in caliber 44-40 only with a

20-inch round barrel. It was listed in Remington's 1901 catalogue at $13.25 for the blued model and $14 for the nickel finish, and weighed a mere 5¾ pounds.

The Remington No. 1½ Sporting rifle, which was short-lived, came along in 1888. Basically a modified No. 1 and lighter in weight, it carried the same action and was offered in about eight rimfire rounds and four centerfire chamberings until about 1897.

The Remington No. 2 Sporting rifle was announced in 1873 and lasted until about 1910. This longarm wore the "medium size" No. 2 action and was chambered for several 22 rimfires: 22 Short, 22 Long, 22 Long Rifle, 22 Extra Long, and also for the 22 WCF (centerfire). Additional cartridge chamberings included the 25-20, 25-21 and 25-25 Stevens, a 32 rimfire, 25-10 rimfire Stevens round and a 22 Maynard centerfire, as well as the 32-20, 38-40 and 44-40. Sights were rather crude on this model. Barrels were tapered octagonal.

The No. 3 Remington-Hepburn, designed by Lewis Hepburn at the Remington Company, was based on a falling-block action patented in 1879. The following year, the first No. 3 rifles were brought out and were gradually expanded with a number of variations, among them a Match Rifle, a Long Range Creedmoor, a Mid-Range Creedmoor, a High-Power Rifle, a Long Range Military Rifle and Schuetzen Match Rifle. Technically, these are not Rolling Blocks, however.

The Remington No. 4, introduced in 1890, was popular and enduring. It had the smallest action and, like the others, could be used to build custom rifles of modest cartridge dimensions. The Stoeger catalogue for 1932 lists a Rolling Block No. 4 as the Model 4—Single Shot chambered for the 22 Short, Long, and Long Rifle, the 25 Stevens, 32 Short and 32 Long. The advertisement noted a 22½-inch barrel, walnut stocks and automatic shell ejector. Overall length was 38½ inches, weight 4¼ pounds, and price was a whopping $6.40 in 1932. It was discontinued the next year.

The Model 5 Rolling Block rifle, offered to the public around the turn of the 20th century, was a real favorite. It was built to withstand the higher pressures of smokeless powder, and its action was as large as the initial No. 1 action. Called the Remington No. 5 Special High Power Rifle, it was certainly high power in its day. Wearing a round barrel, the rifle was available in the popular 32-40 Winchester High Power, as well as the 32 Winchester Special, near clone of the 30-30 except for bullet diameter, and the 38-55 Winchester High Power, the smokeless powder load

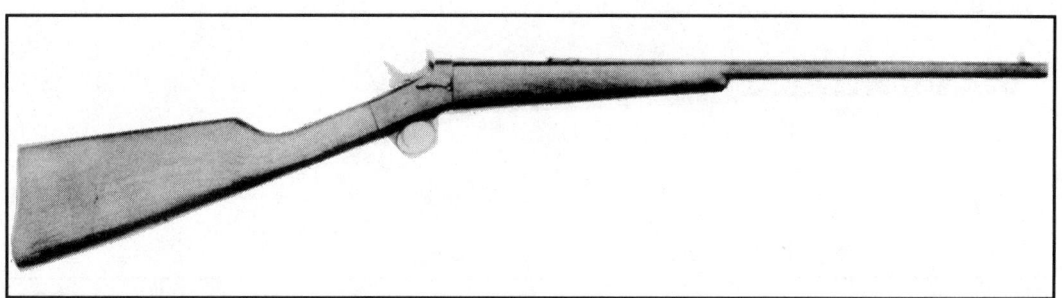

The Remington No. 4 Rolling Block, with the smallest action, was popular perhaps because of its size and weight. Chambered for rimfire cartridges, it was available to hunters until about 1933.

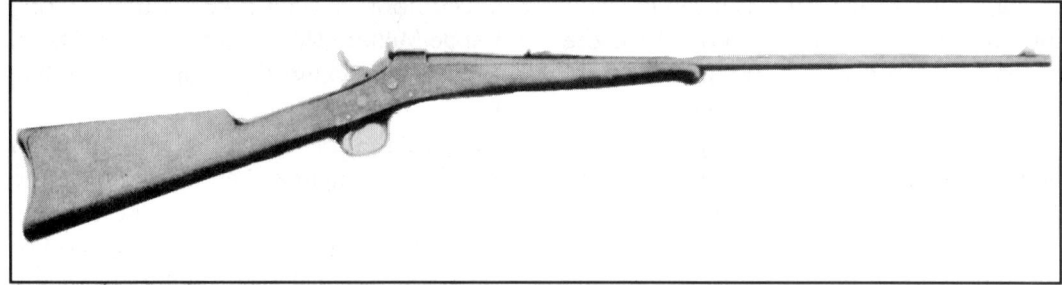

The action of the Remington No. 5 Special High Power was based on the No. 1 design, except was heavy-duty for smokeless rounds. Representing the last of the rolling-block modifications, the action itself weighed over two pounds.

for the regular 38-55. In 1905 the rifle sold for $18. In military configuration (carbine), it was essentially the same, but came in a number of good medium-range cartridges, such as the 30-30 Winchester, 7mm Mauser, 30 US Army (30-40 Krag), 303 British and 8mm Lebel. Many of these no doubt saw sporting as well as military service. In 7mm Mauser, the rifle was big game effective with modest recoil.

The Remington Model 6, listed in Stoeger's 1932 catalogue for $5.45, was a small takedown 22 rifle with 20-inch barrel and very light weight. A steady seller, it was manufactured between about 1902 and 1933 in more than 250,000 quantity.

The last Rolling Block produced was the No. 7 Rifle. The only Rolling Block with a pronounced pistol grip and checkered forend, this was manufactured between about 1903 and 1911. Less than 1,000 made their way out of the plant and collectors consider this a rare find.

For the record, the Remington rolling-block action was built as a single-shot shotgun in 16 gauge with 30- or 32-inch barrel. The shotgun was advertised with a Laminated Barrel for $55, but only $18 for the plain barrel. The Engraved model cost $70, while the Extra Engraved model sold for $80. And a hunter could order the shotgun with swivels for only a dollar extra.

Many Remington Rolling Blocks that saw military duty probably found their way into the sporting field as well. They include the caliber 58 Transformed Long Rifle, or 58-caliber musket already mentioned. There was a New York State Rifle in 50-70

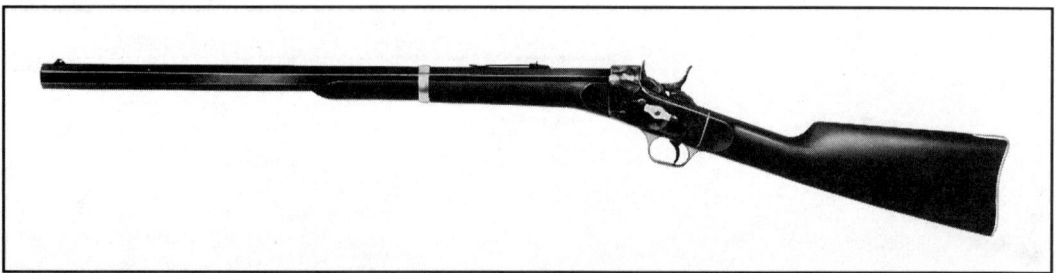

A contemporary portrait of the great Remington Rolling Block rifle, one of the sturdiest sporting arms in history. Note the double hammers, one of which is a real hammer, the other, an "ear" that is pulled back toward the shooter in order to operate the action.

82 LEGENDARY SPORTING RIFLES

The 45-70 Government cartridge is the most-chambered round for the current Rolling Block rifle and can be readily handloaded with numerous bullet styles and weights.

caliber with 36-inch barrel, which weighed 8 pounds 12 ounces and carried five lands and grooves of equal width. This 50-caliber rifle (.510-inch bullet diameter) was rifled with a 1:42 rate of twist, one turn in 42 inches, clearly showing that the bullet had low sectional density and did not require much RPS (revolutions per second) to keep it spinning on its axis. The New York State Carbine and Improved Rifle are the same,

> ### THE REMINGTON ROLLING BLOCK NO. 1 SPORTER AT A GLANCE
>
> **Period of Manufacture:** circa 1866 to 1902
> **Calibers:** Many different rimfire and centerfire, depending on the variation
> **Action:** Built with the large No. 1 rolling-block action designed originally by Leonard Geiger and adapted by Joseph Rider (other action styles were built on later Rolling Block variations)
> **Barrel:** Of steel, blued; 24 to 30 inches, usually octagonal; some round barrels on later models
> **Weight (approx.):** 8 to 9½ lbs.
> **Triggers:** Single-stage or double-set
> **Sights:** Various, including rear Vernier sights mounted on tang; globe front sight; many variations
> **Stock:** Plain straight-grip stock of American walnut; a few special order fancy-grain walnut; slender wooden forend; oil-finished; several shapes of buttstocks and buttplates
> **Furniture:** Casehardened receiver
> **Variations:** A vast number, including the Buffalo Rifle, Deer Rifle, Adirondack Rifle, Long Range "Creedmoor," a Mid-Range Target Rifle, Short Range Rifle, Black Hills Rifle and Light "Baby" Carbine (with saddle ring and barrel band) as well as 58-caliber Musket conversions and military rifles

the first with 22-inch barrel, the second chambered for the 45-70 cartridge. The 43 Spanish Rolling Block rifle and carbine carried a 1:20 rate of twist. The 43 Egyptian version was another military Remington, as was the 41 Swiss. The 1902 Rolling Block rifle was built in caliber 7mm Mauser as well as 8mm Lebel, 7.65 Mauser, 30-40 Krag, 303 British and 7.62mm Russian—all smokeless powder cartridges. The smokeless action of the 1902 was the largest and strongest of the breed. The action itself measured 8.5 inches in length and 1.312 inches across; it weighed 2 pounds 10 ounces with sidewalls .290-inch thick. Modern cartridges such as the 30-06 were chambered into custom rifles using this action.

Original Remington Rolling Blocks were available with double triggers and other refinements, although not nearly as many as Winchester offered for its Single Shot, and the custom arms maker could of course provide such triggers as well as a multitude of other quality features.

The Remington Rolling Block single-shot rifle survived the ravages of time because it was, and still is, a great rifle. It's as simple as that. Other single-shot cartridge rifles have come and gone, but this old standby just keeps standing by. The Navy Arms Company, for example, offers a replica Remington Rolling Block in 45-70 Government caliber in two versions: the Creedmoor with half-octagon/half-round barrel for long-range shooting and a Buffalo Rifle with octagonal barrel. It is available with 26- or 30-inch barrel, walnut stocks and fixed front sight with adjustable rear sight. This modern Rolling Block is well made and accurate. And as long as it's offered in replica form, a modern shooter will have a chance to experience shooting the fine "old" Rolling Block.

THE 1873 WINCHESTER
CENTERFIRE SUCCESS

9

Millions of people who never fired a big game rifle went to a motion picture all about a sporting firearm. The star of the movie was Jimmy Stewart; co-star, none other than the Model 1873 Winchester, namesake of the film. The story was later retold in another production starring Tom Tryon. "One of One Thousand" was the theme of the screenplay, referring to a highly refined Winchester Model '73 rifle selected from a thousand production rifles. Long before the movie, however, the Model 1873 made history as a sporting rifle—and a rifle of westward expansion in the hands of pioneers, lawmen and desperadoes. The '73 was special because it shot special cartridges—centerfires. The rounds it employed did not come close to

Replica of the Model 1873 Winchester sporting rifle offered by the Navy Arms Company.

Jimmy Stewart holds the special One of One Thousand Model 1873 rifle, focus of the film, "Winchester 73."

outclassing those of the big single-shot breechloaders, but they had enough punch to get the job done. The '73 held plenty of ammo, reloaded quickly and spit bullets out like a popcorn machine. In a tough situation, a man armed with a '73 repeater was a lot better off than someone holding a more powerful, but slow-loading, slow-shooting shoulder arm.

Because the '73 used centerfire ammo, its owner could handload ammunition. Offered in the 1875 Winchester catalogue was a reloading outfit for five dollars. In it was a charger, which was no more than a dipper or "cup" of the correct size to hold the right charge by volume of black powder for a specific cartridge. The kit also included a bullet mould to cast correctly sized projectiles. According to an advertisement, "The Reloading Tool, as constructed, removes the exploded primer, inserts the new primer, and fastens the ball [bullet] in the shell [cartridge case], at the same time swaging the entire cartridge to the exact form, and with absolute safety." That last part is important. The brass cartridge case expanded during firing, of course, and had to be forced back to approximate its original dimensions or it would stick in the chamber of the rifle. Since black powder was used, the cartridge case had to be cleaned out (or at least should have been) to reduce the chance of later corrosion, which could cause a misfire or a burst case in the rifle chamber. In the new ammo, brass cases of greater strength replaced the copper cases, which had been fine for rimfire rounds. The design of the centerfire case allowed a much stronger head that withstood comparatively heavy loads, whereas the older-style case often cracked, split or bulged even with the low pressure of blackpowder loads.

The new 1873 was just right for the innovative ammo, and the cartridges chambered in the rifle helped to ensure its fame. Eight out of 10 rifles made were chambered for the 44 WCF, or 44-40 cartridge. The 44-40 was a good round and still is. Winchester still manufactures it today because there are numerous old-time guns as well as a number of modern replicas that use that round. It was considerably more powerful than its 44 Henry rim-

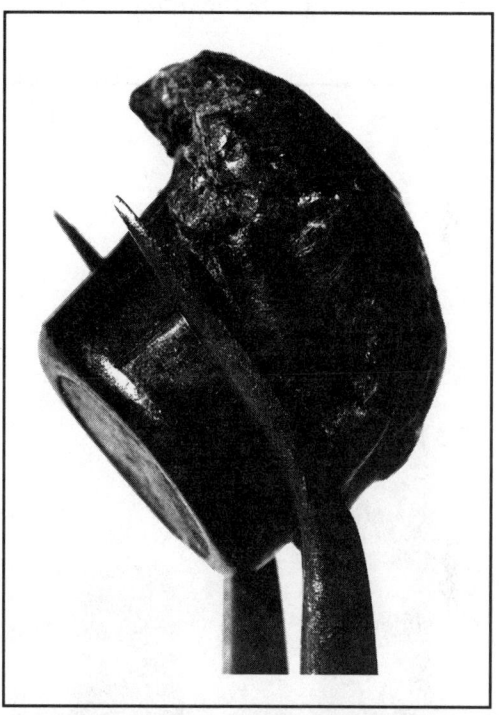

This 200-grain bullet from a 44-40 cartridge was recovered from a bull elk. Even though it is not an elk cartridge, the 44-40 was often used against most North American big game.

fire brother, although the cartridge remained small peanuts when compared with truly potent rounds.

Essentially the same bullet that was used in the 44 Henry was retained for the 44-40. This was a 200-grain lead missile. Even though it was a 44 caliber with 40

1873 WINCHESTER 87

grains of black powder, the actual caliber was and remains .427 inch in diameter, not $^{44}/_{100}$ of an inch. Of course, so many 44-40s have been manufactured over the years in both rifles and handguns that variations in actual bore diameters have cropped up. So much ammo has been made that it's not difficult to find bullet diameters that vary for this cartridge. Bullets of .429-inch and .430-inch diameters, for example, are commonplace. Forty grains of black powder does seem to be the amount actually used, though—at least that is what some very old factory ammunition reveals. W.W. Greener's ballistic data for the 44-40 shows a 200-grain lead bullet in front of 40 grains of black powder (granulation of powder not mentioned). A muzzle velocity of 1245 feet per second is recorded for the factory load, yielding a muzzle energy of 689 foot-pounds, minuscule by comparison with modern ammo or with the big busters of the Model 1886 Winchester and other blackpowder rifles. But this level of ballistic

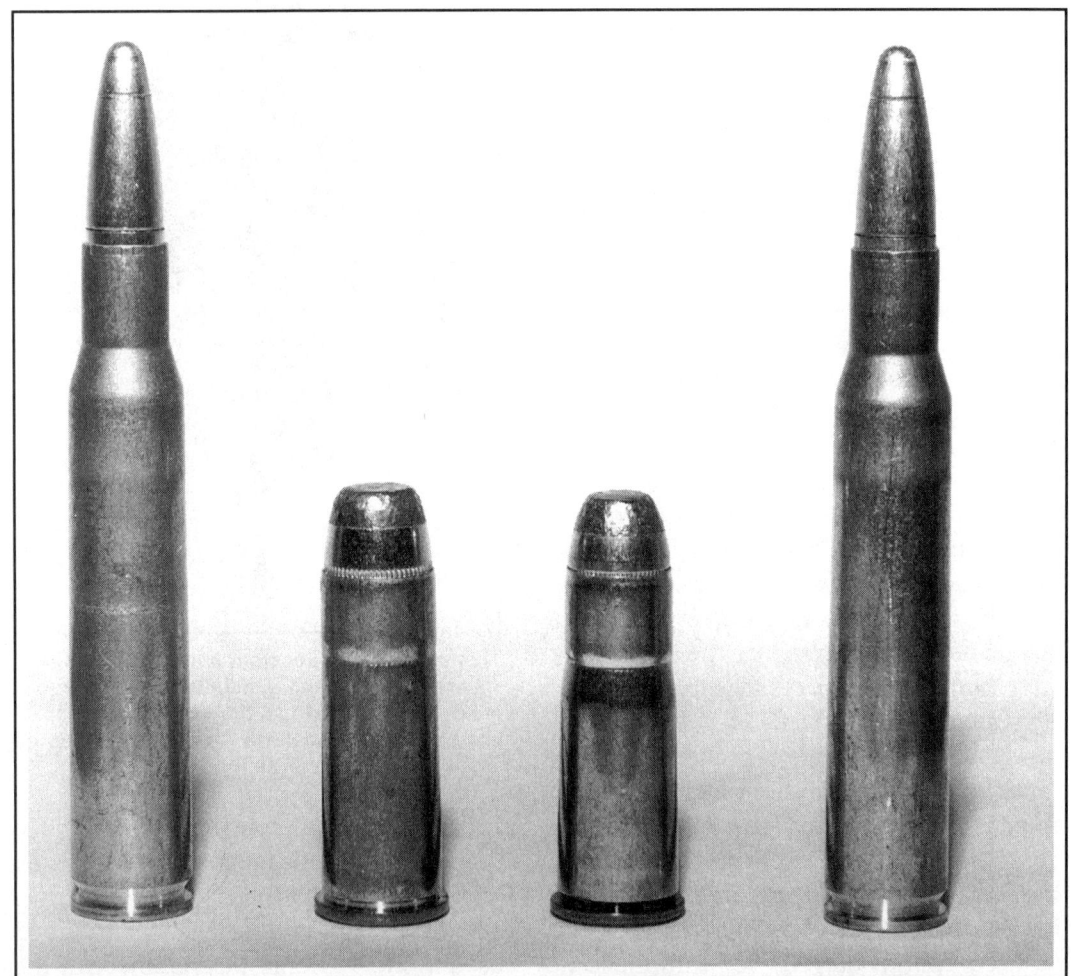

The 44-40 (center left) and 38-40, two centerfires chambered for the 1873 Winchester, are flanked by two 30-06 cartridges for comparison.

impetus is higher than what the 44 Henry Flat rimfire achieved.

Regarding penetration and effectiveness, Greener shows penetration of nine soft pine 7/8-inch thick boards 15 feet from the muzzle. I have a friend who has tagged considerable game, including elk, with a 44-40. And in my collection of recovered bullets, I have a 200-grain jacketed factory projectile retrieved from an elk carcass. My friend, a highly efficient hunter, got his elk with a 44-40. On deer, his farthest shot with that round was about 100 yards; on elk, however, his farthest shot was about 50 yards. Even with close stalking and careful shooting, the hunter gave up on the 44-40 and went to a larger cartridge. Hits that would have resulted in one-shot kills called for a second shot with the 44-40.

Nonetheless, the cartridge proved to be so effective on deer-sized game at close range that in 1879 the Model 1873 Winchester rifle was chambered for an even less powerful cartridge, the 38 WCF. This became known far and wide as the 38-40. It's difficult to say why the company made this move. The 38-40 is a good cartridge, but offers nothing over the 44-40, even in terms of trajectory, to recommend it for big game in place of the 44-40.

The bullet loaded into the 38-40 weighed 180 grains, but loads with 165-grain bullets are also common. Like the 44-40's inaccurate nomenclature, the 38-40 was not 38 caliber, either, because the cartridge held a bullet of .401-inch diameter. Bullets of exactly .400-inch were also used. Here is a true 40-caliber cartridge and should have been called a 40-40. But 38-40 Winchester it was and remains to this day. The cartridge case of the 44-40 is noted in Lyman's 42nd Edition Loading Manual as 1.305 inches long. The cartridge case of the 38-40 is listed in the same text

The 32-20 (left) was one of the centerfire cartridges chambered in the Model 1873 Winchester rifle. Compared with the 30-30 (right), the 32-20 is a small round, but some hunters considered it adequate for deer. It is illegal for big game in most areas today.

as 1.30 inches and in a later Lyman manual as 1.305 inches. Greener's data shows the 38-40 with a 180-grain bullet pushed by 38 grains, not 40, of black powder for a muzzle velocity of 1268 feet per second and a muzzle energy of 643 foot-pounds, quite similar to the 44-40's muzzle energy. In the Greener test, the 180-grain bullet penetrated seven and one-half pine boards. Winchester's 1891 catalogue shows the 38-40 with a 180-grain soft-point bullet at 1160 feet per second and a muzzle energy at 538 foot-pounds.

Another centerfire, the 32-20 Winchester, was made available in 1882. Make that 31 caliber instead of 32, for the bullet generally fired from the 32-20 had a diameter of .311 inch. Greener shows the 32-20 loaded with 20 grains of black powder for a muzzle velocity of 1177 feet per second and a muzzle energy of 354 foot-pounds. The 32-20 is a real canary among eagles when cartridges for the Winchester Model 1886 rifle (next chapter) are considered. The bullet weighed 115 grains in the Greener test and penetrated six and one-half pine boards. Bullets of 80 and 100 grains weight were also popular. Many hunters counted on the rifle for deer-sized game and the 32-20 round was advertised as a deer-slayer. I spoke with an old-timer in Wyoming who showed me his trusted 32-20, declaring that he had put many deer on the meat pole behind his cabin with that very rifle. "Usually just took one shot," he said. I asked him how far his shots generally were and he said the deer were normally within 50 yards of the muzzle.

The Model 1873 Winchester was also chambered for the 22 rimfire, making it the first repeating rifle to use this round,

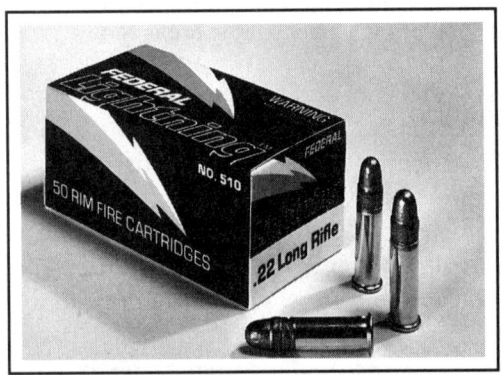

In addition to the centerfire offerings, the Model 1873 Winchester was chambered in 22 rimfire.

according to some experts. The 22 rimfires, Short and Long, were offered in 1879, but the use of these rounds required a special magazine tube. There was no loading gate in the receiver to accept 22 rimfire cartridges. Also, in Winchester's catalogue issued November 1, 1885, the Model 1873 rifle was listed in caliber 22 WCF. The best information reveals that no '73s were ever made in 22 WCF. The next issue of the catalogue mentioned nothing of the '73 in caliber 22 WCF. It's not impossible, however, that a few were made by the company for testing purposes, but no records exist.

An important fact to bear in mind when thinking about the Winchester Model '73 is that Colt chambered all three centerfire cartridges, as well as the 22 rimfire, in that company's sidearms. This started a trend that survives today on a small scale— a rifle/handgun combination chambered for the same cartridge. A man on the trail who had an 1878 Colt Frontier sixgun and a Winchester '73, both chambered for the 44-40 cartridge, for example, didn't have to worry about procuring different ammo to feed either. With a single- or double-action Colt in 32-20 Winchester and a Winchester Model 1873 rifle chambered for the same round, a gifted marksman could do a "heap of work"—from protecting life, limb and property to putting a rabbit or even a deer in the pot. The '73 in caliber 32-20 was listed as a 15-shot rifle. The Winchester promise was almost true: an outdoorsman could load his rifle on Sunday and shoot all week.

Students of the Model 1873 who wish to go beyond this study into the nuances and modifications of the rifle should look into *The Winchester Book* by George Madis. Model '73 rifles were offered in so many variations that it's impossible to examine them all, even in a much longer work. While few 1873s were shipped during the first year of production, a total of 720,609 were eventually sold, according to Winchester figures. Records for 1907 and 1908 do not exist, apparently, but thousands of other entries do. The rifle was manufactured from 1873 into 1919, but its life did not end in 1919 because Winchester '73s were assembled at the plant until 1924. If figures are correct, a total of 18,260 rifles were shipped from Winchester in 1924, a high number, but probably reflective of the company cleaning up on remaining stock in an effort to put the '73

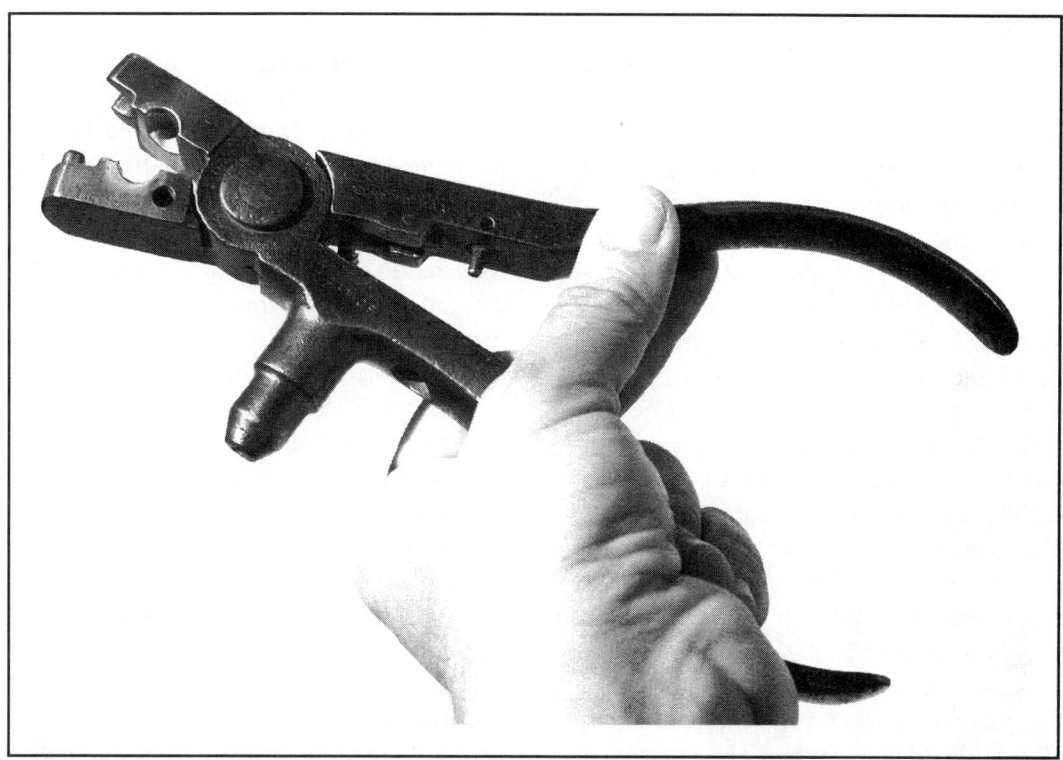
Winchester offered a nutcracker-style reloading tool for the 44-40 and other cartridges. The tool deprimed, primed and seated a bullet.

into the history books for good. That wouldn't happen anyway, incidentally, because the '73 was due for future replication and all of its cartridges would remain in use.

The 1873 began as Serial No. 1, but historians assume that No. 1 was a prototype and never saw shipment. Although the '73 was very much like a Model 1866 in appearance, it was a steel or iron-frame rifle; no brass-frame versions were built. Those who believe they have seen a brass-frame '73 probably came across a Model 66 or plated '73. A few '73s that wore plating could be mistaken for brass, including gold-plated examples.

Although used largely as a sporting rifle, its military use helps to tell part of the rifle's story. The '73 was sold in 1878 and 1879 to Spain as the Spanish Model '73 in both musket and carbine forms, caliber 44-40. A cleaning rod was centered underneath the barrel. The rod fitted into the full-stock musket, which had a barrel band at the halfway mark on the long forestock. The Spanish Carbine wore a special military-style rear sight. The '73 also saw some police work. One story goes that after a skirmish with Apache raiders, the Texas Rangers, equipped with single-shot Sharps rifles, asked permission to buy themselves Winchester Model 1873 repeaters. Permission granted, ten men of the frontier battalion went to Austin and bought the Winchesters. The Rangers purchased their new '73s in 1875—out of pocket. It was worth it. Better to have a fast-action '73 you paid for yourself than

1873 WINCHESTER

an issue single-shot.

In terms of variations of the Model '73, there were more options and extras than stars in the sky. Conveniently, it is possible to break the '73 down into rifle, carbine and musket. The following is a very general picture. The rifle wore a round or octagonal barrel of about 24 inches, with a crescent or rifle-style buttplate and open sights. The Carbine had a 20-inch barrel, and a saddle ring on the left-hand side of the receiver. The Musket had a 30-inch round barrel as standard and a full-length stock. But barrels varied from 14 to as long as 36 inches, with no doubt individual orders differing from these parameters. Furthermore, there were barrel weight options. The 23- to 32-inch octagon barrel of regular weight could be ordered in a "buffalo" weight with a barrel 24 to 36 inches long that measured a full inch across the flats and added as much as two pounds to the overall weight of the rifle.

The early carbines carried barrels that in fact measured 19⅞ inches long, with a true 20-inch barrel appearing only later. Special order carbines with shorter barrels were available, too, the most popular length being 15 inches, then 16 and 18. A sliding trapdoor buttplate could be ordered, crescent style. The sliding plate covered a recess in the buttstock that was suited to hold a cleaning rod. With black powder, guns required cleaning after shooting. Those that were neglected stood a chance of being ruined. So the cleaning rod in the buttplate made sense.

Set triggers were another option. Model 1873 rifles have been discovered with set triggers and no serial numbers. These rifles were probably the result of repairs to triggers, whereby the original trigger was discarded along with the lower tang, which was stamped with the serial number of the rifle.

A dedicated student of the '73 will even want to study dust covers, for they varied over time. The dust cover is the sliding plate on top of the action that protects the mechanism—the same as on the Model 1866. Early '73s had none; then dust covers were made available for any customer who wanted one—no extra charge. For a while, a number of dust cover orders were apparently filled; then they were out again, back again, like a seesaw.

Even rifling style varied. Five- and six-groove rifling was used. Grooves were often wider than the lands—or to say it another way, the rifling consisted of narrow lands. The 32-20 carried a 1:30 rate of twist, one turn of the bullet on its axis in 30 inches. That was altered to 1:24 on some models. The 38-40 had a 1:40 rate of twist, and the 44-40, a 1:36 rate of twist. Surprisingly, the 22-rimfire '73 was built with 1:30 and sometimes 1:40 twist, whereas later a much faster twist was common (and still is), such as 1:16.

Sight styles? You name it. There was an "African Model," so-called because it had a series of folding-leaf sights that could be zeroed for different ranges. There were adjustable open sights and tang sights, wind gauges with spirit levels, the latter listed at four dollars in one catalogue. Globe sights (sights with a circle of metal or a ring) were offered. So was a hinged Beach sight, for one dollar.

One of the more productive ways of discerning variables is to go to an original catalogue and find a specific model that was for sale at a given time. In the E.C. Meacham Arms Company (of St. Louis) catalogue of 1884, there is a full page of Winchester rifles, including three '73s. One is a "32 C.F." (centerfire) in three styles: a Carbine with 20-inch barrel, 12-shot capacity, weight of 7 pounds and a cost of $24. A Sporting Rifle Model 1873 is next, with barrel listed as 24 inches "or under," round only, 15-shot, weight of 8 pounds at a cost of $25. The third 32-20 is also a Sporting Rifle with the same basic dimensions but with octagonal barrel, a weight of 8¼ pounds and a price tag of $27. The two other centerfire calibers are listed too. The 38-40 was offered in Sporting Rifle only, but the 44-40 is a Carbine or Sporting rifle with several options, including "Tools" (presumably reloading equipment) for $4. Also listed are set trigger options.

The 1891 Winchester catalogue shows a Model 1873 with round barrel, any caliber, half or full magazine, for $18, and a "Special Sporting Rifle" with a 24-inch octagonal barrel, case-colored frame and checkered walnut buttstock and forearm, half or full magazine, for $35. Montgomery Ward & Co., Chicago, catalogue of 1895 offered a Winchester 1873 rifle in calibers 22 rimfire Short only, 32-20 and 38-40—no 44-40 in this ad. Prices were about half those listed for the 1884 Meacham ad. The Ward advertisement also carried a Model 1894 Winchester, then brand new, for under 12 dollars. The smokeless version had not yet appeared at the time of the Ward's ad, so cartridges were 32-40 and 38-55 only—no 30 WCF (30-30). The Sporting Rifle was the most popular Model 1873 with a total of 58.4% of the full 1873 lifetime run. But carbines made a good showing at 36.6% of the total. Last on the list was the musket with 5% of the total.

If you consider a rifle that deserved to be thought of in reference to the famous slogan, "Winchester—The Gun That Won the West," the '73 is a good choice. It's a Winchester all the way, a lever-action repeater with all the options, including magnificent engraving for those who cared to order and could afford the luxury. Teddy Roosevelt was one. He had a wonderful firearms collection and among his "ranch rifles" was a custom 1873 Winchester.

What about the "1 of 1000" model?

Here are two handsome replicas of the Model 1873 Winchester that were offered by the Armsport company—a tribute to a fine vintage rifle that modern shooters can enjoy.

1873 WINCHESTER 93

> ### THE 1873 WINCHESTER AT A GLANCE
>
> **Period of Manufacture:** 1873 to circa 1920
> **Calibers:** 32-20, 38-40 and 44-40 Winchester centerfire; 22 rimfire
> **Action:** Lever-action repeater with tubular magazine underneath barrel
> **Barrel:** Rifle, blued steel; 24- or 26-inch octagonal or round with one barrel band usually. Carbine, 20-inch round with two barrel bands usually. Musket, 30-inch round barrel with 27-inch magazine and barrel bands
> **Triggers:** Single-stage type or set triggers optional
> **Sights:** Open; post or blade front; folding-leaf rear; a number of variations, including tang, globe and Beach sights
> **Stock:** Straight-grip plain stock of American walnut; special order fancy-grain walnut; wooden forend; crescent-shaped buttstock on some
> **Furniture:** Iron or steel frame, case-colored; some rifle-style (crescent-shaped) sliding trapdoor buttplates
> **Variations:** Many, for numerous examples of this model were produced; much customizing, engraving, etc. 136 special One of One Thousand rifles were manufactured with exquisite refinements.

Announced in Winchester's catalogue of 1875, the One of One Thousand was acclaimed for its accuracy. In the process of test-firing rifles, when a certain one exhibited above-average accuracy, it was set aside for embellishment. This was indeed a special rifle, one that would excel out of a group of a thousand. There was also a One of One Hundred model which was "not quite so fine," according to Winchester's own admission.

Once deemed worthy of One-of-One-Thousand treatment, the rifle received a double-set trigger system and "Extra Finish." The Extra Finish meant extremely high-grade figured wood with handcheckering, a casehardened receiver or plated receiver, special sights and, in short, all kinds of extras. Only 136 authentic One of One Thousand '73s were made. Most of them are still out there somewhere, for fewer than 40 have been collected in modern days. Each was clearly marked "One of One Thousand" on the barrel. Although the rifle was supposedly born of special accuracy, I believe that the extra accuracy claim was part of the plan to show off a fine piece of workmanship. Whatever the Winchester company had in mind, the fact remains that 136 of them were made and most of them are either lost forever or . . . is there one in your attic?

Sporting rifles that are too good to die, don't. They are collected after manufacture and later copied. Of course a replica of the famous Winchester Model 1873 is currently for sale. The Cimarron Arms Company of Houston, TX, offers an 1873 in a "Short" rifle version with 20-inch tapered octagonal barrel in calibers 22 Long Rifle, 22 Winchester Magnum Rimfire, 357 Magnum, 44-40 Winchester and 45 Colt. Also available is an 1873 "Button" model with half-magazine and a 30-inch octagonal barrel Express Rifle 1873 in all of the calibers mentioned above. Dixie Gun Works of Union City, TN, also offers an 1873 replica in 44-40 only, 11-shot, with 20-inch round barrel. These replica '73s have given modern shooters an opportunity to shoot and hunt with a legendary sporting arm. One of the rifles that "won the West," the 1873 Winchester is still winning a place in the world of shooting.

WINCHESTER'S 1886
A REPEATING POWERHOUSE

10

John Moses Browning we know received $8,000 for the rights to his single-shot design. That $8,000, according to some sources, was also payment for the rights to another Browning design that would become the Winchester Model 1886 repeating lever-action rifle. T.G. Bennett, Winchester's manager, took home a wooden model of a Browning repeater that became the '86, which is probably true—whether or not the gun was included in the $8,000 buy-out. Called the "Golden Jubilee Rifle" by Winchester when it debuted in 1886, the lever-action is workable over a hundred years later. Original '86s are still used today in the big game field, entirely at home in timber or brush on any North American big game. In addition, since

The Winchester Model 1886—a smooth-working repeater with powerful cartridges.

One of the best big game hunting rifles of the late 19th and early 20th centuries, the 1886 Winchester handled well despite its size. It had sufficient accuracy at modest ranges, plus power.

Browning brought out a copy of the '86 in the rifle's centennial year, modern shooters are able to enjoy 1886 replicas.

What made the 1886 so appealing? It was a repeating powerhouse, chambered for potent blackpowder cartridges, including the 45-70. While the Model 1876 rifle was much like the Model 1873 with a larger action and chamberings for strong rounds, including the 50-95, the '86 was a better action overall and it constituted a more agreeable rifle. Bennett probably knew during his 1883 visit to the Browning shop that the design couldn't fail in the marketplace. Browning got a patent on the '86 design in October 1884. Two years later, Winchester gave the first completed '86 serial No. 1—and the rifle was on its way to fame. The '86 overshadowed the '76 so badly that the latter model never stood in the sun again. It became obsolete.

The Model 1886 was the first repeating rifle to use the sliding vertical locking-bolt design. (The Model 1892 rifle also used this system to lock the action.) Two blocks of steel were fitted into slots in the receiver of the action as well as corresponding slots in the breechblock. These strong rails of steel held the '86 action shut tight. It was so good that when the '86 was updated into the Model 71 Winchester in 1935-1936, few changes in the action were necessary to contain the smokeless-powder 348 Winchester cartridge—just as no changes were needed in the '86 action to hold the earlier 33 Winchester smokeless round—except for improved steel capable of withstanding higher pressures. Rugged and reliable are words easily overused when speaking of fine hunting rifles, but no other terms better describe the '86. The rifle enjoyed a long life.

More than 3,000 rifles were sold during the first year of manufacture, followed by several thousand more in 1887. The '86 appeared in catalogues into the 1930s, and is considered out of production by 1935-1936. The year 1932 saw the last Model 1886s off the assembly line, ending with No. 159,994, although a few '86s were constructed into the 1940s from remaining inventory parts. The rifle perished production-wise in the 20th century, because it was costly to make. The receiver began as a 40-ounce piece of stock that had to be milled and worked into shape. The first '86, with round barrel, cost $19.50. Octagon barrel, or half-octagon/half-round models, cost $21. Not that these are high prices for so much rifle. One style of 1876 Winchester sold for $27 in 1884; a 50-95 caliber version sold for $38 the same year. However, in 1886 it was possible to buy a Model 1873 Winchester for about 10 dollars. So by comparison, the '86 was dear.

The most popular model, as far as current literature can detect, was a solid-frame 1886 with standard sights and rifle-style or crescent buttplate. The rifle wore a 26-inch octagonal barrel with a full magazine tube underneath. The magazine, in calibers 38-56, 40-65 and 45-70, carried nine rounds; calibers 40-82 and 45-90 reduced this to eight. The half-magazine on the '86 carried only three rounds (making the rifle a four-shot with one in the chamber).

The "Fancy Sporting Rifle" offered in 1887 was the start of many variations and fancy extras. This rifle sold for $36 and used select walnut for the stock and forearm, which were nicely hand-checkered. The exquisite engraving, however, is what grips the modern rifle lover. Numerous riflemen took advantage of the options on the Winchester Model 1886 and special orders escalated.

Among the variations of the Model 1886 were an extra-heavy (15-pound!) 36-inch barrel chambered for the 45-90 Winchester cartridge. Round, octagon or half-octagon/half-round barrels were available in varying lengths and riflings, including smoothbores. Full magazine or half-magazine models could be purchased, as well as solid-frames and takedowns. Rifle- and shotgun-style buttplates; semi-pistol and straight grips; plain, fancy and checkered wood—all of these options were offered. Stocks with cheekpieces appeared, as well as sling swivels and trapdoor buttplates. Sight styles ran from the ordinary open buckhorn rear with elevator bar for elevation adjustment to Express sights with adjustable-leaf settings for 100 to 600 yards. A peep sight was optional. So was a tang sight (peep mounted on the upper tang of

The 45-70 Government was a popular original '86 chambering, which the modern replica also uses. This is Remington's version with a 300-grain hollow-point bullet.

the rifle) and others. Saddle rings were possibilities too.

One drawback seemed to hover around the '86 like pesky gnats—too big. Some shooters thought the '86 was simply too large, i.e., too heavy to carry on a long day's hunt. Winchester solved this problem with the "Extra Light Weight Rifle," offered in 1897. In 45-70 caliber only with a barrel 22 inches long, it weighed a mere 6¾ pounds. The same model in takedown style, first offered in 1894, weighed 7¼ pounds. Carbines were introduced in 1889 and sold for $19 with 22-inch round barrel. A Musket version came out too.

Despite its bigness, the action was always easy-working. The design did not demand micrometer-close metal-to-metal tolerances for proper function; therefore, the rifle worked when more delicate firearms gave up from invasion of foreign materials or lack of cleaning. Winchester believed that the '86 was one of the company's best developments. So did customers. The action, with its double locking bolts, one on each side of the breech bolt, was stronger than previous models, including the 1876 rifle. And it allowed almost reckless abandon in blackpowder cartridge choices.

The first 1886 rifles appeared in calibers 45-70 Government, 45-90 Winchester and 40-82 Winchester. In 1886, these three rounds offered a lot of power for big game hunting. A hunter could wander in grizzly

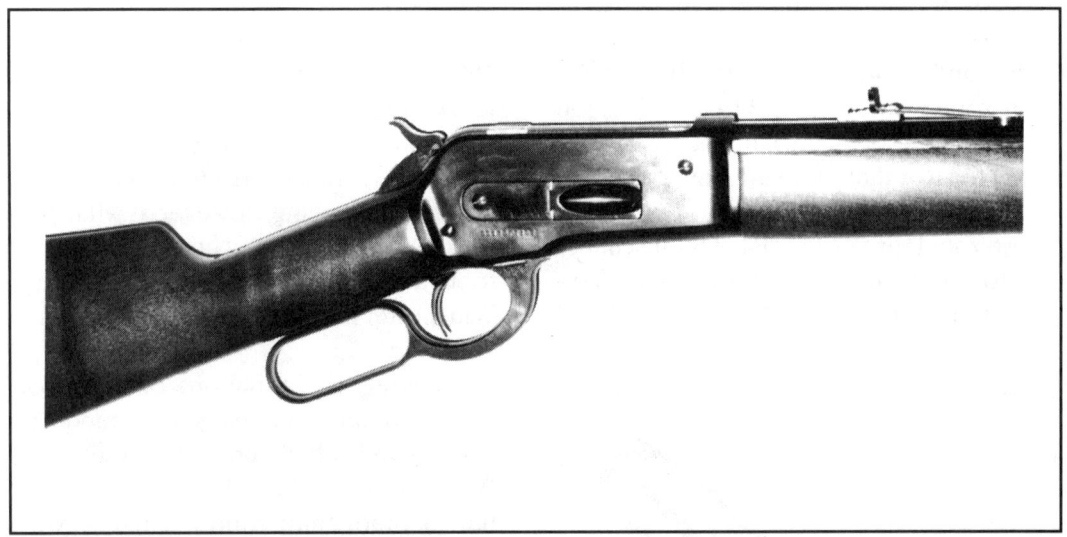

Close-up of the '86 loading port and lever. The full magazine tube underneath the barrel carried nine rounds in calibers 38-56, 40-65 and 45-70; eight in calibers 40-82 and 45-90. The half-magazine option held only three rounds, making the rifle a four-shot, including one in the chamber.

country and feel good about his chances of winning an argument with "the bear that walks like a man." In only one year, three more interesting and useful cartridges were added to the Model 1886 lineup: the 40-65 Winchester, 38-56 Winchester and 50-110 Express. (Typical of gun history, one source notes the advent of the 50-110 chambering as February 1889, not 1897.) The 50-110 was a dandy cartridge for larger-than-deer game, such as moose, elk or grizzlies. And it was worthy of African game, except for beasts like rhino and elephant that "shoot back." Even on lion and other soft-skinned dangerous game, the 50-110 Express, with its 300-grain hollow-point bullet and large caliber, was formidable. In 1894 two more chamberings, the 40-70 Winchester and 38-70 Winchester, appeared—both entirely adequate for most North American hunting. The following year, the rifle was offered in the 50-100-450 cartridge—more bullet weight than the usual 50-110 Winchester loading.

Three years into the new century, the 33 Winchester debuted—one of the finest mid-range cartridges, especially for timber hunting of big game, including moose, elk and bear. With its 200-grain bullet and a muzzle velocity of about 2200 feet per second, the 33 was a smokeless-powder cartridge of greater power than the 30-30 class. Handloaders eventually discovered they could rev 33 Winchester power to approximate that of the later 348 Winchester round. (See Chapter 16 on the Model 71 Winchester for more information.) Because of the superb breech mechanism of the '86, which was of course developed for blackpowder cartridges yielding only modest breech pressure, the addition of stronger steel was sufficient to allow containment of the smokeless 33 Winchester round. No new design features were needed. Winchester had a winner in the '86 chambered for the 33 Winchester. Both cartridge and rifle were excellent in the big game field. In a way, the 33 Winchester put the skids under other 1886 rounds.

In fact, Winchester discontinued the following Model 1886 chamberings in 1910: 38-56, 38-70, 40-65, 40-70, 40-82 and 50-100-450. In 1919 the 45-70, 45-90 and 50-110 Express were dropped. The 45-70 returned to the lineup in 1928, to be retired again in 1931. This whole business of when cartridges were added or deleted from the Model '86 list gets sticky because barrels chambered for various cartridges remained in the Winchester plant long after those cartridges were no longer "officially" offered. So it is possible to find a Model '86 sold in a specific caliber that was supposedly unavailable at the time that particular rifle was built and sold. For a time, the '86 was offered only in 33 Winchester with a 24-inch "pencil thin" (lightweight) barrel.

THE EXPERT'S RIFLE

The 1886 Winchester was thought of in its time as the "expert's rifle." Testimonials were easy to find, for trappers, guides and adventurers of all kinds liked the model. So did plenty of Sunday hunters. In its blackpowder chamberings, the '86 fired big bullets. That was important. High velocity was impossible with black powder, so the only way to boost power was to go with a large bullet pushed by a heavy dose of old-time propellant. What could not be gained in kinetic energy, the way all ballisticians measure "power" these days, was picked up in mass of bullet and also in diameter of the projectile. After all, a bullet from the 50-110 round made a half-inch entry hole. The big lead bullet had high molecular cohesion, too, that is, it did not fragment. So penetration qualities were good due to the retained mass of an intact missile.

In a January 1898 issue of *Outdoor Life*, Dall DeWeese, a well-known outdoorsman in his day, extolled the virtues of his 1886. In "A Moose Hunt in Alaska," DeWeese said, "I have now in camp my special made 40-70-330 metal patched softnose, black powder 86 model Winchester, which I have used for the past four years." Colonel Townsend Whelen later praised the Winchester Model 71 and the Model 1886 rifle that had preceded it. Elmer Keith said in his 1936 book, *Big Game Rifles and Cartridges*, "While dealing with lever action Winchesters, we might as well take up the old 1886 model in .45/70 caliber. This rifle was made for a time with a nickel steel light weight barrel, in solid frame, and chambered for the .45/70/405 gr. soft point

The author shows how to load the Model 1886 through the loading gate port.

cartridge. [With this load, the] rifle . . . has proved a very reliable arm for all species of game in the timber." Keith continued with praise of the rifle and its large blackpowder cartridges for game from deer to grizzlies.

The one hunter and admirer of the Winchester Model 1886 who most stirs my imagination is Ben Lilly. His life story appears in *Great Shooters of the World* (Stoeger, 1990). Lilly lived to hunt. He spent most of his adult life on the trail tracking down stock-killing bears and mountain lions. His favorite rifle was the 1886 chambered for the 33 Winchester cartridge. He liked its power and reliability. Except for Sunday, which he set aside for Bible reading, he hunted every day. Lilly depended on his rifle for his life and his livelihood. "As the smoke from the train blended with the desert haze to the south, Lilly shouldered his battered gunny sack and his carefully oiled .33 Winchester rifle," said Frank C. Hibben in his September 1949 *Outdoor Life* article, "End of A Desert Bear." With that 33 Winchester, Lilly had hunted and killed the big desert grizzly. He had many other experiences with his trusted 1886 Winchester. When I think of the '86, I think of Ben.

My own experience with an '86 was an original that had factory 45-70 rounds. It was an easy-shooting rifle. Recoil was light, due in part to the heavy weight of the rifle. I wrote to Elmer Keith about it, and he sent me his special handload for the 45-70 cartridge. That load significantly boosted the output of the old rifle, and I had great luck with it, using both the Winchester 405-grain soft-point bullet and Remington's bullet of the same weight and style, but with double cannelures. The Model 1886 did its job well. Groups as small as two inches center-to-center for three shots were produced by that rifle. The deer that fell to it generally showed little sign of being hit at first, but toppled over within 50 yards or so. The big bullet, even from the handload that gave it over 1800 fps muzzle velocity, didn't "hardly slow up" on a deer-sized target. I still miss the old piece, having traded it away in a weak moment when a more modern, flatter-shooting rifle seduced me away.

Here are a few more particulars of interest from old-time advertisements for the Model 1886 Winchester:

• The Montgomery Ward & Company catalogue of 1895 listed an octagon-barrel model in 40-82 (firing a 260-grain bullet according to the data), 8-shot, 26-inch barrel, "under 9½ pounds" with a factory price of $21. Wards, however, noted a price of only $14.18 on the rifle at one point, quite a bargain.

• A 1903 advertisement from the Schoverling, Daly & Gales company of New York is interesting because the 33 Winchester smokeless round had just come out. The company made no special note of this in its ad, stating only that the rifle was available in calibers 38-56, 40-65, 40-70, 45-90, 50-100, 50-110 and 33 Smokeless. The '86 rifle sold in all of the above calibers for $21, except the 33 Winchester chambering, which was $25 with its 24-inch nickel-steel barrel and 7½-pound weight (as opposed to the 8¾ pounds of the other calibers, according to Schoverling). A takedown version was also offered in the 1903 catalogue with 26-inch barrel in blackpowder calibers for $25; the 33 Smokeless, $30.

• The J.H. Johnston, Great Western Gun Works company (Pittsburgh) devotes an entire page to the Model 1886 Winchester in its catalogue of 1888-1889. The ad stated that "The system is a new one, as shown in the cut. It is manipulated, like all Winchesters, by a finger lever. This part has a short movement, enabling easy and rapid firing of the gun from the shoulder. The gun is locked by two bolts, having a motion like the old Sharp's breech-block, which show on top of the gun when it is closed. In this position the locking-bolts lie one on each side of the breech-bolts, each fitting into its slot in the frame on the one side, and into a similar slot in the breech-bolt on the other." Interesting interpretation of the workings of the '86.

• The price comparisons are also enlight-

The time and place for the '86 is not yet passed when a scene like this presents itself—big game and timber. With its big bullet calibers, the 1886 is at home here.

Caliber	Bullet (Grains)	Muzzle Velocity (Feet Per Sec.)	Muzzle Energy (Foot-pounds)	Penetration (No. Boards)
38-56 Win.	255	1359	1046	11
38-70 Win.	255	1449	1189	10
40-65 Win.	260	1325	1014	9
40-70 Win.	330	1349	1334	13
40-82	260	1445	1206	12
45-70-405 Govt.	405	1271	1452	14
45-70-500 Govt.	500	1179	1544	18
45-90 Win.	300	1480	1459	13
50-110 Win.	300	1536	1572	11
50-100-450	300	1383	1912	16
33 Win. Smokeless	200	2200	2150	N/A

Ballistics of various chamberings used in the 1886 Winchester. Data based on W.W. Greener and Hornady's Third Edition loading manual.

ening. In the same Johnston ad, the Model 1873 Winchester rifle—with octagon barrel, all calibers from 22 rimfire through 44-40—carried a price tag of $14.75. The Model 1876 with octagon barrel, calibers 40-60 and 40-75, sold for $15.75. The Model 1886 with octagon barrel sold for $15.75 in all calibers (black powder only available at the time), except for the 50-95 Express, which was $20.25. The latter is the same Winchester cartridge case already discussed, but instead of a 100- or 110-grain charge of black powder, it was here loaded with 95 grains. Although many of the blackpowder cartridges of the day were in truth the same case with different bullets and powder charges, they were noted as separate and unique rounds; this book follows the same practice.

It is impossible to divorce the ballistic properties of the 1886 cartridges from the rifle because these rounds helped to seal the fame of the model. For example, in 1895 the 50-100 was offered with two bullet styles, a 450-grain soft-point and a 450-grain full-metal-jacket. A hunter who desired superior penetration had a fine option in the Model 1886 chambered for the 50-100 using the full-patch ammo. The 38-56 Winchester, according to ballistic data supplied by W.W. Greener, carried 56 grains of black powder behind a 255-grain bullet for a muzzle velocity of 1359 feet per second (fps) and a muzzle energy of 1046 foot-pounds. In tests, the bullet was found to penetrate 11 boards. These boards were soft pine, each 7/8-inch thick, the rifle fired from a distance of 15 feet. Each cartridge coming up was also tested against the exact soft pine boards. While soft pine is not necessarily a scientifically acceptable medium for testing bullets, these particular tests are worthwhile because of the comparison values from one cartridge to another—all rounds used the "plain lead bullet." Please see the accompanying chart.

The 38-70 Winchester held 68 grains of black powder, which gave a 255-grain bullet a muzzle velocity of 1449 fps for a muzzle energy of 1189 foot-pounds. Ten boards were penetrated. Perhaps the slightly higher velocity of the 38-70 compared with the 38-56 deformed the soft lead bullet more, hence the former penetrated one board less. On the other hand, simple test variations could be the cause

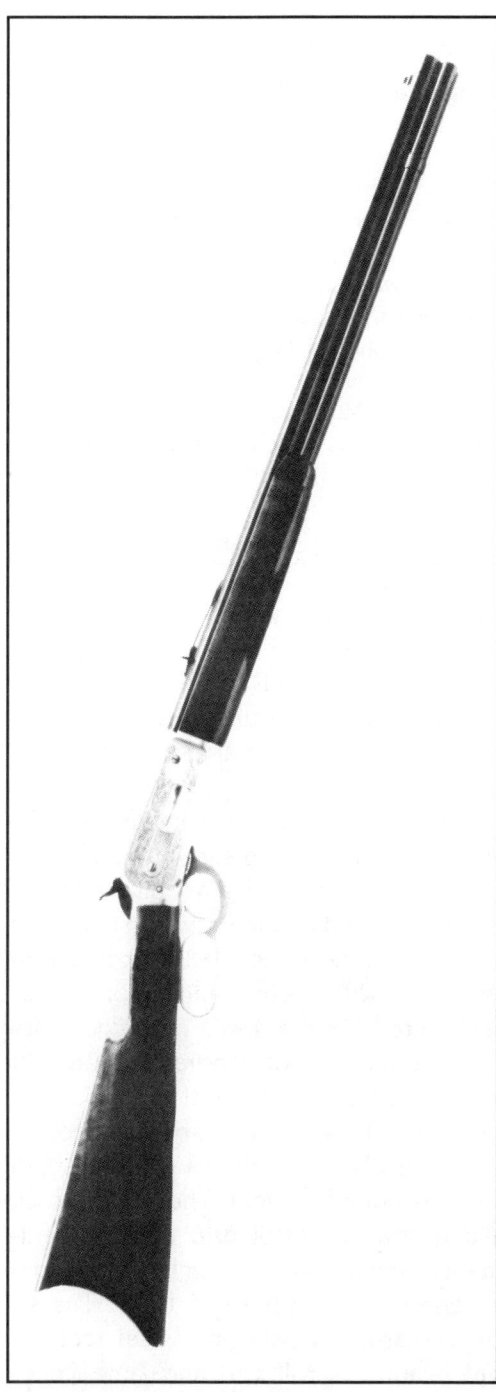

The handsome Browning replica of the 1886 Winchester. In the Hi Grade version, this all-steel rifle with metal buttplate and beautifully engraved receiver makes a coveted addition to any sportsman's collection.

of less penetration. However, the deformation theory seems feasible, because when the 38-56 and 38-70 were compared with full-metal-jacket bullets at their respective muzzle velocities, the 38-56 bullet penetrated 14$^1/_2$ boards, while the 38-70 bullet penetrated 19. The 40-65 Winchester is listed with 65 grains of black powder and a 260-grain bullet, 1325 fps muzzle velocity, 1014 foot-pounds of muzzle energy, nine boards penetrated. And the 40-70 Winchester used 70 grains of black powder with a 330-grain bullet for a muzzle velocity of 1349 fps and a muzzle energy of 1334 foot-pounds, 13 boards penetrated.

The 40-82 Winchester was tested with its 260-grain bullet in front of 82 grains of black powder for a muzzle velocity of 1445 fps, muzzle energy of 1206 foot-pounds and 12 boards penetrated. The 45-70-405 Government with its 405-grain lead bullet and 70 grains of black powder got 1271 fps muzzle velocity for 1452 foot-pounds of muzzle energy and 14 pine boards penetrated at 15 feet from the muzzle. The same cartridge in its 45-70-500 Government designation, firing a 500-grain bullet at 1179 fps, achieved a muzzle energy of 1544 foot-pounds with 18 boards penetrated. The longer-cased 45-90 Winchester using 90 grains of black powder with a 300-grain bullet developed 1480 fps muzzle velocity, 1459 foot-pounds of muzzle energy and 13 boards penetrated. The 50-110 Winchester Express put its 300-grain lead bullet out of the muzzle at 1536 fps for a muzzle energy of 1572 foot-pounds and 11 boards penetrated. But the 50-caliber round in its 50-100-450 loading, in fact 95 grains of black powder instead of 100 grains in this particular test, provided a muzzle velocity of 1383 fps for 1912 foot-pounds of muzzle energy and 16 boards penetrated.

Hornady's Third Edition loading man-

The Model 1886 Winchester at a Glance

Period of Manufacture: 1886 to 1935
Calibers: About 10 different chamberings, the 45-70 being the most popular
Magazine Capacity: Full magazine held 9 rounds (38-56, 40-65 or 45-70 caliber), 8 rounds (40-82, 45-90). Half-magazine held 3 rounds
Action: Lever-action repeater w/side loading port; first repeater to use the sliding vertical locking bolt design.
Barrel: Of steel, blued. Rifle, 26 inches, round or octagonal; Carbine, 22 inches, round; Musket, 30 inches, round. Some half-round, half-octagon—from 22 to 36 inches.
Weight (approx.): From $6^{3}/_{4}$ lbs. (Extra Light Weight) to about 9 lbs. plus
Triggers: Single-stage type or double-set
Sights: Open; much variety
Stock: Straight-grip plain stock of American walnut; many special order fancy-grain walnut with checkering and other embellishments; wooden forend; shotgun or crescent-shaped buttplate; oil-finished, a few varnished
Variations: Many variations, including engraved models, saddle rings attached to some receivers; recoil pads; much customizing, etc.

ual showed a load for the 33 Winchester smokeless round with a 200-grain jacketed soft-point bullet at 2200 fps for a muzzle energy of 2150 foot-pounds. This round was not tested against the pine boards. However, considering trajectory comparisons between the 33 Winchester and those blackpowder cartridges chambered for the Model 1886 Winchester rifle, it's easy to see why shooters often opted for the smokeless round. For example, in order to sight the 40-65 Winchester in for 200 yards, the bullet must strike a foot high at 100 yards. The 38-56 Winchester must be sighted to hit slightly more than a foot high at 100 yards in order to shoot dead on target at 200. And the 50-110 must be sighted almost exactly the same as the 40-65 for a 200-yard zero. The 33 Winchester with its 200-grain bullet at 2200 fps muzzle velocity could be sighted in only $4^{1}/_{2}$ inches high at 100 yards for a bull's-eye at 200 yards. This made the 33 Winchester perfectly adequate at 200 yards in terms of trajectory. Of course, the big blackpowder rounds had sufficient remaining energy at 200 yards to be effective at least on deer-sized game,

if not larger wild animals. But it meant either sighting in so that the shooter had to hold a foot under his target at 100 yards, or sighting in for around a hundred yards and then holding several inches high for a 200-yard strike.

The 1886 Winchester may have faded briefly like the setting sun, but it dawned anew on its centennial in a replica of modern steel. Issued by the Browning company in limited edition, the "1886 Lever Action Repeating Rifle" was a nine-shot sporter chambered for the 45-70 cartridge, a favorite round of contemporary shooters. It was offered in two grades (I and Hi Grade) with 26-inch octagonal barrel composing a rifle of about 45 inches overall length and $9^{1}/_{4}$ pounds weight. The walnut stock had a straight pistol grip and crescent-shaped metal buttplate. Sights included a buckhorn rear with front bead. The Hi Grade carried a pale gray steel receiver with beautiful scroll work and game scenes of elk and American bison. So it is that the 1886 was revived on its 100th birthday and remains a popular sporting rifle in gun collections to this day.

THE WINCHESTER '92
SHORT, SLICK AND VERSATILE

11

Anyone who has watched western movies has seen the Model 1892 Winchester. The '92 has been the most-used of the carbines in films, because it was chambered in the 44-40 Winchester cartridge for which blackpowder 44-40 blanks have been easy to purchase. The famous Model 94 Winchester found its way into many motion pictures too, but the '92 remains king of the celluloids.

A smash hit from the start, the Model 1892 Winchester was born in the year of its name. It is also commonly called the Winchester '92, and the company had stamped some of its rifles "Model 92." One reason for its popularity was its cartridge offerings: the Winchesters 32-20 (32 WCF), 38-40 (38 WCF) and 44-40 (44 WCF). These

The Winchester Model 1892 offered popular cartridges and easy handleability.

rounds were favorites for years. They were short, so a lot of ammo could be loaded into the magazine. They were mild to shoot, with scarcely the recoil of a butterfly's wing. And they were sufficiently accurate for everyday shooting. Mild-mannered rounds in good numbers from an easily managed repeating rifle made the '92 one of the more famous Winchesters.

The 1892 Winchester was less costly to produce than the 1873 Winchester, which it ended up replacing. It had a stronger action than the '73, was easier to handle, as any shooter could prove by taking both rifles to the range, and it was far more trim in appearance. The '92 was, in short, a more modern rifle than the fine '73. Keep in mind that shooters who were used to the '73 were already familiar with the 92's rounds because they were the same. So the transition was an easy one. The '92 was also like the Model 1886 Winchester, right down to the double locking bolts, but smaller in every way and more than two pounds lighter in weight generally than its larger brother. Of course, its smaller size precluded the chambering of the powerful rounds for which the '86 was known. But the '92 did a lot of work for its dimensions. And it was practical. The little rifle worked with total reliability and filled an important niche as a sporting rifle: sufficient power for deer-sized game—the most popular of all big game, handy access to cartridges at just about any crossroads hardware store, and the chambering of three rounds that were used in the excellent Colt revolver.

A fourth cartridge, the 25-20 or 25

The 38-40 centerfire round was a favorite in the Model 1892. Here is an original box containing fifty 180-grain soft-point bullets.

106   LEGENDARY SPORTING RIFLES

WCF, was also chambered in the '92 in 1895. While this was not as popular as the other rounds, it held its own and does represent another respectable cartridge for small game hunting, wild turkey, javelina and similar game. A few Model '92s were chambered for the 218 Bee in 1939. The 218 Bee was a fine little stinger, but it lacked the practical nature of even the 25-20. That's arguable, of course, but some of us would rather hunt a wild turkey or similar game with a 25-20 and an 80-grain bullet over the 218 Bee with its 55-grain bullet, even though velocity is greatly in favor of the latter.

The 44-40 was far and away the workhorse of the Model 1892 cartridge line. And why not? It was the only one of the group that could push a modestly heavy bullet out of the barrel. The 38-40 was a good round, but it gained nothing over the 44-40—and the grassroots shooter usually knows what's best for him and his particular needs. The round, as well as the others in the lineup, was eventually treated to a smokeless powder load, but this was good only from the standpoint of cleanup. Black powder was (still is) sooty stuff demanding careful attention to the bore and even the action of the rifle after shooting. But smokeless powder was non-corrosive. After non-corrosive primers were introduced to match the property of the powder, the shooter truly had convenience on his side. He could shoot a lot of ammo before the bore got caked up. When the rifle needed attention, it took only a short while to rid it of smokeless powder residue. The 38-40 and 44-40 were not much improved in velocity with smokeless powder loads. The 25-20 and 32-20 high-velocity loads, however, enjoyed a considerable advancement in muzzle velocity. But even loaded with smokeless powder, the 38-40 and 44-40 remained slower than honey poured over ice.

Besides its petite size, another reason for ease of operation in the '92 was that the short action was slick and easy to work—fast-acting all the way. The rifle, its sights and ammo were all geared to modest-range shooting, but marksmen who practiced with the 92 did more than all right. The little rifle was snake-fast in the brush, and a solid hit from either the 38-40 or 44-40 was worthy of a deer at close range. Modern shooters do not agree with the use of the 32-20 for deer, but it's true that many 92s were used as deer rifles in caliber 32 WCF. Bullet placement was the key to success with the low-powered 32-20, and most game departments eventually banned its use entirely. For example, in my state of Wyoming, the 32-20 is illegal for big game, period. That's probably as it should be, but it would be difficult to convince a Wyoming homesteader that his little 32-20 wasn't a deer rifle when he had a record of putting venison on the table with it for years—usually with one well-placed shot. Obviously, the deer have not changed in stature or tenacity over time, but conditions have. The old-timer living along a creekbottom left his cabin rifle in arm looking for a 30- or 40-yard shot at a standing target—and often got it. There were no seasons and few other hunters.

THE 92'S APPEALING FEATURES

The Model 1892 rifle usually carried a 24-inch round barrel. The straight-grain walnut stock with straight grip was fitted with a crescent or rifle-style buttplate. Sights were usually open. I recently examined a '92 with full buckhorn open rear sight and post front sight, but of course it's always difficult to determine whether sights are of factory origin or add-ons.

The standard carbine had the usual 20-

The Model 1892 Winchester was available in a full-magazine carbine version (left) and a half-magazine rifle (right). Shooters enjoyed its light weight and caliber versatility.

inch barrel with full magazine tube and a saddle ring. The weight was an easy-carrying 5½ pounds. The half-magazine was more rare. The day these words were written I examined an original Model 1892 Carbine with half-magazine, half-octagon/half-round 20-inch barrel, shotgun buttstock and full buckhorn open sights. This rifle is an example of a special-order '92. Furthermore, this '92 carbine was a takedown. A test proved that the action/barrel remained tight and foolproof. This is not always the case with the takedowns, however. It should be noted that if a shooter wants a '92 of his own for hunting and shooting, he should either consider the solid-frame model or have a gunsmith take a careful look at the takedown model to ensure that it remains tight. As far as carbines go, the '92 was also offered in a Baby Carbine model with 14-inch barrel.

There was a military-minded Musket model with 30-inch barrel and optional bayonet. Of course, the musket was poorest in sales. It was chambered for the 44-40 cartridge, which made sense because, although no powerhouse, the 44-40 was the strongest of the '92 lineup. (There remains, however, in collection a Model '92 Musket chambered for the 32-20 cartridge.)

Of course, Winchester sold 44-40 ammo well above the other rounds. It's difficult to say how shooters of yesteryear reacted to the large capacity magazines of the '92—either using them as reservoirs or to get off plenty of shots. Having known some old-timers, I prefer the first alternative. The rifle with 24-inch barrel packed in 13 rounds. The carbine, with its 20-inch barrel, carried 11 rounds of ammo in the full magazine, five in the half-magazine. And the Musket held 17 of the 44-40 cartridges.

Initially the barrels were made of ordinary steel, as would be required of black-powder rounds. Smokeless powder was still very much in the background in 1892. The first smokeless-powder cartridge, the French Lebel, came into use by 1886. The Lebel was the first smokeless round to see use by a government's army to the best of my knowledge and research. The 30-40 Krag, also smokeless, was employed in the Danish-Jorgensen rifle of 1889. And the 30-30 was the first *sporting* cartridge to use smokeless powder, but it was actually 1895 before that round was generally in the hunting field. So it makes sense that the '92 was built with steel suitable for black-powder cartridges. Later models used nickel steel. Coupled with the strong action, the '92 was capable of handling the medium-range pressure of the 218 Bee. The Model 65, to follow, was built of even more modern steels.

Special orders abounded for the '92 and just about any reasonable feature could be added to the regular model. Deluxe wood has been found on existing '92s. This is generally a high-grade, tight-grain walnut with good figure and excellent oil finish. A fully engraved '92 with octagon barrel and profuse stock carving was sold in 1899. The engraving alone cost $125; the carving of the stock added $35 to the regular price. And how about a '92 with a 34-inch barrel?

All kinds of sights dressed the '92, including full buckhorns, whereby the sides

The open sights on this 25-20 Winchester 1892 look crude, but the rear notch is actually rather precise and narrow. While the buckhorn style does not produce perfect aim, it does not damage aim as some authorities claim.

of the open rear sight stand tall like cattle horns. Some shooters consider this sight useless, because the horns block the target. But they do not. The target would be, or at least should be, aligned with the open notch and front bead, post or blade. While the horns may obstruct some of the superfluous parts of the target, they do not

One of the advantages of the 19th-century rifle cartridges was their interchangeability with certain sidearms. A settler carrying an 1892 Winchester chambered for 44-40 would need only that kind of ammo if he carried this Colt revolver on his belt.

get in the way of an aiming point. I've used them often and hit well with buckhorn sights, although they, of course, have no real function and their demise is not mourned by anyone today. The little Model 92 was usually iron-sighted and those sights were open rear coupled with a bead up front. Winchester's little A-5 scope was attached to the '92 on special request, but the little top-ejector was never a truly great scope rifle.

Montgomery Ward & Co. of Chicago showed the Winchester Model 1892 in its catalogue of 1895. "A New Repeating Rifle," read the advertisement, "The Winchester Model 1892." Wards noted that "The system is the same as the model of 1886," in reference to the double locking bolts. Wards clearly announced to prospective buyers that the '92 would be made only with 24-inch barrels and only with plain triggers. The first part proved unreliable, with 20-inch carbines and special orders, but triggers for the '92 did remain "plain." Straight-grip stock, the ad said, with octagon or round barrels. Factory prices were quoted as $19.50 for the octagon barrel and $18 for the round barrel, but Wards beat those prices soundly. "See our prices," boasted the company: $11.85 for the octagon-barrel model and $10.84 for the round-barrel model. A final quote from the advertisement read: "They are only made as quoted below, using the same tools and cartridges as the Model 1873. See index for quotations on Tools and Cartridges," meaning the 32-20, 38-40 and 44-40 rounds and reloading tools.

Winchester, in its 1916 catalogue, gives the Model 1892 solid coverage. The information imparted is identical to that of Ward's in that the '92 is the '86 in miniaturized form. The gun is light, strong and handsome, Winchester stated. The '92s I've shot were light, strong and handsome. It is interesting that in 1916 Winchester strongly and flatly stated that barrels over 24 inches would not be sold, not even on special order. But the company did offer at the time the options of octagon, round, half-octagon/half-round barrels, full mag-

110 LEGENDARY SPORTING RIFLES

Who could forget John Wayne in his role as Rooster Cogburn? Braced for action with the reins between his teeth, he carried the large loop Model 1892 in one hand and a revolver in the other. He also used a Model '92 carbine in the 1939 classic film, "Stagecoach."

azines or half-magazines and shotgun-style, rubber or crescent-shaped buttplates. Surprisingly, Winchester offered set triggers on customer demand, in contradiction to the statement that the 92 would not be fitted with those. The Take Down model was available, as well as solid frame.

Furthermore, Winchester offered interchangeable barrels in 1916. These barrels were for the 38-40 and 44-40. Recall that these two cartridges were much the same, except for the caliber. Because of such cartridge likeness, a shooter could buy an extra barrel for his takedown rifle and simply "screw it on" and start shooting. In 1916, a war year, Winchester charged the following for its Model 1892: the rifle with 24-inch round barrel, $18; with octagon barrel, $19.50; with half-octagon/half-round barrel, $20. The carbine cost $17.50. The Musket was $19. The most expensive Model '92 in this particular catalogue was the Take Down with 24-inch half-octagon/half-round barrel at $27.

Ammunition for the '92 at this time ran $16 for a thousand 32-20 or $9 for a thousand primed cases. These were loaded with 20 grains of black powder using a 115-grain bullet. Winchester also sold smokeless "high-velocity" 32-20 ammunition at $21 per thousand rounds with this notation: "Model '92 Special Win. High Velocity, Soft Point or Full Patch." Smokeless 32-20 not designated as high-velocity ammo cost a dollar less per thousand loaded rounds. Ammo for the 44-40 and 38-40 cost the same. Either one sold for $19 per thousand rounds, with the 44 using a 200-grain bullet and the 38 a 180-grain bullet. Both of these were offered in smokeless rounds with soft-point or full-metal-jacket bullets: $24 for standard velocity and $27 for high-velocity ammo per thousand rounds.

A NEW MODEL 92: THE 65

The Stoeger *Shooter's Bible* for 1940 did not show a Model 1892, although the 218 Bee cartridge was listed in Winchester's Model 65 lever-action rifle. This is important: the reason the '92 is not shown is that the 65 was a takeover of the earlier model. "For many years veteran users of lower-powered hunting rifles have praised the Winchester Model 92 Repeater," the advertisement boasted. "Taking the basic principles of this rifle, Winchester has developed a new type." That was the Model 65 with pistol-grip stock and a round 22-inch barrel, magazine tube ending at the tip of the forend. It had a shotgun buttstock and was sold in solid frame.

The Model 65 remained chambered for the 25-20 and 32-20 rounds and the open-sighted rifle was billed as just right for turkey, fox, woodchuck and similar game in these calibers, which was factual, especially the turkey part. Few rifle cartridges are better turkey-takers at modest range than the 25-20 or 32-20. In 218 Bee, the 65 was touted as a woodchuck, bobcat, fox and coyote rifle for "average range." The Model 65 was a seven-shooter in the 218 Bee and an eight-shooter in 25-20 or 32-20, including a round in the chamber of each. A look at the 65 clearly reveals where the Model 1892 Winchester had progressed by 1940. As far as the gun scholar is concerned, the Model 65 is considered a minor continuation of the Model 1892. The Model 65 was a marketing nightmare, however. It's timing was all wrong. It had come along in 1933, but production had ceased by 1941. A few trickled out of the factory into 1943.

The Model 53, unveiled in 1924, had experienced a similar fate. For all practical purposes, it too was a Model 1892 in somewhat improved form. The 53 was a

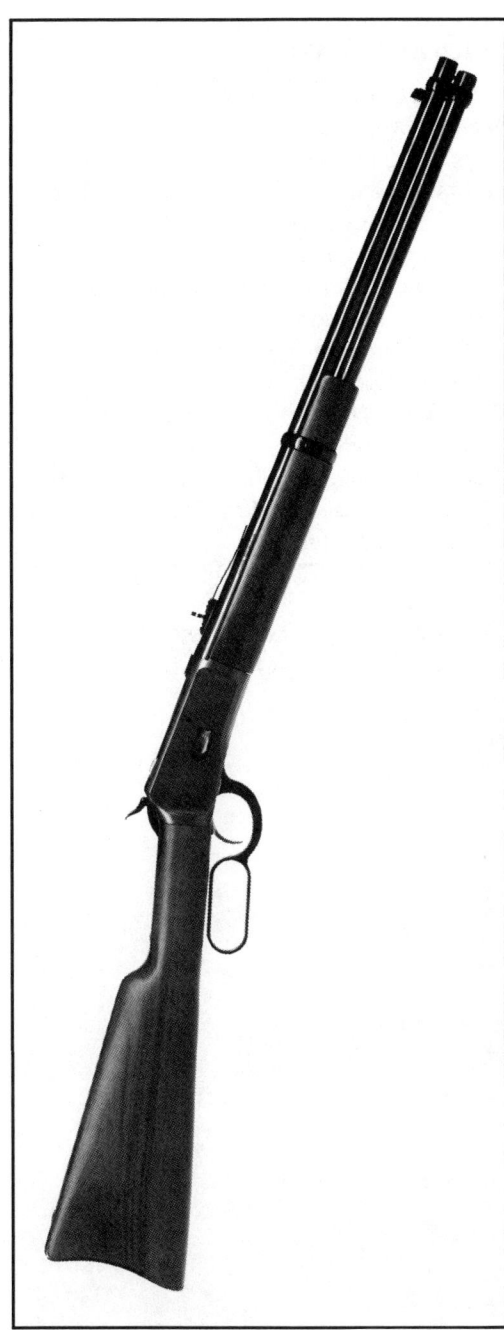

The Model 1892 Winchester was reborn about 1979 in a Browning replica called the Model B-92. A modern re-creation in calibers 44 Remington Magnum and 357 Magnum, the B-92 sported a 20-inch barrel and weighed only 5½ pounds with high-gloss French walnut stock.

pretty little rifle with 22-inch barrel and a magazine containing six rounds. Calibers included the 25-20, 32-20 and 44-40. All sorts of extras were available for the 53, as was the takedown feature and set triggers. The 92 and 53 were sometimes confused and rightly so. George Madis tells us that rifles marked "92" carried all of the features belonging to the 53. The 53 was short-lived and made little impact on the gun world.

Strictly speaking, the Model 1892 Winchester enjoyed a long life—from 1892 into 1931, when manufacture was discontinued. Over a million had been made by 1932, but few in their original configuration sold after that. The last of the breed was numbered "1,004,067." But sales of the 1892 carbine, the Model 53 and the 65 were lumped together and they sold into 1941, so in a broader sense, the years of the Model 1892 Winchester could be considered from 1892 to 1941(3).

Famous sporting rifles often carry on the tradition of the mythological Phoenix bird in that they die and are reborn. New life for the Model 1892 Winchester was infused by the Browning company, which produced an outstanding replica around 1979. In calibers 44 Remington Magnum and 357 Magnum, the carbine was named the Browning B-92 Lever Action. It was an 11-shot beauty that wore a 20-inch barrel and weighed only 5½ pounds with high-gloss French walnut stock.

The Model 1892 was reasonably accurate, amply strong of action and barrel and was chambered for some useful cartridges. In fact, Marlin not long ago brought out a lever-action rifle chambered for the 25-20 and 32-20 rounds. Nostalgia alone cannot account for the continuance of the short cartridges so well-liked in the '92. Those rounds found a niche in the "old

> ## THE MODEL 1892 WINCHESTER AT A GLANCE
>
> **Period of Manufacture:** 1892 to 1931 (early 1940s, if you consider the Model 53 and Model 65 as improved versions); over 1 million manufactured
> **Calibers:** 25-20, 32-20, 38-40 and 44-40; 218 Bee (rare)
> **Magazine capacity:** In 44-40 caliber, the full magazine held 11 rounds (carbine) or 17 (musket); half-magazine held 5 rounds
> **Action:** Lever-action repeater with side loading port
> **Frame:** Smaller version of the Model 1886's
> **Barrel:** Of steel, blued. Rifle, 24 inches usually. Carbine, 20 inches; Musket, 30 inches. May be round, octagonal or part-round/part-octagonal, up to 34 inches
> **Weight (approx.):** 5½ pounds (carbine)
> **Triggers:** Single-stage or set type; plain
> **Sights:** Open; post front, sometimes buckhorn rear; various styles
> **Stock:** Plain straight-grip stock of American walnut or special order fancy-grain walnut; wooden forend; oil-finished, some varnished; shotgun-style, rubber or crescent-shaped buttplates
> **Variations:** Numerous, including engraved models, saddle rings attached to some receivers (carbine); rubber recoil pads; barrel bands on musket and rifle versions, much customizing, etc.

days" and apparently enough shooters deem them useful still that the older ammo for the Winchester Model 1892 has not yet disappeared from the gunstores.

THE WINCHESTER 94
THE SPORTSMAN'S "OLD FAITHFUL"

12

Some rifles sell in the thousands, some in the hundreds of thousands. The Winchester Model 94, or Model 1894 for the year it was introduced, has sold in the millions, with sales pushing 6,000,000 right now. Why has this rifle prevailed so long?

The most famous sporter in the world, the Winchester Model 1894 was the first *sporting* rifle to use a smokeless powder cartridge, the 30-caliber Winchester Center Fire (30 WCF). Two smokeless military rounds—the 8mm Lebel in 1886 and the 30-40 Krag prior to 1892—had preceded the 30 WCF. But by 1895 the 30 WCF smokeless was in full swing.

The Model 94 was a working rifle in a society of working people. It got the job done and it didn't have to be carried

The Model 1894 Winchester in 20-inch barrel carbine version, still produced today.

A rugged Model 94 carbine that has seen a lot of hard ranch use continues to serve its owner in rough country. The Model 94 has long been a workhorse for hunters.

around wrapped up in a horse blanket to keep it pretty or safe from harm. Model 94 rifles were sometimes abused, but they stood up to it. By far, the majority of 94s are still functioning to this day, and that includes rifles that left the factory before the dawn of the 20th century. Of course, very early serial numbers are difficult to locate. The rifle was also mid-sized, not nearly as large or heavy, for example, as the Winchester '86 or '95. The carbine version was even more compact (carbines, for our purposes, are considered rifles). At the same time, the 94 wasn't tiny. It filled a man's hand well enough.

The 30 WCF cartridge was in the mid-range, too. While it was not as powerful up close as a 45-70, for example, when its bullets were carefully placed, the 30 was successful on just about everything. And it shot "flat" for its day. At a time when bullet velocity hovered around the speed of sound, in the 1100-1200 feet-per-second (fps) bracket, the 30 WCF hummed its bullets away at close to 2000 fps. Sighted right on for 150 yards, the smokeless 30 could be counted on to hit a target at 200 yards, and many a practiced marksman bettered that on a regular basis.

Because the '94 shot a smokeless round, upkeep was easier. Corrosive primers were still in use that could harm a bore, and certainly the owner of a Model 1894 smokeless in the early days had to clean his rifle with regularity; but maintenance was a far cry from blackpowder demands. No smoke obscured the target after a marksman touched off the little 30, and here was a repeater that could be counted on to get off plenty of shots without fouling either the bore or action. Recoil was no problem either, since it is generated in part by the weight of the powder charge. Smokeless fuel was much more efficient than black powder, so less powder was required to do the job.

The bullet was pretty modern too. Jacketed bullets had preceded the wide use of smokeless powder. They were of European invention, sometimes called "envelope" bullets. However, American shooters were used to all-lead projectiles. The Model 1894's snappy cartridges fired jacketed missiles. The 25-35 WCF used a jacketed 117-grain bullet. Some sources insist the first 30 WCF bullets weighed 160 grains; others say 165. But just about everyone agrees that muzzle velocity was around 1970 fps, close to the 2000 fps mark. The 30 WCF was way ahead of the 44-40—in short, it was a round that had a solid reputation on the trail and in the hunting camp. On lighter game, such as deer, the 30-30 was as effective as some of the larger blackpowder rounds—faster with chest-strikes. On larger-than-deer animals, such as elk, moose and the large bear, the old-time lead-throwers were probably more certain than the 30 WCF, but good shots with the little 30 did all right on everything. The favorite 44-40 Winchester pushed a 200-grain bullet at around . . . 1300 feet per second? Or was it 1400? Factory ammo, chronographed, showed more like 1200 fps muzzle velocity for under 650 foot-pounds. Chronographed 30 WCF factory ammo, with the 165-grain bullet, averaged about 1970 fps for a muzzle energy of over 1400 foot-pounds.

BLACKPOWDER YIELDS TO SMOKELESS ROUNDS

The original Model 94 that debuted in 1894 was a blackpowder rifle in calibers

The efficiency of the 30-30 Winchester round (left) made it popular with sportsmen. Only about 30 grains of smokeless powder were required to achieve over 2000 feet per second (fps) muzzle velocity, while the 54-caliber round ball on the right required 120 grains of black powder to gain slightly under 2000 fps.

32-40 Winchester and 38-55 Winchester. The barrel steel was not made to withstand smokeless powder pressures. In 1895 an improved Model 1894 was built with much stronger nickel steel, which allowed for use of the 30 WCF. This was truly the Winchester Model 94 that made a hit with shooters, the rifle brought out in 1895. Always short-changed in this story, however, is the 25-35 Winchester. While the 30 WCF is usually noted as the first smokeless sporting round, it is more factual to say two rounds were smokeless sporters, because the 25-35 was announced with the 30 WCF in 1895.

No one will ever know for sure, but it's a good guess that had the '94 stayed with the 32-40 and 38-55 blackpowder rounds into the 1900s, the little meteor might never have made the impact on American shooting that it did. The 25-35 was an expert's deer round. That is, the little 25-caliber 117-grain bullet at something in the neighborhood of 2200 to 2300 fps was never a powerhouse; yet the dedicated sportsman with plenty of hunting experience could favorably tackle big game with the round. One of the largest killer grizzlies in the west was stopped with a 25-35. This was Old Ephraim, a renegade killer that preferred the flavor of livestock. A trapper named Frank Clark tried to get Old Ephraim to set foot in a big snap-jaw trap from 1914 into 1923. Trapper and bear finally came together. According to Utah Department of Fish & Game records, Clark related the bear's demise: "Finally, more out of fear than any other passion, I opened up with my small 25-35 caliber rifle and pumped six shots into him. He fell dead at my feet. . . ."

You can still read the statistics on Old Ephraim on a marker not far from the beautiful city of Logan, Utah:

> **OLD EPHRAIM'S GRAVE**
> (Grizzly Bear)
> **KILLED BY FRANK CLARK**
> **MALAD, IDAHO**
> **AUGUST 22, 1923**–Weight Approx. 1,100 pounds–Height 9 ft. 11 in.
> **SMITHSONIAN INSTITUTE HAS EPHRAIM'S SKULL**

Skeptics may question the statistics. That's a lot of grizzly bear, and the skull's size suggests that Old Ephraim was a monster—a monster taken with the 25-35 from the reliable Model 1894 Winchester. The 25-35 Winchester was a little bit better than its small caliber suggests, because the long bullet could be counted on to penetrate fairly well. The 25-caliber round-nose called for a fast rate of twist, and the Winchester '94 answered with a 1:8, a turn of the bullet in every eight inches of travel. That rate of twist was at least one of the fastest at the time, if not the fastest in a sporting arm. The 25-35 continued to be chambered in the Model 1894 Winchester from 1895 to 1936, when it was dropped, although it reappeared in the '94 from 1940 to 1950.

The 25-35 finally gave way to the larger 30 WCF, as well as the 32 Winchester Special round, essentially a 30 WCF cartridge case, with a 32-caliber projectile. It has a story unto itself. It is said that the 32 Winchester Special cartridge was brought out for shooters who wanted to reload with black powder. The 32 Winchester Special was supposed to be more suitable for black powder than the 30 WCF, according to rumor. Remington's answer to the 30-30 was its own 30 Remington and, sure enough, the company also had a 32 Remington of almost identical ballistics. It seems that going for a slightly larger projectile had some sales appeal, but ballistically the 32 rounds were no better than their 30-caliber look-alikes. The 32 Winchester Special was actually quite popular, and was chambered in the Model 1894 in 1902 and stayed in the lineup until 1973. Some of us believe that the 32 Winchester Special was more likely created as an additional cartridge—something new, another option. In a way, it's disappointing to consider this reason for the invention of the round. However, Winchester clearly announced to the public that the 32 Winchester Special cartridge was indeed special and its 1916 catalogue said the following:

> .32 Winchester Special Caliber. For Smokeless Powder. We have adapted the popular Winchester Model 1894 rifle to handle the new .32 Winchester Special Cartridge, and are prepared to furnish it in solid frame or 'Take Down' style with 26-inch round, octagon, or half octagon Nickel steel barrels and with full or half magazines.

The advertisement continued: "The .32 Winchester Special cartridge, which we have perfected, is offered to meet the demand of many sportsmen for a smokeless powder cartridge of larger caliber than a .30 Winchester and yet not so powerful as the .30 Army [30-40 Krag]." The slant is obviously toward a larger caliber with more power, and Winchester notes a muzzle energy of 1684.2 foot-pounds for the 32 Special, which puts it ahead of the 30-30. Because of the slightly larger bore and bullet, the 32 Special did gain a small muzzle-velocity advantage over the 30-30, but that was lost downrange because both rounds shot 170-grain bullets, the 30-caliber bullet having somewhat better ballistic properties than the 32-caliber version.

By the way, the 32-40 and 38-55 were hardly tossed out the back door when the smokeless cartridge came along. Both were chambered in the '94 from 1894 into 1930.

The king of the Model 1894 cartridges, however, was the 30 WCF, or .30 Winchester. Known also as the 30-30, this designation led many modern shooters to believe it was actually a blackpowder invention. After all, it used blackpowder nomenclature, 30 caliber and 30 grains of powder. The popular name of the round did come from old-time practice, and it did stand for 30 caliber and 30 grains of powder, but this time the 30 grains weight meant *smokeless* powder. The 30-40 Krag was also named for caliber and powder charge, but that round was never a blackpowder number either. The 30 WCF was smokeless from the start. Furthermore, Winchester did not name it the 30-30. It

A cutaway view of the Model 94 shows the major working parts of the famous sporting rifle.

The Remington Core-Lokt bullet design is going on half a century old. This is the type of bullet that helped make the 30-30 cartridge effective on big game.

seems the cartridge picked up that handle along the way, and the firm eventually gave in.

Coupled with its cartridge offerings, the Model 94 was outrageously successful because of Browning's excellent lever-action design. It resulted in a rifle that was reliable and sufficiently accurate for any work it was called upon to perform. Hunters who learned to master the 94 liked it, including Teddy Roosevelt, who hunted antelope with the Model 1894 rifle when it was still new to sportsmen. In *Outdoor Pastimes of an American Hunter*, Roosevelt said:

> I did not have a close shot, for they [the antelope] were running about 180 yards off. The buck was rear-most, and at him I aimed; the bullet struck him in the flank, coming out of the opposite shoulder, and he fell in the next bound. As we stood over him, Joe [Joe Ferris, Roosevelt's hunting partner at the time] shook his head,

and said, 'I guess that little rifle is the ace;' and I told him I guessed so too.

Owners tended to treat the 94 in a personal way. The exact psychology behind the 94 becoming a friend as well as a tool is beyond the scope of this work, but it's true all the same. Many Model 94s carried pet names. "Novia," meaning Sweetheart, was a little 94 carbine from a Mexican ranch. "Turkey Track" hailed from an Arizona ranch. There was "Meatmaker" and "Little Eva," a beat-up 94 that worked hard for its owner during the Great Depression.

The Model 1894 was offered as standard in a rifle version with 26-inch barrel and in a carbine with 20-inch barrel. The rifle weighed about 8 pounds, with the carbine balancing the scale at only $6^{1}/_{2}$ pounds. Anyone who has shot both rifle and carbine may opine that the rifle was a shred deadlier at the target. The longer sight radius and better "hang" of the 26-inch barrel helped the '94 keep nice and steady. If a hunter wanted to own the

Winchester Model 1894 when it came out, he had to part with about 18 dollars American. And herein lies another important reason the 94 has enjoyed such renown over the years: it has always been a bargain. For a modest cash outlay, the "average" hunter had a "deer rifle" and a veteran hunter had a rifle he could use on any North American big game. The price tag was a big attention-getter and still is.

The Model 1894 rifle fell right into place with all Winchesters of the era. It was offered with all of the usual refinements and special features. Barrels varied greatly in length, for example, as well as shape. The carbine usually wore the 20-inch barrel, but a Baby Carbine could be ordered in 14-, 16- or 18-inch barrel lengths. Although the rifle generally carried a 26-inch barrel, a 24-incher was standard on the extra lightweight model. Until 1908 it was no problem to order a special 36-inch barrel Model 1894 rifle in calibers 32-40 or 38-55 Winchester, too. And, of course, saddle rings could be had, and not just on carbines. One existing rifle shows a saddle ring on a special 1894 rifle with extra-heavy octagon barrel. Full magazines and half-magazines were common. Even a single-set trigger saw use briefly. The single-set was only one trigger, but by pushing it forward, it could be set to provide a very light touch. Double-set triggers (two-trigger arrangement), where the rear trigger sets the front or hair trigger for a light touch, were the norm. Embellishments included you name it—from engraving of all magnitudes to wood carving and checkering. And don't forget the takedown model built on the interrupted thread principle.

Because the Model 1894 used the new smokeless powder, the barrel had to be so-marked. A common stamping was: NICKEL STEEL BARREL on one line with ESPECIALLY FOR SMOKELESS POWDER below. For a brief time, it appeared as: EXTRA STEEL BARREL above ESPECIALLY FOR SMOKELESS POWDER on serial numbers from 45,000 to 75,000 in calibers 32-40 and 38-55. Working tough nickel steel was not easy on machinery, so Winchester decided to make a milder steel barrel, but stronger than the old blackpowder barrel, calling it "Extra Steel." When the blackpowder era finally faded away and all cartridges were loaded with smokeless powder by the ammo factories, the Winchester Cartridge Laboratory and the design branch of the company continued to forge ahead with the Model 94. Many rounds were introduced, including current powerhouse loads such as the 307 Winchester, 356 Winchester and 375 Winchester. The first is, more or less, a rimless 308 Winchester—actually a bit less ballistically. The second is a rimless version of the 358 Winchester, but again a bit less powerful. And the third is an updated version of the 38-55, which was always a good round. The new 375 Winchester was simply

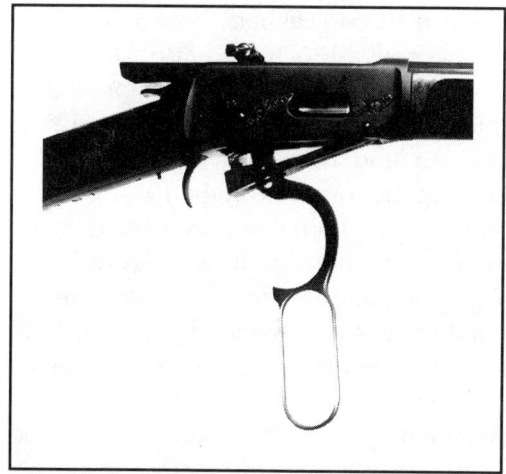

The lever of the Model 94 is shown here in the down position. The down-thrust of the lever cocks the hammer and transports a cartridge up from the magazine on a carrier to firing position.

a stronger-cased 38-55 designed for a tougher Model 94 action.

The Winchester Model 94 is split the same way as the Model 70: pre-64 and post-64, models that were made before and after that date. The model change was not widely accepted by 94 fans and never has been. An important alteration in the post-64 Model 94—a newly designed action—brought the gun fully into the 20th century. Two things about this action stand out. It's much stronger than the old one, thereby capable of handling a more powerful group of big game cartridges, and it has an angle-eject feature. One of the more interesting rounds loaded for the Angle Eject was the 7-30 Waters, developed by modern cartridge expert, Ken Waters. This is essentially, but not exactly, the 30-30 necked down to accept 7mm (.284-inch diameter) bullets. Recoil is light and the 7-30 has plenty of power for deer hunting. The Angle Eject followed the carbine styling, for the Model 94 went almost entirely that route. The carbine simply wiped the rifle out in terms of sales and Winchester decided long ago to all but drop the rifle.

We cannot say, however, that the rifle became extinct. It resurfaced again and again. Two of the finest Model 94 rifles were the "Winchester Model 64" and "Winchester Model 64 Deer Rifle." Many consider this Model 94—for that is exactly what it was despite the model number—the best-looking 94 of the lot. Winchester said the 64 was "the last word in style," and a strong following believed it. But the 94 carbine continued to outsell it so painfully that Winchester dropped the Model 64. The 94 carbine became a standard by shooter demand. Taking the entire sales record into consideration, few 94s were sold with these features: half-magazine, extra short barrels, extra long barrels, rifle-length barrels, half-octagon barrels, engravings, personalizings—special orders with initials, etc.—platings, special buttplates, pistol grips, single-set triggers, double-set triggers, special sights or takedown models. What the shooter wanted, and got, was the Winchester Model 94 Carbine.

Just as the Model 64 was a special Model 94, so was the Model 55 nothing more than a variation of the Model 94. Believe it or not, in 1924 the Model 94 *rifle* was effectively discontinued and the Model 55 was put in the lineup. Of course, the 94 was not truly dropped, just in its rifle configuration; the carbine continued to be made. The 55 was offered to fill any gaps left by the discontinuance of the 94 rifle. It was offered in 30-30 chambering into 1926, then the 25-35 and 32 Special were added to help boost sales. The 55 had a 24-inch barrel, fluted comb, straight-grip stock, half-magazine and a shotgun-style buttplate. In fact, the takedown style was standard for the 55, the solid frame coming along in 1930. In the middle 1930s, the Model 55 just faded away. The fine 64 came along in 1933 in calibers 25-35 and 32 Special, as well as 30-30 and also for a while in 219 Zipper. World War II clipped production of the 64, but it was resumed after the war and built into 1956-1957, then again for a short while in the 1970s because shooters cried out that they wanted the 64 back—until they had it. Sales were poor.

Commemoratives, a phenomenon common to exceptional rifles, honored the Model 94 design by making tribute to special events in our nation's history. Approximately 75 of these were built on the 94 action, chambered mostly for the 30-30, but also the 32 Winchester Special, 32-40, 44-40 and 38-55. The first commemorative, the "Wyoming Diamond Jubilee," appeared in 1966; it was dedicated to Wyoming's 75th year of statehood. Fifteen hundred were made and sold within the state by the Wyoming Diamond Jubilee Committee. A second commemorative appeared the same year, dedicated to the 100th year of the Model 66. It was built on the 94 action, caliber 30-30. Nebraska's 100th year of statehood was honored with another Winchester in 1966. Other commemoratives include the "Canadian '67 Rifle," "Alaska Purchase," "Illinois Sesquicentennial," "Buffalo Bill," "Golden Spike," "Northwest Territories" and "NRA Rifle"—all limited edition runs and numbered from one onward.

Today the Model 94 is represented by the Winchester Model 94 Big Bore Side Eject (not angle eject). This name clearly establishes the fact that spent cartridges are flipped out to the side. Chambered for the 307 Winchester and 356 Winchester cartridges only, the Side Eject Model 94 takes a scope sight centered over the action. It is the carbine, of course, with 20-inch barrel and six-shot tubular magazine. Winchester never did offer a 94 magazine for pointed bullets, although Remington's Model 141 tubular magazine clearly shows that this can be accomplished. The United States Repeating Arms Company (USRA) makes the current Winchesters, which are built of the finest steel and design and are as rugged and accurate as any 94s in history. USRA offers a standard Model 94 Side Eject Rifle (in 30-30 and 7-30 Waters), a Ranger version (30-30 caliber) and a Trapper with 16-inch barrel in the same chamberings as well as the 44 Rem. Magnum (which also holds the 44 S&W Special) and the 45 Colt.

The Winchester Model 1894 is a forever rifle. If not one more were ever made, shooters of the 21st century would still know about it. Model 94 Winchesters are

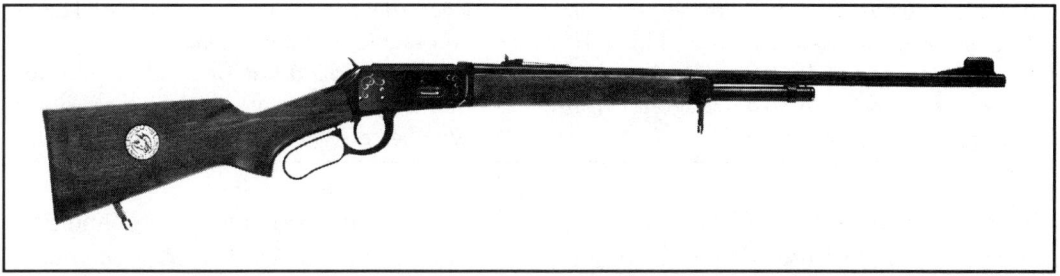

The NRA Centennial rifle (above) that honored the National Rifle Association was a commemorative built on the 94 action in 30-30 caliber. The current Model 94 Winchester Angle Eject carbine (below) expels empty brass out to the side rather than upward. This is a stronger action than that used on past models.

> ### The Model 1894 Winchester at a Glance
>
> **Period of Manufacture:** 1894 to date
> **Calibers:** In 1894, blackpowder calibers 32-40 Winchester and 38-55 Winchester; in 1895 smokeless 30-30 Winchester and 25-35; later 32 Win. Special; contemporary calibers—7×30 Waters, 30-30 Win., 44 Rem. Mag., 45 Colt and others.
> **Magazine Capacity:** 6 rounds usually
> **Action:** Lever-action repeater, originally designed by John Browning with side loading port
> **Barrel:** Of nickel steel or "extra steel" to accommodate smokeless powder, blued. Rifle, 26 inches standard; Carbine, 20 inches standard. May be round or octagonal, from 14 to 36 inches special order
> **Weight (approx.):** Rifle, 8 pounds; Carbine, 6½ pounds
> **Triggers:** Single-stage type or double-set
> **Sights:** Open; adjustable buckhorn-style rear; post or blade front usually
> **Stock:** Straight-grip plain stock of American walnut; special order fancy-grain walnut; wooden forend; shotgun or crescent-shaped buttstock; oil-finished, a few varnished
> **Furniture:** Casehardened receiver, hammer, lever, trigger and buttplate; one barrel band and saddle ring on carbine
> **Variations:** Takedown or solid frame; numerous options, as available on other Winchesters

scattered around the globe. They continue to experience hard use in the wilderness of Alaska and Canada, in the deserts of Australia, Old Mexico, and every part of the United States. Most of us have been through a few 94s. I have. One year I decided I needed a rugged companion rifle for the trail. After thinking on the subject, the same conclusion hit me over and over. I bought another 94. I liked it so much I had it customized by Dale Storey, who builds the Storey Conversion on the 94 action. The rifle has traveled with me for many miles and put plenty of game on the family table, doing what it was built for—faithfully serving the outdoorsman.

THE 1895 WINCHESTER
FIRST BOX MAGAZINE LEVER-ACTION

13

The Model 1895 Winchester was a celebrated lever-action repeater that boasted several firsts, not the least of which was first place in the hearts of dedicated sportsmen. I originally saw a '95 in 1958 when I was living in Patagonia, a village on the Arizona/Mexico border. My friend Robert Bradsher traded a German Luger pistol for one. "Was there ever a lever-action 30-06?" my friend asked. At the time, I wasn't sure. I guessed that there wasn't. He laughed and handed me his newly acquired rifle—a Model '95 in caliber 30-06 Springfield. H.V. Stent, well-known rifleman, hunter and author of his day, praised the Model 1895 on its 50th birthday. In the August 1945 *American Ri-*

The Model 1895 Winchester with its distinctive "box magazine" beneath the receiver.

fleman magazine he wrote: "This year marks the golden anniversary of the Winchester Model '95—my candidate for the distinction of being the highest American development of the sporting rifles." Big words from a noted firearms authority, and Stent could back them up.

Colonel Townsend Whelen for a time considered his Model '95 in 40-72 Winchester a best friend on the trail, carrying the rifle on many wilderness treks. Martin Johnson, the famous film maker of wild animal movies, used only the Winchester Model '95 as his backup gun, stopping charges of lions, buffalo and other dangerous game down to 10 feet from his shoelace. His '95 was chambered for the powerful 405 Winchester cartridge. So was Theodore Roosevelt's reliable "Medicine Gun." Leslie Simson may not be a household name these days, but in the early 20th century he was known as one of Africa's greatest hunters. He's the fellow who backed up Saxton Pope, Arthur Young and Stewart Edward White as these men hunted lions and other game with the longbow in Africa in 1925. The first two names are familiar to anyone in archery today; for them the Pope & Young Club is named. White was a well-known novelist and hunter (who also admired the '95). Simson used several rifles in his capacity as professional hunter, but one of his all-time favorites was the Winchester lever-action '95 in 30-06 chambering. Simson shot his '95s so much he wore two of them out—bore only—you didn't retire a '95 action. Simson was on his way to burning out a third barrel when Art Young bought the rifle from him. Young got on the '95 bandwagon, proclaiming that talk against the '95 and its lever-operated action being too weak for powerful cartridges were seeds of propaganda sewn by those who wanted to promote bolt-action firearms. Some of that was undoubtedly true.

The Winchester Model '95 was built for smokeless powder cartridges, and was chambered for fairly potent rounds, although at the time they were not factory loaded to terribly high breech pressures. The 30-40 Krag was the first, followed by the 30-03, the 30-06, the 303 British, 35 WCF and 405 Winchester. The rifle was also chambered for the 6mm Lee Navy cartridge, known as the 236 Navy, but the

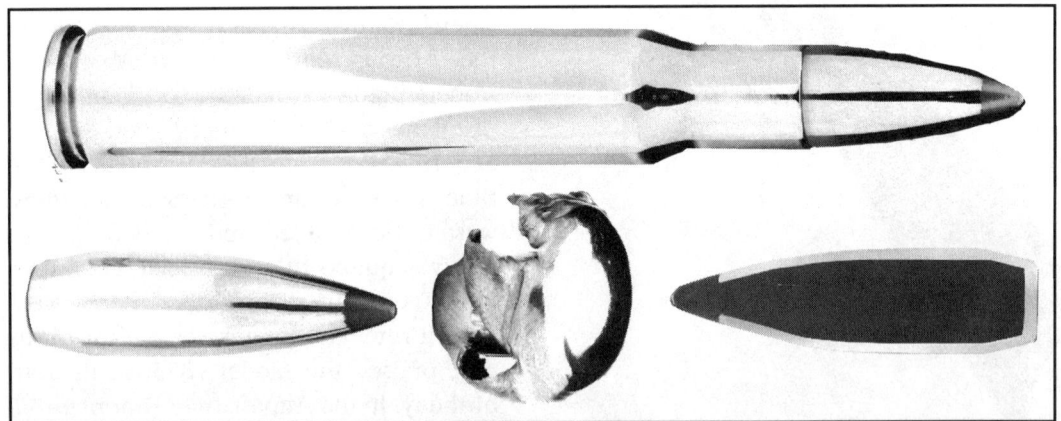

The Model 1895 Winchester is unique in that it is the only lever-action rifle chambered for the 30-06 Springfield cartridge. Federal's Premium load is shown here with recovered 150-grain Sierra boat-tail bullet (center).

The Model 1895 Winchester was manufactured in two versions, a First Model with smooth receiver, and a Second Model (above) with fluted receiver. This close-up clearly shows the box magazine.

rifle was not, as far as records show, distributed in this chambering because the 6mm round did not work well in the '95 action. A musket version of the '95 was built for the Russian military and chambered for the 7.62mm Russian cartridge, as well as two blackpowder rounds, the Winchesters 38-72 and 40-72.

It is true that the '95 received some bad press. It was still selling strong in an era when bolt-action rifles were poised for a takeover, which eventually came to fruition. Talk of the 95's lack of accuracy and weakness of action flitted around gunshops and onto magazine pages. But the '95 was neither inaccurate nor weak. It was, after all, winner of the 1896 Wimbledon Cup Match for 1,000-yard accuracy shooting against the best target arms of the day. Little more need be added to refute those who categorized the '95 as inaccurate. The competition, as detailed in the September 1896 issue of *Shooting and Fishing* magazine (forerunner of *American Rifleman*), was stiff:

> The weather was cloudy... with a strong wind at one o'clock, as unsteady as it is possible to be.... Arriving at the foot of the range, one finds all the aspirants for Wimbledon honors lined up at the firing point.... There... is the veteran pigeon shooter, Colin R. Wise, of Passaic, with the Krag-Jorgensen .30 caliber; Colonel Cecil Clay, of Washington, D.C., with his old Springfield; Lieutenant F.C. Wilson,

of Georgia, with one of C.E. Overbaugh's Sharps-Borchardt Creedmoor .45-110 specials; Captain Stebbins, of New York, with one of the new Winchester-Lee .236 naval rifles; Captain J.C. Postell, of Georgia, with a Springfield military .45-70; Captain T. Cann (the winner) with a new Winchester repeating military rifle Model of 1895....

The ".30 caliber" noted in the article in the 1895 used by Captain Cann had to be the 30-40 Krag because of the year; the 30-03 and 30-06 were a few years away from development at the time.

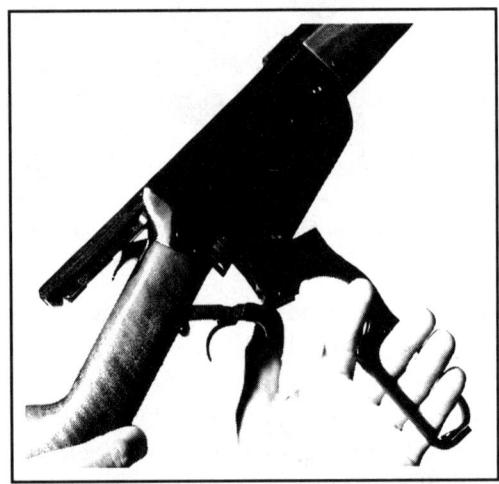

A close-up view of the open action of the Model 1895 rifle.

As for strength, the United States Army Ordnance Board tested the Model 1895 Winchester in 1898 because rumor had it that the rifle might be slated for military use. Winchester provided test rifles and the Army put those rifles through hell. In one test, the '95 fired "ten lots of 500 consecutive rounds in about thirty minutes each, the gun being allowed to stand until cool between each 500 rounds, and to be used only as a magazine arm." In another Army test, two rounds intentionally rendered defective were fired in the '95. These were cross-filed through the rim to ruin the case. But the '95 stood up to all of this abuse. Then overloads were used. Cartridges overloaded on purpose to provide 75,000 PSI (pounds per square inch), the supposed limit of the fine Model 70 bolt-action rifle before its bolt set back, were shot in the '95 in an attempt to ruin the action. Excessive headspace was incurred after shooting the overloads, but the action was not destroyed or left inoperable.

Stent admitted that the '95 had some problems, but for every one of them he cited a positive attribute. In the New York State Ordnance Board Rapid-fire test, for example, the '95 won the day over every other entry, the '95 successfully firing 56 shots in one minute. Stent allowed that the '95 was difficult to field-strip for cleaning, and in turn was tricky to reassemble. He admitted that cleaning the rifle from the muzzle was necessary (as with the Model 94 Winchester), and that the '95 was on the heavy side and could be awkward to load due to the box magazine that was fed rounds from up top and down through the action itself. All the same, he was indignant that Winchester did so little to remedy the problems, while the company did update the Model 1886 into the Model 71 Winchester. In one of the more rare company disclosures, Winchester answered the objection through Edwin Pugsley, the company's main spokesman at the time (1945):

> There were several reasons for discontinuance of the Model 95, the first and most important one being a lack of sales. In the last years of its official existence we sold very few guns. As you know, in manufacturing an arm, as is done by the large gun compa-

nies, it is necessary to set up and run several thousand of the model at one time. In the early days, when Winchester had only a few models, we seldom considered setting up for less than a run of 10,000 guns. In more recent years, however, with the number of models greatly expanded, it has been necessary for us to make shorter runs. Even with these. . . , the Model 95 sold so slowly that it did not pay us to keep it in the line.

Pugsley further explained that as GIs returned from the World War II theater, they brought with them many 8mm Mauser rifles, which in turn stimulated the use of 8mm Mauser ammo. The result was that numerous 30-06 rifles exploded because shooters were not careful to keep 8mm Mauser ammunition out of them. The Model 1895 rifle was strong, but it could not withstand a bullet of about 32 caliber running upbore from a case that was ill-sized to begin with, so shooting 8mm Mauser ammo in a gun not chambered for it caused trouble. And why not? Such abuse wreaked havoc in bolt-action rifles too, but the '95 was singled out as particularly problematic with 8mm Mauser fodder. Pugsley admitted that one reason the '95 was taken off the market was a rumor that suggested it was weak and could blow up while shooting 30-06 ammo. In fact, the rifle failed only when 8mm Mauser ammo was inadvertently and wrongly loaded in the chamber.

Many other reasons for the 1895's death were enumerated by Winchester's man, including poor carrying qualities. A hunter could not easily carry the '95, Pugsley reported, because he could not wrap his hand around the balance point—the magazine was in the way. Pugsley also indicated that loading the magazine from the top was awkward, especially with hunting gloves on. So the '95 went down. But it was around for a good long while before it sighed its last. . . .

BROWNING'S GENIUS FLOURISHES AGAIN

John Moses Browning had come up with the initial design of the Model 1895 rifle. No surprise—since the gun genius had inspired other distinguished Winchester rifles. Browning filed for a patent (No. 549,345) for the '95 on November 19, 1894, which was granted the following November 5. It's fairly safe to assume that Browning's major objective was to fashion a rifle around the 30-40 Krag cartridge. This smokeless powder round (which preceded the 30-30, incidentally) was becoming more in demand by hunters.

In addition, the 30-40 Krag used pointed bullets, which were unsafe in the popular tubular magazine of the day, because this invited detonation. When the rifle recoiled, the point of the bullet of one cartridge was jammed hard in the tube against the primer of the cartridge in front of it. Browning's goal was to design a lever-action rifle that did not use a tubular magazine. A box magazine was ideal because the points of all bullets were directed forward, never touching the primer of another round. That's how the Model 1895 got a box magazine. Of course, it was the first lever-action rifle in the world to wear one—and it worked. Any cartridge with a pointed bullet, or for that matter a round-nosed or flat-nosed bullet, could be used successfully in the Model 1895 Winchester.

Why Winchester decided to accommodate the blackpowder rounds 38-72-275 (38-72 WCF) and 40-72-330 (40-72 WCF) in the '95 is lost in the cobwebs of time.

It's obvious that two blackpowder rounds might satisfy those shooters who, for one reason or another, did not want to buy a rifle chambered for the smokeless 30 US Army, or 30-40 Krag round. Incidentally, rifles with octagonal or half-octagon/half-round barrels could be purchased with these blackpowder cartridges, but were apparently not normally offered with other rounds.

As with most Winchesters of the period, the Model 1895 underwent many developmental changes, as well as minor style variations. The first 5,000 '95s were flat-sided, with one-piece finger levers. Somewhere around serial number 5,000 the fluted receiver came into being, giving the receiver more thickness in the locking bolt region, with the lower part of it milled out to reduce needless weight. The action was smokeless powder all the way. Even the 38-72 and 40-72 could be used with the proper type and charge of smokeless powder, *according to one source, but not a recommendation here.* The 30 US Army, 38-72 and 40-72 were chambered in the '95 from the beginning of the rifle's life.

Winchester had a field day promoting the exciting '95 and its smokeless powder round. Sears, Roebuck & Company ran an

The fast-working lever action of the Model 1895 allows the rifle to remain at the shoulder for repeat shots.

advertisement in its catalogue stating, "This is the gun that shoots two miles." They reminded buyers that the 30-40 Krag was capable of 2400 fps muzzle velocity. With the barrel elevated to about 45 degrees, the Krag was capable of shooting a bullet two miles. So the advertisement was no empty promise. The '95 repeater gave a man five 30-40 Krag rounds out of the box magazine (with pointed bullets, remember) and the bullet was shown to fire through 58 7/8-inch pine boards. The '95 in caliber 30-40 wore a 28-inch barrel. In the same Sears advertisement, the 38-72 was mentioned with a 26-inch barrel—nothing on the 40-72 noted. The 38-72 bullet made it through 25 pine boards, Sears said. The 30-40 was used with "metal patched bullets" in its pine board test. Those were probably of the "full patch" or full-metal-jacket form with no lead exposed at the tip. Sears charged $17.82 for the Winchester Model 1895 in the 1890s, caliber 30-40 Krag, and $14.90 chambered for the 38-72. Those prices are for ordinary Model '95s.

Winchester's 1897 catalogue shows a fabulous Model 1895 with high-grade checkering on wrist and forearm, plus a fully engraved receiver. The flat-sided receiver made it all the better to carry engraving. The remarkable work cost only $12.50 more than the basic rifle.

Schoverling, Daly & Gales of New York City advertised a solid-frame Model 1895 in its 1903 catalogue. In calibers 30 U.S. Army, 303 British and 35 Winchester, it wore round, nickel-steel barrels 26 inches long. All three calibers carried five shots in the magazine and one in the chamber. Weight was about 8 1/4 pounds. Price: $30. The 38-72 and 40-72 Winchesters were also advertised on the same page. However, the 26-inch barrels for these two rounds are

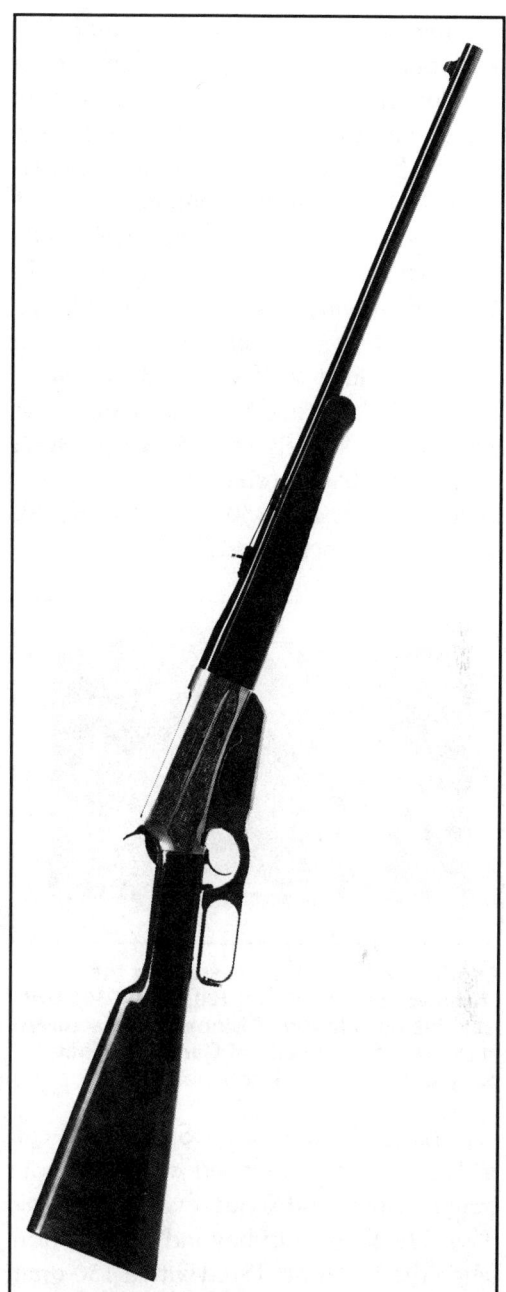

The Browning Arms Company of Morgan, Utah, replicated the Model 1895 Winchester in the mid-1980s in the original 30-40 Krag and 30-06 calibers.

listed as octagonal for $21 (8 1/4 pounds overall) or round for $19.50 (7 1/2 pounds).

No mention is made of nickel steel. This leads one to question the use of smokeless powder in the 38-72 and 40-72 without great care to the type of powder and charge. Both 38-72 and 40-72 carried six rounds with one in the chamber.

Notations on calibers and barrel lengths are faulty in that some research shows the 35 WCF carrying a 24-inch barrel only, yet the Schoverling advertisement lists the Model 1895 in 35 WCF with a 26-inch barrel. The 30 US Army and 303 British are shown with 28-inch barrels, the 38-72 and 40-72 with 26-inch barrels (which corresponds with Schoverling) and the 30-03, 30-06 and 405 WCF with 24-inch barrels.

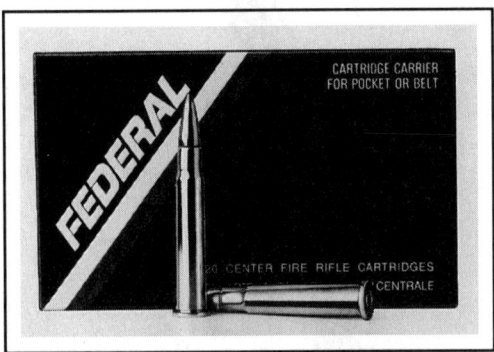

Another cartridge from yesteryear that was chambered in the Model 1895 is the 303 British. This reliable round is now manufactured in the U.S. by the Federal Cartridge Company with a 150-grain soft-point bullet.

As far as the 30-06 Springfield cartridge goes, it was loaded with numerous bullet weights and styles, even in the "old days." However, just beyond its inception, when the 30-06 was listed with a 150-grain bullet at about 2700 to 2800 fps muzzle velocity, it's clear that the loading companies were advertising a 180-grain bullet at approximately 2700 fps and a 220-grain bullet at approximately 2400-2500 fps for use in the '95. This is important because the Winchester Model 1895 was not necessarily developed during the period of more potent 30-06 factory ammo; however, the rifle was safe for the higher velocity 30-06 ammunition that evolved later.

It was the 405 Winchester, however, that changed the complexion of the 1895 rifle entirely. While not quite the powerhouse that advertisements promoted, it was hardly a weakling. The 405 was supposedly developed for the Winchester Model 1895 rifle, another distinction because the rifle was believed by some to have been developed around the 30-40 Krag cartridge and its pointed bullets. An advertised load for the 405 Winchester was a 300-grain bullet at 2350 fps with muzzle energy at 3700 foot-pounds. To be exact, the true muzzle energy was 3680 foot-pounds, but the advertised figure is close enough and merely rounded off for appearance. So the 405 was definitely in front of the 30-06 in terms of punch. The latter, with a 180-grain bullet at 2700 fps muzzle velocity, produced a muzzle energy of 2914 foot-pounds.

The 405 was born around 1904 when the Model 1895 was almost a decade old. The round made it possible for Americans to consider carrying a lever-action rifle to Africa when lever-actions were at their pinnacle of popularity in this country. The 405 Winchester cartridge could be loaded to around 45,000 PSI as a maximum safe pressure without a problem. And of course the Model 1895 action could handle over that PSI. The factory settled on the 300-grain bullet with a pressure of approximately 43,000 PSI, which no longer registered the advertised 3700 foot-pound rating, but was still fairly stout for steam. That combination would develop 3225 foot-pounds, still ahead of the 30-06. Plus the 405 bullet was, after all, heavier with a diameter of around 41/100ths of an inch.

> ### THE MODEL 1895 WINCHESTER AT A GLANCE
>
> **Period of Manufacture:** 1895 to early 1930s. About 425,000 were made, mostly in Musket configuration.
> **Calibers:** Smokeless 30-40 Krag, 30-03, 30-06, 303 British, 35 Winchester, 405 Winchester, 7.62mm Russian; 38-72 and 40-72 blackpowder
> **Action:** Lever-action repeater with box magazine underneath the frame, designed by John Browning. Solid frame or takedown.
> **Barrel:** Of nickel-steel (for smokeless calibers), blued. Rifle, 22 to 28 inches, round; Carbine, 22 inches, round; Musket, 24 to 30 inches, round usually (made in large numbers). Some models with octagonal barrel
> **Triggers:** Single
> **Sights:** Open; rifle-type rear; post or blade front, usually
> **Stock:** Straight-grip plain stock of American walnut; some high-grade walnut; wooden forend; oil-finished, a few varnished
> **Furniture:** Blued receiver flat-sided initially, then fluted
> **Variations:** Not as many special orders as other Winchesters, although variations seen with different buttplates, engravings, etc.

The round was so good that one of our leading ammo experts, Ken Waters, extolled its virtues in his *Pet Loads* book:

> The old .405 Winchester cartridge is still a good one despite its age, better in fact than either the .444 Marlin or .45-70, and while not suitable for ranges beyond two hundred yards, the fact remains that we have never had a better cartridge for taking big game with a lever-action rifle. It deserves to be brought back!

The 405 Winchester remains to this hour the most powerful factory round chambered in a lever-action rifle. It is surpassed only by wildcats, such as the 450 Alaskan, chambered in lever-actions, but not by a commercially loaded round.

A wealth of concise information on the '95 exists in Winchester's own 1916 catalogue. "Made for .30 Army, .30 Government Models 1903 and 1906, .303 British and .35 and .405 Winchester Center Fire Cartridges." The "Take Down" Rifle was offered in the same chamberings for $32.50, $2.50 more than the solid-frame model. No set triggers were offered on any of the rifles. One page features a magnificent Fancy Sporting Rifle with shotgun-style buttplate, rather than crescent-style or rubber buttplate. It carried fine checkering at forend and wrist, plus superior-grade walnut and overall excellent fine finish. A real beauty, it sold for $45. The catalogue also shows a 24-inch barrel Sporting Rifle for $30, the N.R.A. Musket and a 20-inch barrel carbine. The 1916 catalogue lists the ammo as:

- 30 Army w/220-gr. soft-point or full-patch bullet, $50/thousand rounds
- 30-03 or 30-06, $55/thousand rounds
- 303 British w/215-gr. soft-point bullet, $50/thousand
- 35 Winchester w/250-grain soft-point bullet, $55/thousand
- 405 Win. w/300-gr. soft-point or full-patch bullet, $60/thousand

Schematics in this catalogue show the workings of the Model 1895 quite clearly, with abundant information on the action and its function. There is also a parts list for reference.

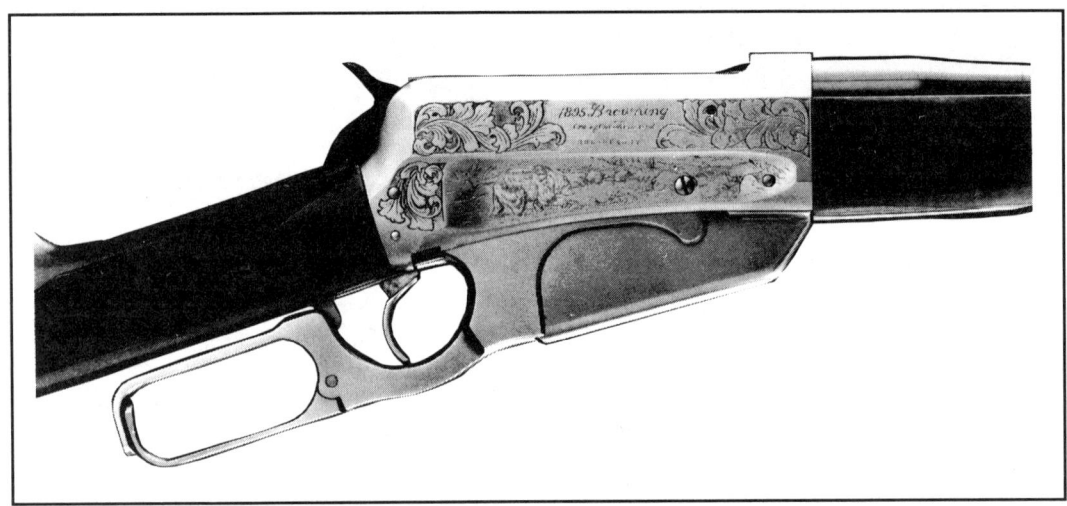

A close-up view of the Browning Model 1895 replica highlights the beautifully engraved receiver and cut-checkering of the High Grade version.

Although not every "legendary" rifle has been offered in a replica model, many of them have, and the Winchester Model 1895 is no exception. Once more, the Browning company is responsible for bringing back the Model 1895 in calibers 30-40 Krag and 30-06. These replicas met with such demand in the 1980s that soon the entire supply was exhausted.

The original '95 didn't sell quite so well, although about 425,000 were shipped from the Winchester factory. First offered in 1896 in the 30-40 Krag, 38-72 and 40-72, the rifle sold well only in 30 caliber. The two blackpowder rounds never soared. The 303 British, added to the list in 1898, was popular in Canada and still is, but it was never a hot item in the U.S. Winchester's excellent 35 WCF came aboard in 1903 and was far superior to its popularity. It was not a big seller, but should have been. The 35 Remington was less powerful, but highly accepted by the public in somewhat similar rifles. In 1904 the 405 Winchester was added to the lineup and it truly was a famous cartridge, even though it is obsolete now. The 30-03 Springfield debuted in 1905, but when the similar 30-06 appeared the next year, it fairly well supplanted the '03. The Model 1895 was chambered for the '06 cartridge in 1908. After that, 30-03 chamberings were on special order only.

But the story continues. Recall that the government of Russia ordered Model 1895 Winchester rifles chambered, of course, for their own military round, the 7.62mm Russian. These muskets were military oriented and cannot be counted as famous sporting rifles, but who knows how many of them saw civilian use after military life? And don't forget Pancho Villa and his boys. Mexican revolutionaries were quite fond of the '95 and considered themselves fortunate soldiers when they were issued the Winchester repeater.

The Winchester Model 1895 made an indelible mark in the history book of famous sporting rifles. Built. Sold. Discontinued in 1932. Replicated. One of the greats, it is still for sale at gun shows and in arms publications today.

THE MAGICAL MANNLICHER
BIG GAME SUPERIORITY

14

The 1800s quietly gave way to the 1900s and a period of startling advancement: airplanes, electricity, cars. Many 19th-century ideas became 20th-century realities. Cities sprawled. Wilderness shrank. Dedicated sportsmen witnessed change as they explored every crack and crevice of yet-unsettled parts of the globe for big game. One rifle dominated the ranks of these wanderings: the Mannlicher-Schoenauer.

Introduced in 1900, this rifle succeeded for the same reasons early Winchesters, Marlins and others made it: reliability and service. A hunter could count on his Mannlicher. She balanced like the Scales of Justice, carried light as a feather, pointed fast and never let a man down.

The renown Mannlicher carbine with bolt action, fullstock and unique rotary magazine.

The slick rotary magazine with non-jamming feed gave a hunter confidence that the second shot would be there if needed. No sporting rifle handled like the Mannlicher. The more a hunter used it, the more faith he had in the little jewel. Familiarity bred praise.

The Mannlicher, more accurately the Mannlicher-Schoenauer (M-S), was best-loved in the carbine version chambered for the do-more-than-its-size 6.5mm cartridge. The carbine's full-length stock was graceful and slim in contour. It fit into a saddle scabbard neatly and withdrew fast, so transporting it was no problem by vehicle or horse. It was light, but never confuse the sensible carrying weight of the Mannlicher carbine with some of our contemporary flyweights that look like they escaped from a miniature toy factory. It was

The Mannlicher is popular with big game hunters today, as it was with turn-of-the-century adventurers. On a modern-day African safari, Sam Fadala (right) used a Mannlicher rifle in caliber 30-06 to down this warthog.

solid and stable, had good sights and proved sufficiently accurate for all big game hunting in the hands of an expert rifleman.

The M-S wore a good trigger—double set was prominent—and its design was ingenious, right down to the cartridge release button that, when activated, put the cargo of the magazine into the shooter's hand. The magazine itself was quick-detachable for cleaning and upkeep. Metal-to-wood fit was excellent and in spite of considerable drop of a rather thin comb to accommodate the iron sight, the M-S was relatively pleasant to shoot, with recoil seeming to come straight back instead of the stock levering up into the shooter's face.

The trim carbine was escorted all around the world for the better part of a half century. In fact, in 1950 an *American Rifleman* article posed a question about the Mannlicher: "Obsolete?" The answer: "Not by a long shot! You'll still find the little 6.5 from Point Barrow to Tierra del Fuego, from northern Russia to Capetown...wherever experienced big game hunters are."

THE M-S SERVES THE SERIOUS HUNTER

The story of the Mannlicher-Schoenauer begins in Steyr, Austria, once known as the "Iron City." The "Society of rifle and barrelmakers of Steyr," a clan of gunmakers that fell apart because Emperor Rudolf II detested the little town, was born back in the 16th century. The Iron City was strongly Lutheran, while Rudolf held to the Catholic faith. Steyr was an asset to the country, however, producing arms and accessories for the Austrian army. Rudolf's army employed the guns and gear, but the ruler would not pay for them. In spite of non-payment, somehow Steyr survived and even thrived, becoming the gunmaking center of Europe. By the 1800s, Steyr was still a manufacturing center and one of its citizens, Leopold Werndl, was independently employed in making carbine barrels, steel ramrods, shoes, lance points and other goods.

Leopold and his wife, Josepha Millner Werndl, were parents to a son Josef born on February 26, 1831. Josef would make a difference in the gun world, for as a young man he dreamed of a machinable firearm action, one that would have superior ability in locking the cartridge in place. His invention was a bolt-action rifle that earned a large army contract from the Austrian Steyr-Werke factory. Other armies wanted the rifle as well. Werndl's turn-bolt action was a success that gained global notice as well as a special name for Steyr: "arsenal of the world." Black powder, at this time, was giving way to smokeless, a wonderful propellant. But an immediate problem was that it produced much higher pressures than black powder. Existing muzzleloaders could not handle that much pressure. The frontloading firearm had to continue in the use of black powder only, lest the gun blow up. Many designs that were successful as blackpowder arms were suspect at best with smokeless powder.

But that was not the case with Werndl's repeating bolt-action rifle. It held up to smokeless powder breech pressure. When the Golden Age of hunting arrived in the late 1800s and early 1900s, many regions were still game-rich and populations were low enough to allow hunters an open hand. The need for a high-quality big game rifle for the serious hunter was clear. Werndl worked on various models and was still developing new ideas when he died at age 58 on April 29, 1889.

Werndl's theories survived him, however, as others took up the quest for a fine hunting rifle capable of chambering powerful big game cartridges. Two men, Ferdinand von Mannlicher and Otto Schoenauer, combined their inventiveness and, building upon Werndl's work, produced the very rifle the hunting fraternity had been waiting for. In 1900, production began on the Mannlicher-Schoenauer rotary-magazine rifle. The overall design belonged to von Mannlicher, but Schoenauer shared in

Ferdinand von Mannlicher, one of the world's greatest gun geniuses. Not only did he invent the famous rifle that bears his name, but many other useful designs as well.

the rifle's fame by perfecting the action that his partner, and others, had been working on.

Schoenauer was a Werndl man, a perfectionist and an arms technician. He was also Director for the Oesterreichische Waffenfabriks-Gesellschaft—the Austrian armory for firearms production—here known as OWG for obvious reasons. Schoenauer perfected the Mannlicher magazine using a star rotor, in which cartridges were held in a circular fashion. It was touted as "flawless." Modern shooters who have not seen the M-S magazine may have seen an off-shoot in the Savage Model 99 with its rotary design.

Mannlicher was a gun genius. His story is told too infrequently today with too little emphasis. He was born in Mainz, Germany, in 1848 and died in Vienna, Austria, in 1904 or 1907, depending on which source you use. "Ritter" was attached to make his full name Ritter Ferdinand von Mannlicher. He was, for a time, chief engineer for the Austrian Northern Railway. Later, he worked for the OWG, the armory famous for its bolt-action repeating magazine rifle.

Mannlicher was as prolific as he was creative. From 1875 to 1904 he invented many gun designs—more than John Moses Browning or Germany's Paul Mauser. Mannlicher's genius accounted for 150 repeating rifle designs and automatic arms blueprints. His automatic rifle was perfected by 1885. It was a light machine gun, which he thought would boost the effectiveness of the Austrian army. It embodied five moving parts, much like those later used in the Browning Machine Gun. The operating principles of Browning's automatic firearms follow closely on Mannlicher's, including the use of an accelerator housing, locking action, reciprocating parts associated with the barrel, as well as in the locking, unlocking and cocking, plus the method of harnessing recoil energy. The M1 Garand was also based on Mannlicher's ideas—the M1 clearly borrowed from the gas bleed-off system invented by him in 1895. The Austrian army did adopt Mannlicher's straight-pull bolt-action rifle chambered for an 11mm blackpowder cartridge, which was reduced in caliber later to 8mm, but retained its blackpowder nature. In addition, the Canadian Ross rifle and the Swiss Schmidt-Ruben, both straight-pull bolt-action models, followed directly on Mannlicher ideas.

Mannlicher knew that smokeless powder was poised for a takeover. While in the employ of OWG, he made his Model 1886 rifle worthy of the higher-pressure propellant and included front locking lugs for strength at the head of his bolt design. Of the numerous patents Mannlicher obtained, one was British patent No. 2915 for a bolt-action rifle with a rotary magazine in its buttstock. The design received no commercial notice. Setting to work again, he acquired British patent No. 632/1888 for another rotary magazine, this one beneath the bolt action of the rifle and operating with a star wheel. Again, commercial success eluded him. Schoenauer and Werndl tried to perfect the magazine, but did not succeed at this time. By 1900, however, a refined Mannlicher-Schoenauer was shown to an enthusiastic group at the *Exposition Universalle* in Paris. This was von Mannlicher's rifle (and to be fair, his magazine idea as well) with Schoenauer honored for improving the magazine. Mannlicher's ideas for a fine hunting rifle had finally been transformed from paper to wood and steel. Improvements on this basic model in the form of Model 1903 in caliber 6.5mm, the Model 1905 in caliber 9×56mm, the 1908 Model in 8×56mm and the Model of 1910 in 9.5×57mm all brought fame to von Mannlicher.

While Mannlicher's reputation with military arms paled, his sporting rifle endures, and at least one hunter—this one—still carries a Mannlicher into the field. The past three seasons running my own Mannlicher has put venison on the table. Abercrombie & Fitch of New York City called the M-S the finest sporting rifle in the world. In its 1919 catalogue, the popular Model 1886 Winchester (*see* Chapter 10) sold for $15.20. A fine Parker shotgun went for $37.50. But the M-S rifle, calibers 6.5mm and 9mm, sold for $75 each. Which is why the Mannlicher was known as the rifle of the rich and famous—they could afford it.

Names of hunters who carried the Mannlicher would make a Hall of Fame for great outdoorsmen. WDM "Karamojo" Bell owned a Mannlicher rifle and spoke highly of it. He used it to procure meat for his camps in Africa. Bell found that the little 6.5mm, which was also noted as a 256, was ideal for providing meat for his workers and himself. Bell's large-scale meat-gathering is often misconstrued as the work of a game hog, but it was not. Bell had many mouths to feed, so it was common for him to take a dozen head of game in a day. His rifle had to be reliable and the Mannlicher fit the bill. Being one of the greatest marksmen of his or any era, Karamojo tried the petite 6.5mm for elephant hunting. In writing about the experience, Bell said, "I once had a carbine Mannlicher-Schoenauer with a 20-inch barrel down to 5½ pounds with a hollowed-out walnut stock that was simply lightning on elephant." He liked the carbine's short bolt-throw as well as its short length.

Walter Winans (1852-1920) was a firearms authority of his day and an Olympic Gold Medal winner with both revolver and rifle. This author, who illustrated his own books, preferred a Mannlicher. So did the famous ivory hunter, Frederick C. Selous. Likewise Sir Alfred Pease, who said, "With the .256 I have killed many lions, as well as pachyderms and antelopes from greater kudu downward, it is no weight to carry on foot or on horseback, and the mechanism is of the simplest and strongest kind; wet, sand, mud, tumbles, and croppers

The Mannlicher has been the carbine of choice by hunters from all over the world. Used on palatial European estates to ranches in the western United States, the full stock carbine is recognizable anywhere.

have never injured it." Ernest Hemingway carried a Mannlicher and also wrote the rifle into his work a time or two. Vilhajalmur Stefansson was a famous Arctic hunter and explorer who carried a Mannlicher Model of 1903. The little carbine served Stefansson well during the 12 frigid winters he spent on the northern ice. Author of books on African hunting, Denis Lyell, preferred a Mannlicher. He said, "Should I be going to hunt in Africa still having a .256, I would just as soon use it as any other rifle." Another adventurer, Blayney Percival, said, "I shot most of my lions, say forty, with the .256." Baron Bror von Blixen, whose wife authored *Out of Africa*, based on their life in the Dark Continent, was a Mannlicher man too.

Roy Chapman Andrews, the world famous American naturalist, relied on the Mannlicher for large game. Andrews shot Chinese tigers as well as Marco Polo sheep with the slender rifle. Big bore enthusiast, Elmer Keith, may have detested smallbores, but not the Mannlicher. He considered the 6.5mm stronger than its bullet size indicated. In a June 1950 *American Rifleman* Keith said, "I would prefer the 6.5mm 160-grain soft-point load for all work on our largest beasts like elk, moose, and really big bear, to any magnum .25-caliber cartridge in existence, regardless of how high its velocity." Major C.H. Stigand, another famed African hunter, voted for the Mannlicher. So did Colonel Richard Meinertzhagen and Count Vasco de Gama, both international hunters of note.

What was this magical Mannlicher? A.F. Stoeger, Inc., was responsible for bringing the Mannlicher to America in numbers. The widely read catalogue presented Mannlicher sporting arms for years. The catalogue of 1932, for example, includes the famous Mannlicher carbine in 6.5mm chambering with 18-inch barrel. Also offered were the 8mm, 9mm and 9.5mm in carbine form with 20-inch barrels. The 30-06 was chambered in either a 20-inch carbine or 24-inch barrel model. These were standards for the Mannlicher. Special models included a takedown.

A LOOK AT THE MANNLICHER

Let's take a look at a "real live" Model 1905 carbine in 9mm. Weight is 7 pounds 2 ounces with an overall length of 40½ inches. She wears an original carrying strap, a cleverly designed one-piece unit attached to a regular rear swivel with the front swivel attached via a bolt through the breadth of the forend. The 20-inch barrel is slender and in a way just right—long enough to reach cartridge potential, or nearly so, and short enough to be handy.

A blued nosecap dresses the meeting place of barrel end and forend. A serrated blued-steel buttplate holds a trapdoor, within which rests a cleaning rod plus cutouts for two cartridges. The latter makes sense. Trapdoor compartments that do not offer cartridge contour allow rounds to fly forward, pushing bullets deeply into the cartridge case. The perfect fit of the Mannlicher cartridge cavities guards against this problem. The stock of high-grade (not super) wood has nice wraparound checkering at the forearm, plus two checkered panels at each side of the wrist. The rotary magazine is removed by a smart spring-loaded plunger device. A bullet tip or a similarly shaped instrument is pushed into the forward hole in the floorplate, which allows the floorplate to turn by 90 degrees. That movement frees the magazine, which can then break down swiftly for cleaning and oiling. The trigger guard levers into the rear of the floorplate and is held in place by a screw at the back tang. The mild pistol

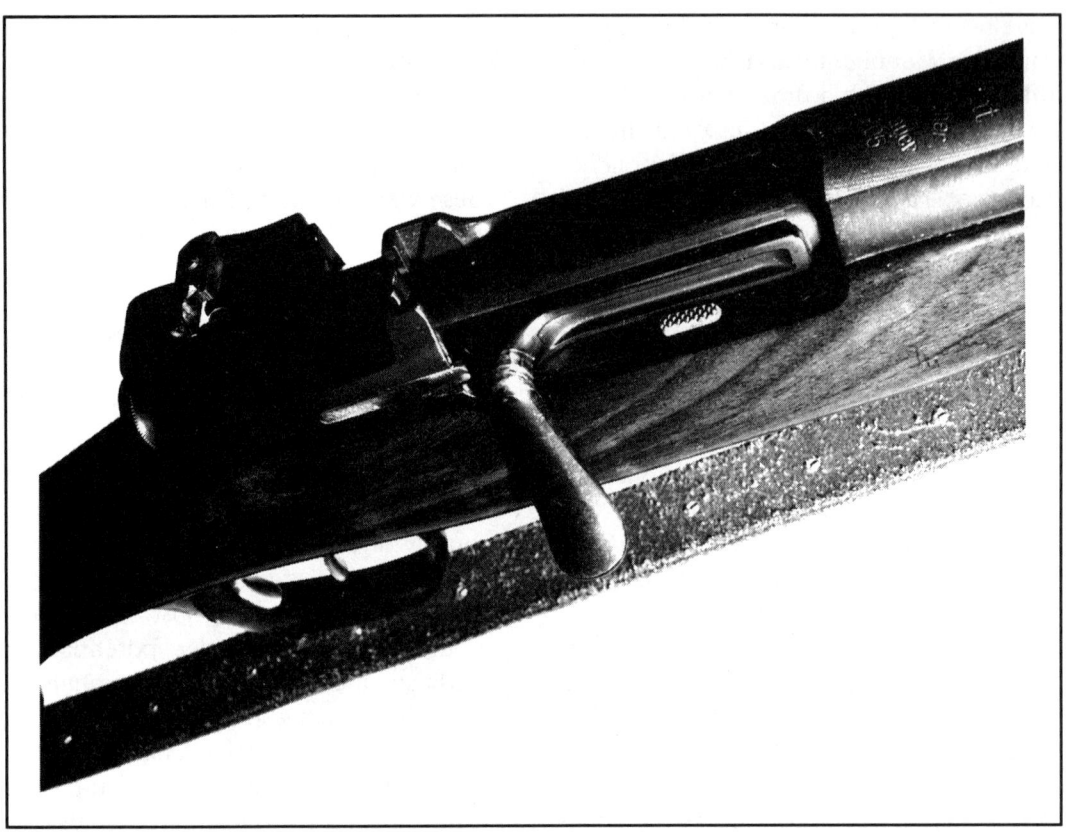

A close-up view of the original Mannlicher action reveals the cartridge release button, forward right of the bolt handle. Pushing this knurled rectangular button with the action open releases the cartridges from the magazine into the shooter's hand. So many shooters admired the Mannlicher that a Mannlicher Collector's Association was formed.

grip—partly responsible for the fast-handling quality—is fitted with a metal cap.

The underside of the butterknife bolt handle is serrated for grip. Forward of the bolt handle is a magazine release catch. A push inward on this catch releases the cargo of cartridges from the magazine and the rounds are directed into the waiting hand of the shooter. This excellent device means that rounds do not have to be worked through the action to clear the magazine. The butterknife bolt handle was despised by some experts who said it didn't offer enough grip area, but the flat-sided handle maintained the slender lines of the rifle; in fact, it offered plenty of area to get ahold of. Detractors said further that the bolt handle was too far forward, rather than resting right above the trigger guard. True, but hunters had no problem getting used to this setup and it's doubtful that so much as a split second was lost in operating the bolt because of handle location.

The sights on this particular Mannlicher are entirely adequate for brush and woods hunting. The front sight is a standard gold bead on a ramp. A blank is fitted into a rear dovetail slot in the barrel that would normally contain a rear sight. Instead of an open sight, this carbine wears a Lyman No. 36 peep, which is a spring-loaded aperture sight that swings out of the way as the bolt is drawn to the rear. The base of the bolt handle pushes the sight back. Then the sight springs back into place. The Lyman No. 36 sold for $10 in the 1930s and was billed as a "No tap or drill needed" sight. There was a Mannlicher peep sight, which devout collectors prefer over the Lyman rear sight, but the latter works admirably well. Behind this sight rests a bolt-release button that allows the withdrawal of the bolt for breech-end cleaning.

The military-like safety on this model is not as graceful as it might be, but is entirely workable. A wing over the cocking piece revolves upward to lock the bolt and deactivate the sear. A quick thumb-push on the wing moves the safety from an upright to a left-hand position, bringing the carbine into battery. A shooter knows when the safety is on immediately, because it blocks the view through the peep sight until the safety is pushed off. The safety wing can also be switched to full right, which locks the bolt. So this is, in effect, a three-position safety. Far left wing: fire. Upright posture: on safe, but bolt can be operated. Far right wing: on safety, bolt locked.

This Model 1905 has the double-set trigger. M-S models could be ordered with single triggers as well. In 1958, trigger options cost $14 for single, $20 for double set. Since the triggers were interchangeable, a shooter could have both types in one rifle. The double-set trigger was extremely light and sharp in the set position. In the unset position, the primary trigger was double-stage; slack had to be taken up before the trigger engaged. In the set position, the trigger broke at only seven ounces. This was just fine.

Grassroots American shooters, however, were not crazy about the double-set trigger nor the M-S safety nor the slim stock design, which was built with iron sights in mind. Changes were in demand. Besides, scope sights were not at home on the original-style Mannlicher. Steyr offered factory scope mounts, but they were ultra-high. The two-piece bolt cocked on opening. A cocking knob extended to the rear when the rifle was cocked. Lock time, as compared (for example) with the speedy Model 700 Remington, was slow. The butterknife bolt handle was workable, but shooters seemed to want a knob instead. Some said the carbine had a "weak action." No doubt the two-piece bolt offered nowhere near the strength of the Mauser. Yet, these arguments all ran from the light of practical field use. In the field, the bolt handle was agreeable, and the action was strong enough to accommodate some fine cartridges.

All of these "preferences" had to be addressed. Before long, the original Mann-

One of the best cartridges chambered in the original Mannlicher was the 9mm Mannlicher, or 9×56mm (far left), shown here in comparison with other medium-bore rounds: (left to right) the 35 Whelen, 358 Winchester and 348 Winchester.

licher sporting arm received more than a facelift—it became a whole new firearm. The M-S was in trouble partly for price too. In 1932 a hunter could buy a perfectly reliable Model 54 Winchester (*see* Chapter 15) for $53.40. That same year, the M-S carbine cost $82.50, and in 30-06 chambering, the price tag was $107.25. More revealing are 1939 figures: the fine Model 70 sold for $61.25, while the Mannlicher carbine tipped $140, with the 30-06 going for $175. Over a 47-year period of operation, the factory turned out only 74,000 of the original-style Mannlicher rifle, or 3.5 rifles per working day (according to research figures).

As with so many great sporting rifles, it's difficult to remove the cartridge from the firearm in a fair-play assessment of greatness. The Mannlicher rifle itself was, on the face of it, the true reason for greatness. Although its cartridges were second in stature, the 6.5×53mm became a giant killer in the hands of expert riflemen. It truly was not a powerful cartridge when compared with the other Mannlicher rounds, and even less impressive compared with the 30-06 and larger rounds. A 6.5mm—about 26 caliber—160-grain bullet left the muzzle at around 2300 fps. Muzzle energy was almost a ton at 1880 foot-pounds, but the 30-06 with a 180-grain

Contemporary Mannlichers (this one is Ruger's Model 77) are chambered for many excellent big game cartridges, including Federal's High Power 308 Winchester.

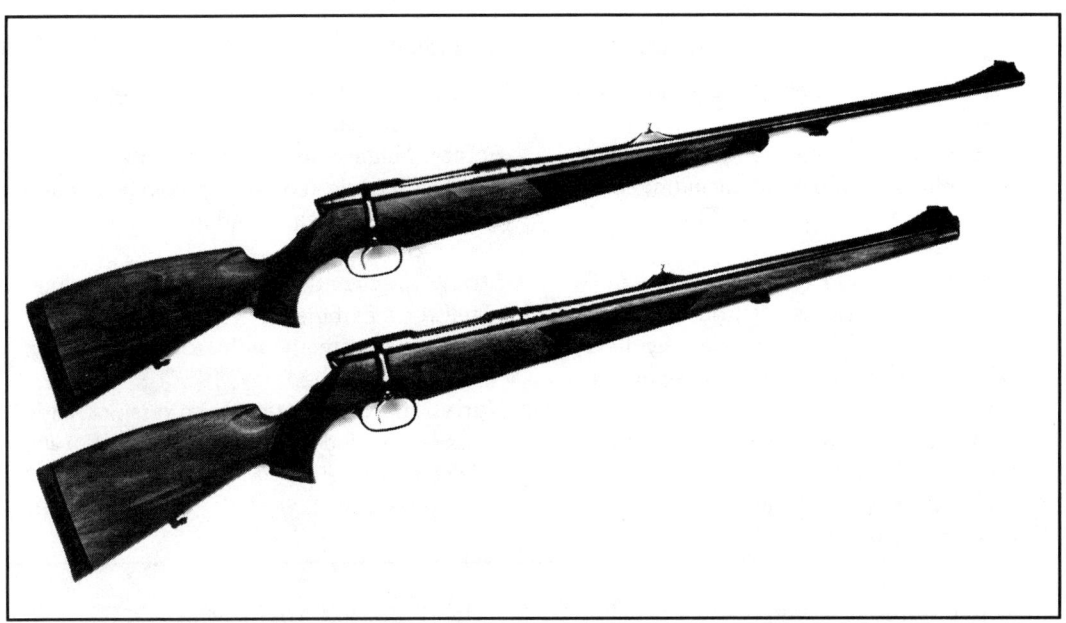

Modern-day Mannlichers in rifle and carbine styles still carry the bolt action and some of the superior features of the original, including superb metal-to-wood fit and a steep price tag.

bullet at 2700 fps gained over 2900 foot-pounds, close to a ton and a half. But a 6.5mm 160-grain bullet is long for its caliber, with a high sectional density of .328. But was it lofty in sectional density? Yes, but it did not outstrip many other projectiles by much and some not at all in the sectional density department.

The 6.5mm was absolutely deadly, as Keith said, on large animals because fine hunters employed it. They put the bullet where it belonged. Furthermore, the 6.5mm was light-recoiling and that can make a difference in how well a rifle is managed. But on the face of it, the other Mannlicher rounds were more deadly, though far less appreciated, than the 6.5mm. The 8mm, or 8×56mm, Mannlicher round pushed a 170-grain bullet at over 2400 feet per second, but a better bullet from this cartridge was a heavier (about 200 grains) projectile at around 2100 fps. There were other loads for the 8×56mm, including a 227-grain missile at 2300 fps from a handload. To be fair, the 6.5mm benefited from handloading, too, and the 160-grain bullet could be shoved at 2500 fps for 2221 foot-pounds of energy. No matter. A 227-grain jacketed bullet at around 2300 fps carries 2667 foot-pounds of energy. The 6.5×53 or 6.5×54 was loved. The 8×56 was liked.

The 9×56mm didn't enjoy as much praise and today ranks last in appeal among collectors. The 9×56, according to sources provided by the Mannlicher Collector's Association (MCA), suffered from varying chamber dimensions and bore dimensions, especially the latter. A true 9mm bullet would be .354 inch in diameter. Many Model 1905 rifles were just that. But some were .356 inch. And a Model 1905 slugged (bore measured) for this work came out just shy of .358-inch bore diameter. Some claim this situation is rare to non-existent, just a lot of poppycock made up by collectors and put in print by gunwriters. However, the facts seem to stand up.

> ### THE MANNLICHER AT A GLANCE
>
> **Period of Manufacture:** 1900 to date, with adaptations
> **Calibers:** 6.5mm, 8mm, 9mm, 9.5mm initially; plus about 30 more, including 30-06, 243 Win., 257 Roberts, 270 Win., 264 Win. Mag., 308 Win.
> **Action:** Bolt action ("butterknife" handle) with cartridge release button and rotary magazine. Originally designed by Ferdinand von Mannlicher, improved by Otto Schoenauer.
> **Barrel:** Of steel, blued. Rifle, 24 inches, round; Carbine, 18 or 20 inches, round
> **Weight (approx.):** Carbine, 7 pounds plus
> **Overall Length:** 40½ inches w/20-inch bbl.
>
> **Triggers:** Double-set usually; single option; interchangeable
> **Safety:** Military-like 3-position safety
> **Sights:** Open, iron originally; gold bead ramp front; peer rear; variations, including scopes
> **Stock:** Checkered pistol-grip stock of walnut; fullstock carbine or halfstock rifle; steel trapdoor buttplate with storage cavity on some; oil-finished
> **Variations:** Solid or takedown versions; early models include the 1903 (6.5mm), 1905 (9×56mm), 1908 (8×56mm) and 1910 (9.5×57mm)

Nonetheless, the 9×56mm was an excellent round. A carbine in that caliber that has been in my camp the past three seasons drives a 225-grain bullet at 2500 fps with a handload and a 250-grain bullet at 2300 fps. These are maximum figures, of course, built carefully in one particular rifle only, and they do not represent the average ballistics of the original 9×56mm.

However, a factory load listed in *American Rifleman* magazine for June 1966 shows a 247-grain bullet at 2160 fps for a muzzle energy of almost 2600 foot-pounds. The handload with the 225-grain projectile at 2500 fps is worth over 3000 foot-pounds. The 9.5×57mm Mannlicher round was chambered in the 1910 Model. It was more of the same, only with larger bullets. Also called the 9.5×56mm, 9.5×56.7mm and 375 Nitro Express Rimless, the 9.5 put a 260-grain bullet on the line at 2150 fps with a factory load for 2670 foot-pounds and could be handloaded for over 3000 foot-pounds of energy. Having hunted with the 9×56mm, I know its worth.

The original-style Mannlicher was chambered for as many as 30 other cartridges, among them: the 7×57, 8×64 Brenneke, the 30-06, an 8×60mm powerhouse, the starchy 9.3×62mm and a larger-yet 10.75×68mm. After World War II came the 243 Win., 257 Roberts, 257 Weatherby Mag., 6.5×68mm, 270 Win., 264 Win. Mag., 308 Win., 8×68mm, 338 Win. Mag. and even the 458 Win. Mag.

The grand rifle lives on today in modern versions still imported from European shores, but the original Mannlicher is gone, probably never to return. An authentic replica would pose problems with which modern shooters would not be willing to cope. The Mannlicher has a strong contemporary following, however, in the Mannlicher Collector's Association. The MCA serves all of those who are interested in the noble Mannlicher. The group is comprised not only of die-hard collectors who have many Mannlichers in their holdings, but to quote an officer of the group: "Some of our members are still looking for their first rifle." That's the kind of loyalty the Mannlicher generated by the adventurers of the past—and continues to enjoy to this hour.

MODEL 70 WINCHESTER
THE RIFLEMAN'S RIFLE

15

The term "Rifleman's Rifle" was for years synonymous with the Model 70 and is still bound to the bolt-action repeater classed throughout the world as one of the finest sporting arms of all time.

The story of the Model 70 really begins with Winchester's Model 54. Although this rifle gets more than its share of criticism, it was a fine bolt-action sporter and a proper forerunner of an even better rifle. The Model 54 ricocheted into the Roaring Twenties, Serial No. 1 arriving in 1925. About 3,000 of the model were sold in the first year, not nearly as many as one might expect of a sleek bolt-action rifle chambered for cartridges that are still prominent today. Its cartridges were superb. The Model 54 was offered in caliber 30-06—

The current Model 70 Winchester Standard Grade with swept-back bolt style.

the No. 1 cartridge in sales west of the Mississippi River to this day and perhaps the best "all-around" cartridge in the world—and the 270 Winchester Centerfire (270 WCF), the only true 7mm cartridge of any consequence. (Cartridges called 7mms, such as the 7×57 Mauser or the 7mm Remington Magnum, fire bullets of .284-inch diameter. That is not a true 7mm. It is 7.2mm. The 270's .277-inch bullet, on the other hand, is 7mm on the nose, or precisely 7.0358mm.) The cartridge was well-received at its inception, and eventually became one of the most popular big game rounds ever. As this is written, the four best-selling rounds in the West are (in order) the 30-06 Springfield, 270 Winchester, 7mm Remington Magnum and 243 Winchester.

The Model 54 was also chambered for the 30-30 cartridge, which didn't make much sense, and the public let Winchester know it. The 30-30 chambering was last in sales for the 54, with the other calibers running like this: 30-06, 270, 250 Savage, 22 Hornet, 8mm Mauser, 7.65mm Mauser and 9mm Mauser. Additional chamberings included the 7mm Mauser, the faster-than-anything 220 Swift and the excellent 257 Roberts. Being a handsome, workable bolt-action rifle using some of the best cartridges of the 20th century still didn't spark shooters to run headlong for the Model 54, however. That fact remains a mystery, but it is why the Model 70 went on the drawing board.

For starters, the Model 54 had a two-stage trigger with what was known as "military creep." Slack was first taken up and then the trigger could be fully operated. Lock time—the time elapsed between release of the trigger (breaking of the sear) and cartridge detonation—was not fast. This problem was corrected with an up-

The post-64 Winchester Model 70 African model is chambered for the powerful 458 Winchester cartridge.

dated model with 50% less firing pin travel. The new system was called the Speed Lock by Winchester. But the 54 still had prob-

gas porting of the 54 was less than perfect. The Model 54 Sniper's Rifle in 30-06 with receiver sight and 26-inch stainless steel barrel had a military look about it. The heavy barrel was 1 1/4 inches across at the breech and 7/8 inch across the muzzle. In the 1932 Stoeger catalogue, this model sold for $186.95, while the sporter, with 24-inch barrel, sold for $53.40; 20-inch carbine barrel went for $49.50. Calibers shown were 30-06, 270, 250 Savage, 7mm Mauser, 7.65 Mauser and 9mm Mauser.

Although the Model 54 remained for sale into 1943, with approximately 50,000 produced in total, it was in fact superseded by the Model 70 in September 1936. Many arms enthusiasts have long believed that the first Model 70 barrels were in fact Model 54 tubes put into service. This seems to be supported by looking at the Model 70 Winchester that bears Serial No. 1. Remarkably, that rifle has been recovered for posterity. More remarkably, the Model 70 Winchester bearing the first serial number was not kept by the company as a historical monument. It was shipped down the road as if it were no more important than any other serial number. Numbers 2, 3, 4 and so forth were also shipped away as "working guns" to be used by the public at large. Serial No. 1 was purchased by a Texas gentleman who simply wanted a good hunting rifle. In his advanced years, the man gave the rifle as a gift to his nephew, Mark Worthington. Worthington, a rancher, carried the Model 70 with its only-one-in-the-world serial number for years.

After 10 years of use, Worthington took his Model 70 to a pawn shop, "because I knew it was old and might have some collector value. I just wanted to hear what he [the pawn shop broker] would say about it." The pawn shop man in effect said, "You give me the rifle and I'll pay for

This Winchester Model 670, a "sub-model" of the Model 70, wears a Weaver scope sight.

lems. While the safety was functional and effective, it was more suited to iron sights than a scope. And at least in theory, the

it to the tune of a four figure cash settlement." Worthington wasn't interested in selling, so he took No. 1 away with him, filled, however, with curiosity. Why such a high offer on an old work rifle? Later, he took the rifle to a collector of Winchesters and another cash price was immediately offered, this time in the high five figures. Now Worthington's interest was piqued. He consulted the uncle who had given him the rifle. The gentleman had purchased the rifle in 1937 when he was on a Colorado elk hunt. He wanted more than the usual 30-30 for elk, so the new Model 70 in 30-06 caliber looked pretty good as it rested in a Colorado hardware store. He didn't get an elk with the rifle, but he did end up taking plenty of Texas game with it before giving No. 1 to his nephew.

The story is compelling because of claims that Model 70 Winchesters were being sold in 1936. Of course, No. 1 could have rested in the Colorado hardware store for a year or more before it was sold, so its purchase in 1937 does not prove that Model 70s weren't for sale before that time. The rifle's serial number on the ring of the action is a mere "1" with no other designation. So Mr. Worthington had never paid any attention to it. The marking that interested him far more was the caliber, which was posted as ".30GOV'T'06," an abbreviation for 30 caliber Government 1906, the round we call the 30-06 today. No. 1 was an ordinary Model 70, the Standard Rifle as it was called, or Standard Grade. When Worthington's uncle picked it up at the Durango hardware store, the rifle was outfitted with a Lyman receiver sight. But shortly thereafter it was treated to a 10X J.W. Fecker scope sight. The rifle shot remarkably well, so the Fecker scope stayed. Worthington received No. 1 in 1977 and didn't look into its history until 1987.

Many experts have looked and are still looking at the rifle as well as No. 2, which was located in Pennsylvania. The barrel of Mark Worthington's Model 70 No. 1 was probably built in 1935, and it's fairly sure it was originally intended for a Model 54 Winchester. It has the pre-war type safety, which was much improved later on.

One of the more interesting viewpoints on the Model 70 Winchester is in an article written by F.C. Ness, a former arms authority with *American Rifleman* magazine. In "The New Model 70 Winchester" that appeared in November 1936, Ness says, "The Model 54 Winchester has passed into history." Ness goes on to explain that a few more 54s were due to appear in caliber 22 Hornet only, but that "The New Year of 1937 will usher in an improved Winchester bolt-action rifle, the new Model 70, which will supplant the old Model 54." Ness said much about the advantages of the new 70: "Gone is the 'canoe-paddle' forestock, the high-angle

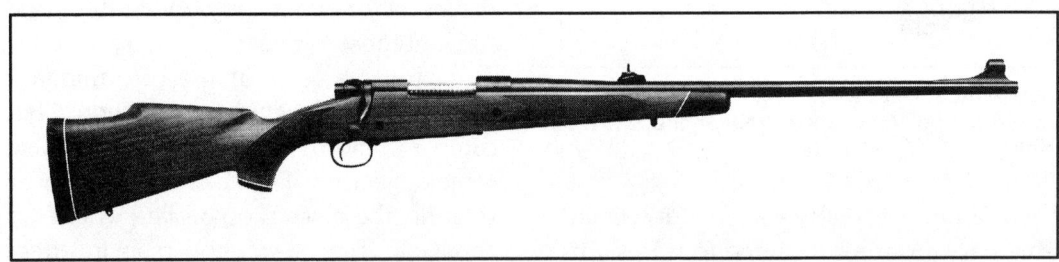

The Winchester Model 70 in the Magnum version, post-64 production with Monte Carlo stock.

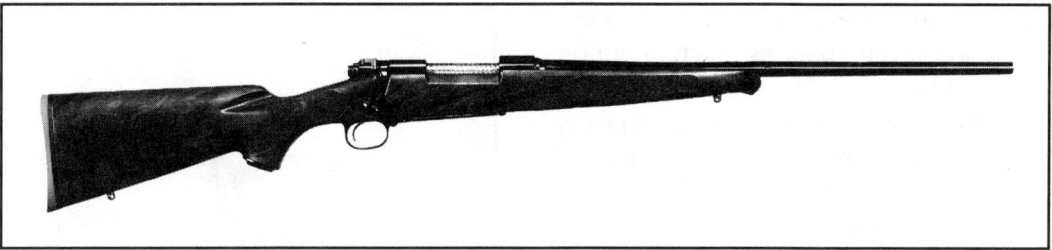

The modern Model 70 Featherweight comes in several powerful big game calibers. Note the schnabel forend and handsome cut-checkering on this beauty.

bolt handle with vertical safety, the sear bolt-stop, the much-criticized trigger, the solid floor plate and poor trigger guard."

Gone indeed. The Model 70's forestock was clean and smooth, hand-filling enough, but not so large that it promoted a choking grip and loss of fluidness in shooting. The bolt was swept back, not only much better looking, but angled correctly so that the hand automatically found the knob, which was situated in line with the trigger guard. The wing safety was improved on the Model 70, but would undergo further development to become as fine a three-position safety as known to the industry. Lock time was fast. And the new trigger was about as good as factory triggers get. On my own Model 70, the factory trigger was set by a gunsmith in 1959, one year after the rifle's purchase, and only touched again in 1990 by another smith who tuned the trigger for a crisp break at under two pounds. The trigger guard was milled, the floor plate hinged.

Ness explained that the 70 would be offered with a standard 24-inch barrel, an optional 20-inch barrel and a 26-inch barrel in 220 Swift only. Steel was of the latest and finest quality throughout. At the time, Winchester was concerned with a target Model 70 as well as a sporter because of the high interest in paper-punching. The company was proud of its National Match Target Model and Bull Gun. The Match Target Model 70 had a floated barrel, rather than full-length bedding. The Match rifle had a 24-inch barrel, the Bull Gun a 28-inch heavy barrel.

One of the best things that happened to sporting rifles occurred with the Model 70's attention to the bolt lift, which favored scope mounting. Although the telescopic rifle sight was still off in the distance as a fully accepted aiming device in the 1930s and 1940s (believe it or not), the scope would take over within the next decade or so and the Model 70 was ready to wear it properly.

The splash made by the Model 70 Winchester as it entered the shooting pool was not as great as one might expect, nor as great as it should have been. But the 70 was on its way to great fame with a reputation as the finest bolt-action sporting rifle of all time. That opinion would not be shared by everyone, but thousands of hunters expressed their admiration for the Rifleman's Rifle. So here we stand toward the end of 1936 with a new bolt-action rifle that was promised in calibers 250-3000 Savage, 220 Swift, 270 Winchester, 30-06 Springfield, as well as the fine 257 Roberts, the long-lived 7×57mm Mauser and the powerful 300 H&H Magnum.

THE 70 LIVED FOUR LIVES

The Model 70 is still in production, and has lived at least four interesting lives.

First was the pre-World War II version. These were paid about as much attention as would be given any factory rifle of the era. Checkering was clean-cut. Bluing was good. All appointments were well-attended to. Even the wood of the stock was of a better grade than later models possessed. These facts are not so much a reflection of the Winchester company as they are of the times. Gunmakers could afford to put more hands-on effort into their products because labor was cheap. So the first Model 70s are forever known as the pre-War models, running from 1937 to the beginning of World War II. The war years were a natural break for Model 70 production.

The second phase of Model 70 identification begins around the close of World War II and runs into the 1950s. These were fine rifles, but with probably a little less of the hand-touch and not quite so many special orders. The early 1950s into 1963 marks the third period of Model 70 production (as far as students of arms are concerned). Wood was beginning to be a problem, and the Model 70 was given the same treatment other rifles received— good sound wood, but without as much figure as might be found in previous years.

The year 1963 marked the end of the "original" Model 70 Winchester. Production cost vis-à-vis sale price was a big problem. One expert declared that if the old Model 70 were retained, it would eventually have to double in price. Who would buy it? Through intelligent engineering, Winchester found a way to continue the Model 70 intact, but without so much handwork. Furthermore, a minor negative feeling about the strength of the original Model 70's action existed, although unfounded. Researchers discovered what Winchester was more than happy to tell the public anyway, that a Model 70 action

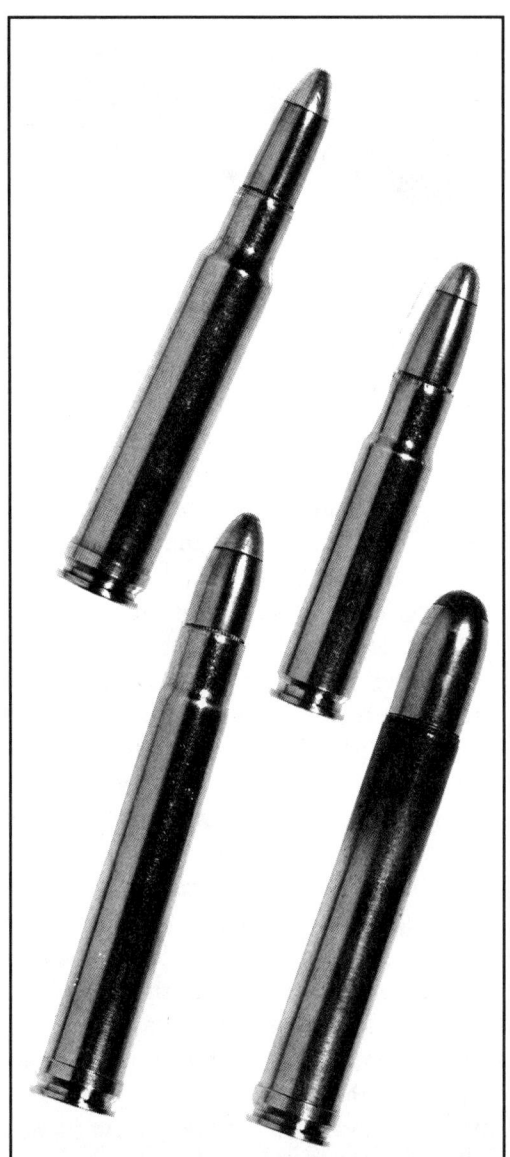

The Model 70 Winchester has been chambered for many great big game cartridges over the years, including the 338 Winchester Magnum (top left), 358 Winchester (top right), 375 H&H (bottom left) and 458 Winchester Magnum.

was good for around 70,000 PSI before it "set back" the bolt. This was a conservative figure, like saying a car will stand up to only 100 mile-per-hour driving before it breaks. Yet nobody can legally drive 100 miles per hour, so that margin of strength is more than adequate. The same for the old Model 70 Winchester. Cartridges were not then, and cannot now be, loaded into the 70,000 PSI range with safety. So the action was and still is entirely adequate in strength for all normal loads.

The post-1963 Model 70 received a new bolt capable of withstanding more than 100,000 PSI. The new bolt encompassed the entire head of the cartridge so that if the head of a round gave way, it would be enshrouded by the bolt, without any escape route for brass debris. It was true: the post-1963 Model 70 was stronger. Lost in the bargain was the claw extractor. Not to say that the smaller extractor was less useful, but the claw did have a lot of grip on the cartridge case for extraction purposes and a swelled case was usually pulled free. This small point did not hurt the new Model 70, but its overall appeal fell off as far as many riflemen were concerned. The fourth phase of the Model 70 Winchester was here.

The "new" Model 70 made such an impact that the rifle would forever be separated into "pre-64 Model 70" and "Model 70" production. Custom gunmakers today often pay several hundred dollars for a pre-64 Model 70 just to steal the action from the rifle so they can build a custom arm around it. For a while, the Winchester people tried various ways to convince American shooters that the new Model 70 was better—and in many ways it was. They tried free-floating barrels, but some of those models had barrel channels routed out considerably more than necessary. The 70 just didn't look the same.

Later, when the United States Repeating Arms Company (USRA) bought Winchester, they steadily improved the rifle. No hunter who buys a Model 70 Winchester today is making a mistake. The rifle is strong as a mountain and slick as the surface of a frozen lake. It's accurate to boot and entirely reliable, with the same general appointments, such as three-position wing safety, all previous models enjoyed. It's difficult to keep up with Model 70 changes, for there have been many, along with a multitude of chamberings for some of the best rounds ever developed.

Here is a recap of Model 70 chamberings, since the long life of the rifle is tied to many of these fine cartridges, while other rounds, some very good ones at that, went by the wayside. The pre-64 Model 70 was chambered for the 22 Hornet, 220 Swift, 243 Winchester, 250 Savage, 257 Roberts and 264 Winchester. The latter was a hummer of a cartridge that was destined for small sales in spite of its good ballistics. Built on a shortened 300 Magnum case, this 26-caliber round simply did not generate the punch developed by the 7mm Remington Magnum, designed on the same case. The latter ended up a world leader among rounds, the former a second-runner only. The pre-64 Model 70 was also chambered for the 270 Winchester, of course, as well as the 7×57 Mauser and a 7.65×53mm cartridge seldom encountered today. The 300 Savage was chambered in the rifle, as was the 308 Winchester, 30-06 Springfield, 300 H&H Magnum, 300 Winchester Magnum, 338 Winchester Magnum, 35 Remington, 358 Winchester, the fine 9×57mm Mauser, 375 H&H Magnum and the powerful 458 Winchester Magnum. You can readily see that the rifle was loaded for any game in the world because of the wide array of cartridge choices.

The post-63 Model 70 continues to carry a bevy of superior long-range cartridges in the lineup, including the 7mm

Remington Magnum, which as noted before has been selling in the third slot after the 30-06 and 270 "out west." The current Model 70 Winchester is also chambered for the 223 Remington, 22-250 Remington, 25-06 Remington, 280 Remington, 270 Weatherby Magnum, 300 Weatherby Magnum as well as many of its original rounds, such as the 264 Winchester, 375 H&H and 458 Winchester.

Many different variations exist, such as the Super Grade, in keeping with tradition, for there has been a Model 70 Super Grade for generations, and a Featherweight, also from the old lineup. New are the synthetic stock Model 70 (Winlite) and a Ranger series introduced in 1985 as a lower-priced 70 with all of the attributes of the regular rifle, except for some of the refinements; plus the Ranger has a hardwood stock. It shoots fine.

The Model 70 has had a long and interesting life. An indication that Winchester considered the 70 no more than an upgraded Model 54 is clear in the initial asking price of the rifle. The original Model 70 (Standard Grade) sold for $61.25, only a few dollars more than the Model 54, yet it carried many upgraded features over the 54. Also, to be fair about it, the last of the 54s were also improved models. The 70 didn't take the world by storm for, according to sales figures, the best-selling caliber—30-06—of the first genre Model 70 rifles (1936–1943) amounted to a figure of only 27,758 rifles. George Madis quotes some factory figures of sales for the prewar Model 70 by caliber:

- The 270 Winchester: 6,053 rifles
- The 22 Hornet: 3,390 rifles
- The 220 Swift: 2,931 rifles
- The 300 H&H Magnum: 2,812 rifles
- The 257 Roberts: 1,877 rifles
- The 375 H&H Magnum: 871 rifles
- The 7mm Mauser: 729 rifles
- The 250 Savage: 625 rifles
- The 300 Savage: 607 rifles
- The 35 Remington: 117 rifles
- The 7.65mm Mauser: 31 rifles
- The 9mm Mauser: 22 rifles

From 1945 to 1951, over 160,000 Model 70s were manufactured. But from 1952 to 1963 almost 360,000 more were produced. In all, well over a half million pre-64 Model 70 rifles were manufactured. That's a lot of rifles, but nothing close to the Model 94 lever-action Winchester. Today, there's an interesting phenomenon concerning the Model 70. Post-1963 models are quite valuable as "shooters," but not "collectors." Pre-64 models are sought after for collections as well as actions. The problem with the latter situation is the robbing of actions from otherwise fine Model 70 rifles. Now what happens to the rest of the rifle? It's not unknown for good barrels to be used as replacement barrels on pre-64 Model 70 rifles that are shot out. Now comes along a collector who finds a specific Model 70 pre-64 rifle in good condition, but it is wearing the wrong barrel. In truth, the collector value of such a Model 70 is reduced considerably, although the rifle's action remains a high-ticket item.

My first bolt-action rifle was a Model 70. I'd read Jack O'Connor's books and articles so many times that the words were all but worn from the page. He liked the 270 Winchester, so I liked it. In 1958, after a long summer of pearl diving—also known as washing dishes at a restaurant from 6 PM to 3 AM—I had enough money for the 70. The rifle's career included 14 Coues deer of record book status. But one day I noticed that groups were spreading ever wider. The gunsmith who examined the ri-

> ### THE MODEL 70 WINCHESTER AT A GLANCE
>
> **Period of Manufacture:** 1936 to present, usually divided into pre-1964 (often pre-WWII and post-WWII), 1964-type and 1972-type
>
> **Calibers:** Pre-64—22 Hornet, 220 Swift, 243 Win., 250 Savage, 257 Roberts, 264 Win., 270 Win., 300 Savage, 300 H&H Magnum, 300 Win. Mag., 308 Win., 30-06 Springfield, 338 Win. Mag., 35 Rem., 375 H&H Magnum, 7mm Mauser, 7.65mm Mauser, 9mm Mauser, 458 Win. Mag.; post-64—includes many of the original rounds plus 7mm Rem. Mag., 223 Rem., 22-250 Rem., 25-06 Rem., 280 Rem., 270 Weatherby Mag., 300 Weatherby Mag., and others
>
> **Action:** Strong bolt action with claw extractor; post-64 models had stronger action minus the claw extractor
>
> **Barrel:** Of steel, blued. Rifle, 24 inches; Bull Gun, 28-inch heavy barrel; optional lengths on various models. Post-64 models had swaged (free-floating) barrel.
>
> **Weight (approx.):** 6½ lbs. (Featherweight) to 13¼ lbs. (Bull Gun), depending on caliber, model and barrel length
>
> **Sights:** Various. Generally, open rear; hooded ramp front; African sights for African model, e.g.; scopes optional
>
> **Stock:** Straight or pistol-grip stock of American walnut or hardwood; special Varminter, ISU, Monte Carlo or Marksman stock; newer stock of fiberglass. Oil-finished or laminated. Many options (checkering, etc.), including schnabel forend
>
> **Variations:** Many, encompassing a long period of production, including types of cheekpieces, checkering, recoil pads, sling swivels, ebony forend tips and pistol-grip caps, etc.

fle shook his head. "'Looks like a factory smoke stack in there," he said. And it did. The bore was shot out. I put the rifle aside for a while, taking up a different model in caliber 7mm Rem. Mag.

Then one day it was time for a custom rifle. Frank Wells was the builder. I wanted to know what action to use for my new handmade rifle. Frank got a puzzled look on his face. "Your old Model 70, of course," he said. I protested that it might not be strong enough to contain the cartridge I had to have, the 7mm Remington Magnum. Frank looked puzzled again. That was a couple decades ago. The custom pre-64 Model 70 rifle has seen many hunting seasons since then, put a good deal of fine meat into the freezer and did nothing other than function perfectly.

One final aside: the rifle was always sufficiently accurate for big game hunting, but never a tack-driver. Until one day at the range I fired three shots at 200 yards and the bullets printed into an inch. I tried it again. Three shots later, again at 200 yards, not 100, the group was in the inch center-to-center realm. I chalked it up to luck. Next time out, however, the excellent groups repeated. I asked two members of the gun club to witness the next three-shot group, which they did. The cluster was .75 inch at 200 yards. They signed the target and it now stands at DGS, Inc. custom gun shop in Casper, Wyoming. The rifle still shoots that accurately.

The puzzle was easily answered. The fine Douglas air-gauge barrel was always capable of superb accuracy, but the full bedding of the barrel was not to its liking. Along the way, the forend of the rifle warped slightly downward, relieving pressure only at that point. For reasons no one can prove, that particular barrel bedding brought out its potential in accuracy. Other

Author Sam Fadala in action with his custom Model 70 Winchester. Crafted by Frank Wells, the arm was built on the action of a pre-64 Model 70 purchased in the 1950s.

rifles bedded exactly the same way have proved that the pressure relief toward the forend is not always the answer, but it was for this particular Rifleman's Rifle.

The Model 70 Winchester's future is assured. If no further 70s were made, the model would remain one of the finest and most famous of all sporting arms ever developed. It isn't that any single feature of the 70 is light years ahead of other rifles; it's the marriage that makes the difference. When the designers at Winchester got together in 1933 to plan a better Model 54, it was the beginning of something special.

WINCHESTER MODEL 71
A MODERNIZED LEVER-ACTION

16

The Model 1886 Winchester gave hunters what they wanted—a heavy-duty repeating rifle capable of taking a beating in any terrain. One day, however, Winchester awoke to the fact that the '86 was a greybeard. It remained fairly popular, with its steel-smooth dependability and fine 33 Winchester smokeless cartridge. But American business relies in part on "something new," so the boys at Winchester went to work modernizing the '86 and its cartridge. The result was the Model 71.

This new model was also a lever-action rifle. With a solid frame and visible hammer, it was strong, reliable and slick as a greased ball bearing. The 71 was an immediate success. It may have seen even more popularity, but the bolt-action rifle

The Winchester Model 71—a rifle built on the Model 1886 action in 348 Win.

was already showing itself to be the hunting firearm of the future. The 71 and its cartridge were specialized; the 348 Winchester was a round of modest range in a world being taken over by the 30-06 and the 270, as well as other "high-intensity" loads of flatter trajectory.

American Rifleman magazine announced the Model 71 in its February 1936 issue. F.C. Ness, one of the better known arms authors and a tester for the publication, said the 71 was built to supplant the

The 348 Winchester cartridge was descended from the 33 Winchester, just as the Model 71 was designed after the Model 1886 rifle. The 348 cartridge is shown broken down into case (left), powder and 200-grain Remington bullet.

Model 1886. He promised that the new rifle handled like a dream, and felt that the Model 71 was "a modern rifle for the old-timers." He meant that the rifle was modernized, with a powerful cartridge, but that it performed like the old guns, being a lever-action rifle so much like the '86. Woods and timber hunters who demanded high quality in a firearm found it in the 71. It was built in the Winchester tradition, which was no more or less than American insistence on excellence, for all the rifles of the era were well-made commensurate with their grade and cost.

The Model 71 appeared in 1936, not only by way of introduction, but in reality. Records show the first 71 in the Winchester warehouse by November 2nd. Now enters some of the usual controversy concerning firearms history: was there a turnaround in model numbers? Did the Model 71 truly precede the Model 70? Here is one version of the story: The company believes that its Model 70 Winchester bolt-action rifle predates the Model 71. The new bolt-action Model 70 was also a replacement arm. As the 71 was designed to replace the 1886, the 70 was designed to replace the handsome Model 54 Winchester bolt-action rifle. But chronology reverses itself. Four Model 71 rifles were shipped in late 1935, so that by 1936 the 71 no longer wobbled on the legs of a newborn colt, but was galloping into gunshops all over America. During 1936, 7,812 Model 71 rifles were shipped from the factory.

But it was January 1936 before the first Model 70 Winchester left home. Looking through the rear window of a time machine, the ever-famous Model 70 could well have been the Model 71 and vice versa. Of course, being gun history, there are disparaging reports to sift through. A Winchester fan emphatically declares in a letter that he bought a Model 70 Winchester before January 1936 and that there is an error in the records. He further states that he kept the bill of sale because the 70 was so new. I suppose it is no more important to know which model truly came first than it is to ponder whether the chicken preceded the egg. It is interesting to note that factory records are not entirely flawless, let alone complete. By 1936, however, the Model 1886 Winchester was half a century old. The beloved rifle and its rounds had made history. Ben Lilly, mentioned in Chapter 10, took it upon himself to pursue cattle-killing renegades of the day, both mountain lions and grizzly bears, with his 33 Winchester.

So the Model 71 came on the heels of a romantic as well as practical firearm. But the 71 arrived too late to be included in the real romance of the old-time hunting rifles. Timber hunters loved the 71, of course. It was made for them. The somewhat short 13¼-inch length of pull (distance from center of trigger to center of buttstock) allowed the 71 a quick jump to the shoulder without snagging on heavy, cold-weather hunting clothes. The sights coupled with the open rear sight on the Model 22K.

As for the barrel, it was round and 24 inches long, providing superb balance to the 71. The rifle carried four rounds in its tubular magazine, with a round in the chamber. In later years, the 71 would be called one of the smoothest operating lever-action rifles of all time. So when hunters said that five fast shots could be fired rapidly, they were right.

Handling was not necessarily improved by the somewhat large forearm of the two-piece 71 stock, but there was a reason for this larger-than-usual forend: absorption of recoil by the left hand for a

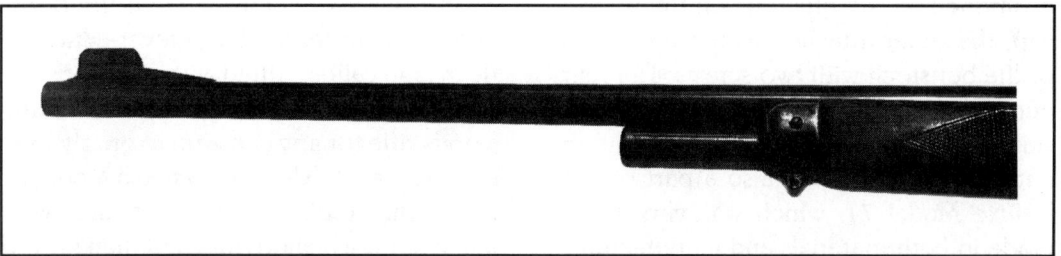

Rather than a full magazine, the Model 71 had a tubular half-magazine, in which only blunt-nosed bullets were allowed.

were meant for fast-shooting, too, helpful in timber and brush. A peep sight was mounted in a rather ingenious fashion on the breech bolt. This sight became known as the Winchester 98A breech bolt peep. Why that intelligent setup was later altered defies imagination. This peep readily aligned itself with the eye and was small, out of the way and neat. A dovetail slot was put on the barrel, but this was filled with a blank, which was later replaced with a rather ordinary open rear sight on the standard grade Model 71. However, a number of Model 71s were fitted with the Lyman 56 receiver aperture or peep model later on. A 31W front sight option was right-handed shooter, or the reverse for a left-handed shooter. Of course, the lever-action 71 was equally at home for either right-handed or left-handed marksmen. A stout forearm tends to encourage the shooter to grip the rifle too strongly. This slows down an otherwise fast swing, which does nothing for hitting a moving target. But the 71 with its 348 Winchester cartridge was no popgun, so the larger stock made sense. Right away, we see the Model 71 as different from the earlier Model 1886, because the 71 was never offered in a great variety of styles or chamberings. As noted in Chapter 10, Winchester 1886s came in all sizes and weights, chambered for a variety of blackpowder cartridges, plus the 33 Winchester smokeless round. The 71 enjoyed few alterations, only one chambering and was seldom special-ordered. It was made steadily in Standard and Deluxe grades, except for 1941 when it was not made at all because of the war. For a brief time in 1937, a 20-inch barrel was installed on the 71, but that reverted to the 24-inch length for the life of the rifle, as did its eight-pound weight.

Originally, an upgraded version of the Model 71 did not carry any special designation. It was simply there. However, a Deluxe model was offered with a checkered pistol grip and forearm, as well as a pistol grip cap. Integral sling swivel eyes were positioned on the rifle, one on the forend cap, the other attached to the underside of the buttstock with two screws. The rear butt sling eye was a milled piece, not a stamped part. A factory mounted sling on detachable swivels was also a part of the Deluxe Model 71, which was very high-grade in both materials and manufacture.

The Model 71 was always solid frame, no takedowns. There was, however, a major change in the tang, which collectors instantly notice. The long $3^7/_8$-inch upper tang of the early 71 was shortened by an inch in later models. The comb of the stock was brought more forward at this time, reducing "felt recoil" on the face.

Winchester had been proud of the Model 1886 and its 33 Winchester cartridge. That pride continued in the Model 71 and its 348 cartridge. The Model 71 was a better '86. Interior and exterior design was improved, resulting in a smoother action, superior trigger and beefy forend stock. The higher comb of the 71 was comfortable. The pistol grip was hand-filling. The action of the Model 71 remained very much like the '92 in that it had two vertical locking bolts positioned at the latter fourth section of the sliding bolt. Although the double locking bolt concept was a good idea, the two bolts did not make the action capable of withstanding the kinds of pressure associated with the best bolt-action arms of the same era, nor was such strength necessary considering the nominal factory pressures of the 348 cartridge.

A FINE, FAST-HANDLING WOODS RIFLE

Testimonials for the Model 71 were easy to find. Even arms authors who did not usually choose lever-action "big bores" liked the rifle. Jack O'Connor, who liked medium calibers, spoke favorably of the 71 in his 1964 edition of *The Rifle Book*. The "Winchester Model 71 lever-action rifle in .348 caliber, fitted with receiver sight and gun sling. This is a fine, fast-handling woods rifle for any game up to grizzly bear and moose." O'Connor owned a Model 71 for a while, took a few head of game with it, including a bighorn ram, but then moved on to bolt-action rifles with flatter-shooting cartridges.

Two other famous shooter/writers of the day also liked the Model 71: Elmer Keith and Colonel Townsend Whelen. Whelen was a bolt-action fan and as one would expect, he did not stay with the Model 71, although he tried it and liked it for what it was. He felt the rifle and round capable for all North American game up to 200 yards and even 225 yards. Whelen warned in his 1940 text, *The Hunting Rifle*, that the chamber of the 71 should be kept extra clean and shiny and especially oil-free. Dirty chambers did nothing for extraction, and oily chambers thwarted case cling. In other words, a slick chamber promoted bore thrust, whereby the cartridge case instead of hanging onto the walls of

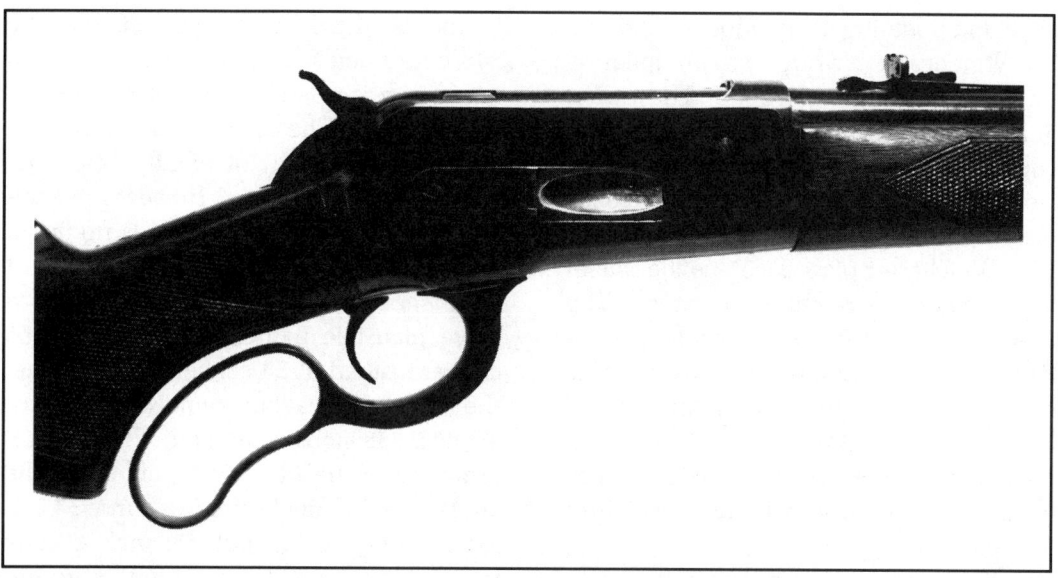

A close-up view of the loading gate on the Model 71, a copy of the gate that adorns the Model 1886.

the chamber tended to come back hard against the face of the bolt. Part of the problem was the slope-shouldered case, which had a tendency to thrust rearward in the chamber.

Elmer Keith liked the Model 71 and its 348 cartridge better than most because, as anyone who has read about Keith or who was friend to the man knows, Elmer favored fat calibers and big bullets over the "babies." Keith praised rifle and round in his 1936 book, *Big Game Rifles and Cartridges*. He said, "It is the finest balanced, sighted and stocked lever action rifle that has come to my notice."

In addition to writing in *American Rifleman*, F.C. Ness noted in his book, *Practical Dope on the Big Bores*, that the Model 71 appeared on the 50th birthday of the Model 1886 Winchester and that the rifle was a definite improvement, especially in the trigger, which was capable of breaking at 3.5 pounds. Ness called the 71 a "moose gun." He especially praised the fine 210-grain bullet loaded in Peters factory 348 Winchester ammo.

Praise came from all quarters. Al Barr was one of the best-known shooter/writers of early *American Rifleman* fame. He had good results with the rifle and its ammo. Grassroots hunters also admired the 71. I met a Canadian hunter in the Yukon one day, cradling a Model 71 Winchester comfortably across his forearm. I asked him what he thought of the rifle. He answered in a thick Scottish/Canadian accent as he patted the stock of the rifle. "Aboot ah mile from 'ere, up in thu moontains, ya kin see it from 'ere, me 'n' this rifle met up wi' ah b'ar, aboot as close as yer face is ta moine now. An ah put a slug inta tha' bear quick-er'n ya kin wink an' 'e goes steeraight down!" I asked him if maybe he'd thought of trading the Model 71 for something a little more modern. He looked at me as though I should have known the answer to that stupid question.

Although love of the 71 was certainly for the rifle itself, the cartridge was a fine one, too. As the Model 71 was a continuance and updating of the Model 1886, the 348 Winchester cartridge was an updating of the 33 Winchester round. They were quite close ballistically. In fact, a knowledgeable handloader can come pretty close to producing 348 Winchester ballistics from the old 33 Winchester cartridge. Why Winchester picked a 33-caliber bullet in the first place remains a mystery. Why they continued a similar size bullet (34 caliber) in the 348 compounds the enigma. Not to say that there is anything at all wrong with 33- or 34-caliber projectiles. On the contrary, they are excellent, as proven by the modern 338 Winchester, which fires 33-caliber bullets.

But hunters have not stampeded to 33-caliber firearms and certainly not to 34s. Caliber 35 has been more prominent. Why didn't Winchester build a 358 instead of a 348? It would have been interesting to sit in on those conversations that pertained to choice of caliber. My guess is that the 348 continued where the 33 left off, and that's why it was chosen, not because of its size per se. The cartridge was supposed to be named the 34 WCF, 34-caliber Winchester Center Fire. However, 34-caliber bullets are about as rare as finding a hundred dollar bill stuck to the bottom of your shoe. So Winchester went with a more plausible name: 348, indicating 35 caliber instead of 34 caliber. All the same, the 348 is a 34-caliber round with the projectile .3458 inch in diameter. What's more, bore size of the 71 is .340 inch across the lands. The 33 Winchester was a true 33 caliber, shooting a bullet of .338 inch, exactly the diameter of bullets used in the present 338 Winchester Magnum cartridge. So the 348 was an oddball—no mistake about it.

It was also a dandy big game round. Since the Model 71 was chambered only for the 348, and since the 348 helped to make this rifle famous, it's only fair to assess the ballistics of the cartridge. It is, of course, a slope-shouldered round with a great deal of body taper. It's rimmed, not rimless, and because of that, case style looks far more like an enlarged 30-30 than a 30-06 or other modern rimless round. In an attempt to check on the potential of the round with modern powder, I loaded a 200-grain bullet and a 250-grain bullet with H-4350, IMR-4350 and IMR-4831, three propellants recommended by powder companies. The best velocity obtained with a 200-grain bullet was 2661 feet per second (fps) at the muzzle. That's a muzzle energy of 3145 foot-pounds. The 250-grain bullet left the muzzle at 2283 fps for a muzzle energy of 2894 foot-pounds. These velocities were taken 12 feet from the muzzle and would be slightly higher if worked back to actual muzzle velocity. Winchester provided three factory loads for the 348.

The two most popular bullets for the 348 Winchester cartridge were the 250-grain (center) and 200-grain (right) compared with a 180-grain 30-caliber bullet (left).

Cartridge	Bullet (grains)	Muzzle Velocity (feet per second)	Energy (foot-pounds)
33 WCF	200	2200	2150
35 WCF	250	2195	2670
348 Win.	200	2535	2855
348 Win.	150	2920	2840

The ballistics shown above were compiled by Al Barr for *American Rifleman* in 1949. The firearms and loads were tested by the H.P. White Laboratory.

However, it was not the only company to offer ammunition for the Model 71 Winchester rifle. Peters had excellent 348 loads as did Remington.

Three bullets were popularly loaded in the 348: 150-grain, 200-grain and 250-grain. The 150-grain bullet was offered in an attempt to make the 348 what it was never intended to be, a flatter-shooting round for far-off shots. At about 2900 fps, the 150-grain churned up a muzzle energy of over 2800 foot-pounds, but the bullet had low sectional density and lost its speed relatively fast. Nonetheless, it was dynamite on deer-sized game. The 200-grain bullet was a better all-around choice.

The 250-grain bullet was the best of the three for close-range timber shooting no matter what the game animal, including grizzly bears and moose. Loads with this bullet died for a while, then were revived. Rumor held that the load with the 200-grain bullet, at least from Winchester, was not entirely correct and that higher-than-desired pressures resulted. Perhaps. When the 250-grain load returned, it was just fine, especially in the Silvertip design, which was quite popular.

It's easy to stand on the threshold of the 21st century and comment about a cartridge designed in the early 20th century. However, conjecture soon creeps in. Solid comparisons with other cartridges of the moment, however, clearly prove why the 348 was considered excellent. In the accompanying chart, the 348 is compared with the popular 33 WCF and 35 WCF, two cartridges in the same class. As you can see, the 348 Winchester with its 200-grain bullet is sufficiently ahead of the 33 Winchester and 35 Winchester to deserve merit. As noted, however, the 33 Winchester could be handloaded to duplicate 348 power closely.

Some shooters felt the Model 71 Winchester carried the kick of a mule, and that its recoil was in fact excessive, even for the fine ballistics it delivered. A fellow writer pointed out that he shot seven elk with the 348 with seven shots. What could be more perfect? But he traded the rifle away for a 7mm Remington Magnum, which also dropped elk quickly but didn't "kick" as hard as the old Model 71. Dale Storey, who owned a couple Model 71s in his earlier days of shooting, agreed with the high-kick assessment. The custom gunmaker said jokingly, "They didn't run out of Model 71 Winchesters. They ran out of men to shoot them." On the other hand, many shooters did not find the recoil of the 71/348 objectionable, pointing out that the rifle was for hunting only, not bench-shooting, and that at the moment of truth, with a big bull elk in front of you, recoil didn't count for anything. Accuracy, of course, always has meant a great deal in a big game rifle, and the Model 71 was sufficiently accurate for big game hunting—and then some.

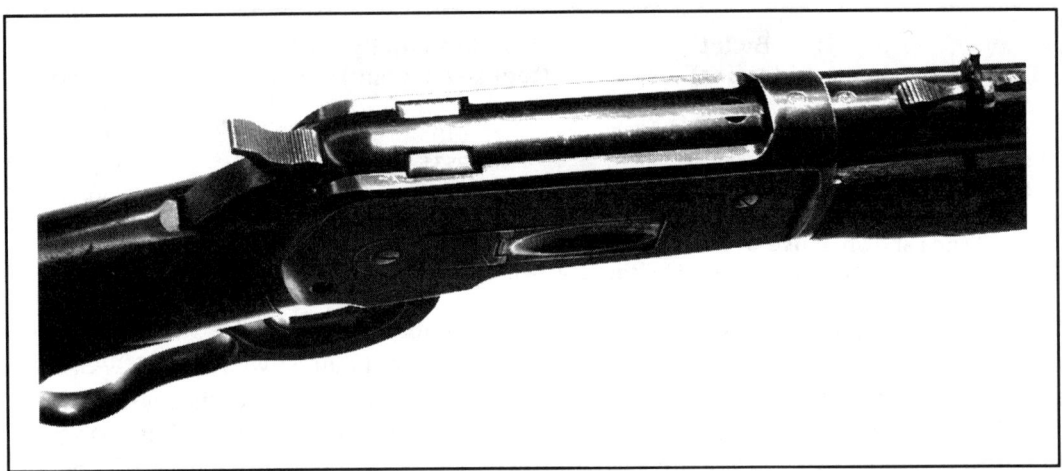

This view zeroes in on the double locking bolts of the Model 71 Winchester action. Note also the rear open sight with semi-buckhorn styling.

It is no surprise that results varied among shooters, because marksmen do not share the same shooting ability. Some shooters were better able to handle the powerful rifle from the bench; therefore, they got good accuracy results. Others were probably buffaloed by the big rifle and they shot poorly with it, giving the Model 71 no chance to prove itself. Elmer Keith did not obtain great accuracy from his 71, but he managed to keep his bullets inside of an eight-inch ring at 200 yards. Since 200 yards is closing in on the limit of intention for the 71 and its 348 round, that's not bad. Al Barr contended that as the barrel grew hotter, accuracy suffered. Barr fired 10-shot groups at 200 yards. But he allowed the barrel to cool between shots. His witnessed groups were only 3.75 inches center to center at 200 yards. Barr found that when he fired more rapidly, whereby the barrel was allowed to heat up, groups opened to seven and eight inches. My own Model 71, using handloads with Barnes 250-grain bullets, printed four-inch groups at 200 yards, off the bench, but with only three-shot strings, not five, and certainly not 10.

Do keep in mind that these groups were made with a peep sight, not a scope. The Model 71 was a top-ejector. Spent cases pop straight up, as with the old-style Model 94; therefore, scopes were never entirely at home on the 71. Trajectory was truly not a problem, however. In a test, the 250-grain bullet was made to strike three inches high at 100 yards, a normal sight-in for a modern big game cartridge. So sighted, bullets clustered on target at 200 yards. That's plenty flat-shooting for the woods.

So what put the skids under the Model 71 Winchester? The 71 had—'still has—a fine reputation. But it was on the gunrack in 1936 and moribund by 1958. Number 47,254 was the last of the 71s, according to files. Many factors were the cause of its demise. First, while the lever-action remains as workable as ever, the big game rifle of the hour is a bolt-action. The 71's action was and still is good, but it's not a bolt model, nor will it chamber the fast-shooting cartridges associated with bolt-actions.

Second, the 71 would never wear a scope properly, and this is the age of the scope sight. Even for woods hunting, shooters have found that it's tough to beat a scope. Third, inflation of price affected sales. In 1939, a Standard grade Model 71 cost $49.95, while the Deluxe ran $57.75. By 1957, the price was up to $110 for the plain model and $135 for the fancier Model 71. Winchester's own Model 70 competed with the 71. A hunter could buy a Model 70 chambered for the 270 or 30-06 for close to the same dollar asked for a 71.

As handloading became a hobby with shooters, marksmen learned they could load their own ammo for less money and have custom-grade fodder to boot. The 71 was not a reloader's dream. Bolt-actions gave less case stretch and handled reloads better than lever-action models.

Hunters always want to shoot farther. Although Jack O'Connor got a sheep with his Model 71, the "average" hunter knew he was much better off with a flat-shooting rifle for the long shots. The Model 71 with its blunt-nosed bullets was not the ticket. And sharp-pointed bullets were not proper in the tubular magazine, even if the 348 could shoot them at high speed.

The newer Model 88 Winchester, introduced in 1955, was also a lever-action rifle, but it could use pointed bullets. Chambered for modern cartridges such as the 243 Win., 284 Win. and 358 Win., the 88 had better long-range ballistics and could be made more cheaply. But if it were so grand a rifle, it would have survived, but it did not.

Some shooters still argue that the Model 71 kicked too hard for what it delivered, while others argue that this is poppycock. No matter. I don't think a reputation for hard recoil hurt the Model 71's longevity, although it is difficult to prove

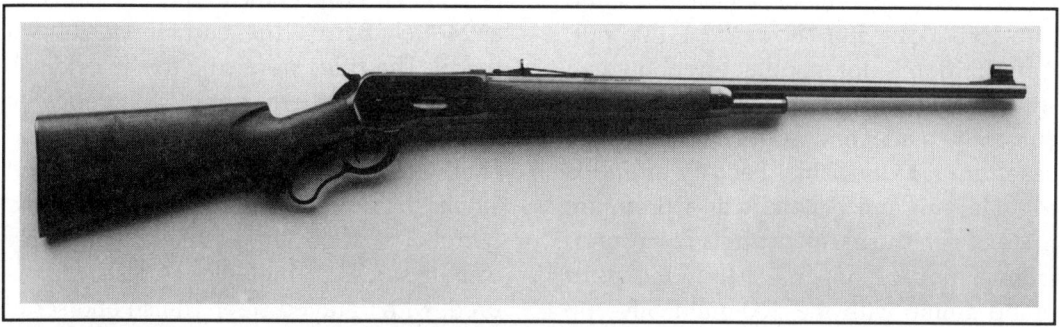

In 1987 Browning introduced a replica Model 71 in rifle and carbine versions. The Grade I rifle (above) has a 24-inch round barrel, while the High Grade carbine (below) sports a 20-inch barrel, checkered pistol grip and forend and engraved receiver.

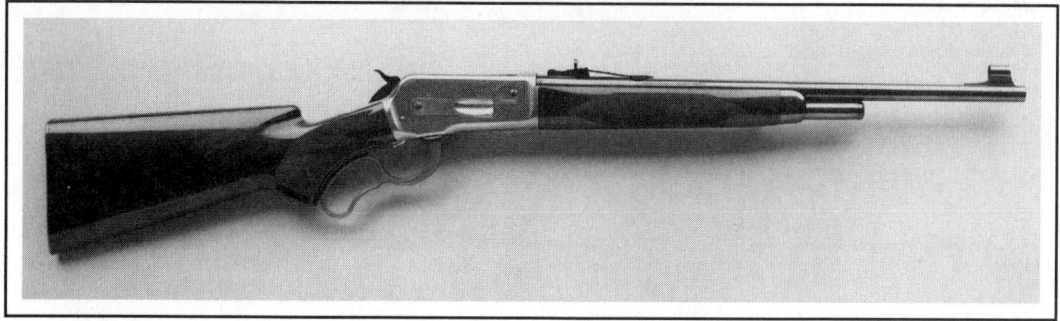

> ## The Model 71 Winchester at a Glance
>
> **Period of Manufacture:** 1935 to 1958
> **Caliber:** 348 Winchester
> **Magazine Capacity:** 4 plus 1 in the chamber; half-magazine
> **Action:** Solid-frame lever-action repeater built on the Model 1886 action
> **Barrel:** Of steel, blued; 24 inches, round; 20-inch barrel made only in 1937
> **Weight (approx.):** 8 pounds
> **Sights:** Usually open rear, semi-buckhorn style; hooded ramp front. Some with Winchester 98A breech bolt peep, Lyman 56 receiver aperture, 31W front sight on Model 22K
> **Stock:** Pistol-grip stock of American walnut; "stout" forend. Fancy Grade had checkered pistol grip and forend, high-gloss finish, sling swivels.
> **Variations:** Few, except for sight selection. Made only in two grades, Standard and Deluxe (Fancy)

one way or the other. The bottom line is that the 71 is gone and has been for a long time in spite of the fact that it remains one of America's premier hunting rifles. Gone out of manufacture, but not out of mind.

The Model 71 Winchester was made to last and last—for lifetimes, not one lifetime. Of the 71s made, it's a good bet that the vast majority remain at least intact and safe to shoot. Gun shows bear this out. Ammunition is not manufactured, but can still be found. Bullets in caliber 348 are currently made and sold, and cartridge cases are also available. Factory ammo is for sale, too, but generally at a premium price at gun shows. In testing a few rounds from a box of Super-X 348 Winchester brand ammo with the 200-grain Silvertip bullet, the average velocity was 2528 fps at 12 feet from the muzzle. So the rifle is still available in good used condition, and ammo can be obtained as well.

Furthermore, the Model 71 was rebuilt as a replica. It was too famous a sporting rifle NOT to resurface. Browning Arms came through again in 1987. The company introduced the Browning Model 71 replica of the original Winchester 71 in two models: standard rifle and carbine. The rifle had a 24-inch barrel, the carbine, a 20-inch barrel. The rifles were true to the original. Furthermore, there were two grades of Browning 71s to choose from, Grade I and High Grade. The Grade I featured walnut stocks, blued receiver, magazine tube and barrel. The High Grade model had fancy walnut stocks, a high-gloss finish, checkered, with "grayed steel" finish and scroll engraving. Gone, but not gone—that's the 71.

REMINGTON AUTOLOADERS
FIREPOWER WITH FINGERTIP CONTROL

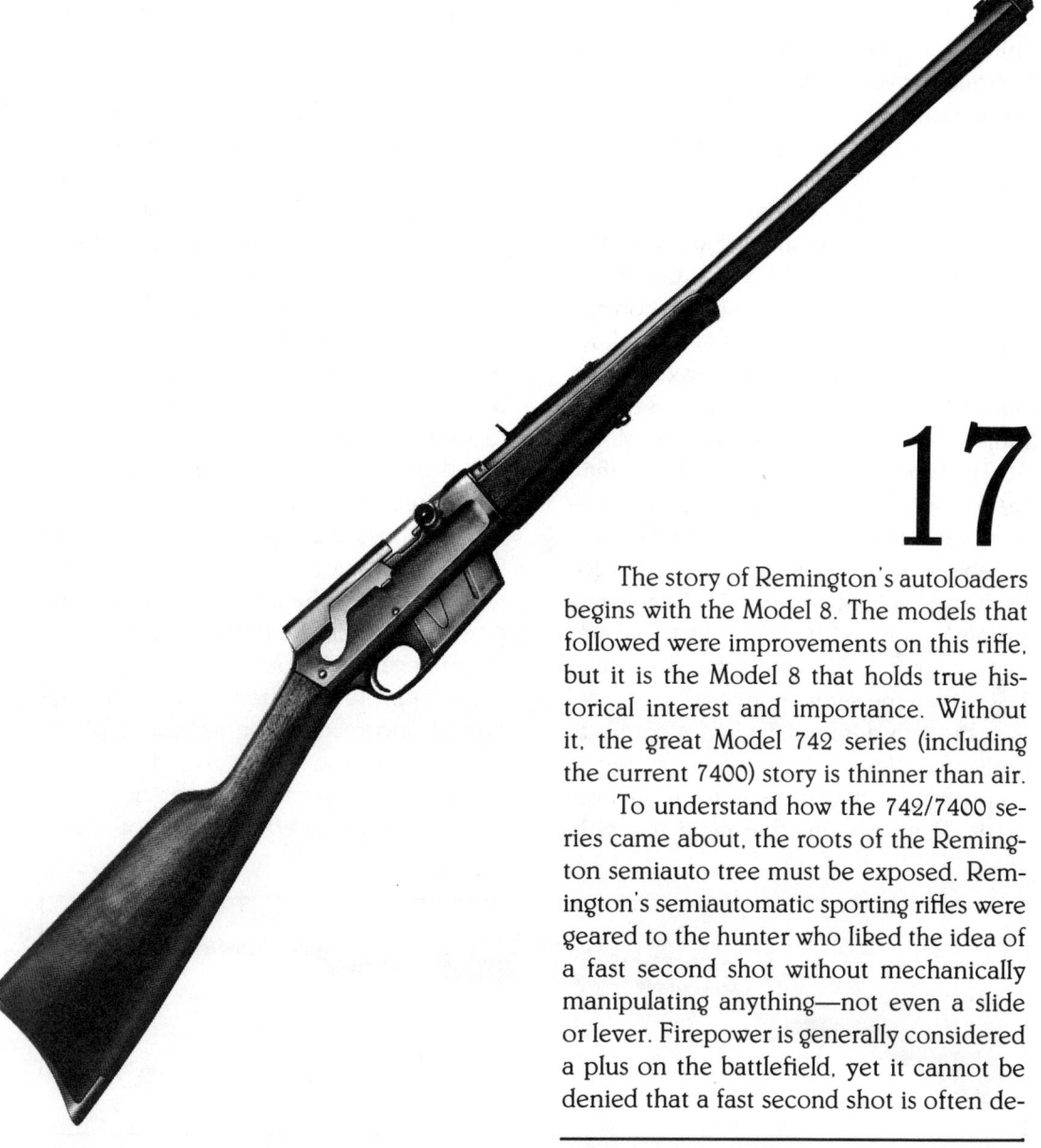

17

The story of Remington's autoloaders begins with the Model 8. The models that followed were improvements on this rifle, but it is the Model 8 that holds true historical interest and importance. Without it, the great Model 742 series (including the current 7400) story is thinner than air.

To understand how the 742/7400 series came about, the roots of the Remington semiauto tree must be exposed. Remington's semiautomatic sporting rifles were geared to the hunter who liked the idea of a fast second shot without mechanically manipulating anything—not even a slide or lever. Firepower is generally considered a plus on the battlefield, yet it cannot be denied that a fast second shot is often de-

The Remington Model 8—a unique, American-made autoloader.

sirable on the hunting field as well. Furthermore, a medium caliber, such as the 30-06, grows in effectiveness when multiple bullets can be delivered rapidly. Consider a bull moose standing broadside at 75 yards. One shot well-placed from a 30-06 will surely do the job. But the wise hunter may add another and even another if the animal remains standing after bullet number one arrives on target. That's when a fast-action rifle comes in handy and a certain brand of sportsman has always bought that theory. Remington figured that out a long time ago. The company has sold many thousands of semiautomatic big game rifles and continues to serve those outdoorsmen who want firepower with fingertip control.

Is a semiautomatic faster than a slide-action sporter? Two Winchester 22-rimfire rifles were tested side by side: a semiautomatic Model 69 and a slide-action Model 61. The latter spit out ten bullets faster than the former. That's because the Model 61—or at least this particular Model 61—was capable of firing with the trigger pulled back and held back as the slide handle was furiously pumped back and forth. In this demonstration, the slide action was quite faster than the semiautomatic.

But let's agree that when it comes to big game rifles, nothing is quite so fast in emptying the magazine as the semiautomatic. Remembering that rapid fire without confidence is useless, Remington had to offer the sportsman a semiautomatic big game rifle that could be relied on. Jamming is one of the nastiest words in a hunter's vocabulary. If a semiautomatic has a propensity for jamming, it is worthless to the hunter.

John Moses Browning was the owner of the design that was the heart of Remington's Model 8 semiautomatic big game rifle. Browning became associated with Remington early in the 20th century. His semiauto design, U.S. Patent No. 659786 granted October 16, 1900, was the impetus behind the Model 8. That rifle appeared in 1906, making it the earliest successful big game rifle of semiauto nature. The Model 8 used a recoil-operated action. A portion of cartridge energy that would normally be translated into recoil was put to work to force the action into motion. It is believed that this recoil-operated action reduced recoil. Because of its design, the Model 8 was capable of handling some fairly decent cartridges. That is an important point. Had the 8 not functioned with powerful rounds, the future 742/7400 rifles might never have come about. The bolt in the action turned (revolved). Two lugs locked into recesses on each side of the barrel where the barrel extends into the receiver. This specific manner of closing the breech provided the kind of action

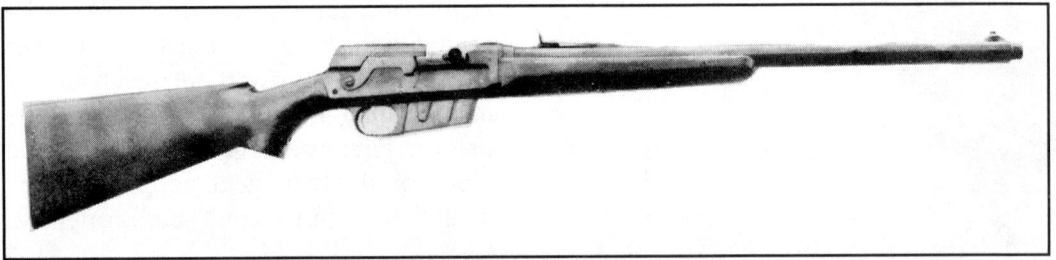

The Model 81 Woodmaster was an improved Model 8 with semi-beavertail forend, half-pistol grip walnut stock and a change to the shotgun-style buttplate.

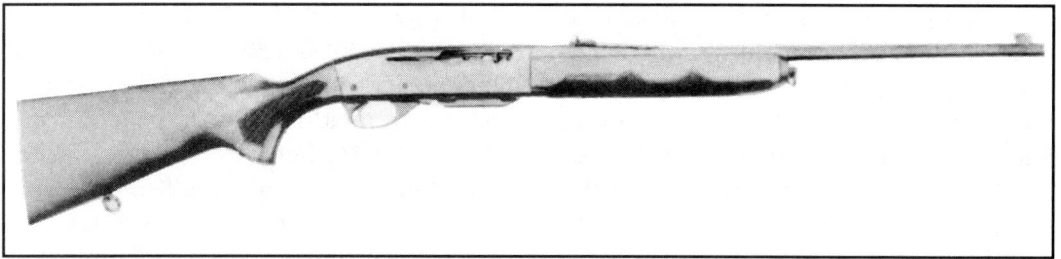

The 740 Woodmaster was another of Remington's refinements of autoloaders. This rifle, with detachable 4-shot magazine, appealed to sportsmen who were fond of the 30-06 cartridge.

strength necessary for high-intensity cartridges.

Remington called its Model 8 "autoloading," a perfect description. It did load automatically, but was not an automatic. "Automatic" assumes continuous fire with one pull of the trigger, while "autoloading" means that the trigger must be activated and released again for each fired shot. The Model 8 would not fire again until the trigger was released. Although noted in some literature as a detachable box magazine, Remington did not offer such a magazine on the sporting version of the Model 8. However, the later Model 81 was available in a special police rifle with a 15-shot detachable magazine, 35 Remington caliber. Originally, a clip was part of the magazine, but the clip was later eliminated. After shooting the contents of the five-shot magazine, the bolt remained opened. You'd reload the magazine and release the bolt forward to run the first round home into the chamber. Then simply pull the trigger and shoot five times.

The Model 8 enjoyed several good features and a few poor ones. It had, as already noted, sufficient strength to contain good cartridges for big game hunting. And the breech of the Model 8 was enclosed so that if anything went wrong—and there is no indication that anything did—the shooter would have plenty of metal between the problem and his face.

That kind of engineering lent confidence to a marksman. He knew he could trust the rifle because it was designed to be safe. Another safety feature was a trigger design that prevented accidental discharge. In theory, at least, the Model 8 could be dropped and the rifle would not go off because of a "balanced trigger system." Furthermore, the safety on the Model 8 was excellent. It allowed a shooter to tell by feel if the rifle was in battery or on safety. The safety was large and easy to work and there were no complaints of safety failure.

Trigger pull received both high and low scores. The trigger was advertised as extra light, supposedly breaking at $2\frac{1}{2}$ pounds pressure. That would be quite light for most off-the-shelf hunting rifles prior to adjustment by a gunsmith. However, while some Model 8 triggers may have broken at $2\frac{1}{2}$ pounds, trigger pull weight varied. A shooter could not be certain of what he would find from one Model 8 to another in regard to trigger letoff.

Another decided black mark for the Model 8 was its looks. It was not a real beauty, and carried a military appearance about it. The square-back receiver coupled with the box magazine seemed to be the cause. Furthermore, the Model 8's barrel recoiled rearward within a sleeve when the rifle was fired. The sleeve gave the rifle the appearance of having an extremely heavy barrel, which it was not.

A projection from the bolt allowed the action to be worked manually, which was necessary in checking for a clear or loaded chamber, as well as introducing a round into the chamber. One more note on loading procedure to clarify the fact that the Model 8 did not have a detachable magazine. Loading the Model 8 was actually accomplished by bringing the bolt rearward with a pull-back on the projection described above. This exposed the magazine from the top. Pre-loaded clips could be used, and were offered for a while, then dropped. The clip could be employed in "stripper" fashion by pushing downward with the thumb on the top cartridge and thereby forcing all five cartridges from the clip into the magazine. Rounds could also be loaded one at a time directly into the magazine by pushing them downward. When the magazine was full, the projection was tugged back just a little more to release the bolt. The bolt slammed forward, forcing a cartridge into the chamber. The rifle could also be fired one shot at a time.

Interestingly, the Model 8 was a takedown from the start. The piece broke in the middle, more or less, and could be stacked in a short carrying case of about two feet. The manner in which you took down the Model 8 also allowed for easy cleaning. Furthermore, as long as the assembly screw was kept tight, the Model 8 would not "shoot loose," a trait not every takedown could boast.

The cartridges for the Model 8 closely resembled the Winchester line in power, but the one big difference was that they were rimless. Rimless rounds worked better than rimmed in the semiauto or autoloading action. Initially, Remington provided rounds in calibers 25 Remington, 30 and 32 Remington. Although the cases were different, these rounds were similar in ballistics to the 25-35 Winchester, 30 Winchester (30-30) and 32 Winchester Special. It's safe to say that these three Remington rounds were designed with the Model 8 in mind. The 35 Remington was not. When the Model 8 appeared in 1906, the 25, 30 and 32 arrived with it. The 25 was the least popular of the trio. The 35 Remington, which was added to Model 8 chamberings in 1908, proved the most popular of the four and is still factory loaded to this day and chambered in new firearms. It was much like a 35 Winchester in power, although the latter had a little more steam. A Model 700 Remington bolt-action rifle can be ordered in 35 Remington, for example.

So the floating-barrel Model 8 recoil-operated autoloader worked well and was chambered for good cartridges. Also, accuracy was good enough for big game hunting—not superb—but adequate. The barrels of the Model 8 were listed as 6-groove for the 25 Remington and 7-groove for the other calibers. Rate of twist was 1:10 for the 25 Remington, not as fast as Winchester's twist for its 25-35. The 30 Remington used a 1:12 twist, the 32 a 1:14 rate, and the 35 Remington a 1:16 rate of twist. Groups of about $3\frac{1}{2}$ inches were noted for the 25 Remington. But the other rounds produced groups about an inch larger at 100 yards. However, these groups were for 10-shot strings, not five-shot or three-shot strings, which makes a difference.

Stoeger's No. 18 catalogue of 1932 says of the Remington Model 8: "The only high power autoloading rifle made in this country that positively locks the cartridge in the chamber until the bullet has left the muzzle and thus prevents loss of killing power. Powerful enough for any big game found on this Continent. Shoots as fast as

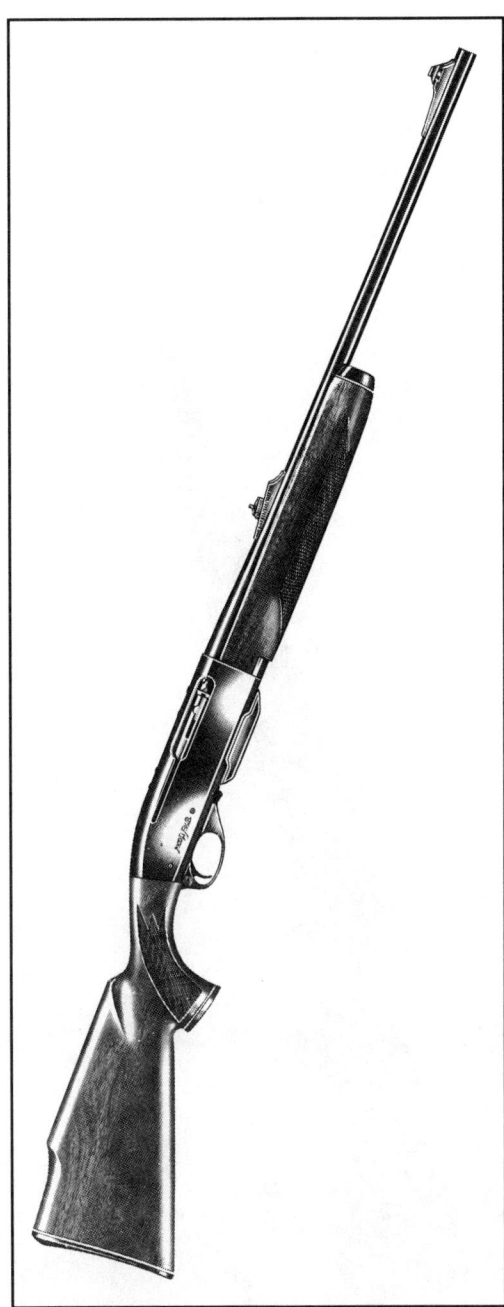

The Remington Model Four, introduced in 1981, was another sleek variation on the Remington semiautomatic big game rifle.

the trigger can be pulled. Double locking lugs. Positive operation."

The Model 8 was offered at the time in five different grades: Standard, Special, Peerless, Expert and Premier. This is telling because it indicates that Remington, as well as some shooters, considered the Model 8 more than just a workhorse. The vital statistics for all show a five-shot magazine—not detachable—a takedown feature bringing the overall length to only 23 inches, a weight of 7 3/4 pounds, hammerless of course (no exposed hammer), 22-inch barrel, American walnut straight-grip stock with optional semi-pistol grip, rifle-style steel buttplate with step-adjustable buckhorn rear sight and white metal bead front sight. Also noted in 1932 is "Trigger pull exceptionally light." Calibers were the three basic rounds plus the 35 Remington. In 1932 the Standard Grade sold for $64, Special Grade $92.40, Peerless Grade $165 and Expert Grade $242. Premier Grade went for $319. By comparison, in 1922 a Winchester Model 94 standard grade sold for $36.30 and a Winchester Model 54 bolt-action rifle, $53.40.

In 1936, the Model 8 gave way to the 81, basically an improved extension of the 8. The Model 81 was chambered for the 300 Savage as well as the 30, 32 and 35 Remingtons; the 25 Remington was eliminated. Now the rifle had a name: Woodmaster. And it had a semi-beavertail forearm and a shotgun-style steel buttplate to replace the former rifle-style buttplate. The Woodmaster had a "Half-Pistol Grip" stock, according to the Stoeger/Remington reference, which in fact was a small pistol grip. All other features were essentially the same, with the advertised weight more realistically stated as about eight pounds. The same grades remained. A Model 81A was Standard grade at $70.58; the 81B Special Grade cost $79.86; the 81D Peerless grade $165.98; the 81E Expert Grade $232.57 and the 81F, Premier grade sold for $299.17.

REMINGTON AUTOLOADERS 171

(No 81C is noted.)

The Model 8 was a good rifle, but the Model 81 was better because it was refined. And Remington knew that a much more sleek semiautomatic big game rifle was possible. Anyone who had anything to do with guns knew it. All a shooter had to do was look at the Krieghoff High Powered Autoloading Rifle. This was a relatively sleek semiauto chambered for the 30-06 cartridge. It was gas-operated rather than recoil-operated. The barrel didn't move. The rifle had a tube beneath the barrel that looked like a long magazine, but was instead a housing for the "action rod." The rod was activated by gas bled off toward the muzzle. The Krieghoff was advertised as "racy" with "pleasing contour," and in the 1930s it cost $500!

It would be a long time before Remington had such a rifle. But at last it arrived. The Model 81 was discontinued in 1950 and it was not until 1955 that a new Remington autoloader was for sale far and wide in America. In one sense, the Model 8 and Model 81 were parents of the new Remington, which was called the Model 740 Woodmaster. In another way, they resemble each other about as much as a cat and a canary.

The best way to describe the Model 740 is to admit that it was sired by Remington's slide-action Model 760. The gas-operated Woodmaster was all but jam-proof with clean fresh ammunition. And of course, there was no slim barrel sliding inside of a "stove pipe," as some shooters called the barrel jacket of the 8 and 81. The breech of the 740 was solid—no place for gas to escape should a case rupture, an unlikely event in the first place. A four-segment interrupted thread locking system was put to work on the 740 Woodmaster. The bolt head with multiple lugs locked well

Remington's Model 742 BDL deluxe version is typical of the handsome lines of the semi-auto Remington rifle. This one wears the Monte Carlo stock with basket weave checkering.

172 LEGENDARY SPORTING RIFLES

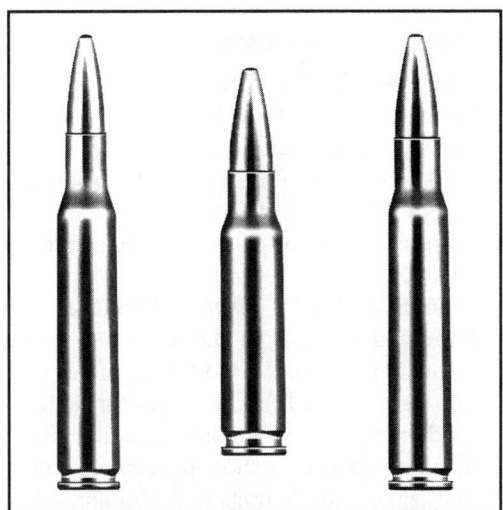

The Remington semiauto big game rifle is chambered for the 270, 308 and 30-06 rounds. They are shown here (left to right) in their Extended Range loadings with a 140-grain bullet in the 270 and 165-grain bullets in the 308 and 30-06.

in place, so just about any cartridge could be chambered in the new Remington. A gas port in the barrel provided the power that worked the action of the 740. Of course, gas pushed the bullet upbore in a normal fashion, but once the bullet was past the gas port, which was about 8.5 inches from the breech, some gas was put to work pushing an action bar sleeve. Dual action bars were driven rearward. Mechanical timing made it all come out right. The action functioned perfectly in the 740. The bolt returned to lock up the next round in the chamber and rapid fire was secured.

The hammerless 740 handled better than the 8 or 81 and was much more trim than either. It required less "hardware" to make it work, so the 740 was better balanced. This time there was a box magazine that held four rounds of ammunition. Remington was smart in bringing out the 30-06 first. The 30-06 was considered more than adequate for all North American big game, and now hunters could have that great cartridge in a semiauto big game rifle that handled like a shotgun. The rifle could not get out of adjustment in any way. The 740 was superseded by the 742 in 1960. Outwardly, the two rifles appeared the same. They almost were. However, the 742's barrel could be removed from the receiver more easily than the barrel of the 740—a plus for gunsmiths. The 740 was just about foolproof, but the 742 enjoyed a few minor alterations that made it even more reliable. These rifles weighed about 7½ pounds in 30-06 caliber. Advertisements for the 742 reminded hunters that they could have a 220-grain bullet from the 30-06 with five quick shots. More calibers were added, among them the 280 Remington (a 7mm bullet on a case slightly longer than the 30-06), the 243 Winchester, the 308 Winchester and the 6mm Remington. The 742 was offered in various grades

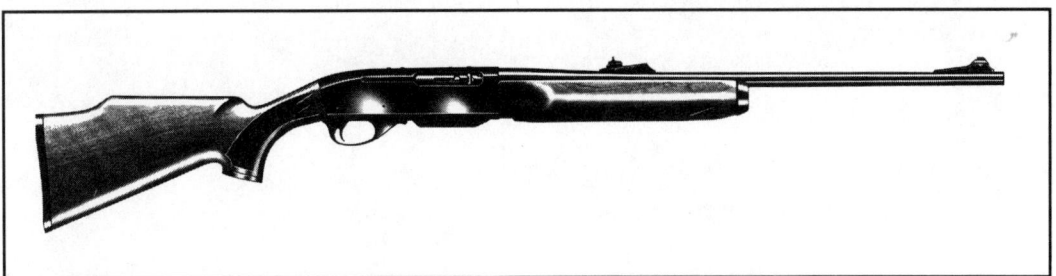

The Model 7400 is an updated version of the Models Four and 742. A reliable rifle in many fine calibers, it is a real looker, especially in this high-gloss stock version.

> ### THE AUTOLOADING REMINGTON MODEL 8 AT A GLANCE
>
> **Period of Manufacture:** 1906 to 1936
> **Calibers:** 25, 30, 32 and 35 Remington rimless
> **Magazine Capacity:** 5-shot, not detachable; clip in early version
> **Action:** Hammerless, takedown recoil-operated semiautomatic; positive lockup with double locking lugs
> **Barrel:** Of steel, blued, 22 inches, floating; 6-groove (25 Rem.), 7-groove (other calibers)
> **Weight (approx.):** 7 3/4 pounds
> **Triggers:** Balanced trigger system in which gun would not go off if dropped
> **Safety:** Large and easy to work
> **Sights:** Open step-adjustable buckhorn rear; white metal bead front
> **Stock:** Straight-grip stock of American walnut; rifle-style steel buttplate
> **Variations:** Five different grades: Standard, Special, Peerless, Expert and Premier. Optional semi-pistol grip and other extras.
>
> **MODEL 81 WOODMASTER**
> Refined version of the Model 8 with shotgun-style steel buttplate, half-pistol grip, semi-beavertail forearm and 8-pound weight. Made 1936 to 1950
> **Calibers:** 30, 32 and 35 Remington rimless plus 300 Savage
> **MODELS 740/742 WOODMASTER**
> Improved versions of the Model 81 with great similarity to the Model 760 Slide Action (see chapter 19). New features included solid breech, 4-segment interrupted thread locking system, 4-shot detachable box magazine, chamberings in 30-06 and 308 Win. (Model 740) plus 6mm Rem., 243 Win., 280 Rem. (742). Model 740 made 1955 to 1960; Model 742 made 1960 to 1980
> **MODEL 7400 REMINGTON**
> Improved Model 742 with same caliber offerings (plus 270 Winchester), 22-inch barrel, in various grades with a variety of extras. Made 1981 to date

with different refinement.

Today, the Remington semiautomatic big game rifle with number 7400 is the best Remington autoloader of all. With four-shot magazine, the 7400 Remington Autoloader is chambered for the 243 Winchester, 270 Winchester, 280 Remington, 308 Winchester and 30-06. Barrel length is 22 inches (18 1/2 for the carbine), weight about 7 1/2 pounds and overall length 42 inches. It comes with open sights, but is all set up for a scope. Available in various grades with a variety of extras, its prices range from three to four digits. Introduced in 1981, the Model 7400, formerly the Model 740, formerly almost the Model 81, which is formerly the Model 8, is here to stay for a long time.

REMINGTON'S MODEL 700
A HIGH-POWER BOLT-ACTION

18

The Remington Company, one of the oldest arms makers in the world, began, the story goes, with Eliphalet Remington Jr. asking his father for a rifle. When Dad said no, young Remington decided to do something about it. He built his own rifle. Eliphalet gathered scrap iron, which he welded to form a gun barrel. He went from his home in Ilion to Utica, 15 miles on foot, to have the barrel rifled. His father, who was a smith, was impressed. When people saw the Remington rifle, they wanted one. Remington senior supported his son and before long the business outgrew the small shop.

As with many companies of early America, a government contract helped the Remington concern. Actually, the

The Remington Model 700 ADL with laminated stock—a pleasure to own and to use.

contract was awarded to Amos & Company of Springfield, Massachusetts, for Jenks carbines, probably to be used if unfriendly action with Mexico materialized. When Amos & Company declined, Remington bought the contract and went to work. The government was happy with the results. When the Civil War broke out, Remington was remembered. Another government contract kept the company working to capacity. Eliphalet Remington died on August 12, 1861, but E. Remington & Sons continued as a corporation. Even with their manufacturing of commercial typewriters (they were the first in America), the bottom fell out of the business. A few bad financial moves, and Remington was knocked against the ropes. Hartley & Graham of New York purchased the company. Hartley made an especially astute decision by creating the Union Metallic Cartridge Company to meet a demand for good commercial ammunition. We have all seen ammo with UMC on the headstamp. This mark denoted the ammunition company that was linked with Remington.

UMC, founded in 1887, expanded through the purchase of two small ammunition companies. Hartley guided the concern until his death in 1902 when his grandson, Marcellus Hartley Dodge, cemented a merger that brought UMC and Remington truly under one corporate roof. World War I saw the plant increase from 4,500 to 20,000 workers. In 1933, E.I. DuPont de Nemours & Company, who had a strong financial base, bought a controlling interest in Remington. DuPont took over the Chamberlin Cartridge and Target Company, the Charles Parker Company, maker of the famous Parker Shotgun, and the Peters Cartridge Company.

World War I and its aftermath no doubt marked the beginnings of a bolt-action big game rifle for the famous Remington firm. During WWI, Remington produced over a million and a half bolt-action military rifles for both the British and U.S. governments. These Remington arms were based on the Enfield action—a strong, long-bolt design. When the war ended in 1918, Remington found itself the owner of many Model 1914 actions as well as an abundance of barrels. Nothing was done with them immediately. However, it was soon evident that the American soldier, who was also a hunter, had taken a fond look at the bolt-action rifle. Assuming that a bolt-action sporting rifle might make it in the 1920s, Remington reworked Enfield actions to produce a smoother-looking product. It got rid of the big "ears" at the rear of the action that safeguarded the back sight—practical in wartime, unnecessary on a sporting rifle.

THE MODEL 30 LAUNCHES A REMINGTON LEGACY

In 1921, the Remington Model 30 was introduced. It is with this rifle that the saga of the famous Remington Model 700 begins. The Model 30 was one of the first high-power bolt-action big game rifles to really "make it" in America. The original 28-inch barrels were lopped off to 22 inches. Remington chambered these for various cartridges, including the 25 Remington, 30 Remington, 32 Remington and 35 Remington rounds. Good cartridges, the first three were ballistically much like the 25-35 Winchester, 30-30 and 32 Winchester Special, with the 35 Remington offering a little more close-range punch than its mates. Also offered was the 7mm Mauser later on, as well as the 30-06. The Model 30 chambered for the 30-06 was, in truth, about all a careful hunter needed for everything, except dangerous bear. (Those who challenge this may remember the two Yukon miners, both carrying 30-06 rifles, who were attacked by a grizzly bear. They struck the bear in the chest with a total of seven shots. Still, the bear killed both men. Nonetheless, under most normal circumstances, the Remington Model 30 in caliber 30-06 was up to the task.)

Early 30-06 Model 30s were made with barrels intended for the 303 British cartridge. The barrels had groove diameters of .311 inch instead of .308. Remington recognized that although this was not a big problem, better accuracy would result from

The Remington Model 30 continued to undergo improvements, especially in stock design. Also further work was done on the Enfield action, which originally cocked on the closing of the bolt. The 30 wasn't a bad-looking rifle, but it always bore a military look. The S-shaped bolt handle was retained, for example, as well as the original-style safety. Various models were introduced, including a carbine intended for law enforcement people. A Weaver scope could be purchased as a factory add-on. The scope, of course, improved the rifle's potential to put bullets

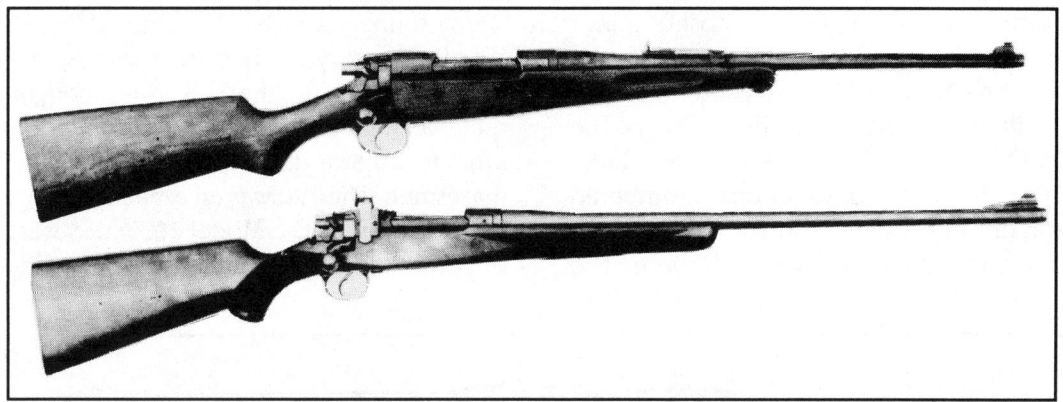

The Models 30 and 30s bolt-action sporters, forerunners of the legendary Model 700, were manufactured between 1921 and 1940. Built on the Enfield action, they retained a military appearance that modern Remington bolt-actions have eliminated.

a more reasonable bullet fit in the bore. The Model 30 was given a barrel with a groove diameter of .3085 inch. The five-shot magazine gave a hunter plenty of ammo. Sights on the early Model 30 were American standard all the way, a buckhorn open back sight coupled with a gold bead up front that was affixed to a barrel band. A Lyman 48R peep (receiver) sight could be readily attached to the Model 30 because the receiver was pre-drilled and tapped. The rifle weighed in at around 7½ pounds, depending on caliber, and carried nicely.

in the bull's-eye, but the double-stage military trigger did nothing to promote field accuracy. More calibers were offered for a while, including the 8mm Mauser, possibly due to ready access to huge quantities of it. The 7.65 Mauser and 257 Roberts were also offered, while the Remington rounds were dropped. Not that they were so bad, but why have a strong, and actually quite large, bolt-action chambered for rather petite cartridges that would fit into a much smaller action? It didn't make sense.

The 1932 Stoeger catalogue listed a

couple of rather typical Remington Model 30 rifles: the 30A Standard Grade and 30S Special Grade. The first was chambered at the time for the four Remington rounds already mentioned plus the 7mm Mauser and 30-06. The barrel was 22 inches long, the stock semi-pistol grip and fitted for a sling. Checkering was standard. This Model 30 cocked on the opening of the bolt handle. The single-stage trigger is noted as "short, snappy, light"; gone is the military two-stage trigger. A 20-inch barrel carbine cost $48.70 at the time, while the standard 30A ran $52.75. The more refined 30S with pistol-grip stock, hooded front sight, Lyman 48 receiver sight, and a host of minor refinements, such as pistol-grip cap, cost $66. The 30A and 30S were good rifles, free of their original military rifle problems. The 1940 Stoeger catalogue shows the Model 30 in 30A and 30R variations, chambered for the 30-06 only, and the 30SL, chambered for either 30-06 or 257 Roberts. The 30A with 20- or 22-inch barrels cost $60.49; the 30R, not checkered, ran $55.44; the 30SL with Lyman sight cost $73.61. For comparison, the Winchester Model 70 standard grade ran $61.80 at this time.

The Remington Model 30 was a good bolt-action rifle, but it was inevitable that Remington update its bolt-action offering with a new rifle. The Model 700 story continues with at least three more major bolt-action rifles. The Model 720, another excellent firearm, was briefly in the lineup. An astute NRA official described the 720 as "A far cry from its parent, the M1917 Enfield." First offered in 1941, the 720 went off line when the U.S. entered World War II. Not very many were made. As the NRA pointed out, the U.S. Navy bought quite a number of 720s as presentation arms to be awarded to Marine and Navy marksmen. The 720 was an exceedingly refined version of the Model 30, which was, of course, an off-shoot of the military En-

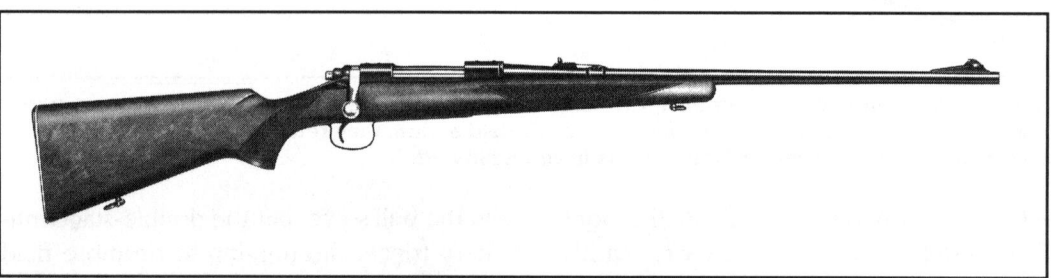

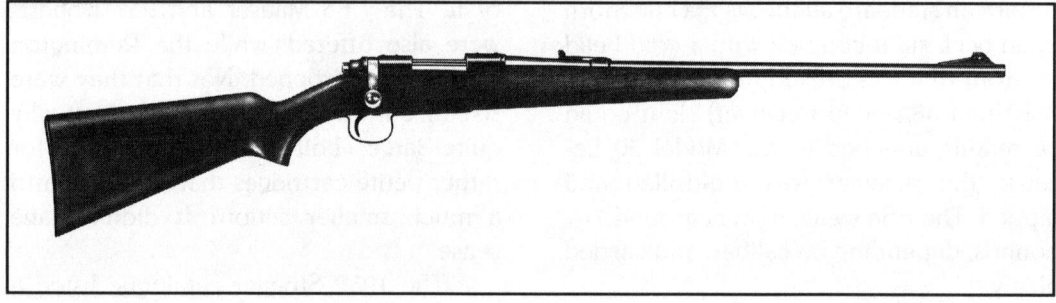

The Model 721 B Remington (top) and its shorter-actioned brother, the Model 722 A (bottom), were produced from 1948 to 1961. Excellent rifles with reasonable price tags, they were both improvements of the Models 30 and 720.

field. It had a swept-back bolt handle that cocked on opening, a single-stage trigger (with optional two-stage trigger), a nice walnut stock of clean design, hinged floorplate and checkering. Calibers 257 Roberts, 270 Winchester and 30-06 were chambered in barrels of 20-, 22- or 24-inch lengths. Quick-release sling swivels were standard. In 1941, the Model 720 cost $68.20. The addition of the Lyman peep sight raised the cost to $80.55. Not cheap—but a bargain all the same for a fine sporting rifle.

From the beginning, the Enfield-inspired Remington bolt-action sporting rifles had many good features to recommend them. One was the manner in which the bolt operated to allow low (natural) scope sight mounting. This would pay off in two sub-models of high merit, the Remington Models 721 and 722. They were essentially the same, except for action length. Since there was no sense having a 30-06 bolt length for a shorter round, Remington wisely decided to match bolt length to cartridge.

To put things in perspective, recall that DuPont took over in 1933. Remington was well behind Winchester and Savage in sales at that time. DuPont intended to shut down Remington rifles and continue with other products instead. George Read, a DuPont engineer and head of an investigating committee, saved Remington rifles from going down the drain. Read was impressed with the rifles the company turned out, in spite of lagging sales. He liked their quality and design. World War I had established Remington as a capable company in regard to production. But gearing up for a short-lived boom necessitates winding down when the boom fizzles. So long range, Remington did not benefit appreciably from WWI arms production.

MODELS 721 AND 722—YOU GOT YOUR MONEY'S WORTH

Revving up for World War II production forced Remington to modernize its operation. A new bolt-action rifle was needed as part of Remington's renewed plunge into sporting rifle sales. Models 721 and 722 served that function. They were profit-oriented from the start, but they also gave a shooter more than his money's worth. Merle "Mike" Walker, an engineer, was instrumental in the development of the 721/722. Later on he promoted one of the finest small cartridges of all time, the 222 Remington. Walker knew what he was doing. His ideas were brilliant, though down to earth and workable.

Originally an organic chemist, Walker had the ability to learn firearms from a design platform. In a pre-World War II setting, Walker had helped Remington with many projects, including the development of an anti-tank cartridge that provided over 4,000 fps muzzle velocity. Before the end of the war, Walker and the men who worked with him had a pretty good idea for a Remington bolt-action rifle that would not have to sell for a bundle, but would work like a better priced firearm. It would be especially accurate and built on an extremely strong action design. The 721/722 and the 700 that followed all share similar characteristics—the strong action already noted, but also fast lock time and a good trigger. The model offered the possibilities of a target rifle without the high price of one. The hunter had what was truly a low-cost big game bolt-action rifle chambered for high-power cartridges in the 721 action length. The 722 provided a host of marvelous mid-sized rounds, including the 222 Remington, which would make the gun one of the most accurate out-of-the-box rifles of all time.

Hunters can order the popular Model 700 bolt-action in a host of calibers with a magnificent assortment of options. Above rifles are just a sampling.

It's important to stress the fact that the 721 and 722 were essentially the same rifle, with the latter being shorter in the bolt by more than 3/4 inch. While the Model 720 was not a financial success, because it took about 250 operations to produce the bolt and receiver, the Model 721 or 722 was much simpler to build, requiring only

180 LEGENDARY SPORTING RIFLES

about 60 passes. Fine instruments, they did not yield to manufacturing expediency in any way.

The only element of the 721/722 that posed a minor concern was the tiny extractor. The claw extractor of the pre-64 Model 70 Winchester, just like those of the Mauser 98 and Springfield, was replaced with a tiny unit located in the head of the bolt. Clean and proper ammo posed no problem. Dirty ammo or cases reloaded too many times might cause less than slick extraction. The problem was not much of a threat on the 721/722, nor on the current Model 700. The trigger on the 721/722 was again improved, not at all the reworked military trigger of the Model 30.

Button rifling, a Mike Walker development, created an excellent 721/722 bore. Another positive aspect of the rifle was overall weight. Hunters wanted a light rifle. The 721/722 were about right, in the 7- to 7¼-pound bracket—not so feathery light that they were hard to control in the field, but easy to carry. The 721/722 could be advertised as super-strong because they were tested and retested to see how much abuse they could withstand. They were tested for bolt strength and gas leakage. The strength of the action was ascertained in part by loading bullets into the bore in front of a cartridge so that the projectile in the cartridge had to drive not only itself through the bore, but also the bullets in front of it. Talk about a bore obstruction! The 721/722 action held up to unmerciful pressures that destroyed other actions. They were also tested exhaustively for fatigue. Testing proved that all was not perfect with the prototypes, so when a problem was found, it was worked on until remedied.

The 721 and 722 were chambered "smart" from the start. Walker and company did not allow outdated rounds to end up in them. Of course the 30-06 was offered and the 270 Winchester, which was enjoying brisk sales. That only made sense. For the hunter who wanted a bit more than a 30-06, the 721 was chambered in the fine 300 H&H Magnum round. At the time, this cartridge did not develop its full potential from factory loads, but handloaders could make the 300 H&H cook.

The shorter-action 722 began life with three cartridges: the 220 Swift, 257 Roberts and 300 Savage. The 220 Swift was the fastest-shooting round available. The 257 Roberts was a great one for deer, especially when a handloader got hold of the round and put the correct bullet and powder charge together. A handloader who owned a 721/722 could have a field day, and we are, of course, speaking only of careful prudent loads from loading manuals, not wild-eyed home recipes. A recent chronographing of a 300 Savage handload shooting a 165-grain Speer bullet showed a consistent muzzle velocity just shy of 2800 fps. More surprising was a 190-grain bullet at 2500 fps, all with good case life and obviously safe pressures. So the 721 and 722 were wisely chambered for some of the best rounds of the day, especially for handloaders.

But the show was yet to begin. In 1950, the little 722 rocked the world with a new round: the 222 Remington. Imagine a scaled-down 30-06 round and you're picturing a 222. A 50-grain bullet took off at 3200 fps. In bigger and better America one might think the 222 would be headed for trouble because of the much faster 220 Swift. Not the case. The Swift was great, but almost too much in many situations. The 222 was highly accurate and mild. Yet, it was capable of 300-yard varmint shooting. Many other rounds were and still are

This custom Remington 700 has had its safety changed over to a wing-type three-position safety. Note the special engraving.

being chambered in the 721/722, although the rifles have once more undergone change and the 721/722 no longer enjoy manufacture.

THE MODEL 700 SURPASSES THEM ALL

The great Model 700 has taken over. It may seem to have taken a while to reach the real topic of this chapter, but the story of the 700 cannot be told without including its predecessors. Furthermore, the Model 700 is essentially a refined Model 721/722—truly refined. Every feature is in fact improved, from stock design and finish to overall looks and performance. Its current cartridge lineup, as of 1991, includes the following rounds in both short-bolt and regular-bolt sub-models:

- 17 Remington
- 222 Remington
- 223 Remington
- 22-250 Remington
- 243 Winchester
- 6mm Remington
- 25-06 Remington
- 270 Winchester
- 7mm BR (Bench Rest)
- 7mm-08 Remington
- 7mm Mauser
- 280 Remington
- 7mm Remington Magnum
- 308 Winchester
- 30-06 Springfield
- 300 Winchester Magnum

182 LEGENDARY SPORTING RIFLES

- 300 Weatherby Magnum
- 8mm Remington Magnum
- 338 Winchester Magnum
- 35 Remington
- 35 Whelen
- 350 Remington Magnum
- 375 H&H Magnum
- 416 Remington Magnum
- 458 Winchester Magnum

It is impossible to list them all because there are special order 700s from the Remington Custom Shop as well as fine short-run Classic rifles in many different calibers.

The Model 700 comes with an extraordinary selection of options. The Model 700 ADL, for example, has no floorplate for those who don't mind running unfired rounds through the rifle to expel them. It's a fine version of the 700 at a savings. The BDL grade has a floorplate and other minor embellishments over the ADL. The ADL and BDL are the backbone of the lineup. A test of the BDL in caliber 7mm-08 proved that the little cartridge is absolutely fine, with good ballistics and high accuracy potential. Out of the box, the 7mm-08 produced five-shot groups of .75 inch at 100 yards from the bench with factory ammunition.

The BDL Varmint Special model wears a heavy 24-inch barrel and weighs nine pounds. It is chambered for the 308 Winchester, the 7mm-08 and, of course, for varmint rounds from the 222 through the 6mm Remington. There is a KS version with Kevlar (synthetic) stock called a Mountain Rifle and a similar AS Model 700. The powerful Safari 700 and the handsome Model Seven are out there for those who want sweet-carrying rifles with shorter bar-

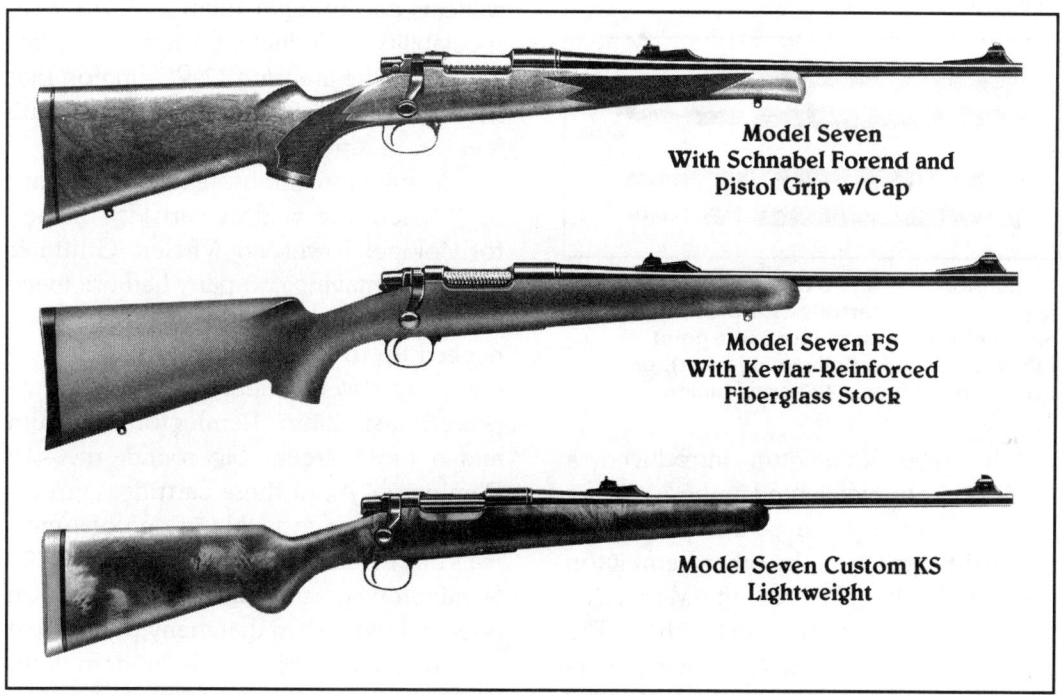

The handsome Remington Model Seven, an off-shoot of the Model 700, is a compact rifle with 18½-inch barrel that is available in numerous excellent calibers and stylings.

> ### THE REMINGTON MODEL 700 AT A GLANCE
>
> Improved, refined version of Models 721/722, which originated with the Model 30 of 1921
> **Period of Manufacture:** 1962 to the present
> **Calibers:** You name it - a sportsman's dream (see text, page 000)
> **Action:** Strong bolt-action repeater, built originally on the Enfield action
> **Barrel:** Of steel, blued, 22 or 24 inches usually, round
> **Weight (approx.):** 7 to 7½ pounds, depending on caliber and barrel length; heavy barrel, 9 pounds
> **Sights:** Ramp front; sliding ramp open rear
> **Stock:** Checkered Monte Carlo pistol-grip stock of American walnut
> **Variations:** Numerous; ADL and BDL models plus Classic, Custom, Mountain, Safari, Peerless and Premier grades with options, including hinged floorplates, satin finish, synthetic stock, schnabel forend, rubber butt pad, engraving, grip and/or forend caps, etc.

rels. The Model Seven KS with synthetic stock can be purchased in the potent 350 Remington Magnum cartridge for hunting big game in timber country. This rifle weighs under 6 pounds and wears a barrel only 18.5 inches long. And don't forget the custom shop, which can refine the 700 in four grades—I, II, III and IV.

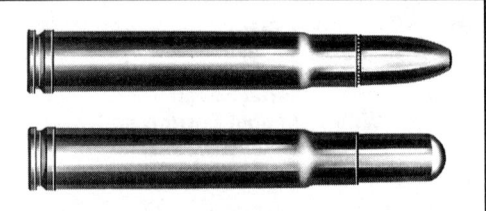

Remington developed the powerful 416 Remington Magnum cartridge for the Model 700 Safari rifle. In both pointed soft-point (above) and solid (full metal jacket), the 416 cartridge fires a 400-grain bullet.

In 1956 Remington introduced a Model 725 not highlighted in the 700 story because it was short-lived and not significantly different from the other Remington bolt-action rifles. In 1962, the Model 700 debuted and of course is still with us. The 700 results from the fine 720 that was gone in 1942 and from the excellent 721/722 rifles that it replaced.

Remington has never been afraid to take a plunge, not only in rifle manufacture, but also in cartridges. One of the finest long-range western big game rounds, the 7mm Remington Magnum, bears the Remington name because the company saw in the original wildcat the super potential of a Big 7. Remington tamed many wildcats and brought them to factory respectability, including the 7mm-08, the fast 25-06 and the amazing 17 Remington that shoots a tiny 25-grain bullet at over 4000 feet per second.

Remington also brought out a factory 35 Whelen, the wildcat cartridge named for Colonel Townsend Whelen. Griffin & Howe riflemaking company had originally built rifles in this round, which is a 30-06 necked up to hold 35 caliber bullets. The company also engineered the long-range powerhouse 8mm Remington Magnum and a more recent big round, the 416 Remington. All of these cartridges are excellent and are available in one of America's biggest success stories, the Model 700 Remington sporting rifle. It's been shown over and over again that many of the great ones had to be replicated in modern times because they were too good to die. The Remington Model 700 has replicated itself.

THE REMINGTON PUMPS
RELIABLE AND TRAIL READY

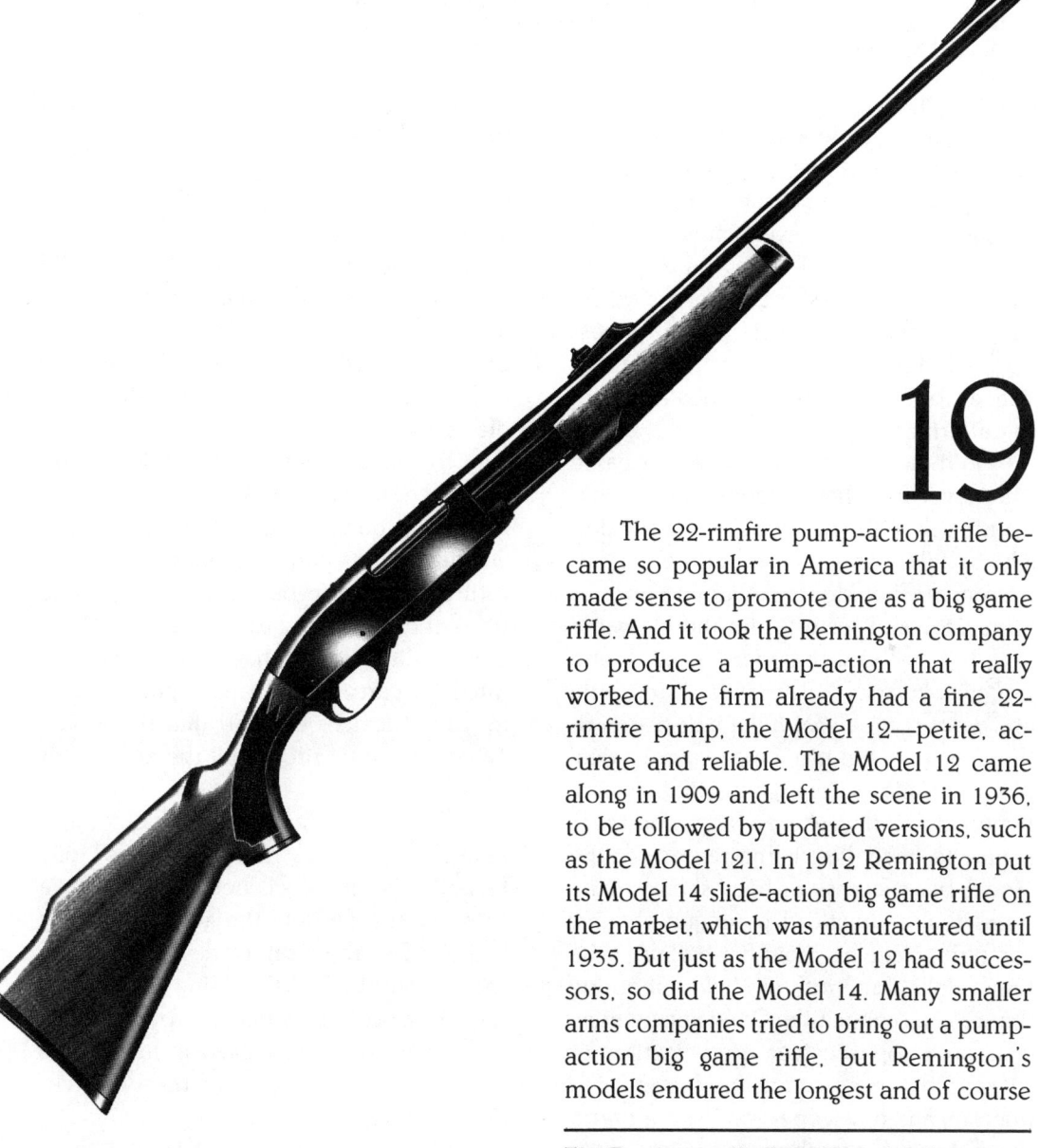

19

The 22-rimfire pump-action rifle became so popular in America that it only made sense to promote one as a big game rifle. And it took the Remington company to produce a pump-action that really worked. The firm already had a fine 22-rimfire pump, the Model 12—petite, accurate and reliable. The Model 12 came along in 1909 and left the scene in 1936, to be followed by updated versions, such as the Model 121. In 1912 Remington put its Model 14 slide-action big game rifle on the market, which was manufactured until 1935. But just as the Model 12 had successors, so did the Model 14. Many smaller arms companies tried to bring out a pump-action big game rifle, but Remington's models endured the longest and of course

The Remington Model 7600—a modern pumpgun with a strong action and reliability.

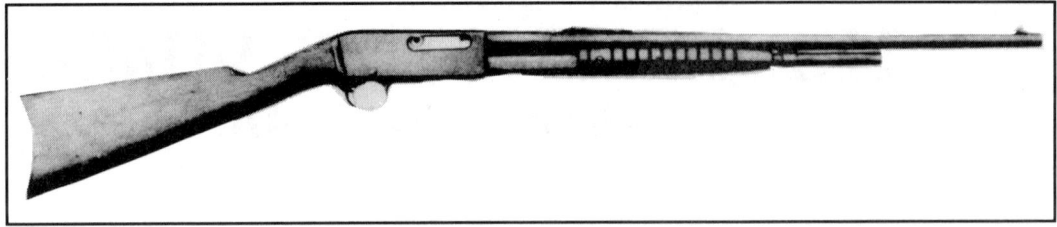

Remington's Model 14 was one of the first successful pump-action sporting rifles that dated back to 1912. With a "spiral-type" tubular magazine, the arm was chambered in calibers 25, 30, 32 and 35 Remington.

are still on line.

While the slide-action 22-rimfire certainly influenced the popularity of the pumpgun for big game, the pump shotgun probably affected it even more. J.D. Pedersen, a long-time Remington engineer, came up with the basic design of the Model 14 "trombone" action rifle. A hammerless action and solid breech gave the rifle credence from the start as an innovative, up-to-date rifle.

Remington's pump-action big game rifle never had that "experimental" look. Contrast it with the Model 8 autoloader, which did possess an experimental appearance. The Model 14 pumpgun was born sleek and ready to hit the big game trail. It weighed well under 7 pounds and was well-balanced. The slide-action rifle could not compete with the bolt-action rifle all around, but it still made a great deal of sense. Today's Remington is in fact ideal for woods hunting where a fast second shot is nice to have. Fast is the reason for the Model 14's success. It's been shown many times that a practiced pumpgun shooter can often place his rapid-fire bullets in the target right along with the fellow shooting the semiautomatic rifle. Good appearance, a smooth top receiver, side-ejection of spent cases, easy scope mounting—if a hunter wanted a scope—and some pretty good cartridge chamberings promoted the Model 14 and its offspring.

Perhaps too much is made of the fact that the Model 14 was a "safe" rifle. In spite of the fact that all big game rifles are capable of functioning safely with proper ammo, Remington's Model 14 got especially high marks because of the solid steel wall between the chambered cartridge and the shooter. The Model 14's solid breech blocked out dirt and debris as well. Pull the trigger. Shoot. Work the slide handle. Shoot again. It couldn't be simpler. Add to this the fact that the rifle had no tendency to jam, and that the breech locked up quite close to the head of the cartridge. That particular fact lived on in future Remington pump-action big game rifles and that's why to this day the Remington slidegun is chambered for high-intensity cartridges. Three separate built-in safety devices ensured that the Model 14 could not be fired until the action was fully locked.

The trigger and sear did not enter into relationship until the action was fully locked. The sear-lock held the sear in a firing pin notch until the action was fully locked. The third safety device was that the action blocked the firing pin so that the pin could not strike the primer until the action was fully locked in its forward or closed position. One of these devices alone would have been an asset to the overall safety of the Model 14, but three simply gave it triple insurance. The safety of the Model 14 functioned as a sliding lock. It rested behind the trigger, not entirely ideal. In front of the trigger would be more natural for the shooter's finger progress, but nevertheless it was an excellent safety and quick to operate. Lying behind the trigger, however, created a solid block. The trigger could not be activated when the safety was in the *on* position. Also, the safety functioned to tell the shooter if the rifle was cocked or uncocked. If uncocked, the safety would not go on at all—not until the interior hammer was in the rearward battery position.

The extractor of the Model 14 was also positive in function. The rifle was known to extract even swelled brass. Naturally, badly swelled cases would present a problem, just as they do with any action, including a Mauser 98-type with claw extractor. Reloading for the Model 14 and later Remington big game pump-action rifles was/is satisfactory, and lockup of the actions in such models as the 760 and 7600 allows very little case stretch. Of course, full-length resizing of fired brass is a good idea to aid later case extraction.

The Remington Model 14 was a takedown in the very best sense of the word, for the 14 did not shoot loose. A takedown screw allowed the rifle to "break in half." This feature reminds us very much of the 22-rimfire pump-action rifle, which could also be broken down by activating only one screw with fingers or the aid of a coin to loosen the screw. Furthermore, when the Model 14 was in its takedown mode, it was truly compact at only 27.5 inches in length.

THE 14'S SPECIAL MAGAZINE

One of the most fascinating aspects of the Model 14 was its tubular magazine. This type of magazine usually insisted on blunt-nosed bullets because sharp-nosed ones might set off the primer of the round in front during recoil. In the Model 14 this could not happen, because its tubular magazine was of the "spiral type" in which cartridges were retained "end to nose" and offset within the tube. The magazine tube was entirely reliable and why all tubular magazines were not similarly built is a good question.

A loading gate on the underside of the Model 14 allowed cartridge feeding without a hitch, although loaded rounds did have to be worked through the action for removal. The use of pointed bullets was possible with the Model 14, but in fact did not develop to any great extent, due to two facts. First, blunt-nosed bullets were popular during the era of the Model 14 and, second, the cartridges chambered into Remington's pumpgun, while good, were not long-range rounds to begin with. They were good woods numbers and were adequate for shots up to about 200 yards. These rounds were the familiar Remington series, the 25, 30 and 32. The 35 Remington soon came along as well. But the 25 Remington was dropped due to lack of buyer interest.

Stoeger's 1932 catalogue listed the Remington Model 14 as a "High Power Slide Action Repeating Rifle" in calibers 25 Remington, 30, 32 and 35 Remington. The 14A was listed as the standard grade model, a hammerless takedown rifle with solid breech, 22-inch barrel, checkered American walnut stock, buttstock and forend, with half-pistol grip, rifle-style steel buttplate, step-adjustable semi-buckhorn rear sight and white metal bead front sight. Literature on the subject suggests that the Model 14 was tapped and drilled for a peep sight at some point in its manufacture. And of course a scope sight was easy to add, since Model 14 scope mounts were available. Six shots with one in the chamber was noted as cartridge capacity. A weight of 6¾ pounds was listed as average. The Model 14A standard grade sold for $48.75 in 1932, toward the end of its production life.

Other variations included the 14C Special Grade at $82.50, a 14D Peerless Grade for $149.60 and a 14F Premier Grade at $303.60. The 14R was the carbine version of the rifle, noted as "furnished with ring on left side of the receiver, no extra charge" for saddle use; the price was $48.75, same as the standard grade model. A Whelen-type sling strap for the 14 could be added to the rifle for $2.60 in 1932.

By 1936 the Model 14 was replaced by the Model 141. This was Remington's way of showing an updated model, as they had done with the Model 12 pumpgun that became the Model 121. The rifle was now called a Gamemaster Repeater and possessed no mechanical improvement. The 141 was available in calibers 30, 32 and 35 Remington, caliber 25 Remington by now being dispossessed. The 30 Remington was a 30-30 Winchester for all practical ballistics purposes and the 32 Remington was ballistically a Winchester 32 Special.

The 35 Remington, however, was somewhat unique. This cartridge earned a reputation by its larger caliber, providing a bullet that "made a bigger hole," and by the fact that a 200-grain projectile was the norm. Velocity did not surpass the 2000 fps mark by much, but still, this round was more than anything a 30-30 could put out power-wise. One particular bullet offered by Remington was 200 grains in weight with a lot of lead exposed at the tip. This bullet expanded well enough on deer and black bear and helped to earn the 35 Remington a good reputation on such game. Good shots took the Models 14 and 141 into the field, and with the 35 Remington

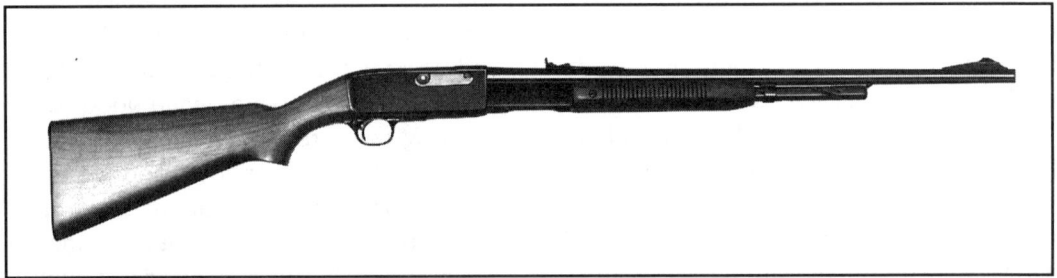

The Remington Model 141 Gamemaster was a reliable big game rifle produced from 1936 to 1951. The unique tubular magazine design allowed pointed bullets, but seldom were pointed bullets used in the 141.

cartridge and its fine bullet these men were highly successful on all big game that they hunted, including moose. So the Gamemaster in 35 Remington proved an excellent combination.

While the 141 was not, by design, a better rifle than the 14, it carried some excellent refinements. The front sight was one. By comparison, the front sight of the 141, which rested on a ramp, made the 14's look rough. The 141 had a longer barrel by two inches. Its 24-inch barrel allowed a slightly longer sight radius and a slightly improved off-hand weight balance. The stock was also mildly improved with a more pronounced pistol grip. The forend was of semi-beavertail style with flattened bottom.

Stoeger's catalogue of 1939 listed the 141 as "the same as the famous Model 14, but with important new improvements." The 141A Standard Grade rifle sold for $53.95 in 1939 and was offered in other grades. The carbine version with 18.5-inch barrel sold for the same price. The 141C sold for $89.45, the D for $147.80 and the F Premier for $284.20. The 141 had "extras" that included a checkered stock for $4.40, a soft rubber recoil pad fitted to the rifle for $5.50, full pistol grip with grip cap for $4.40, a sling for $2.20 and a gold name plate for $6.60. In short, as well as being a fine rifle all around, the 141 was a Model 14 that you could dress up.

THE MODEL 760 TAKES OVER

But as fine as the 14 and 141 were, they could not withstand the forces of progress. The 14 fell to the 141 and the 141 was phased out in 1951, to be replaced the following year by an entirely new rifle: Remington's high-quality Model 760. Remington designers were hard at work in the 1940s developing a new pump-action big game rifle and they found it in the 760. If the 141 was sleek, the 760 was more so.

If the 141 worked smoothly, the 760 was at least its equal. While the 141 locked up well, the 760 action was even stronger. And if the 141 chambered good cartridges, the 760 eclipsed it in that arena too.

In 1953, gunwriter Warren Page, who wrote for *Field & Stream* magazine, cheerfully announced the 760 as a rifle that slide-action fans would go crazy over, especially if they were shotgun fans. How much like a shotgun was the 760? The rifle's receiver started life as the same forging as a Remington Model 11-48 autoloading 28-gauge shotgun. The trigger and safety parts of the 760 were a match-up for Remington's Wingmaster Model 870 shotgun (the same setup as the 11-48, too). Furthermore, the 760's stock was shotgun-style. In short, a lover of the pump-action shotgun couldn't go wrong with a 760.

The new rifle was also called the Gamemaster. It was chambered for a variety of excellent cartridges, including the fine 35 Remington, 300 Savage and the 257 Roberts, for the hunter who wanted an excellent light-recoiling pump-action deer rifle. But the really big news was that the 760 was chambered right away for the 30-06 Springfield. The 35 Remington was a darn good close-range round, but at

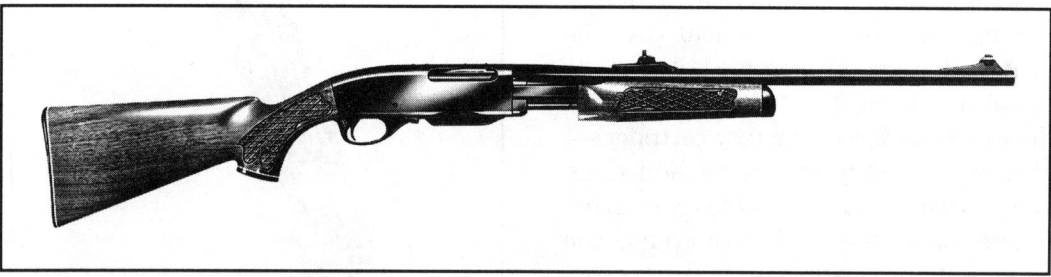

The Model 760 Gamemaster carried the same name as its forerunner, the Model 141, but wore a very different appearance. Available in many chamberings, the 760 pump-action was manufactured from 1952 to 1980.

longer ranges the bullet looped toward earth like a rock. The 30-06 put a good deal of extra performance distance in the Model 760. So did the 270 Winchester, another popular round. Later on, the 760 was also chambered for the 223 Remington, 243 Winchester and 280 Remington.

The reason the 760 could handle such premium big game rounds was the lockup system. The barrel screwed into a barrel extension, which included the breech-bolt locking lug recesses (not the lugs, but the recesses for the locking lugs). The system (rotary multiple-lug breech bolt) encompassed 20 locking lugs, or 20 interrupted screw thread sections that cammed around 20 matching sections within the barrel extension itself. This arrangement gave the action a lockup between the bolt and the barrel, as it were. The 760 was tested with the same overloaded factory cartridges—blue pills—used to test bolt-action rifles. They contain about 70,000 PSI (pounds per square inch) pressure and of course can damage the action.

The first 760 slide-action 30-06 carried a 22-inch barrel and a weight of 7½ pounds. Of course, the 760 enjoyed the same safety features that had become well-known on the 14 and 141. The rifle could not be fired until the action was fully closed and locked. Even if the trigger were pulled during the closing of the action, the rifle would not go off, according to the literature supplied by Remington. "Trigger must be pulled and released for each shot," Remington said. Once again there was a solid receiver and this time the Gamemaster was advertised for a scope sight, which it naturally mounted dead center on the receiver. Side ejection was positive. "New extraction principle," said Remington, which was successfully proved on the famous Model 721, and positive side ejec-

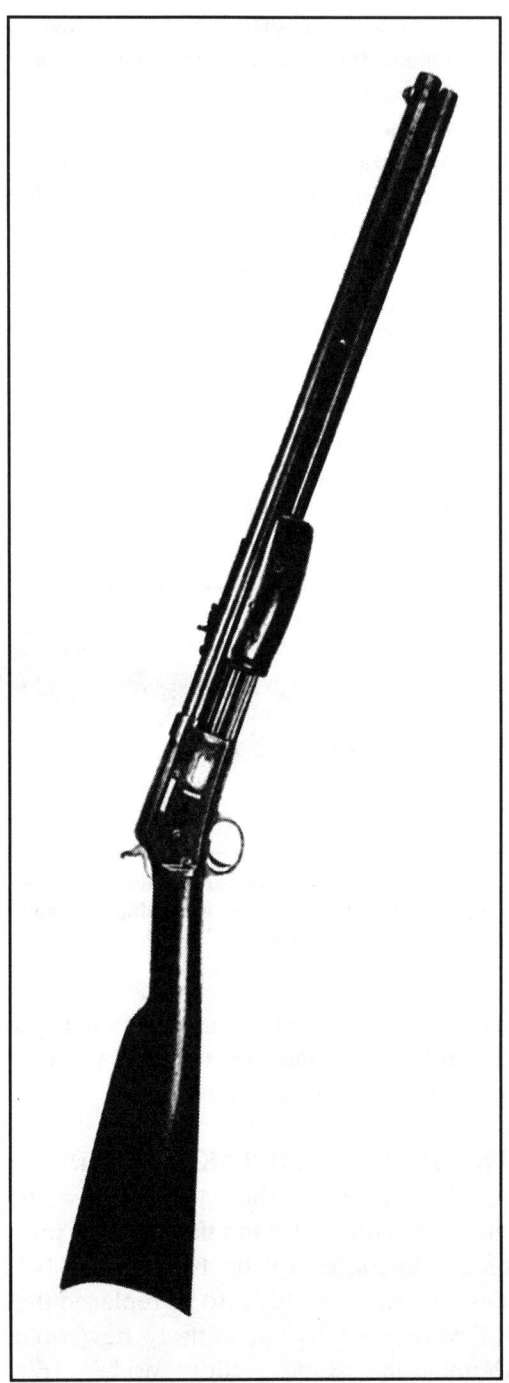

The slide-action big game rifle made famous by Remington actually dates back to the Colt Lightning sporting rifle. In calibers 32-20, 38-40 and 44-40, the Lightning's tubular magazine held 15 rounds.

tion. The trigger was advertised as smooth without backlash. It was a good hunting trigger, albeit not as crisp as that on Remington's Model 700 series, which offers an exceptional trigger pull.

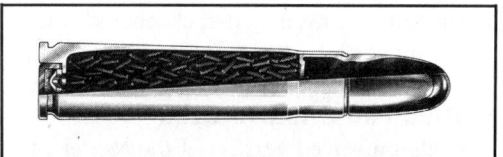

The 35 Remington cartridge made early Remington slide-action big game rifles potent at close range. This is a cutaway view of the 35 Remington with a 200-grain bullet.

The 760 was not advertised as a takedown model. Nor should it be misconstrued as one. However, shooting enthusiasts found that the rifle could be broken down, especially with the use of a special wrench because lockup occurred at the barrel extension. Taking the 760 down would not result in later headspace problems. The forearm hanger was unscrewed, which in turn allowed the breech-bolt mechanism to disengage for complete bore cleaning from the breech end.

Truly good news for the 760 fan came with accuracy tests. While this rifle did not exactly whip the 721 or 722, it could put five shots inside of two inches, center to center, at 100 yards from the bench, and that was better than practical hunting accuracy demanded. Warren Page saw right away that the 760 could be rechambered to wildcat cartridges that were built on the 30-06 case. He mentioned the 35 Whelen. It is interesting to note that the newest Model 760, today's Model 7600, is chambered for the 35 Whelen. A five-shot rifle with a four-shot clip, the 760 of course used pointed projectiles. The safety remained at the rear of the trigger guard. In 1953 the Model 760 cost $104.50.

Today, the 760 remains on line with Remington in the form of the Model 7600. An improved version of the 760, the Model 7600 came along in 1981. The rifle is chambered for the 243 Winchester, 270 Winchester, 280 Remington, 308 Winchester, 30-06 and 35 Whelen, and has also been used to chamber wildcat cartridges. One of the very best of these wildcats is a 338-06, much like the 35 Whelen, but with better downrange ballistics. This 33-caliber wildcat is of course built by opening up the neck of 30-06 brass to accept .338 inch bullets. Ballistics include a 200-grain bullet at 2700 fps and a 250-grain bullet at 2400 fps for muzzle energy figures of 3238 foot-pounds and close to 3200 foot-pounds, respectively. The cut-checkered walnut stock of the Model 7600 is better suited to a scope sight because of its high Monte Carlo comb. With a 22-inch barrel, the 7600

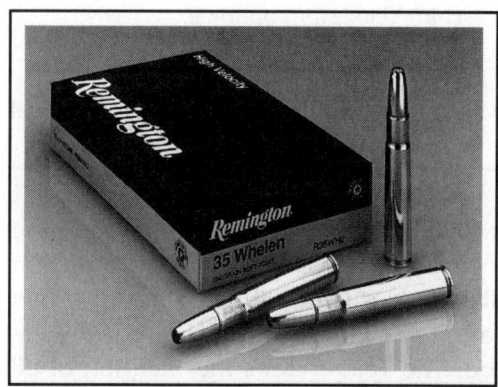

The current Remington Model 7600 big game rifle offers even more power in its 35 Whelen chambering with either 200- or 250-grain bullet.

weighs about 7½ pounds and measures 42 inches overall. The 7600 is an entirely modern rifle in all respects.

Some shooters say the 7600 is a bolt-action rifle that happens to function with

The Remington Model 14 at a Glance

Period of Manufacture: 1912 to 1935
Calibers: 25, 30, 32 and 35 Remington
Magazine Capacity: 5 plus 1 in "spiral-type" tubular magazine, side ejection
Action: Hammerless, takedown "trombone" pump-action with solid breech, smooth top receiver, grooved walnut slide handle
Barrel: Of steel, blued, 22 inches
Weight (approx.): $6^{3}/_{4}$ pounds
Safety: Three separate safety "devices:" action had to be fully locked before trigger and sear functioned together; sear-lock held sear in a firing pin notch until action was fully locked; action blocked firing pin from striking the primer.
Sights: Open step-adjustable semibuckhorn rear sight; white metal bead front. Drilled and tapped for scope mounts.
Stock: Checkered half-pistol grip stock of American walnut; rifle-style steel buttplate
Variations: Different grades with varying embellishments—Special (14C), Peerless (14D), Premier (14F) and saddle-ring carbine (14R). Sling strap optional.

MODEL 141 GAMEMASTER
Basically an improved version of the Model 14 with 24-inch barrel
Period of Manufacture: 1936 to 1951
Calibers: 30, 32 and 35 Remington
Improvements: Ramp front sight, better weight balance, more pronounced pistol grip, semi-beavertail forend
Variations: Extras included checkered stock, soft rubber recoil pad, full pistol grip with grip cap, sling, gold name plate

MODEL 760 GAMEMASTER
Sleek, improved version of the Model 141 with 22-inch barrel
Period of Manufacture: 1952 to 1980
Calibers: 222 Rem., 223 Rem., 6mm Rem. (244), 243 Win., 257 Roberts, 270 Win., 280 Rem., 300 Savage, 30-06 Springfield, 308 Win., 35 Rem.
Weight (approx.): $7^{1}/_{2}$ pounds
Improvements: Very strong action with rotary multiple-lug breech bolt, more modern outward appearance, positive side ejection

MODEL 7600
Improved version of the Model 760 Gamemaster with strong action and safety
Period of Manufacture: 1981 to date
Calibers: 243 Win., 270 Win., 280 Rem., 30-06, 308 Win., 35 Whelen
Variations: Offered in a multitude of grades with various options

---

a slide. Its modern-style bolt and fine lockup action make this pumpgun function like a bolt-action rifle. Shooters who reload for it have good results with good case life too. The 7600 follows the tradition of all Remington pump-action rifles with a multitude of grades. Currently, it is the only pump-action rifle to occupy the particular niche in firearms that belongs to a high-power slide-action model. Even though the Model 7600 is the only one in the series still manufactured, the 14, 141 and 760 are often seen at gun shows as well as in the field. They may no longer be made, but these reliable, trail-ready Remingtons are hardly retired.

SAVAGE MODEL 99
ACTION SO SMOOTH

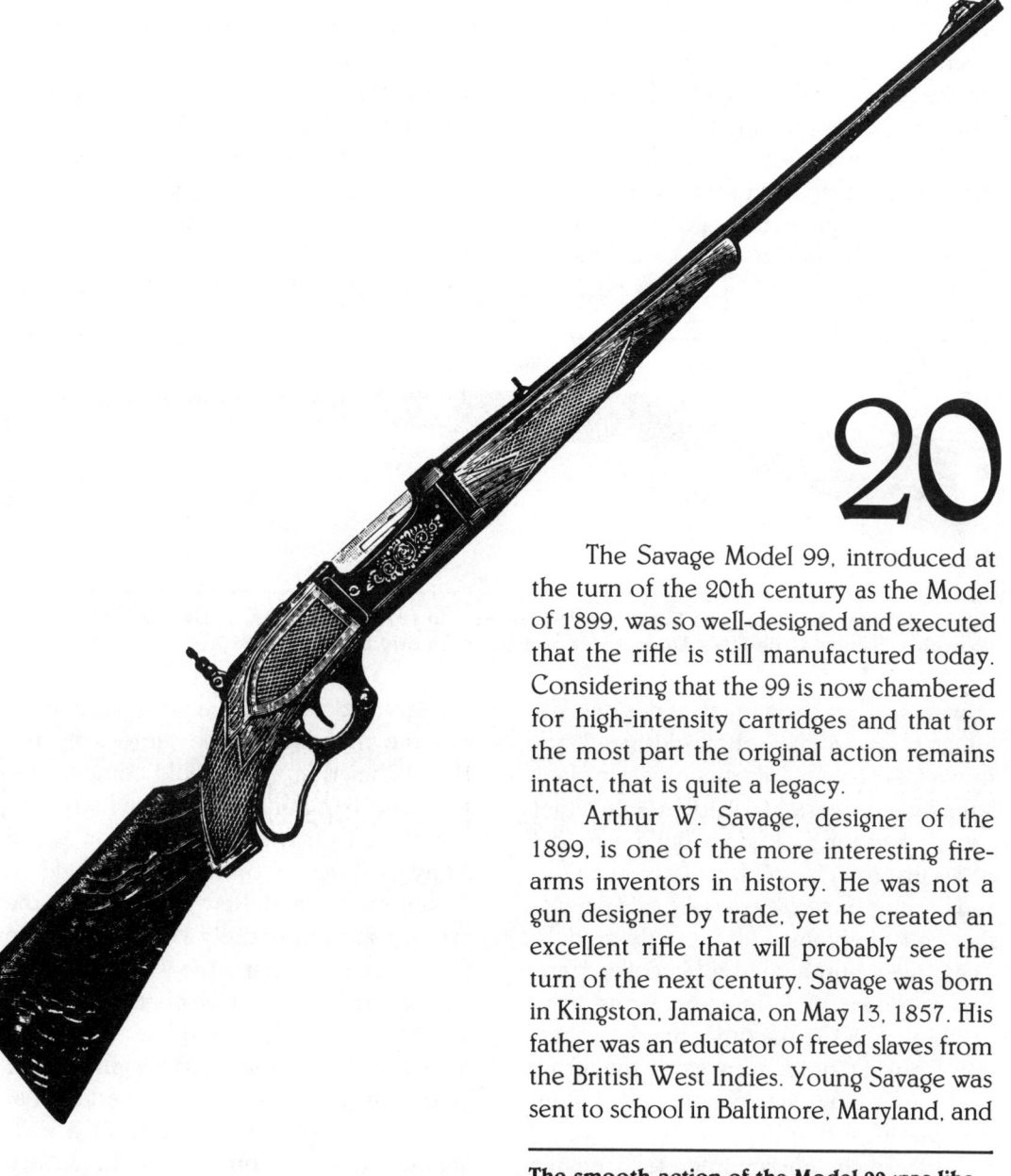

20

The Savage Model 99, introduced at the turn of the 20th century as the Model of 1899, was so well-designed and executed that the rifle is still manufactured today. Considering that the 99 is now chambered for high-intensity cartridges and that for the most part the original action remains intact, that is quite a legacy.

Arthur W. Savage, designer of the 1899, is one of the more interesting firearms inventors in history. He was not a gun designer by trade, yet he created an excellent rifle that will probably see the turn of the next century. Savage was born in Kingston, Jamaica, on May 13, 1857. His father was an educator of freed slaves from the British West Indies. Young Savage was sent to school in Baltimore, Maryland, and

The smooth action of the Model 99 was like "glass on glass." This is a Model 99K.

was also schooled in Britain. He became an artist for the *London Graphics* paper and from that post moved on to Australia where for two years he traveled the outback. He married and with his wife Ann, he decided to raise cattle. Within nine years, they owned the largest cattle ranch down under. The Savages eventually had seven children and sold the cattle ranch to run the family coffee plantation in Jamaica. When Savage apparently tired of running the plantation, he left it in the hands of an overseer. Savage then went to work for the Belt Line Railroad as manager of the lines.

It's likely that at this point Savage abandoned the coffee operation because

action. He was familiar with this rifle from Britain and apparently felt the firearm would benefit from repeater status. What may have been a design that never saw production is an action idea for the 30-40 Krag cartridge. Savage was a thinker and proved to be an inventor. However, he was not a factory man. His early models were never built because they were a manufacturer's nightmare, demanding numerous operations. They were not cost-effective. Even those that were eventually built, Savage farmed out to other plants. He finally discarded all hopes of making the Martini into a respectable repeater.

Savage latched onto a new plan using

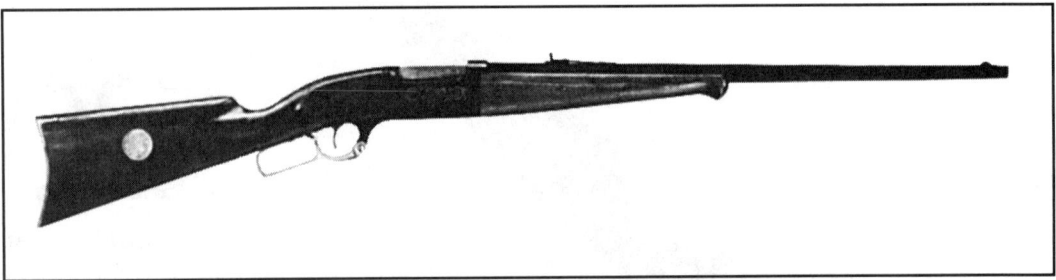

The Model 99 was basically an improved Model 1895. In 1970 to commemorative its 75th year in operation, Savage issued this Anniversary replica of the original Model 1895.

he wanted to work on firearms designs. His interest lay in an action designed for smokeless powder only, but his early plans left a lot to be desired. History records that Savage had the Colt plant build a model of his first rifle. It could not have been too bad because Savage eventually sold patents that he had obtained on his early models. These were purchased by Marcellus Hartley, president of Remington Arms from 1888 to 1902. On the other hand, the patents couldn't have been earth-shattering because Remington never put any of them into production.

Originally, Savage intended to make a repeater out of the single-shot Martini

a rotary spool magazine. This, of course, was the magazine made famous by the Mannlicher rifle. Savage did compete for a government contract for a military rifle chambered for the 30-40 Krag or 30 US Army cartridge. In ordnance trials held on Government Island, New York, in 1892, the military was not entirely satisfied with the Savage rifle. Perhaps the Army was not happy with a rifle that weighed 10 pounds, was 53 1/4 inches long and had a pregnant magazine protruding in front of the trigger guard. Furthermore, it's fairly certain that the military mind leaned toward a bolt-action rifle at this time. Only the Savage and one other entry at the 1892 trials were operated by an under-lever.

Arthur Savage switched to a sporting rifle, rather than pursue a military piece, and chose a 32-20 sporting rifle to start. His first patent, applied for in June 1887 and granted in July, was for the repeating Martini with the tubular magazine in the buttstock. This was a patent picked up by Marcellus Hartley. An improvement on this patent, dated February 28, 1888, was also assigned to Hartley and of course never put into production. A patent for 1891 shows the Martini again, but with a different magazine style. Savage's patent for February 7, 1893, shows progress, revealing a tilting breechblock rifle with a rotary magazine. This patent was eventually assigned to Childs, Reynolds and Risley, the latter name which would be connected with firearms (including military guns) for many years.

The patent of September 27, 1895 is of most importance, for this is the father of the great Savage 99 rifle. This patent, for the Savage Model 1895 rifle with a cocking indicator, would reside with the Savage Repeating Arms Company. The story of the 1895 goes back at least to 1892. Savage had at that time a fantastic little lever-action rifle for the 32-20 cartridge. Those who owned or tried the '92 rifle claim that the action was one of the smoothest-working types ever. The 1895 model is vital to the Savage 99 story because the 99 is basically a 95 with modifications. So few, in fact, that Savage would in effect turn a Model 95 into a Model 99 for five dollars.

The Savage Model 95 made an impact on the shooting world. It possessed smokeless powder strength and was ready to take on some extremely interesting and useful cartridges. It had a solid breech, was hammerless and operated more or less on a "spring-loaded" firing-pin system, using coil springs instead of flat springs. The solid breech offered an enclosed action. Empty cartridge cases were shucked out to the side, not straight up. The trigger was entirely safe, although it retained a bit of creep due to design, but nothing to hurt hunting accuracy. The 95 was a natural for the scope sight from the start. The rifle's lines were smooth and clean and the action was foolproof. Those who have shot the 95 system will attest to the fact that jamming is not a trait of this great rifle. The cocking indicator, a pin on some models, protruded through the top of the receiver. By feel, a hunter would know that the action was cocked and ready to go. The exact type of indicator varies with models, but the idea goes back to early examples.

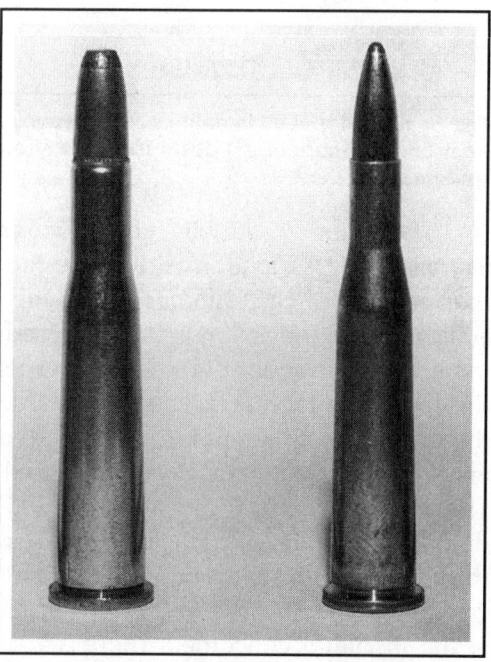

Two cartridges chambered in the Model 99 Savage were the 25-35 Winchester (left) and 22 Savage Hi-Power (right). The latter, originally a wildcat attributed to Charles Newton, is a necked down 25-35. It is also known as the "Imp."

The Savage Model 99 in caliber 250 Savage with scope sight is easy to control in the field. It can be fired without taking it down from the shoulder to work the lever. Fast-action was always the trademark of the 99.

The action on the 95 (and 99) works like glass on glass due in part to the fact that cocking of the hammer is not fully achieved until the action is almost closed. In return, the lowering of the lever to expel the spent cartridge case does not include the cocking of a hammer, so all imparted energy is directed toward ejecting the shell. The action is cammed shut rigidly. In addition, because the cartridge is enclosed in the receiver with no avenue for rearward gas escape, the action is "gas-proof" as far as the shooter is concerned. There is a rebounding firing pin that won't get snapped off. The ejector on the 95 was a good one from the start. Another feature is the cartridge number indicator, a rotating brass piece that shows a number through a tiny window cut in the receiver. The number is zero when the magazine is empty or it shows the exact number of rounds in the magazine.

Reliable. That's the best word to describe the Savage. Add it up: action strength; darn good cartridges; no protruding hammer; and easy scope-mounting when scopes would become popular. The rotary or spool magazine was just about perfect, too. It had worked on the Mannlicher and it worked equally well on the Savage. Furthermore, Savage ammo could carry the pointed bullet for far better long-range effect, because there was no tubular magazine with bullet points up against primers.

A further plus for the Savage rifle was

its potential for accuracy. A throughbolt held the buttstock in place and having no tubular magazine also meant no connection difficulties or pressure point problems. In a sense, the barrel was free-floating on the Savage 95. Bedding was not a detriment to accuracy. The 95 is, in all effects, the 99 and that's why it is given space here.

One more point before leaving the 95: it was chambered for the 303 Savage cartridge. On the face of it, this is nothing to get excited about. But when a gun student looks closer, the 303 Savage was a rather clever idea. In the first place, it appeared fairly much in the same time frame as the 25-35 Winchester and 30 Winchester (30-30), but the 303 Savage is never credited as a first among smokeless sporting rounds. Recall that the Winchester sisters both arrived in 1895. The 303 Savage likewise. Second, possibly because Savage originally considered his 303 a military number, it carried a heavier bullet than the 30-30. That's conjecture from some experts. Perhaps Savage decided on a heavier bullet strictly for close-range penetration improvement on big game. We will never know for sure. The fact is, the 303 did shoot a 190-grain bullet, while the 30-30 carried 170- and 180-grain bullets. Although the 30-30 and 303 Savage are not interchangeable cartridges, they are of about the same powder capacity and near performance twins when loaded equally. But Savage had hunters thinking of the 303 as a bigger 30-30. Savage always had a way of selling a round to the hunter.

Savage probably did miss the boat by failing to use a pointed bullet in the 303, because the 95 could take it. The Winchester 94 could not. Better downrange ballistics would have resulted. In my own tests, the 303 with pointed bullets was chrono-

The original tang sight on the Model 1899 is shown here in the up position ready for use.

graphed with Oehler skyscreens downrange, and the streamlined projectiles retained velocity/energy far better than round-nosed or flat-nosed bullets from the same cartridge and rifle. Known as the 301 Savage in England, the 303 was well-received by American hunters. Something that has been all but forgotten is the fact that the 303 Savage did not come out with 30-caliber bullets. A micrometer revealed that samples of UMC factory 303 Savage ammo were loaded with bullets of exactly .311 inch. That is 31 caliber, not 30. Later on, the 303 Savage was loaded with 30-caliber bullets. The same micrometer measured a 190-grain Silvertip bullet in Winchester's 303 Savage ammo at 30 caliber—exactly .3085 inch.

Incidentally, not all old 303 Savage ammo carried the 190-grain bullet. A cartridge, with a Savage headstamp marked "S.A. Corp." for Savage Arms Corporation, was loaded with a 180-grain bullet, but again diameter was not .308 inch. Nor was it precisely .311 inch. Bullets averaging 178.5 grains in weight had a diameter of .310 inch. No wonder the English called it a 301 Savage instead of a 303 Savage. In another test, I used an old Remington brand. Bullets were again .310-inch diameter at 180-grains weight.

Ballistics for the 303 were checked for this chapter using original ammunition in excellent condition and an Oehler chronograph. From a 26-inch barrel, a 180-grain bullet achieved a muzzle velocity of 2052 fps. New Winchester brand 303 Savage ammo gave a 190-grain Silvertip bullet 1951 fps. Expert hunters took these ballistics into the field and had great success with the 303 in the Savage Model 95.

An advertisement for the Savage 1895 shortly after its appearance stated that "The Savage is a hammerless rifle made on scientific principles and is one of the most powerful shooting rifles yet produced." The ad continued: "A steel boiler plate 3/8-inch thick has been perforated by a bullet—caliber 303—fired from a Savage rifle at a distance of thirty feet and it will penetrate 35 pine boards 7/8-inch thick." The 303 Savage cartridge is the only round shown for the new rifle and denoted: ".303 for Savage Smokeless." Velocity of the round was 2000 feet per second. The notice further stated that the Savage kicked its

Sam Fadala assembles his Model 99 takedown by first screwing the barrel into place in the receiver, then attaching the forearm.

empties out from the side, not the top, and that the barrel was 26 inches long with open sights. The magazine held five rounds. Price of the Savage at its beginnings were $21.50, which was higher than the Winchester Model 1895 box magazine rifle advertised for $17.82 on the same page of the same catalogue. Plus, the Winchester was chambered for the 30 US Army (30-40 Krag). The Savage, however, was promoted as a modern-style rifle, which it was in comparison to Winchester's 1895 top-ejection model.

It is interesting to note that the initial Savage 1895 rifles were not built by Savage. They were made by the Marlin company and bear Marlin's proof marks, the well-known encircled JM insignia. Marlin may have built Savages from 1895 to 1899, rifles with 26-inch round barrels and 22-inch carbines. A discrepancy in the literature points out a round barrel for the Model of 1895, but Sears offered a Savage 95 with an octagon barrel. The Savage Repeating Arms Company went under the laws of the State of West Virginia beginning on April 5, 1894. Major offices were in Utica, New York, and eventually the company did switch to New York State laws as the Savage Arms Company until 1915.

The story of the 1895 Savage ends in 1899 with the famous Model 99... almost. Actually, Savage brought out a commemorative Model 1895 lever-action rifle on the 75th anniversary of the company in 1970. Called the Anniversary Model 1895, it was of course mechanically the Model 99 throughout with rotary magazine. This commemorative was chambered for the 308 Winchester cartridge. Styling was reminiscent of the original 1895 with a 24-inch octagon barrel, cartridge indicator and crescent-shaped buttplate. Inlaid into the right side of the buttstock was a brass medallion that read, "Savage Arms Co. 75th ANNIVERSARY." A gold-filled engraving on the right side of the receiver read "Model 1895" with embellishment all around. The rifle was advertised at a price just short of $200. The commemorative Model 95 was another good Savage rifle.

THE MODEL 1899 PERFECTED

The Model 1899 Savage appeared in 1899, as we know, and it eclipsed the Model 1895 Savage from which it stemmed. The patent granted October 3, 1899 served the Model 1899 rifle. No major changes were recorded in the overall workings of the Savage lever-action big game rifle from the 95 to the 99. Of course, many minor adjustments were implemented as new models took over. The hammer indicator and sear arrangement, for example, were altered slightly. The safety changed altogether on later models; a safety on the top tang was far easier to operate than the original safety that was a sliding bar rear of the trigger located in conjunction with the lever.

Like the 1895, the Model 1899 was chambered for the 303 Savage. It was soon augmented with many different calibers and styles. Numerous variations on the Model 99 theme exist, and should not another 99 be made, there are as many as a couple million 99s in existence today—not all different styles of course. But by 1907, the 1899 was offered in a takedown version and special order models were common. Two representative examples have crossed my path. One is a Model 1899 with 26-inch half-octagon, half-round barrel in caliber 303 Savage. It wears a checkered semi-pistol-grip stock of fine grade wood and a perch belly buttstock that help to dress this beautiful Savage rifle. Two-inch 100-yard groups with peep sight were the best obtained in bench-testing. But the largest groups were under three inches, same sights. Handloads gave the 150-grain bullet 2700 fps with perfect extraction and long case life.

The second 99 is a takedown that belonged to Arnold Bowen, my father-in-law. He hunted with the rifle for years and put many elk in the freezer. In 300 Savage caliber with serial number just under 280,000, the handy takedown bagged all sorts of big game for Arnold. It is still a reliable and handsome rifle. It has "shot loose," but remains safe and sufficiently accurate for close- to medium-range big game hunting. The takedown system is simple screw-on, not interrupted thread, and both front and rear sights are attached to the barrel; the rear sight is not on the receiver. So the rifle remains sighted in even when the threads have become worn.

In 1907 the Savage 99 was offered in blackpowder caliber 38-55 Winchester. Of course, Savage could hardly avoid chambering the 99 for the 30-30. The cartridge was simply too popular to ignore. The 32-40, 25-35 and the Marlin 25-36 were also chambered.

Charles Newton, of Newton cartridge and rifle fame, came up with a wildcat in 1912 that interested Savage. The round was built by necking down the 25-35 Winchester case to 22 caliber. It was called the Imp by some, but the official name was the 22 Savage Hi-Power or Savage 22 Hi-Power. A 70-grain .228-inch bullet left the muzzle at about 2800 fps. Of course hunters had to try the Imp on everything from mice to pachyderms. Results varied. Good marksmen got grizzly bears with one shot. Poor hunters and shooters probably had some bad luck on big game with the Imp. One hunter declared the Imp deadly on tigers and lived to brag about it. But Imp muzzle energy was not much beyond around 1200 foot-pounds.

The next round to come along was better for game, although it was truly not much more than a deer cartridge. Of course, people took it out for everything, including moose and Kodiak bears. It was the 250 Savage of 1914. Smart Savage marketing came through again. Charles Newton was behind this round, too, and history fully supports that Newton intended the 250 to shoot a 100-grain bullet around 2800 fps. In other words, it would be something like the Imp, only better. Newton asked for the 100-grain bullet, but Savage was clever. The company knew that high velocity sold guns. They decreased the weight of the projectile until a clean 3000 fps was obtained. That is why the original 250 Savage round carried an 87-grain bullet. The company called their new baby the 250-3000 Savage in reference to muzzle velocity. Later, a 100-grain bullet was added, but not soon enough for Newton to see it; he passed away before his original intention for the 250 was realized.

Although Savage operated an ammunition plant for a while, ammo was usually produced by other companies. Nonetheless, Savage continued to play a research role in ammo development. And that is how in 1920 the fine 300 Savage was born as a "small 30-06." Those of us who carefully handload the 300 Savage know that it can come quite close ballistically to the 308 Winchester. Savage planned a high-intensity high-pressure short round that would just about duplicate 30-06 ballistics. They actually came fairly close to succeeding, because the 30-06 was not loaded up to its potential at the time. A standard 30-06 load was a 150-grain bullet at 2700 fps. It is easy to push that bullet at over 3000 fps today with 30-06 handloads and also to reach 2800 fps with a 180-grain bullet from the '06. Savage had a fine round in the 300, however, and hunters knew it. A good standard load soon became a 180-grain bullet at darn close to 2400 fps. Personal handloads see 2500 fps with a 180-grain bullet in the 300 Savage, 24-inch barrel, and almost 2400 fps with a 190-grain bullet. It means plenty of power for big game at modest range.

When the short "hot" rounds came along, such as the 243 Winchester, 308 Winchester and 358 Winchester, the Savage Model 99 was ready to accept them—with no changes needed in the action. That alone speaks for the quality of the rifle. In caliber 358 Winchester, the 99 was truly what its early advertisements suggested: a rifle for all big game in North America. The 250 Savage was dropped for a while, but it returned to the lineup. Why not? It's a fine little cartridge.

The Model 99 always sold well. A look at the 1940 Stoeger *Shooter's Bible* tells why it was a bargain. That catalogue held two full pages of 99s. The light 99-F takedown featherweight at 7½ pounds in calibers 22 Hi-Power, 250-3000, 30-30, 303 Savage and 300 Savage sold for $53.50. The 99-H Carbine with 20-inch barrel sold for $45.40. The 99-R solid frame went for $54. And the top-of-the-line 99-K listed at $85.75. The K was described as the takedown model in all calibers previously mentioned for the 99-F, with tang peep sight, special checkered walnut stock, semi-pistol grip, engraved receiver and barrel, stoned action and other features.

Arthur Savage's major role was his gifted invention of a great lever-action rifle that began as a repeating Martini, became a 32-20 sporter, transposed into a Model 1895 and then became the Model 1899 Savage we all know as the Model 99. But

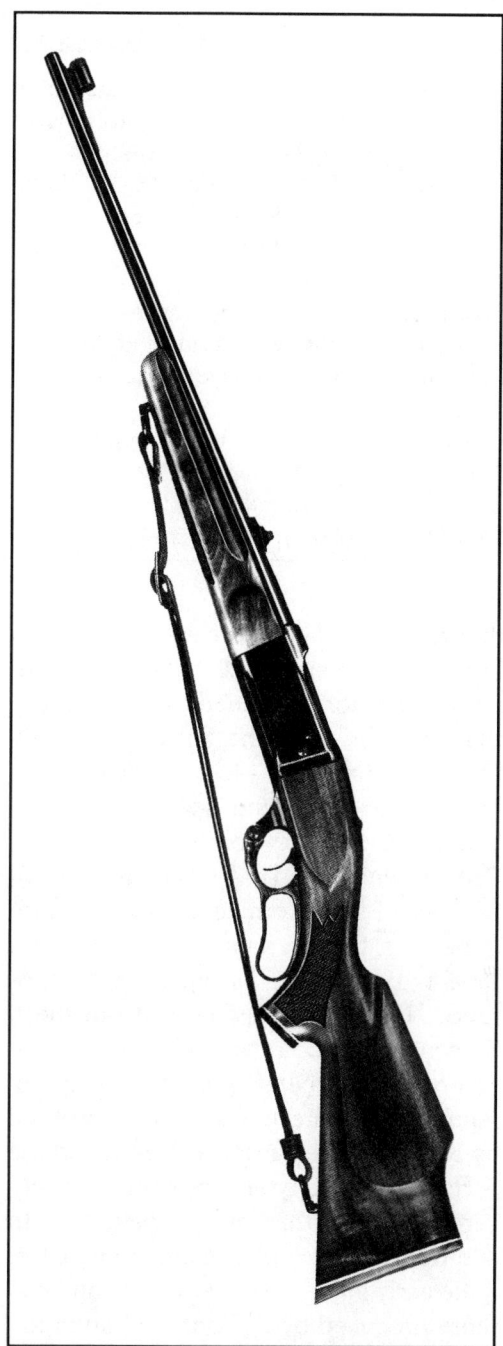

One of the many excellent Savage Model 99 variations is the Model 99-CD Deluxe with checkered Monte Carlo stock, cheekpiece, pistol grip with cap, hooded ramp front sight, swivels and sling. This modern version has a detachable box magazine.

SAVAGE MODEL 99 201

> ### THE SAVAGE MODEL 99 AT A GLANCE
>
> **Period of Manufacture:** 1899 to date (about 1920 called the Model 99, previously Model 1899; patterned after Model 1895)
> **Calibers:** 22 Hi-Power (Imp), 25-35, Marlin 25-36, 250-3000 Savage, 300 Savage, 303 Savage, 30-30, 32-40 and 38-55; other modern caliber offerings
> **Action:** Smooth-working lever-action repeater with rotary magazine and side ejection; later models have detachable box magazine
> **Barrel:** Of steel, blued; round, octagonal or half-round, half-octagonal; 22, 24 inches usually; other variations
> **Weight (approx.):** $6^{1}/_{4}$ to $7^{1}/_{2}$ pounds
>
> **Safety:** Original safety was sliding bar rear of the trigger; later top tang safety
> **Sights:** Open rear; bead front on ramp; other variations, including scope mountings
> **Stock:** Straight- or pistol-grip stock of American walnut; special order fancy-grain walnut with checkering; schnabel forend on early models; oil-finished; many variations
> **Variations:** Numerous, many custom models with various options, including slings, grip caps, type of checkering, fluted forends, different buttplate styles, etc. Carbine, Deluxe, Featherweight and Military models offered as well as various grades.

before Savage died at the age of 81 in San Diego on September 22, 1938, the company he had formed added up to a lot more than that. In 1915, the Savage company had been purchased—lock, stock and barrel, as the old saying goes—by Driggs-Seabury Ordnance Company of Sharon, Pennsylvania. The Driggs-Seabury Corporation had been formed under Delaware State laws, but the name was changed on June 1, 1917 to the Savage Arms Corporation. In 1920, Savage bought out the J. Stevens Arms Company in entirety. Stevens was run separately for a time, but in January 1936, Stevens was fully absorbed by Savage Arms. Savage also acquired the A.H. Fox company and Fox shotguns became a part of the Savage lineup too. In addition, Savage had its name on powders quite early in the smokeless game and had them produced by DuPont; and ammunition bearing the Savage trademark was made by UMC (Remington). So what started out as a repeating Martini, etc., etc., actually grew into a large, thriving corporation.

But the Model 99 goes on. Sales of the rifle probably now surpass the two million plus mark (exact figures are not available). In 1960 Savage marked its millionth 99 with a special engraved rifle presented to the NRA. The 99 was built right to last a long time and is stimulating more and more interest from collectors. Currently, the 99 is offered in the C version in calibers 243 Winchester and 308 Winchester, cartridges that make the most sense in sales. A push button detachable four-shot clip has replaced the spool magazine. The barrel of this 8-pound repeater is 22 inches long. A checkered walnut stock with Monte Carlo comb lacks the distinctive schnabel forend of some previous 99s. The rifle wears open irons; but of course takes to a scope like a kid to candy. A rubber buttplate dresses the back end. The safety is on the top tang, far handier than its original location. But all in all, the 99 remains much the same firearm that Arthur W. Savage intended. And that in itself, almost a century after the 99 sprang from its inventor's mind, is remarkable.

MARLIN'S MODEL 1894
SIDE-EJECTING SAFETY

21

When the most famous sporting rifle in the world, the Winchester Model 1894, came out, it had a rival: the Marlin Model 1894. More accurately, the competition existed between the Marlin Model 1893 and the Winchester Model 94, for these two rifles are of the same action length and can chamber the same cartridges. But that competition is not the major reason for offering the reader a look at the fine old rifle. The Model 1894 Marlin was so good that it is yet with us, although there is another tale, a lesson in advertising.

While Winchester's Model '94 was associated with "the gun that won the West," Marlin's Models '93 and '94 were offered to the public of shooters as superior firearms, period. No fanfare. Marlin advertised

The compact Model 1894 carbine is easy to handle for woods shooting or camping trips.

The Marlin 1893 (above) and the 1894 were "sisters" in design. The '93 handled the longer 30-30 cartridges, while the '94 used the medium-range calibers.

its 1894 as the "Marlin Model 1894 Safety Repeating Rifle." The word "safety" was included in the name of the firearm because it was not entirely unknown at the time for a cartridge case to burst. This condition was bad, but not quite as dangerous as it seems unless the whole back half of the case gave way. A slight crack in the case would allow gas to jet around the action of the rifle, but chances of a shooter being seriously injured by a split cartridge case or minor head rupture were slim with low-pressure blackpowder rounds.

Nonetheless, Marlin liked the idea of reminding the buyer that the company's fine rifle ejected its spent case from the side of the action, not from the top as did the Winchester brand. Furthermore, the topmost portion of the action was solid steel with no ports of any kind. Later on, this factor would lend to easy telescopic sight mounting, another advantage over the top-ejecting Winchester rifle. However, at the time, scopes were not commonly placed on the average hunting rifle so the advantage was not an immediate one. The action of the Marlin was also stronger than the Winchester action. In fairness to the great Winchester rifle, however, it must be pointed out that the advantages of the Marlin at that particular time were not sufficient to cause a shooter to buy the Marlin over the Winchester. Furthermore, the modern Winchester is also side-ejecting and has a very strong action—strong enough to contain several different high-power cartridges.

A Marlin advertisement placed in the Schoverling, Daly & Gales catalogue of 1903 stressed the Marlin '94 as the "Safety" model. Chamberings were listed as the following metallics: 25-20 Winchester, 32-20 Winchester cartridge, 38-40 Winchester and 44-40 Winchester. These were all good cartridges in their respective niches. The catalogue noted that "Cartridges made for Colt Lightning and Winchester Rifles can be used." The Marlin 1894 was offered in various barrel lengths—24, 26, 28, 30 and 32 inches—in both round and octagonal configurations. Carbines were available with 15- or 20-inch barrels and half-magazines. Prices in this advertisement were in accord with barrel style and length—from $13.35 for a round 24-inch barrel to $19.35 for a 32-inch barrel; the octagonal barrel cost about a dollar more. Also noted in the advertisement was a Musket model with a 30-inch barrel for $14.25 and for $2 more an angular bayonet to fit it. Finally, the prospective buyer was assured that "All 1894 models have casehardened frames."

The story of the Model 1894 is of course intertwined with Marlin, the company, and the Model 1881, Marlin's first lever-action factory rifle. At 18 years of age, John Mahlon Marlin (born May 6, 1836) became apprenticed to a gunmaker. He became a professional pistol-maker and was so noted in the city directory of New Haven, Connecticut. In 1863 the directory showed Marlin residing at a boarding house at 130 James Street. By 1870 he was still listed as a pistol-maker, now living in his own home on Mansfield Street. He obtained patent No. 222,064 in 1879 for an underhammer, lever-action repeating rifle with tubular magazine, somewhat like a Spencer. Only one prototype was made and the rifle never saw production. However, it is clear that Marlin had other ideas for future rifles. Eventually, a rifle with "Marlin" engraved on it would have a side loading port. Ejection would come from the top and the action would be lever-operated. It would be of the "bolt" class, whereby a sliding bolt would hold the cartridge in place in the chamber.

That rifle was the Model 1881, the first lever-action longarm Marlin produced. It was chambered for two excellent black-powder cartridges, the 40-60 Winchester and 45-70 Government. This is an important point. Had the rifle been chambered

This shooter enjoys a session with the Marlin 1894 CL "Classic." Chambered for the 25-20, 32-20 and 218 Bee cartridges, the CL imparts only minimal recoil.

for lesser rounds, it no doubt would have remained a fine shooting machine; but in its original chamberings, the Marlin 1881 was a repeating powerhouse for the times. Some big bore single-shot rifles beat it for punch, but not by a wide margin when the 45-70 was the cartridge of comparison. The rifle had a tubular magazine that held 10 cartridges, so firepower was available with ballistic power. An octagonal barrel of 28 inches and a heavy receiver made the Marlin a big rifle that weighed 9 to 11 pounds, depending upon specifications. That was massive. Furthermore, when it first came out, it cost $32, which was a lot of money. Making the Model 1881 was not a cheap proposition and the price tag reflected a value, not an inflationary figure.

Jamming was an occasional problem, however, and the rounds did not feed with perfection from the tubular magazine into the action. The bulkiness of the rifle was also a drawback. The Marlin Model 1881 was eventually reduced in overall size and weight by virtue of shorter barrels. Barrels of 28 to 30 inches were shortened to 24 inches. In order to trim weight, a smaller receiver was designed with less bulky action. The improved rifles became the "40-60 Light," at about 8$1/4$ pounds, and the "45-70 Light," weighing about 8$1/2$ pounds. The new '81 was chambered for two superb blackpowder cartridges of the hour: the 38-55 Winchester and the 32-40 Winchester. The former provided excellent power for close- to mid-range deer-sized game and plenty of hunters used the round on moose-sized mammals as well. The 32-40 was always noted for accuracy and it, too, was amply powerful for deer and black bear. The Marlin Model 1881 turned out to be the first truly successful large caliber lever-action repeater on the market, and about 50,000 were sold, according to old, somewhat rusty records.

THE NEW SIDE EJECTION

John Marlin had further improvement in mind and wanted his lever-action repeater to feed rounds more reliably and smoothly. And he did not care for the top-ejection of fired cartridge cases. Precisely why he did not like this aspect is not known for certain because, as alluded to earlier, scope sights were not in vogue anyway. Besides, the '81 action was amply strong to contain any cartridge of the day, especially since the rifle was geared to shoot blackpowder rounds, which yielded modest breech pressures. But Mr. Marlin gathered engineers around him to work on improvement. The result was a new action—and a new rifle. Before long, the generic Marlin rifle was quite different from its predecessor, and equally different from its peers of Winchester lineage. Marlin Models

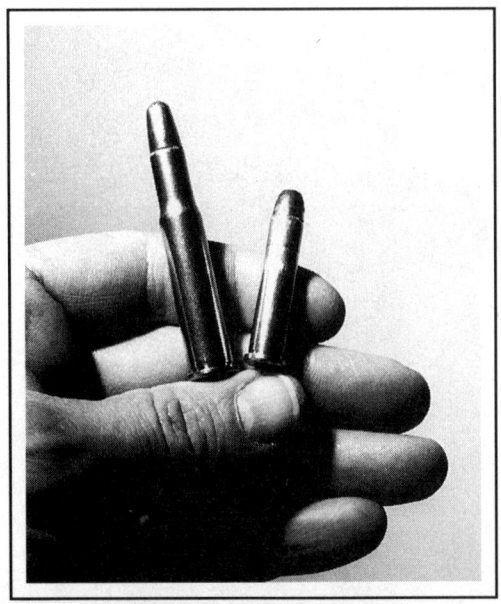

The 32-20 cartridge (right) chambered in the Marlin Model 1894 is small compared with the 30-30, but it is excellent for wild turkey, javelina and other small game hunting.

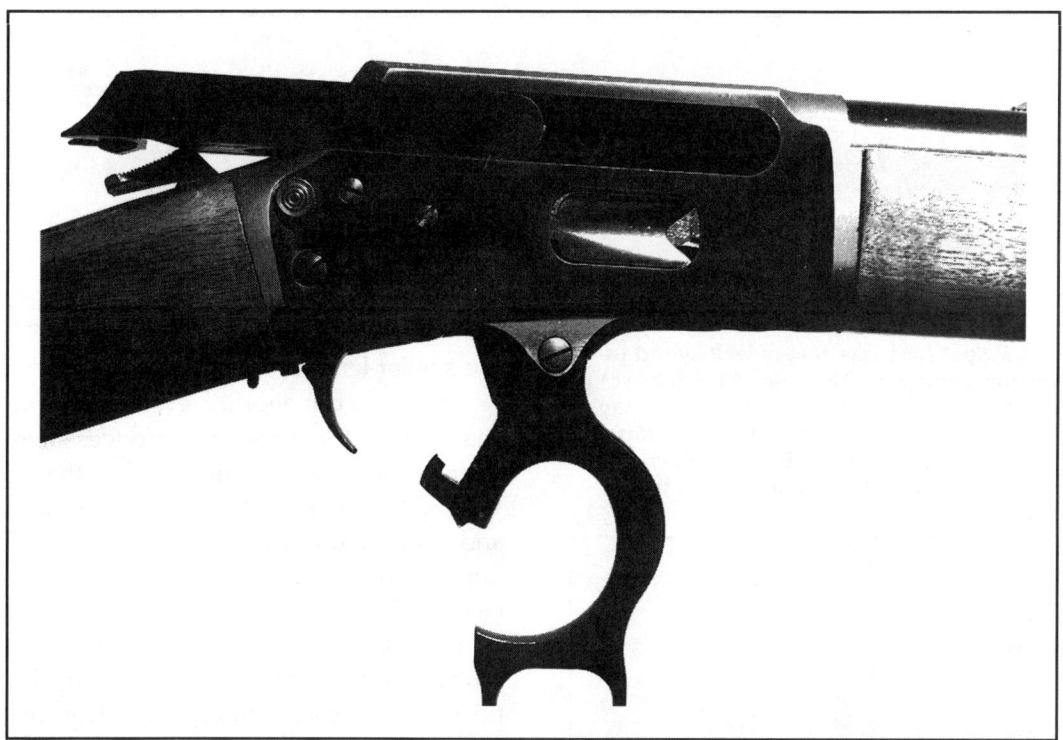

The open action of the Model 1894 reveals the solid top receiver whereby spent cartridge cases are expelled from the side.

1889, 1893, 1894 and 1895 were truly fine examples of the gunmaker's art, even if these guns were born, essentially, on an assembly line. They were entirely sound in all respects: accuracy, reliability, smooth-working and chamberings for a host of useful cartridges.

Marlin's original claim to lever-action fame was a repeater chambered for powerful cartridges. However, the ever-increasing popularity of smaller rounds, such as the 25-20, 32-20, 32-40 and others, took away much of the impetus attached to the Model 1881. Gun inventor L.L. Hepburn helped steer the Marlin company onto a different track. A Model 1888 Marlin surfaced, based on the Hepburn patent of the same year. The Hepburn rifle was clean-looking with simple lines. Chambered for the 32 WCF, 38 WCF and 44 WCF, it was top-ejecting like the Marlin Model 1881.

Hepburn returned to the drawing board and proceeded to create a new design that would be known as the Marlin Model 1889. It would mark the Marlin line forever. The Model 1889 was built in various dimensions, and again in calibers 32, 38 and 44 WCF. Some of the '89s were beautifully appointed, with fine wood, semi-pistol-grip stocks and handsome engraving on the receiver and other metal parts. The Model 1889 was unique. Truly, it was the immediate forerunner of the Model 1894 and other fine rifles. Now Marlin attached the name "New Safety Repeating Rifle" in deference to the solid top frame and side ejection.

The Model 1893 or '93 was an especially good rifle that emerged between the models 1889 and 1894. The '93 is not

MARLIN'S MODEL 1894 207

The Model 1894 was always well-suited to shorter cartridges. The new 1894S (above) is chambered in calibers 41 Magnum, 44 Magnum and 45 Colt. Federal Cartridge utilizes a 240-grain Hydra-Shok™ bullet (below) in its 44 Magnum loading, which adds up to one versatile round.

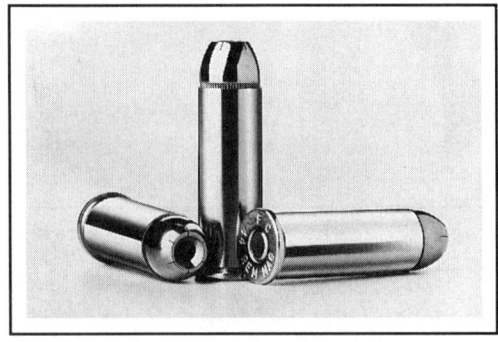

discussed here because the Model 336 coming up is a better representation of Marlin's 30-30. A more detailed discussion appears in Chapter 23.

However, the new Model 1894, the focus of this chapter, was essentially the Model 1893 designed to handle shorter rounds rather than longer ones. It was offered in calibers 25-20, 32-20, 38-40 and 44-40 with round or octagonal barrels. Hepburn's important improvements of a better locking bolt and distinctive two-piece firing pin were continued in the Model 1894. But the frame of the new '94 was shorter, which brought it back into the realm of 44-40 length cartridges. This was another reason the Marlin '94 could not compete with the Winchester 1894 chambered for the 30-30 and similar-length rounds.

Bringing out another lever-action rifle chambered for shorter cartridges may seem to have been a mistake, but the 32 WCF, 38 WCF and 44 WCF were popular and considered adequate by many deer hunters. The 38-40 and 44-40 were in fact ballistically strong enough for deer and even black bear at close range. Our modern viewpoint condemns the use of the little 32-20 for such game, and indeed the 32-20 is illegal in many hunting regions. The '93 and '94 can be considered a pair for our purposes, one for 30-30 and similar-length ammo, the other for shorter fodder. The Marlin Model 94 rifle was capable of carrying a large supply of ammo because of a long magazine tube coupled with short cartridges. The two-piece firing pin was also a built-in safety. Naturally, when the rifle was in the battery position with the action fully closed and locked, the two parts of the firing pin were in line. However, if the action was so much as slightly ajar, the pin parts automatically misaligned, rendering the rifle in a "safe" posture. In short, the '94 could not go off with the action open. The sliding bolt was also improved.

Another ad, this one in Montgomery Ward's catalogue for 1895, described the Model 1894 in glowing terms, as most ads do when trying to sell any product. The difference here was that the words were

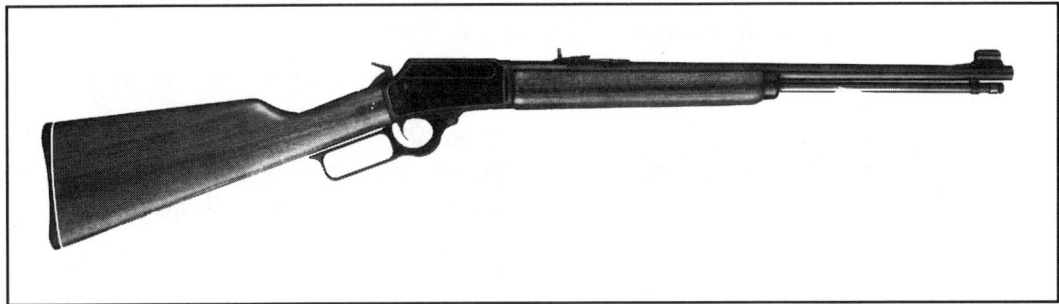

understatement concerning the fine Marlin sporting piece. The "New Marlin Rifle," promised the ad, is "An entirely new model. Every rifle warranted. Model 1889 and '94. The easiest working and handiest rifle in the market." It was all true. "Ejects the empty shell at the side instead of at the top. The newest feature in repeaters." The Montgomery Ward notice was highly accurate, except for the statement "Simple in construction." That promise strayed off the trail of total honesty. In fact, all lever-actions were more complicated in design than the single-shot rifles of the era. A falling block is one thing. A lever-operated system that has to cock a hammer, expel a fired cartridge case, bring a new round up from the magazine, lock the round in the chamber, and so forth, is hardly "simple."

Wards called the new Marlin accurate, which indeed it was. The wish book company suggested that the main reason for accuracy was the Model 94's use of the Ballard system of rifling. Marlin was, in effect, Ballard, and Ballard was Marlin at the time anyway, so this statement rings of truth. The '94 was offered in various choices. One was the 32 WCF, which carried 15 rounds, had a 24-inch octagonal barrel and weighed 6½ pounds. The ad also indicated the chamberings for the 25-20 WCF, 38 WCF and 44 WCF. The Model 1894 Marlin hovered around 7 pounds in

The new Model 1894M (above) is chambered for the 22 Winchester Magnum Rimfire cartridge. This round (below), offered by Federal Cartridge, employs a 50-grain hollow-point bullet. Depending on ammo brand, the load may move at between 1800 and 2100 fps.

weight. Price in 1895 from Wards was $12 to $14. If a modern shooter had a time machine to scoot him back to 1895 for a while, he'd soon understand why the Marlin 1894 was well-received, in spite of the fact that Winchester's rifle of the same model designation, though of course a different rifle, would out-sell it.

The '94 proved so good that it was updated in 1969, and as this is written the Marlin 1894 remains available. The Marlin Company brought back the Model 1894 rifle because it is suited to the modern 44 Remington Magnum handgun cartridge. The tradition of having a rifle and sidearm

> ## THE MARLIN MODEL 1894 AT A GLANCE
>
> **Period of Manufacture:** 1894 to 1935; reissued 1969 to date
> **Calibers:** Original, 25-20 Win., 32-20 Win., 38-40 Win., 44-40 Win.; modern, 22 WMR, 357 Magnum, 41 Magnum, 44 Magnum, 45 Colt (also available in 25-20 and 32-20)
> **Magazine Capacity:** 15 rounds (full magazine); 6-shot half-magazine available
> **Action:** Strong lever-action repeater with solid top receiver and side ejecting feature
> **Barrel:** Of steel, blued. Rifle, 24, 26, 28, 30, 32 inches; round or octagonal; Carbine, 15 or 20 inches, round; Musket, 30 inches with angular bayonet
> **Weight (approx.):** 6½ to 7 pounds; Baby Carbine, 5½ pounds
> **Sights:** Open; buckhorn rear; blade front
> **Stock:** Straight-grip plain stock of American walnut; a few special order engraved fancy-grain walnut; varnished
> **Finish:** Color casehardened frame, receiver, hammer (later blued), lever, buttplate; blued barrel and magazine
> **Variations:** Carbine with full magazine, saddle ring on left side of receiver; Baby Carbine with half-magazine; Musket with angular bayonet. Various options—checkering, buttplates, engravings, etc.

chambered for exactly the same cartridge (such as the 44-40 Winchester rifle and 44-40 Colt revolver in the 1800s) has never died. The Marlin people knew this. So the Model 1894 is back in the saddle again, literally as well as figuratively—almost a century after its inception. In caliber 44 Magnum the little carbine offers plenty of close-range power for deer and similar game. And chamberings have expanded. From 1969 through 1984 the Model 1984 was chambered for the 44 Magnum; in 1979 the 357 Magnum round was added. Later the 41 Magnum, 22 Magnum Rimfire and the 45 Colt cartridge (often incorrectly called the 45 Long Colt) were offered.

In 1988 Marlin fans got a big surprise: the company once again chambered its Model 1894 in calibers 25-20 and 32-20. A step backward? Not so. Many hunters have found that these two old-time cartridges are just right for certain applications, especially close-range hunting of javelina in the Southwest and wild turkey wherever a rifle is allowed for that sport. Since neither cartridge has high bullet speed, the two low-intensity rounds are not destructive of meat. Yet they harvest modest-sized game well because each uses bullets far heavier than those associated with 22 Magnum Rimfire, a cartridge allowed by law on these species in many areas. Furthermore, objectionable recoil in a Model 1894 Marlin rifle chambered for the 25-20 or 32-20 exists only in the mind of the shooter. The rifle chambered for these mild cartridges is easy to shoot with accuracy.

The Marlin Model 1894 rifle is back in the hands of American sportsmen as a newly manufactured rifle. And it wears a scope sight as naturally as any of today's bolt-action models. This is why it was chosen, from a fine firearms company with a long line of great rifles, as representative for this book. If the '94 is considered a short-action version of the '93, which is entirely plausible, it remains true that the fast-action high-capacity rifle has yet to reach its zenith—for modern ammunition has made today's Marlin 1894 an entirely adequate, easy-handling, woods deer rifle.

THE 1895 MARLIN
PUNCH WITH REPEATABILITY

22

Consider that you are at the helm, steering the ship of an organization called the Marlin Firearms Company. You boast many good rifles in your lineup, but the rifle that started it all is defunct. Yet, that rifle offered something few firearms of the era—the late 1800s—could offer the big game hunter: a repeater with lots of power. Yes, the Marlin Model 1881 had it all—almost. Calibers 40-60 Marlin and especially 45-70 Marlin (the company did attach its name to these two rounds) in rapid fire gave the big game hunter a lot of confidence. However, the Model 1881 had flaws. Marlin's trademark turned to side-ejection and a solid-top receiver. But if the 1881 were updated, the company would once again have a reliable powerhouse re-

The improved New Model 1895ss in caliber 45-70 Government.

peater. The year is 1896. You have an exceptional rifle in the Model 1893. If you're guiding Marlin's future through the waters of progress, you consider altering the great '93. And that's just what the company did.

The result was the Model 1895, one of the best rifles to emanate from the famous plant. Recall that the Sharps rifle was so efficient in its day that a large-caliber Sharps remains viable in our own time. The same praise can be bestowed upon the original Model 1895. It was so good when

Marlin used this logo emphasizing solid top receiver and side ejection in its catalogue advertisements between 1908 and 1915.

it appeared in 1896 that it was revived by Marlin to serve serious and dedicated marksmen of the 20th century.

Essentially, the Model 1895 is a Model 1893, which allows a double-duty approach to the rifle. Many of the characteristics of the '93 also pertain to the '95. Because the '95 is so much a '93 in design, it's no surprise that the germ for the '95 action is the work of inventor L.L. Hepburn. The Marlin 1895 is basically an expanded Marlin Model 1893. A larger receiver, larger barrel and larger magazine give the '95 its claim to fame, which is the chambering of excellent cartridges: the 38-56, 40-65 (the Marlin 40-60 under a different name), 40-82, the 45-70 loaded with either 405- or 500-grain bullets and the 45-90. As usual, these designations refer to caliber and powder charge. In 1897 the 40-72 WCF cartridge was added to the Model 1895's list of chamberings. Much later, in 1912, the rifle enjoyed another chambering for one of the best medium-range big cartridges of the era, the smokeless powder 33 Winchester, a round that gave rise to the even more potent 348 Winchester (see Chapter 16 on the Model 71 Winchester).

One of the reasons the Marlin Model 1895 is included among the great rifles of all time is the interchangeability of its cartridges. The Marlin catalogue of 1896 reveals the various names attached to a single cartridge of the period. The reason for different names for the same cartridge stems from the fact that companies liked to lay claim to a round as their own. They got away with this because apparently few restrictions denied a manufacturer the right to call a cartridge its own, even if no one at the company actually came up with the design initially.

Another more obvious reason for various names attached to a round is the old-time method of naming a cartridge based on the specific load. For example, the 45-120-550 Sharps was a 45-caliber round loaded with 120 grains weight of blackpowder behind a bullet weighing 550 grains. What was the 45-100-550? The same cartridge of course with the identical case, but loaded with 100 grains of black powder. The use of smokeless powder sometimes brought a cartridge name change. The 32-40 High Pressure and 38-55 High Pressure cartridges were in fact the 32-40 Winches-

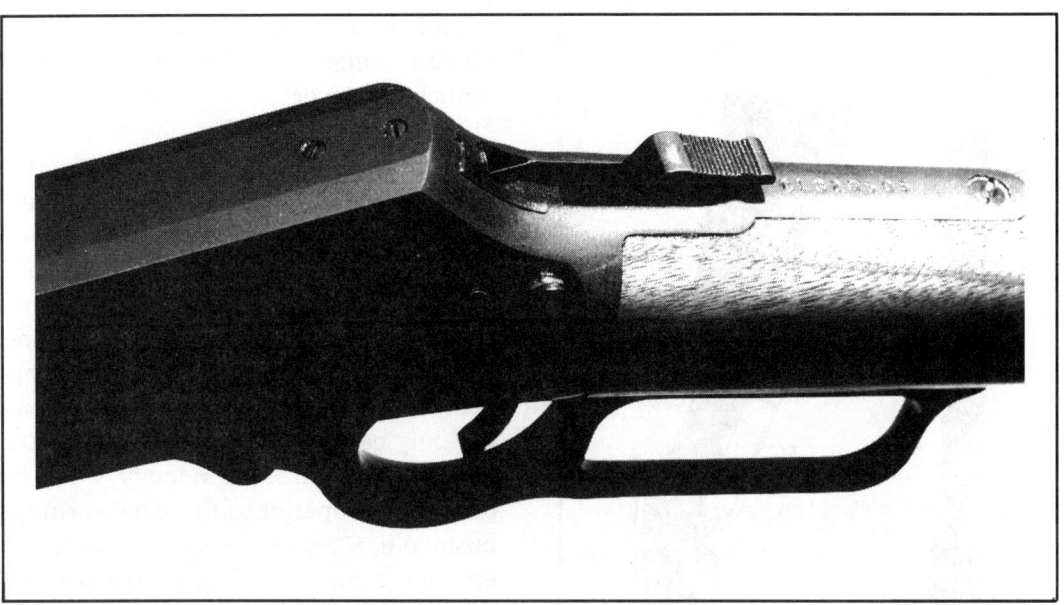

The solid top receiver, this one drilled and tapped for a scope sight, was advertised from the beginning as a safety-minded design. It would actually have more merit when scopes became popular.

ter and 38-55 Winchester, but in smokeless loadings. In this instance, however, the latter number does not indicate the powder charge. It remains a part of the nomenclature only because the cartridges were so-named to begin with, but certainly not because the 32-40 load carried 40 grains of smokeless powder or the 38-55 held 55 grains. Not that the latter figure never represented a smokeless powder load. As we learn from studying the 30-30 cartridge, it was designed from the beginning for smokeless powder. In this instance, the latter figure does represent a smokeless powder charge, for the 30-30 was originally loaded with approximately 30 grains of smokeless powder.

The 1896 Marlin catalogue also listed the 40-82, which was the 40-82 WCF (Winchester Center Fire) round. In another loading it was called the 40-70-330, meaning 40 caliber, 70 grains of black powder and a 330-grain bullet, while the cartridge case—the 40-82 Winchester—remained the same. The 40-65 Winchester was identical to a round Marlin called the 40-60 Marlin. Therefore the 40-65 WCF and 40-60 Marlin employed the same cartridge case. The 45-70 was of course the 45-70 U.S. Government cartridge, but this fine round picked up many different handles, including: 45-70 Marlin, 45-70 Winchester, 45-70-405 U.S. Government, 45-70-500 U.S. Government, the 45-70-330 Gould's Express, 45-70-350 and 45-70-285. The reduction of bullet weights in the 45-70 suggests an attempt to increase muzzle velocity. The only way to accomplish this with black powder would be the use of a lighter projectile. After all, the cartridge case was already about as full as it could get. No more black powder could be imparted therein. So the only way to boost speed was to cut back on bullet weight. Reason: a slightly flatter trajectory. It is doubtful that in actual field practice the lighter bul-

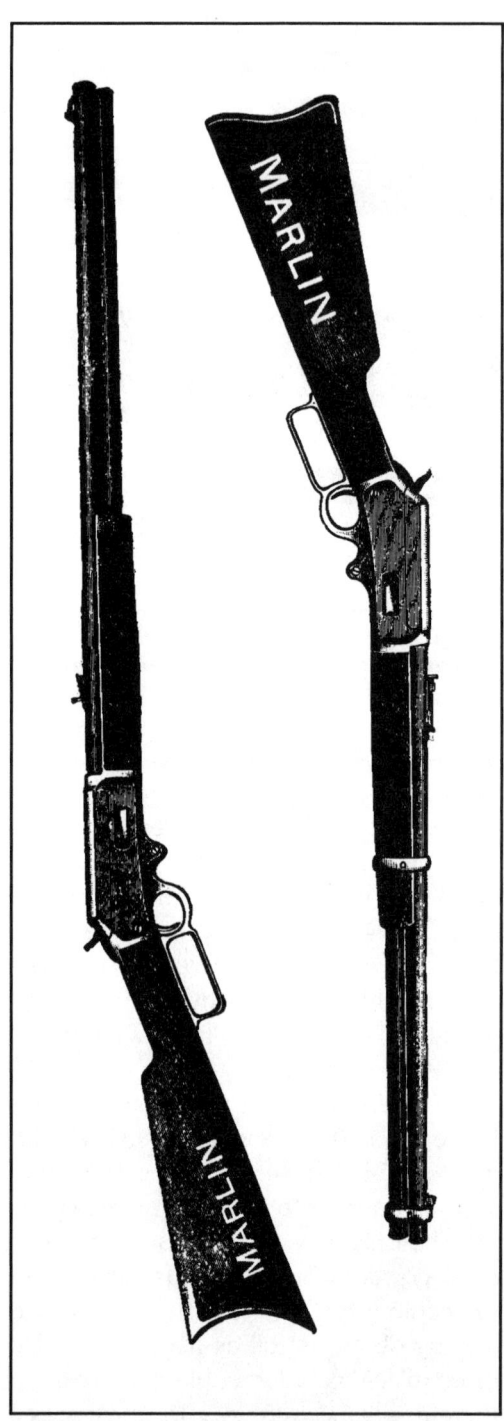

The Marlin Model 1895 in rifle version (left) with crescent-shaped buttplate and various lengthed barrels and carbine (right) that came with 15- or 22-inch barrel.

lets retained enough extra velocity at even modest range to offer much greater "shocking power."

One more cartridge—the 45-90—was mentioned in the catalogue in connection with the Marlin Model 1895. This round was also known as the 45-90 WCF, the 45-85-350, the 45-82-405 and the 45-85-300 Express. Although the term "Express" referred to what the ammo manufacturer deemed an especially potent load, it appears that a little extra muzzle velocity was the only gain. The fine 45-90 with a 500-grain bullet, even at low velocity, would be ballistically superior to the same cartridge pushing a 300-grain bullet at what would amount to no more than a modest speed increase. Arguably, the 45-90 was not worlds ahead of the 45-70 in practical big game harvesting. However, it is equally undeniable that the round was capable of containing a full 20 grains more propellant than its smaller brother. And if the "Buffalo Rifle" in caliber 45-120-550 was a thumper, then surely the 45-90 with a heavy bullet was in the same league. The difference was that the 45-90 chambered in the Model 1895 Marlin offered punch with repeatability. A hunter didn't shoot once, then go about reloading. A hunter fired, worked the lever and shot again. . . and again. Furthermore, a practiced rifleman did not have to remove the '95 from his shoulder to reload. Sure, there was recoil, but it was minimal. And a hunter could easily retain the rifle's buttplate against his shoulder without lowering it after a shot. The lever was flipped down-up smartly and a new round brought into battery. With little loss of sight picture and hasty regaining of that picture, the '95 man sent with accuracy another missile on course—and not just any projectile, but a heavy bullet backed by a decent powder charge.

Various styles of the Marlin Model 1895 rifle were offered to outdoorsmen: the standard model; a carbine with 15- or 22-inch round barrel; and a takedown model credited to L.L. Hepburn. In its takedown mode, the '95 was reduced to the length of the barrel, fitting into a short case for easy transportation. This version could be procured with a round, octagonal or half-octagonal barrel in lengths of up to 32 inches, and in calibers 38-56, 40-65, 40-70, 40-82, 45-70 and 45-90 as well as the smokeless 33 Winchester. Furthermore, certain barrels were interchangeable on one given action. As Marlin's advertisement quoted, "... by purchasing extra barrel parts as many as seven take-down rifles on one action" were possible.

Marlin proclaimed that its takedown Model 1895 was "Strong as the regular rifle, no looseness, no danger of coming apart owing to accident or carelessness. No wear. No adjustments necessary. Can be placed in a 'Victoria' case. As light and compact to carry as a shotgun." Words of truth—mostly. The boast goes perhaps a little too far in that due to design and in spite of an ingenious "locking cam" that was turned into place to secure the barrel, there was some wear. The takedown model could not be counted on to remain tight forever, whereas the regular Marlin '95 could. However, the takedown was entirely reliable. A hunter on the go could pack his '95 into a small space, and after assembly he had a powerful short- and medium-range repeating rifle ready for action. The rifle was well-made.

The Winchester company believed infringement had occurred regarding this takedown model, however. The firm sued Marlin for copying what they insisted was their own takedown system. The courts said otherwise, though, and Winchester lost. Marlin continued to produce takedown rifles exactly as they had before the law suit.

It is only fair to point out that one reason Marlin and other companies were

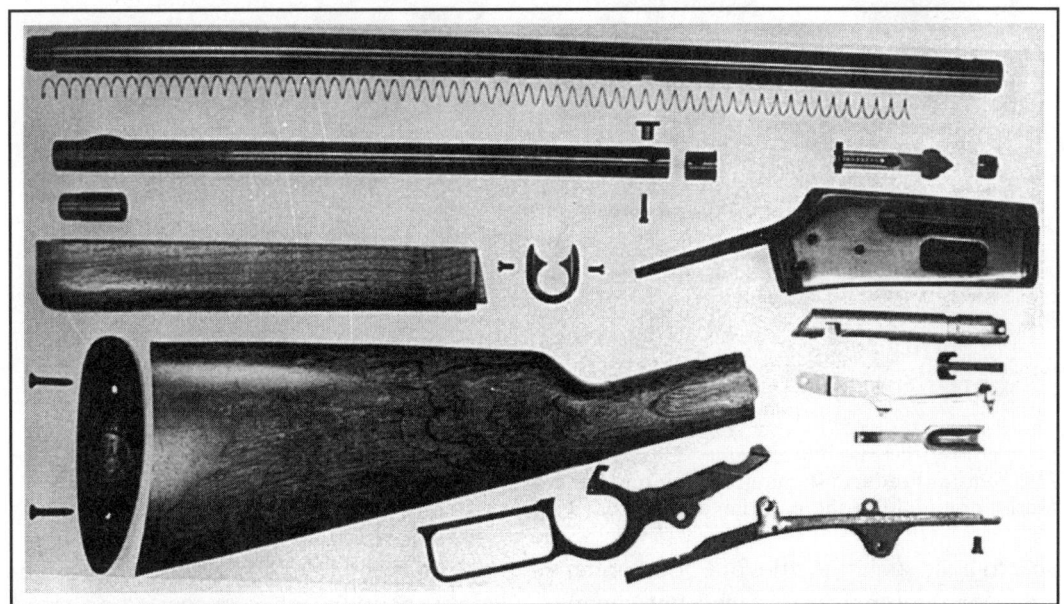

The breakdown of the "New Model 1895" shows just how few parts constitute the modern rifle.

This famous Frederic Remington painting became a symbol of Marlin. Entitled "Danger Ahead," Marlin copyrighted the painting and has used it since 1900.

able to build such fine rifles at a good price, even for the times, was skilled but cheap 19th-century and early 20th-century labor. Experts at all working levels produced high-level execution, while expecting no more than "a living" from plying their trades.

This was true of machinists as well as engravers. Marlin could proudly proclaim, as the company did in an 1896 advertisement: "Marlin. The only Repeaters with SOLID TOP RECEIVERS, SIDE EJECTION, BALLARD BARRELS." High quality inside and out was the byword of the company.

The 1895 enjoyed all of the special appointments associated with other Marlin rifles, including beautiful engraving of the receiver. It was ideal for such work because of the receiver's large flat surface, something later bolt-action rifles would certainly lack. In general, hammers, levers and steel buttplates were color casehardened, not blued—a handsome touch. At no extra cost, the customer could request a blued receiver. Barrels and magazine tubes were blued, of course. The straight-grip walnut stock could be ordered with semi-pistol grip, which was "clean" and did not interrupt the flow of the stock. Fine checkering was also an option. The crescent or rifle-style buttplate was the normal shape for the steel version, but as an option a rubber buttplate was also offered—same price, same shape. The standard carbine had a sling ring on the left side of the receiver, but a customer could have this touch left off.

Length of pull—the distance from the trigger to the center of the buttstock—was on the short side. The rifle stock was somewhat short because it allowed a shooter to snap the '95 to his shoulder quickly without hang-up of any kind, on clothing or the shoulder itself. While a shorter length of pull might allow the face to ride too far forward on the comb of the stock, shooters got used to holding their heads back so that this problem did not arise. The 1895 for its size was therefore fast-handling—another plus for the rifle.

Sights followed the simple traditional pattern. The shooter of today is scope-conscious, or at least he is aware that a micrometer aperture (peep) sight affords an excellent aiming device. Therefore,

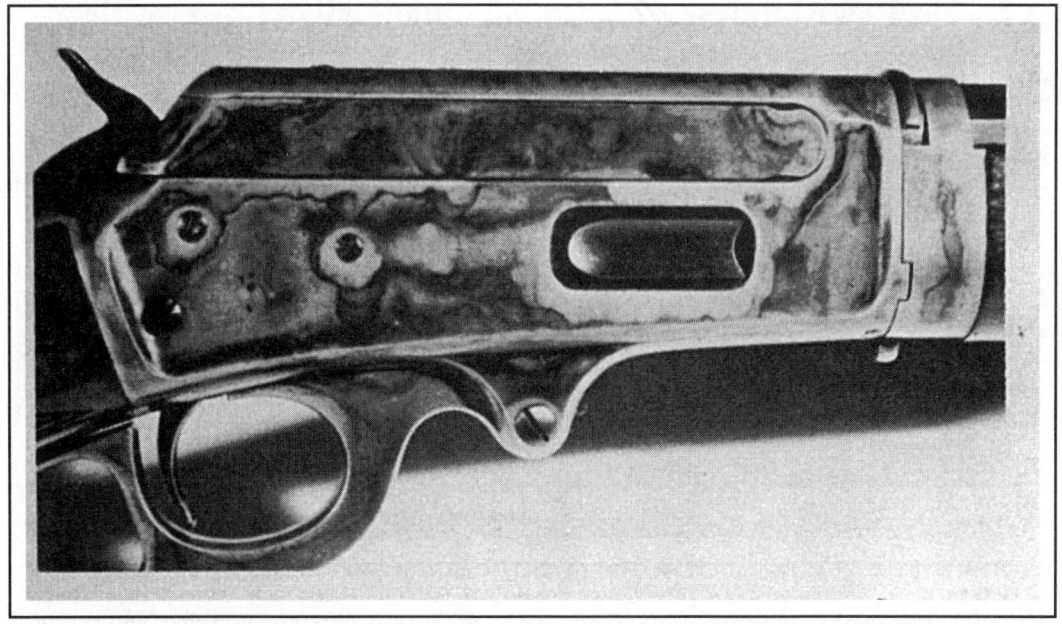

Close-up view of the ornate pattern of Marlin's case-color finish on the Model 1895.

when he looks at what seems a crude open rear sight and simple blade or bead front, he may tend to lift an eyebrow. The ordinary open sight of the 1895 was entirely adequate for big game hunting, however, when the rifle was in the hands of a seasoned outdoorsman. After all, this was not a long-range rifle. It was a short- to medium-range hunting tool. The usual sights were absolutely adequate to the task assigned the rifle—big game hunting. Furthermore, the top tang was also drilled and tapped for a tang peep sight for those who desired an additional aiming device. Over the years, the Marlin company provided many different styles: one employed a vernier gauge; some were large, others small. Many had large-disc/small-aperture arrangements, which indicates target shooting as their purpose. The Lyman Rear Sight, a tang aperture with screw-up/screw-down elevation adjustment, could be fitted to a Marlin as well.

The top of the receiver also had two drilled and tapped holes for L.L. Hepburn's top-mounted receiver sight. Called the Marlin Combination Receiver Sight, it was especially interesting because the peep disc was of the folding variety. This sight offered numerous advantages, because the folding leaf provided a peep sight or an open sight, depending upon its posture. It also offered

The August 1912 supplement to Marlin's 1911 catalogue highlights the "new" Model 1895 Special Lightweight rifle in 33 High Power Smokeless caliber. With shotgun rubber buttplate and 5-shot capacity, it weighed only 7³/₄ pounds.

> ## The Marlin Model 1895 at a Glance
>
> **Period of Manufacture:** 1896 to 1917 (New Model 1895 introduced in 1972)
> **Calibers:** 38-56, 40-65, 40-72, 40-82, 45-70, 45-90; 33 WCF Smokeless introduced in 1912
> **Magazine Capacity:** 5 or 8 shots; half- or full magazine
> **Action:** Lever-action repeater with side ejection, solid top receiver
> **Barrel:** Of steel, later special "smokeless" steel, blued. Rifle, 20, 24, 26, 28, 30, 32 inches; round, octagonal or half-octagonal. Carbine, 15 or 22 inches, round.
> **Weight (approx.):** 7 to 7 3/4 pounds, depending on barrel length
>
> **Sights:** Open; buckhorn-type rear (Rocky Mountain style); German silver blade or bead front. Special Hepburn-designed Marlin Combination Receiver Sight with folding leaf.
> **Stock:** Straight-grip plain stock of American walnut (or black walnut); checkering on special orders; varnished; some semi-pistol grip models
> **Finish:** Color casehardened receiver, hammers, levers and steel buttplates; blued barrels and magazine
> **Variations:** Solid frame or takedown. Some engraved models, sling ring attached to carbine receivers; buttplate options, etc.

a long sight radius (distance between rear and front sight). In addition, because it was mounted on top of the receiver in front of the hammer, in no way could the rifle's recoil drive the peep sight into the eye of the marksman, an accident that could occur with the tang sight. Nor did the sight get in the way of the shooter's grip on the wrist of the rifle as a tang sight might do if a marksman happened to grasp the wrist where the tang sight was usually placed. Rifles manufactured after 1903 were automatically drilled and tapped for this sight. Early 1895s could be fitted with the sight after the fact. Marlin charged $3.25 for the sight, 30 cents to drill the holes and 60 cents to tap them. The words "Marlin Safety" that appeared on the top of the receiver were stamped forward after 1903, so that if a receiver sight was installed, the words would not be obscured by the sight.

In the early years, several thousand Model 1895s were sold; hunters didn't run out to buy them. And they were improved along the way. The sub-model of 1912 was quite special. One of the special lightweight models, it stood apart from other '95s because it was chambered for the fine 33 Winchester smokeless round. Of course, the barrel steel had to withstand the higher pressures generated by smokeless powder, and so the 24-inch round barrels (later 22) were of the "Special Smokeless Steel" type. This unique Marlin '95 wore a half-magazine with five-shot capacity in takedown or solid frame and weighed only 7 3/4 pounds. Its shotgun-style buttplate was fashioned of rubber. In solid frame, it sold for $18.50; in takedown, $22.

While this highly functional version of the '95 was excellent due to design and construction, it was of course the 33 Winchester cartridge that made the rifle even more desirable. Marlin said, "The .33 caliber cartridge is one of the most powerful of all modern high power cartridges, throwing a heavy bullet with extremely high velocity (over 2,050 feet per second), very flat trajectory, deep penetration and tremendous shocking and killing power. It quickly brings down moose, bear, deer and all other big game." More on the 33

Winchester is offered to the reader in Chapter 10 on the Winchester Model 1886. Ben Lilly, the famous bear and lion hunter, carried an '86 chambered for the 33 Winchester. But what did Marlin mean by a big bullet? A missile of 200 grains weight. Velocity in the 2000 fps domain was later increased to about 2200 fps for the 33 Winchester. It was a reliable cartridge chambered in a strong and highly reliable Model 1895. That is why the original contention stated early in this chapter is easily defended: the '95 chambered for the 33 Winchester could still be relied on for medium-range big game hunting. High velocity? Flat trajectory? For the times, yes. Today, no. However, a Model 1895 chambered for the 33 Winchester was a solid 200-yard hunting rifle when it first arrived on the scene—and it still is today.

The Rocky Mountain rear sight and German silver blade front sight continued as prominent on the special 1895 in 33 Winchester. The barrel continued to bear the words "Special Smokeless Steel" on the left-hand side. A bead front sight later replaced the blade. Straight- and semi-pistol-grip stocks were options, as were many extras, including barrel lengths from 15 to 32 inches, full-length or half-magazine tubes, even shorter ones. Incidentally, certain examples of 1895s go against catalogue specifications. That may be due to special orders or experimental models intended to affect improvements.

Toward the end of production, only the 33 Winchester and 45-70 calibers were chambered in the '95. Then it was gone. However, from 1972 to 1979, it was put back on line as the New Model 1895, a lever-action in caliber 45-70. In 1980, a New Model 1895S was offered to hunters until 1983, when another improved version, the New Model 1895SS emerged. Today, the '95 is not truly represented, although Marlin's Model 444SS Lever-Action Sporter is available. Chambered for the 444 Marlin cartridge, the 444SS has a 22-inch barrel rifled with Marlin's excellent Micro-Groove system. It's a five-shot rifle with tubular magazine. Although the 444 is essentially a Model 336, not '95, the spirit of the Marlin Model 1895 rifle lives on in a powerful big bore repeater made by the same company. Marlin's Model 1895 has proved that it was too good to fade away.

THE MARLIN MODEL 336
LONG LASTING, NO NONSENSE

23

According to the Marlin Firearms Company, its "Models 39 and 336 are the oldest shoulder arm designs in the world still being produced." The Marlin Model 1891 preceded the current Model 39, as the Marlin Model 1893 rifle preceded the current Model 336. A little Marlin history helps unravel the 336 story. Recall that John Mahlon Marlin opened a gun shop in New Haven, Connecticut, in 1870 and allied himself with the right inventors to create solid, reliable repeating firearms of high quality. When Marlin died in 1901, the business was carried on by his two sons. Mahlon Henry Marlin, born in 1864, took over as president and treasurer of the company in July of 1901. He acted as plant manager, a position his father had enjoyed.

The Marlin Model 336T "Texan" in 30-30 Win. caliber with traditional side ejection.

John Howard Marlin, born in 1876, was vice president and secretary of the company.

Business continued as usual, with Mahlon ever-interested in new manufacturing techniques and product improvement. Yale graduate John Howard was a salesman and traveler. He enjoyed shooting matches and social gatherings. The brothers made what appears to be a good team. Their interests were apparently diverse enough to compliment each other. Expansion of the Marlin company began with the acquisition of the Ideal Manufacturing Company on May 16, 1910. Although not a bad move, had the company expanded within its own walls, the future may have been brighter. Marlin was, of course, a purveyor of many goods besides guns: baby buggies, shaving cream, game recipe publications, gun cases, slings, gun oil, rust retardants, cleaning kits and more. When the demands of arms manufacture prevailed at the beginning of World War I, the Marlin company was not equipped to mass produce the guns required of warfare. They turned down a huge contract for rifles because they did not feel that the plant was capable of filling the order with any immediacy. The brothers did not wish to expand their operation with new buildings and machines, probably for fear that after the fracas, Marlin would be left with too many buildings to maintain and costly machinery they might not be able to sell.

In spite of all the sidelines, Marlin was truly a sporting arms company. Marlin continued with *The Ideal Handbook*, a loading manual considered a bible to

The Model 336CS carbine version is available in 30-30 or 35 Remington with full magazine and 20-inch barrel with Micro-Groove® rifling. The carbine can wear a hooded front sight and open rear sight (above) or can be scope mounted (below). Hunters have learned that even in the brush, a scope sight is a plus.

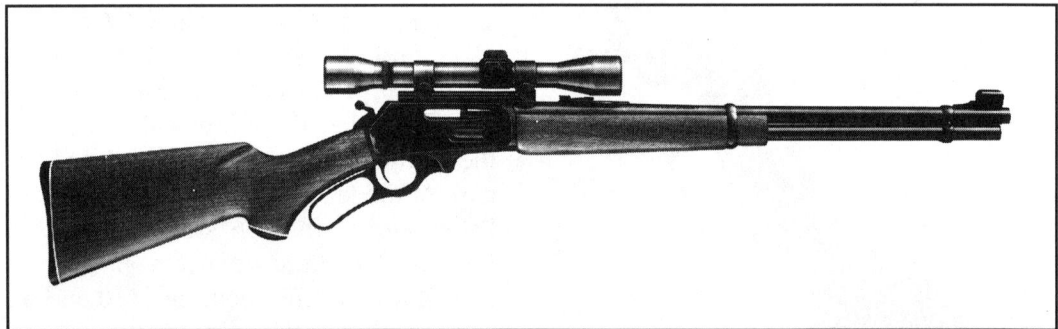

handloaders of the era, which also included non-firearms products. It is important to remember that the brothers seemed to prefer a continuation of the company much as it had been run in the past, in spite of company expansion. However, Marlin was not in tune with the times, and the family business came to an end.

Perhaps the purchase of the Ideal Manufacturing Company, which was later sold to Lyman in 1925, and the manufacture of other hardware items, including a combination shoehorn/buttonhook, decoy anchors and handcuffs, had something to do with the Marlin brothers selling out in 1915 to a New York syndicate. The company was renamed the Marlin Rockwell Corporation. Machine guns for war were the business of the new Marlin firm. These guns, created for allied forces, were turned out in great numbers. But at the close of the war, the need for machine guns sank as peace settled in.

Rockwell was no sporting arms manufacturer, for sporting guns were just not their cup of tea. The company reeled under the impact of peacetime desires for hunting rifles rather than fighting guns. By 1923, Marlin was on the auction block. The story goes that the auction was well-attended by only children and a few stray dogs, except for one serious fellow, Frank Kenna. He bid $100 for the Marlin operation—and got it. However, Kenna also had to accept the liability of a $100,000 mortgage that went along with the purchase of the firm. Frank Kenna Sr. became president of the new Marlin Firearms Company, a post he held until 1947. That year Roger Kenna took over and remained president until 1959 when Frank Kenna Jr. assumed the position.

The name "Marlin" was once again on sporting rifles, although it is true that in 1936 another high-selling item on the market—a razor blade—bore the Marlin name. Marlin razor blades sold by the millions, but that aspect of the business was eclipsed by sporting rifles after Frank Kenna Jr. took over. By the close of the 1960s, Marlin razor blades were no more. The new Marlin company had only to reach back into its previous history to bring out great sporting rifles. They intelligently built upon that glorious past rather than proceed with brand new designs from the drawing board. They also continued to produce under the aegis of quality and fine design.

THE MODEL 336 TAKES SHAPE

There were five models in the 336 family: the Model 1893, followed by the 93 (mostly a name change) and the Model 1936, then the 36 and finally the 336.

The Model '81 had locked up with the action closed. The front portion of the finger lever came to rest against a shoulder at the front of the bolt. Marlin's Model of 1889 had incorporated side-port loading, side-ejection of the spent case and a solid top receiver. The parent rifle of the 336, of course, had these same traits. The Model 1893 was good enough to continue in very much the same mechanical form for a very long time, one day to become the Model 336.

A careful look at the Model 1936 reveals stock, forearm and sight changes over the Model 1893, but in truth nothing startlingly new. These almost cosmetic alterations were instituted to compete with the Winchester Model 1894. A fluted comb stock was added to improve its appearance. The new pistol grip also "modernized" its looks. That this feature aided shooting is debatable. Some marksmen prefer the hand-filling effect of the pistol grip, while others find this feature of no practical value. The forend became a semi-beavertail in place of the previous straight version. The flattened underside of the forearm proved helpful in shooting from a solid rest, which some shooters believed gave you a better hold on it. Meanwhile, not everyone liked the larger forearm. A stranglehold on the forearm does nothing to improve smoothness of swing for a moving shot, and many expert offhand marksmen prefer a looser grip on the front portion of the rifle stock. But these changes were effected to make the Model 1936 more competitive in the marketplace. The new sights were supposed to improve aim, but that, too, is arguable. The front sight, noted as the Huntsman model, became a ramp fitted into a dovetail notch and on the ramp was a silver aiming bead. The rifle was also virtually jam-proof and the trigger was good (not great).

Accuracy of Marlin's 1936 and the later 336 was always good, with a potential for superb bullet-clustering. Out-of-the-box Marlins created group sizes entirely adequate for hunting big game or small. Walter Rodgers, a noted hunter/author, said: "I was using a .30-30 Marlin rifle, and had repeatedly shot heads from wild turkeys with it." L.R. Wallack built a special rifle using a Marlin Model 336 action. His rifle had a 27 3/4-inch heavy barrel of 15/16-inch diameter. It was a Marlin Micro-Groove™ barrel supplied by Marlin. A trademark of Marlin, Micro-Groove™ rifling used multiple lands and grooves to impart minimal engraving of the bullet surface, while enabling the bullet to spin on its axis. Chambered for the 30-30 Winchester round, not some hotshot bench cartridge, the rifle created many witnessed groups of only one-half inch center to center at 100 yards. I bench-tested a Marlin rifle that was rebarreled by

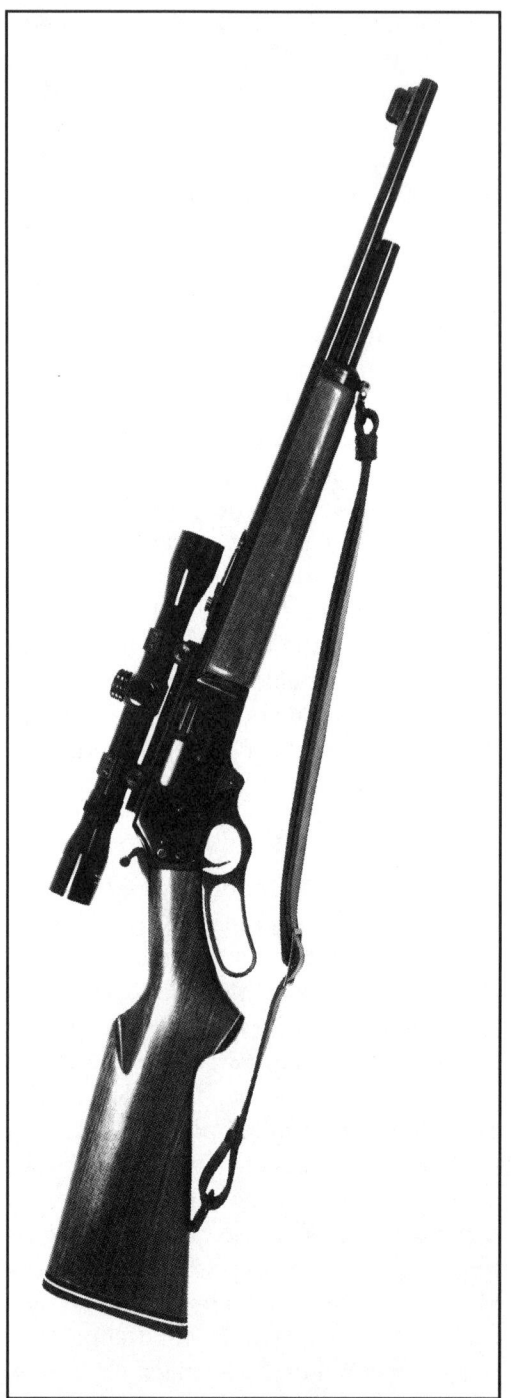

The Model 336ER (Extra Range) was chambered for the powerful 356 Winchester cartridge. It was offered for a few years in the mid-1980s.

Dale Storey. Although the barrel was not of target design, the rifle grouped its bullets into under an inch for five shots at 100 yards.

The function of the 1936 and 336 was (and is) operator-simple because the mechanism takes care of all the work. Upon pulling the trigger, the visible hammer is released from the full-cock posture to fall forward, where it smacks the back of the firing pin, driving the nose of the firing pin into the primer of the cartridge. This detonates the primer, which in turn ignites the powder charge. To fire again, the finger lever is flicked down-up. As the lever is cranked downward, the bolt is unlocked, so that it can slide rearward. As the bolt slides back, the spent cartridge is expelled out to the side of the rifle. The bolt has pushed the hammer rearward into the fully cocked mode. The down-thrust of the lever has also brought a cartridge up from the magazine upon a carrier, presenting the cartridge to the open chamber of the rifle. The lever is returned to its original or closed-action position with an upward snap. It is the up-thrust of the lever that causes the forward movement of the bolt, which drives the cartridge into the chamber. In the closed station, the action is locked. Cocked and locked, the Model 1936 (or 336) is ready to fire again with a pull on the trigger.

The Marlin catalogue of 1936 showed three primary examples of the 1936: carbine, sporting carbine and rifle. Calibers for all three were the 30-30 Winchester and 32 Winchester Special, in direct competition with Winchester's Model 94. The Marlin stock, noted as full pistol grip with a "Sure Grip," or "SUREGRIP," semi-beavertail forearm and shotgun-style buttstock, were also shared features of the three. Both the sporting carbine and rifle wore hooded

The 356 Winchester that was chambered in the Model 336ER for a while is very much like a rimmed 358 Winchester with plenty of power. Here is the 356 shown with 200-grain (top) and 250-grain (bottom) recovered bullets.

front sights, while the carbine was shown without it in the advertisement.

The Model 1936 Carbine wore a 20-inch round barrel (octagonal barrels were not in vogue). The full magazine held 7 rounds with one in the chamber; advertised weight was 6½ pounds.

The 1936 Sporting Carbine also carried a 20-inch barrel, but had a two-thirds magazine with similar overall weight. The shortened magazine made the sporter a six-shot (5 plus 1 in the chamber) repeater. The pistol grip, deliberately noted as "full" in the ad, was more pronounced than pistol grips of many previous models.

The 1936 Rifle carried the longer 24-inch barrel with weight listed at 6¾ pounds, and maintained the six-shot two-thirds magazine.

Other minor traits set apart the Model 1936, but they are minimally important to this study. It's more important to recognize the fact that the Model 1936 was another fine rifle, fully reliable and accurate.

Next in line toward the famous Marlin 336 was the Model 36. Whereas the Model 1936 was advertised in 1936 and truly hit the market in 1937, the Marlin Model 36 surfaced before 1937 was out. A Marlin advertisement for the three sister Model 36s—carbine, sporting carbine and rifle—showed the first without a hooded front sight. Ballard-type rifling was maintained. Weights were listed as the same and all 36s were offered in 30-30 Winchester or 32 Winchester Special. The 36s eventually went to the blued receiver, but with no more color casehardening. A later 36 was available with a sandblasted receiver. The fluted comb was gone on the 36. Checkering of the stock was available on some models, as were swivels and slings.

When the 36 became the Model 336 in 1948, the die was cast: Marlin had its most famous big-bore repeating rifle. By 1979 the company announced serial number 3,000,000, an engraved rifle with gold inlay, which it presented to the NRA museum. Marlin had sold 3,000,000 Model 336 rifles. The company was careful to note that this figure included all designations of the rifle. They also added that the number was approximate and conservative, and that at least 3,000,000 were in fact made and sold. The Hepburn "good idea" remains alive today in the 336, one of the best lever-action rifles of any era.

The change that distinguishes the Model 336 from other lever-action rifles and from its predecessors is the round bolt, effected in 1948 and retained to this hour. Some say 1949 because the Model 336 was more readily available in that year, but 1948 is probably the more accurate date.

VARIATIONS ON A THEME

Numerous variations of the Model 336 have come from the factory since 1948. The Model 336A was a handsome rifle version of the model, and the 336A Deluxe, a further embellished version. The 336C ("C" for carbine) was highly popular from the start. In order to offer a look-alike for the

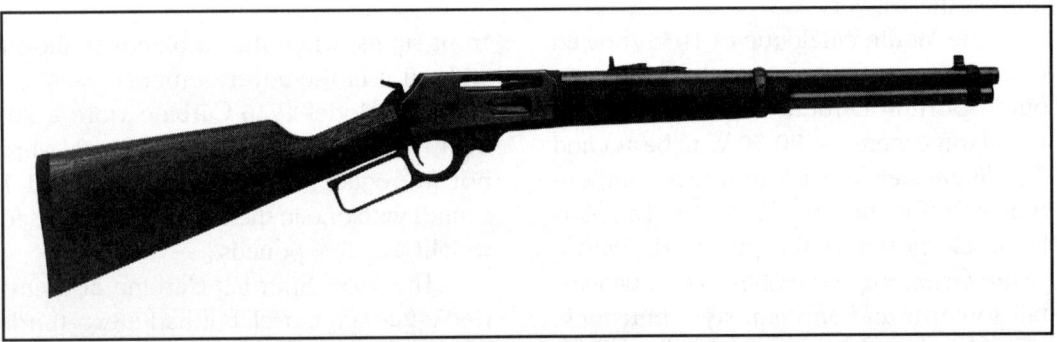

The handsome Model 336LTS in 30-30 is a short, handy Marlin that deer hunters of brush country can greatly admire.

fast-selling Model 94 Winchester. Marlin built a 336T, the "T" for Texan (1954–1983), with straight stock and no pistol grip. There was also a TDL model, a Deluxe Texan, made in the 1960s.

The Model 336SC was, as the initials suggest, a sporting carbine, and the 336SD, a Deluxe Sporting Carbine. From 1955 through 1960 Marlin had its Model 336SC Zipper model. This should have been a workable combination, but somehow it was not. The 219 Zipper, a 22-caliber centerfire cartridge, was highly accurate in bolt-action and single-shot rifles, but in the Model 336 the Zipper was not at its best. Varmint hunters demanded high accuracy when shooting at small targets, especially at longer ranges. The 336 in this version did not fill the bill, although the Marlin 336 lever-action repeater was and is capable of excellent accuracy.

A 16¼-inch short-barreled Marlin, called the Marauder, arrived in 1963, but survived only one year. A 336 Magnum Model, chambered for the 44 Magnum round, debuted the same year and lasted only one year too. While the 44 Magnum was at home in the Marlin Model 1894 action, it was not well suited to the 336 action length.

In 1970, Marlin came out with a 100th Anniversary Commemorative, followed in 1972 by another commemorative in honor of Zane Grey. The rifle, available in 30-30 Winchester chambering only, celebrated the 100th anniversary of the popular novelist's birth and was inscribed "Zane Grey 1872–1972." Only 10,000 Zane Grey rifles were built and were numbered "ZG1 through ZG10000." Each had a Zane Grey medallion on the right-hand side of the receiver. The Zane Grey 336 had a full octagon, 22-inch barrel with a full-length magazine tube and a pistol grip.

The rifle version Marlin Model 336A that sold from 1948 to 1962 reappeared in 1973 and was made until 1980. In 1973 the company tried a little nostalgia and offered the Marlin Model 336 Octagon for one year. In 1983 through 1986, the Marlin Model 336ER was available, the "ER" standing for Extra Range. This was chambered for the 356 Winchester, something like a rimmed 358 Winchester, which certainly is not bad. The ER rifle was also advertised in 307 Winchester, which never

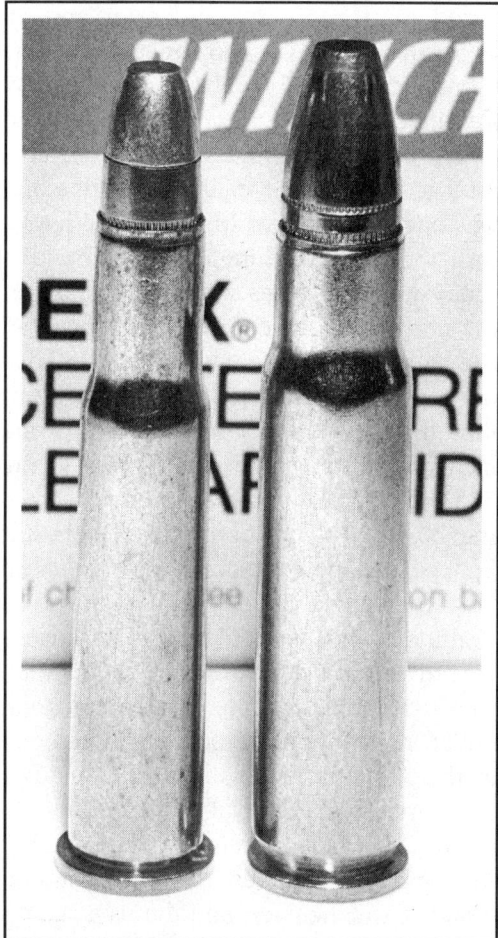

This side-by-side look at the 30-30 cartridge (left) and the 356 Winchester (right) gives an excellent perspective on the size differences between these Model 336 chamberings.

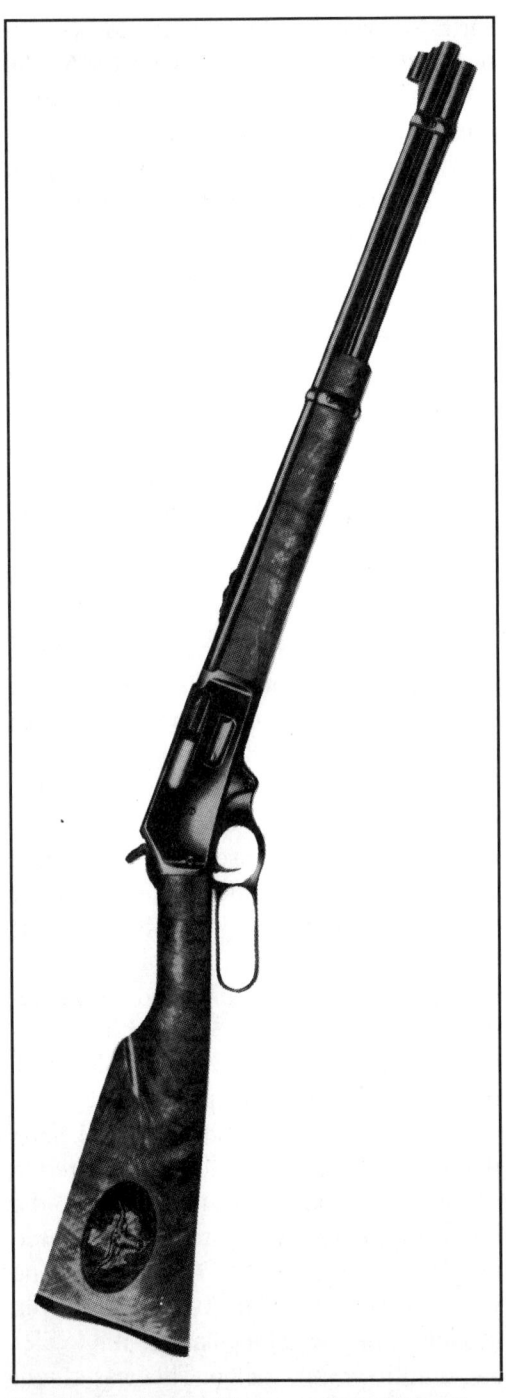

The Marlin Deluxe Texan made in the early 1960s sported a select walnut stock and forearm. The buttstock was embellished with a hand-carved longhorn steer, behind which was a map of Texas.

became a reality.

Other 336s include models 336CS, a TS and an LTS, along with a Model 375 that lasted from 1984 to 1987. Second guessing the public of shooters is no easy task. Marlin's Model 375, chambered for the 375 Winchester, was a fairly powerful modernized version of the excellent 38-55 Winchester. The cross-bolt safety was added to the Model 336 in 1984 as a full safety and this feature remains on Marlin's current rifles.

The present Marlin 336CS is chambered for the 30-30 Winchester and 35 Remington. In 1950 and for several years thereafter, the 336 had been offered in 35 Remington, so bringing it back may seem a surprise. After all, the 356 Winchester is a more powerful 35-caliber cartridge and was once chambered in the 336. Why return to the 35 Remington? The round is today and always was a fine brush and timber cartridge for deer and black bear. In the hands of an expert hunter and marksman, a rifle chambered for the 35 Remington is capable of taking any big game in North America. On the face of it, the 35 Remington may not seem far ahead of the 30-30 Winchester or 32 Winchester Special with their 170-grain bullets at about 2200 fps muzzle velocity. However, the 35 Remington has an obvious caliber advantage. It begins $5/100$ of an inch "wider" than the 30-30's bullet and it enjoys a 200-grain bullet at about the same muzzle velocity as the 170-grain bullets from the 30-30 or 32 Winchester Special. That's only 30 grains advantage in weight, to be sure, but looked at another way, the 35 Remington bullet is 15% heavier, and that is a significant figure. After all, ballistics is a game of inches and grains—inches of trajectory and mere grains weight, with one grain being only $1/7000$ of a pound. Thus the 35 Rem-

> ### THE MARLIN MODEL 336 AT A GLANCE
>
> **Period of Manufacture:** 1948 to present
> **Calibers:** 30-30 Win., 32 Win. Special, 35 Rem., 356 Win. (disc.)
> **Magazine Capacity:** Full or two-thirds tubular magazine with 4 to 6 shots (plus 1 in the chamber)
> **Action:** Lever-action repeater with improved round breech bolt and side ejection
> **Barrel Length:** Ranges from $16^{1}/_{4}$ to 24 inches, usually round, but an octagon version made in 1973
>
> **Weight (approx.):** From $6^{1}/_{4}$ to $7^{1}/_{4}$ pounds
> **Safety:** Cross-bolt safety on current models
> **Sights:** Open rear; hooded front sight; or scope mounted
> **Stock:** Pistol-grip plain stock of American walnut; semi-beavertail forend; shotgun-style buttplate
> **Variations:** Several—among them the 336A, 336CS, 336ER, 336LTS, 336 Marauder, Octagon, Sporting Carbine, 336T Texan, deluxe models and commemoratives, etc.

ington made a good name for itself at close range on deer and black bear in woods and brush in the fast-action Marlin. Of course, the newer 356 Winchester and 375 Winchester offer even more authority for the same type of big game hunting. But it's easy to see why the 35 Remington remains an entirely viable "brush and woods" cartridge. In the 336 lever-action, the combination is remarkably effective.

What about the 444? Marlin's 444, 444S and 444SS are all built upon the 336 design. However, the 444 was mentioned in Chapter 22 because in spirit this is the old Model 1895 idea: big power from a lever-action, certainly far more punch than possible from even the 356 Winchester chambering. To be absolutely correct, the 444 belongs in the 336 family. The Marlin 444SS, the 336 in the 444 Marlin chamber-

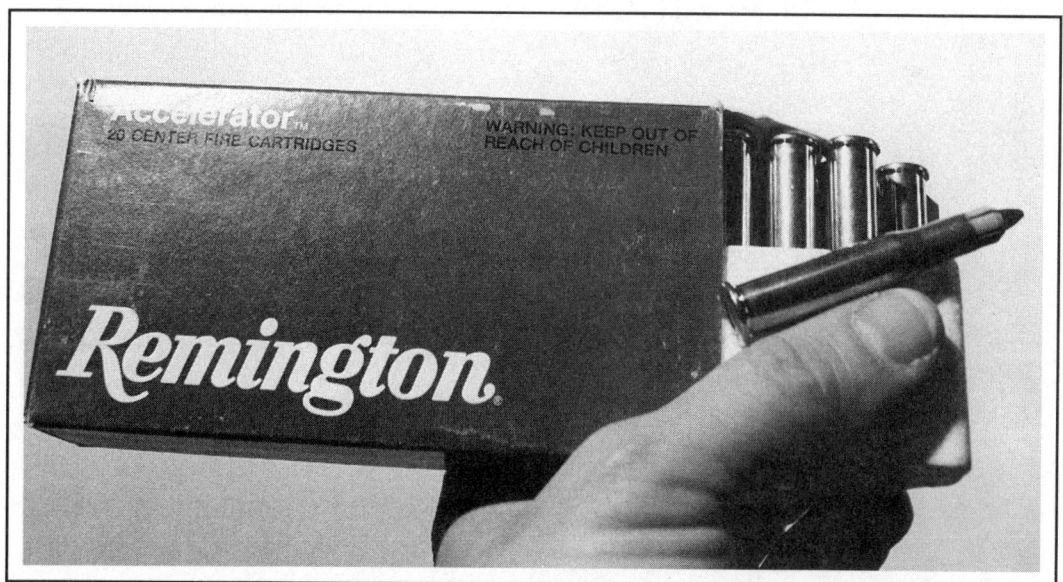

Model 336 rifles chambered for the 30-30 get a bonus in Remington's 30-30 Accelerator ammo, which uses a 55-grain 22-caliber bullet held in a plastic 30-caliber sabot.

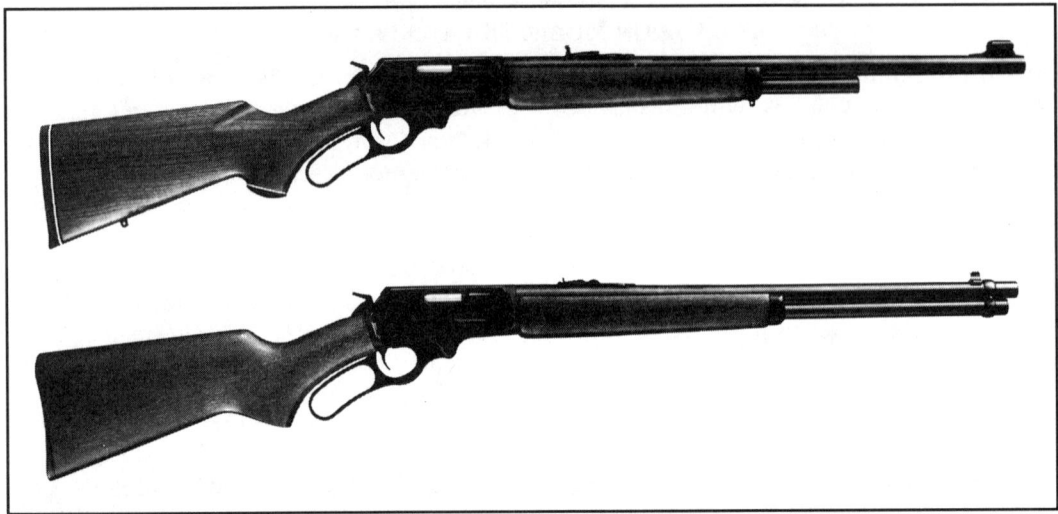

Two offshoots of the Model 336 are the Marlin 444SS (top) and the Marlin 30AS (bottom). The 444SS is chambered in the 444 Marlin and has a 22-inch barrel with five-shot tubular magazine. The 30AS, in 30-30 caliber only, is the 336 lever-action carbine at a savings.

ing, has a 22-inch barrel and five-shot tubular magazine (4 + 1).

The current Marlin 30AS with its stained hardwood stock is a 336 lever-action carbine at a savings. In 30-30 caliber only, the 30AS models are similar to the Glenfield models, which are solid Model 336 rifles at reduced prices for those who are not concerned about a walnut stock. No matter which model you choose, dollar for dollar the Marlin Model 336 remains what it always was—a value for the hunter who demands a reliable no-nonsense rifle for close- to medium-range conditions.

SPRINGFIELD SPORTERS
A "BEST" IN CUSTOMIZING

24

In 1903 the U.S. Army decided to adopt a Mauser-like bolt-action rifle as its own. Word of this quickly reached the White House. President Theodore Roosevelt insisted upon seeing and shooting the new arm to satisfy himself that indeed the rifle was what the Ordnance people claimed. He wrote to Brigadier General William Crozier, the Chief of Ordnance, and asked that a Springfield rifle equipped with special sights be sent to Washington, D.C. When the new rifle arrived, "rough and ready" Roosevelt took it out on the south lawn and gave it a try, reports say. He loved the Springfield and when a bill came for it, T.R. sent his personal check for $42.13. This Springfield, you might say, was the first "sporterized" Model 1903.

A sleek, original 1903 Springfield rifle housed at the Springfield Armory Museum.

SPRINGFIELD SPORTERS 231

Gunmakers have long taken military firearms for their actions alone. They have built some of the most beautiful rifles in the world around the modified actions of military firearms. Sporterized military rifles became extremely popular at the end of World War II, largely because of the well-liked Mauser and Springfield rifles that flooded into the U.S. The term "sporterize" means to alter a military arm in some way. Generally, it involves removing the "army sights" and lopping off the superfluous full-length stock. From that point, further refinements can be made. Using the Springfield action, American shooters have enjoyed the rifle as a sporterized hunting/shooting rifle as well as a custom rifle.

A study of custom Springfields would read like a "Who's Who" of great riflemakers. It would also include the names of many famous marksmen, hunters and gunwriters, such as Colonel Townsend Whelen, Jack O'Connor, Warren Page, Al Barr, General Julian Hatcher, and more contemporary arms authorities and authors, such as Jim Carmichel and Jon Sundra. These shooters have made room on their gun racks for custom-made rifles built on a military action.

Today, many military actions are still entirely suitable for the construction of fine and expensive custom rifles. Gil Van Horn, who builds some of the finest custom arms in the world, selects military actions for his creations. He often selects Mauser actions very carefully for his work. He then hones the action until it is super smooth in function, using the methods and materials he feels are the best. The current Van Horn custom rifle carries a price tag in the

This sporterized Springfield was crafted by Dale Storey in caliber 338 DGS, a 338 built on a blown-out and necked-up 7mm Mauser case. Highly accurate in the field, the rifle has a medium-weight octagonal barrel.

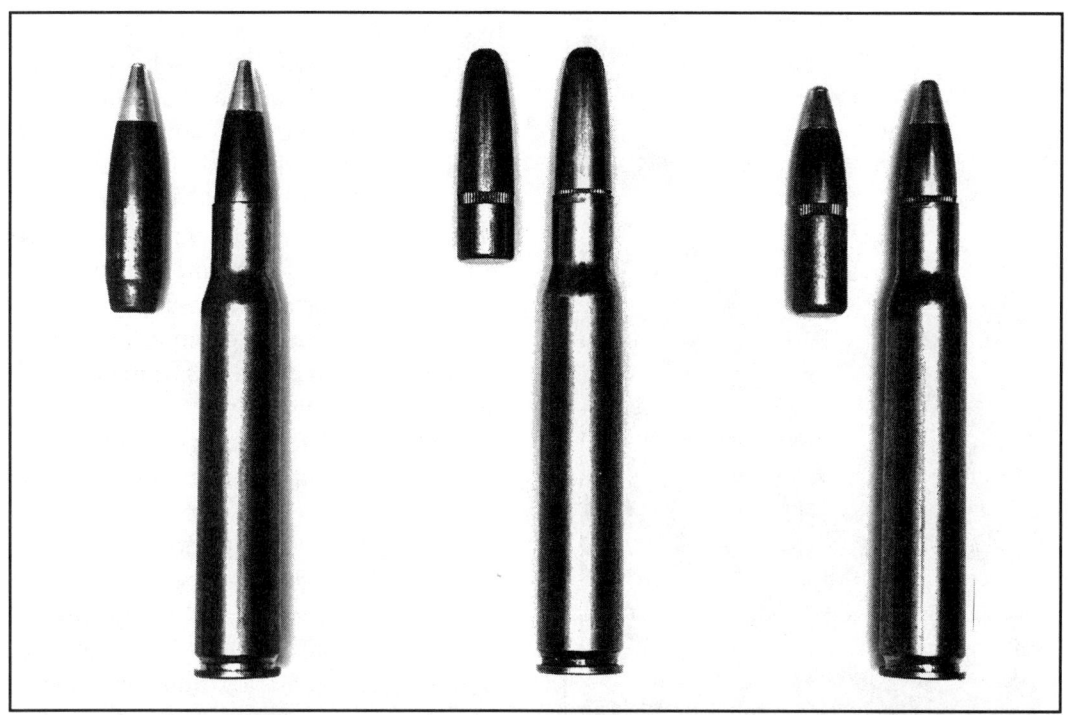

American sportsmen revered the 30-06 Springfield cartridge almost as much as the rifle's fine action. This was due in part to the versatility of the cartridge. Here are three 30-06 loads with three different 180-grain bullets. The Silvertip boat-tail on the left is for long-range shooting; the center round-nosed soft-point gives "reliable expansion"; and the flat-based Silvertip on the right has been a trusted bullet for years.

$10,000 range.

The Springfield was America's answer to the Mauser. The U.S. Army saw a need for an accurate repeater that would chamber a powerful long-range cartridge. Through long study and deliberation, the Springfield rifle was born. Named for the Springfield Armory, the military arsenal that developed it, the "New Springfield" was introduced in 1903 and is known as the Model of 1903, the 1903A3 being a popular designation among arms aficionados. The 1903 saw action in 1917 and 1918 during World War I.

World War II necessitated a rush into arms production. The Springfield Armory tooled up for the production of the Garand rifle, an "automatic" chambered for the 30-06 Springfield cartridge. The Rock Island Arsenal had been building Springfields, but the arsenal sold its tools, dies and equipment to the Remington Arms Company. Remington commenced to build over a million 1903 and modified 1903 rifles at this time; their rifles could be 1903s, 1903A3s or 1903A4s. While Winchester was building Garands, the L.C. Smith-Corona typewriter company produced Springfields. They made over 200,000 Model 1903 rifles. So Springfield rifles were products of the Springfield Armory, Rock Island Arsenal, Remington Arms and Smith-Corona.

To add to the variety of Springfields produced, it is believed that certain shop foremen had their own ways of doing the

SPRINGFIELD SPORTERS 233

Military rifles like this original 1903 Springfield army version have been "sporterized" into fine hunting arms.

job best, so they applied their methods to the production of rifles, resulting in another set of variations that color the Springfield riflemaking picture. Many receivers were heat-treated "by eye"; that is, the expert doing the job decided simply

by looking at it when the receiver was properly hardened. The result was a variation in "metallurgical toughness" of Springfield receivers. Of course, every receiver was up to the pressures developed by the 30-06 military cartridge. Minor problems in steel toughness (ductility across the grain, for example) showed up later when custom armsmakers chose Springfield actions to chamber some very hot rounds, such as the 220 Swift and some high-pressure wildcats (various 25-06 rounds). A general rule of thumb was applied to designate stronger actions versus weaker ones.

The greatest change took place in later Springfield production because of demands for a stronger action. All Springfields with serial numbers below 800,000 were singled out as "low number models," while Springfields with numbers higher than 800,000 were called "high number models." The former were considered too weak by some gunmakers to trust them in the chambering of truly hot modern ammunition. The problem with low-number Springfields, some said, was a brittleness of steel. More than one gunmaker contended that the steel receiver of these low-number models could be cracked by a swift blow from a hammer. Other than serial numbers, no other way is known to determine the stronger from the weaker Springfields.

The model designations did not of themselves allude to strength. For example, Remington's Model 1903A3 Springfield meant that the rifle had a receiver sight and a longer handguard. When the 1903A3 was built without a front sight, it was called a 1903A4 because it was fitted with a Redfield Jr. scope mount and a Weaver 330 model scope sight. The bolt handle was bent on the 1903A4 to accommodate the

234 LEGENDARY SPORTING RIFLES

scope tube. L.C. Smith also made 1903A3 Springfields. Gunmakers complained that many of the Remington and L.C. Smith Springfields were thrown together without regard for refinement. A war was on. Speed of manufacture was essential.

AN OUTSTANDING SPORTER

Michigan-born Stewart Edward White was one of the first well-known hunters to carry a Springfield sporter and to use it in Africa. His daring feats are described in *Great Shooters of the World*. Both White and Teddy Roosevelt carried their Springfields over African soil in the early part of this century and, upon returning to America, they wrote about the rifle and its conquests. White used full-metal-jacket bullets in his Springfield and during his extensive African hunting (three safaris), he dropped between 300 and 400 head of game. The red-headed hunter/writer proved in front of on-lookers that the Springfield could shoot like a dream. White demonstrated his and his rifle's ability before famous riflemen Captain C.E. Crosman and Harry Ross; White shot groups from the sitting position that matched or exceeded groups fired from prone by both Crosman and Ross.

The word got out "big time." Hunters wanted to partake of that sort of reliability and accuracy. Plus the 30-06 Springfield cartridge was applauded as highly as the rifle itself. The cartridge that first appeared in the 1903 Springfield was the 30-03, however, not the 30-06. Just as the 30-06 means "Ball cartridge, caliber 30 Model of 1906," 30-03 means "Ball cartridge, caliber 30 Model of 1903." The 30-03 Springfield round was almost identical to the 30-06, just slightly longer in the neck. The 30-03 was originally loaded with a 220-grain bullet at about 2300 fps. This was in keeping with military tradition, using a long round-nosed projectile, such as the 175 round-nosed military bullet, for the 7mm Mauser cartridge. But that trend changed. In 1906 the 30-03 became the 30-06 by shortening the neck by .07 inch in length and changing the bullet and load. The first 30-06 load, according to research, used a 150-grain

The buttplate of the Springfield army version was used to hold a takedown cleaning rod. Hunter S.E. White said the buttplate was "big enough to carry the baby in."

spitzer bullet at 2700 fps muzzle velocity for a flatter trajectory. In 1926, the U.S. Army again changed the service load with a 172-grain boat-tail bullet at about 2700 fps, although the load was reduced to develop around 2640 fps.

It's easy to see how the Springfield could become so popular with big game

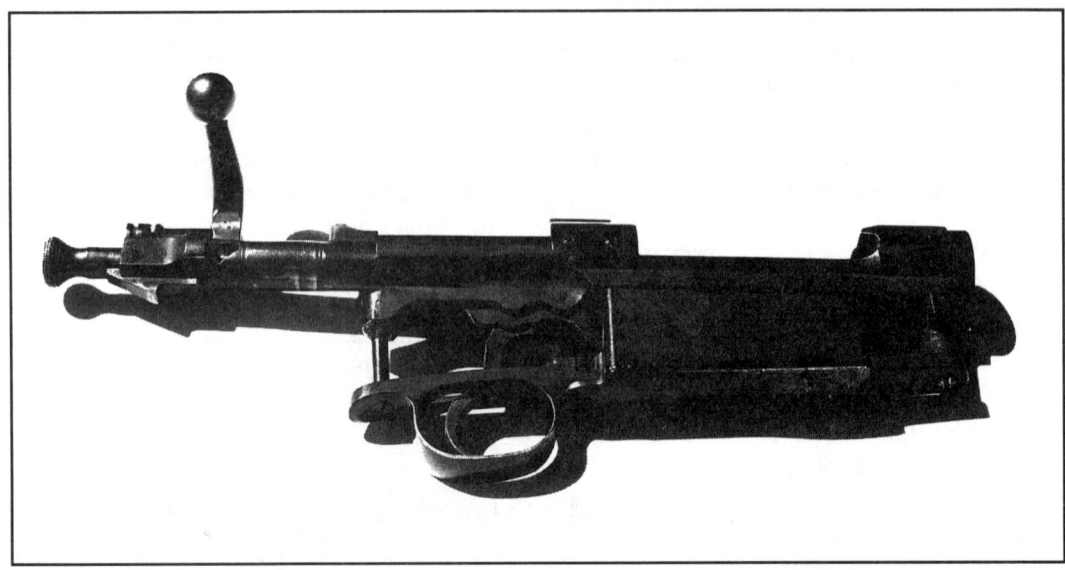

This view of the Springfield action is with the bolt thrown open. The long cocking bolt knob on the end of the action (far left) is sometimes removed when the action is used to tailor a custom Springfield sporter.

hunters. The rifle was accurate and the cartridge powerful. Custom gunmakers got busy. The Springfield action was divided into four general classes. The original Model 1903s made at the Springfield and Rock Island arsenals were named the "casehardened Springfields" by some gunmakers. Serial numbers ran up to 285,507 at the Rock Island Arsenal and 800,000 at the Springfield Armory. The second group were Springfield-made and were "double heat-treated," not casehardened; these numbered 800,001 to 1,275,765. The third grouping includes all Rock Island Arsenal rifles with serial numbers above 285,507 as well as all Springfield-produced rifles above 1,275,765 made of nickel steel. The Remington and Smith-Corona rifles constitute the fourth group. These were equal in strength to, if not always as handsome as, the best arsenal Springfields. So custom gunmakers had many versions from which to choose.

S.E. White's Springfield sporter in 30-06 spread the fame of rifle and cartridge, and many other accomplished shooters of the day demanded the same. White's exploits included great marksmanship. Cunninghame, the professional hunter who had guided Roosevelt, proclaimed in a letter to T.R. that White had to have been the best game shot who ever hunted Africa. T.R. had used the Springfield in Africa prior to White. White simply copied Roosevelt's battery—a Springfield rifle, a lever-action 405 Winchester and a double-barreled big-bore rifle. Louis (Ludwig) Wundhammer, the gunmaker who customized White's rifle, is now celebrated in the field as one of the all-time greats, but at the time was not yet recognized for his work. According to White, the Wundhammer Springfield sporter boasted these features: first, a pistol grip that "permitted clasp and at the same time left the trigger finger independent"; second, a cheekpiece that allowed the stock of the rifle to meet the shooter's face in the same place every time the rifle was

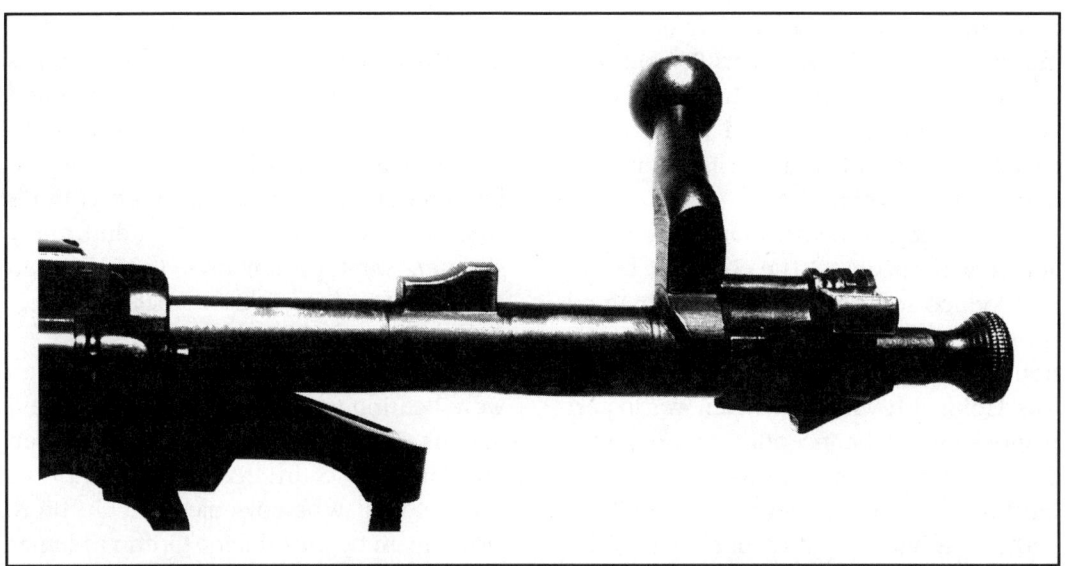

This view of the Springfield action shows what appears to be an extra lug. In fact it is not a locking lug, rather a safety lug, patterned after the Mauser. The lug fits loosely into a recess of the receiver and, in theory, if the two front locking lugs give way, this extra lug will help retard the bolt from rearward motion.

mounted for shooting; third, a shotgun-style buttplate noted as "wide"; a "trapdoor in the buttplate big enough to carry the baby in"; and a gold bead front sight coupled with a Lyman aperture (peep) rear sight. Wundhammer built five Springfield sporters to start. While White could not recall who received the fifth, he did know of the other four recipients: Robert Cameron Rogers, John Colby, E.C. Crosman and of course himself.

An army of the finest gunmakers in the land began to build custom Springfield rifles. Forever emblazoned in the annals of American gunmaking were Thomas Shelhamer, Leonard Mews, John Hearn, Alvin Biesen, Jim Howe, August Pachmayr and Bob Owen. Owen is often considered the most influential gunmaker in terms of the classic-style American stock. An Owen rifle is extolled as "clean." The lines are never abrupt and the workmanship is flawless. Owen built many custom rifles on the Springfield action. Although it was the 1920s when he promoted his own stock style and handmade rifles, his work appears to this day in collections and sometimes for sale at high-command prices.

Another individual who helped popularize the Springfield action as the basis for collectible custom rifles was E.C. Crosman. He was rather adamant about the Springfield, often to the discredit of just about all other rifles. He considered "fancy Mausers with rustless barrels and seven dollars worth of engraving which looks like a million" as made correctly some of the time, but, "What of it?" He thought the bolt fit of Mausers to "have more play when they are clear open than the tail of a cow in fly-time." Crosman said the Model 54 Winchester was "a pretty fair bolt action, but not so good" as the Springfield. The Remington bolt-action rifle, he stated, had a poorly designed stock even in its better grade, and as for the Mannlicher, its bolt handle was "about half way up to the muzzle so a fellow can't work it from the shoulder." He added that the Mannlicher was "just another squarehead gun. Got set-triggers. Can you beat it?" Give that man a Springfield every time.

The rifle company of Griffin & Howe agreed with Crosman. The company began to produce some of the best Springfield sporters ever made. They remain to this hour as premium rifles on gun collectors' lists. Colonel Townsend Whelen was in part responsible for the inception of the Griffin & Howe riflemaking enterprise. Seymour Griffin was a cabinetmaker by profession and also a hunter and reader. In 1910 he purchased a Springfield rifle. He read *African Game Trails* by Teddy Roosevelt and became interested in what the former president had to say about the Springfield as a hunting instrument. Put an army rifle into the hands of a cabinetmaker and he's bound to throw the stock away and build one of his own—which is exactly what Griffin did. His new stock was crafted of fine French walnut. Everyone who saw Griffin's rifle became excited about it, and many shooters wanted their own. Griffin began to circulate a few of his restocked Springfields among friends.

Meanwhile Crosman and Whelen were beating the drum for the Springfield and its 30-06 in the game field. Whelen and Griffin met in 1923 by invitation of the Colonel. Whelen sealed the Griffin & Howe team by introducing Griffin to James V. Howe. Howe was a perfectionist in metalworking and the foreman of the tool shop at Frankford Arsenal, which was headed by Whelen. So in 1923 Griffin &

When the actions are placed side by side, you can see that on the finished Dale Storey Springfield sporter, the Springfield action has been cleaned, polished and reblued and the cocking knob removed.

The little things make the difference. A Springfield sporter can be as handsome and unique as any custom rifle anywhere. Dale Storey embellished the floorplate of this action, for example, with a Sid Bell elk and added a moose and goat to the scope rings.

Howe became a bonafide operation with four men at the top: Griffin became president, Howe became secretary, a man named Holsworth was acting treasurer and Colonel Whelen himself was company advisor. Howe didn't last long and sold his share of the firm for $500 and moved on. Griffin replaced him with other craftsmen of high merit and things went smoothly until 1929 when the Crash struck. The Great Depression caused many prospective buyers to change their minds about orders. Abercrombie & Fitch weathered the Depression well enough to be in a buying position from which Griffin and his associates could not back away. Under A&F, the Griffin & Howe company produced many fine rifles until 1941, when gunbuilders turned their attention to the war effort. Griffin & Howe had never been big and had made only about 2,800 rifles total. But they are credited with putting fine Springfield sporters into the hands of discriminating marksmen and hunters who cherished them.

Eventually, just about anyone who was considered a professional custom riflemaker used the Springfield action to build guns. Not that Springfield actions were used exclusively, for a number of armsmakers preferred Mausers, as the next chapter explains. However, custom Springfields were certainly not difficult to find. Whelen's Springfields became well-known, for example, and they had been made by a number of smiths. Fred Adolph had stocked one of them; James Howe, another. Whelen also had a Griffin & Howe sporter and a Springfield crafted by the famous Adolph Niedner. The Niedner Springfield was built in 1935 from a high-number action. Very accurate, it was chambered for the 257 Roberts with a 26-inch barrel. Niedner had done the metal

SPRINGFIELD SPORTERS

> ### THE MODEL 1903 SPRINGFIELD AT A GLANCE
>
> **Period of Manufacture:** 1903 through WWII
> **Calibers:** 30-06 Springfield, plus others in custom versions
> **Action:** Strong bolt-action used in later sporterized rifles; usually four classes—(1) the weakest, low-number casehardened Springfield Armory-made Springfields (to serial number 800,000) and Rock Island Arsenal-made (to serial number 285,507); (2) Springfield-made "double heat treated" with serial numbers above 800,000 to 1,275,765; (3) all Rock Island rifles above serial no. 285,507 and all Springfield-made rifles of nickel steel above serial number 1,275,765; (4) all Remington- and Smith-Corona-produced Springfields
> **Barrel:** Of steel, blued, 26 inches, but varies depending on customizing
> **Sights:** Open; gold bead or blade front; aperture (peep) rear; many scope sights used; depends on customizing
> **Stock:** Straight-grip plain stock of American walnut; trapdoor buttplate on originals; customs stocks vary
> **Variations:** Any number of variations may be found on sporterized models, depending on who did the customizing

work, but Thomas Shelhamer had stocked it in Circassian walnut. The rifle was stocked to be fired from either shoulder, so that the Colonel could use either eye in his later years when he had trouble with his sight. Whelen kept the rifle until just before his passing in 1961.

In his book, *The Hunting Rifle*, (1940) Colonel Whelen praised the Springfield Model of 1903 as a hunting rifle:

> This work would not be complete without mention of this famous hunting rifle with which many of our hunters have done, and are continuing to do such fine work. About 1909 the more skilled and studious of our hunter-riflemen became aware that they could shoot with far better accuracy, and hit surely at far longer ranges, with our Springfield Model 1903 Service (military) Rifle than with any hunting or sporting rifle regularly manufactured at that time. Accordingly some of us proceeded to have those military weapons remodeled into sporting type, this remodeling consisting of replacing the military stock with a sporting one with pistol grip, more refined lines, and proper dimensions, replacing the military sights with Lyman hunting sights and perhaps a telescopic sight, and smoothing and bluing the rough military barrel.

Whelen concluded that "in many cases these Springfield sporting rifles proved to be far superior to any other hunting rifle, and they made a very enviable reputation for themselves." Today, more custom rifles are built on the Mauser action, partly because far more Mausers are available the world over. But the Springfield sporter's story has been written in indelible ink. It's here to stay.

SPORTING MAUSERS
POTENT AND ACCURATE

25

The 30-06 cartridge had a great deal to do with the fame of the Model 1903 Springfield as a sporting rifle. The original military Springfield could be "cleaned up" through sporterizing using the original barrel, sometimes turned down, polished and blued, with no further effort. Modern handloads for the 30-06 provide maximum velocities of almost 3100 feet per second (fps) for a 150-grain bullet and a shade over 2800 fps for a 180-grain bullet. The 30-06 remains the number one big game cartridge west of the Mississippi River and more than a little popular east of it.

However, at the close of World War II, a great many German Mauser rifles found their way into the U.S. A large number of them were chambered for the 8mm

The excellent Kimber Model 89 embodies features from the Mauser military action.

Mauser (7.9mm), a round not all that much shorter than the 30-06 and about 32 caliber instead of 30. The 8mm Mauser was a fine hunting cartridge capable of good work on all big game when a crack shot was in charge of directing the bullet. But it was impossible for the 8mm Mauser to compete with the 30-06, especially since American factory loads were not up to par; i.e., a popular load being a 170-grain bullet at modest velocity.

When the Mauser Model 98 came out in the latter days of the 19th century, the rifle was first a military number, chambered for the 8mm Mauser cartridge. Very soon the rifle became a sporting arm. Both versions were made by Mauser-Werke in Oberndorf, Germany, which also sold Model 98 actions to different arms companies around the world, so the actions were plentiful. One example of a Mauser-made sporter was the "Standard Model" rifle, a refined version of the German Service Model 98 in calibers 7mm Mauser and 8mm Mauser. It wore a straight-bolt handle and 5-shot box magazine and had a M/98 military-type stock. Another example, more "sporting" in design, was the Special British model, the Type "A" Sporting Rifle. This arm was chambered in the 30-06 (7.62×63) plus 7×57, 8×60, 9×57 and 9.3×62mm. It had a 5-shot box magazine, a 23½-inch round barrel and weighed about 7¼ pounds. While it retained the military-type single trigger, its rifle-style stock was improved with Circassian walnut, a checkered pistol grip and forend. The action carried the familiar bolt and the rifle was available with any number of options, including double-set triggers, shotgun-type safety, folding peep rear sight or three-leaf rear sight, etc.

The 8mm Mauser cartridge came to be considered a sporting round and was chambered in various hunting rifles. The round is also known as the 7.9×57mm, meaning a bullet of 7.9mm diameter and a case 57mm long. The 7×57mm, for all practical purposes, is an 8×57mm necked down to 7mm. Originally, the bullet diameter was .318 inch and weighed 236 grains in round-nosed configuration for a muzzle velocity of 2100 fps. Improved since then, the bullet diameter of the 8mm

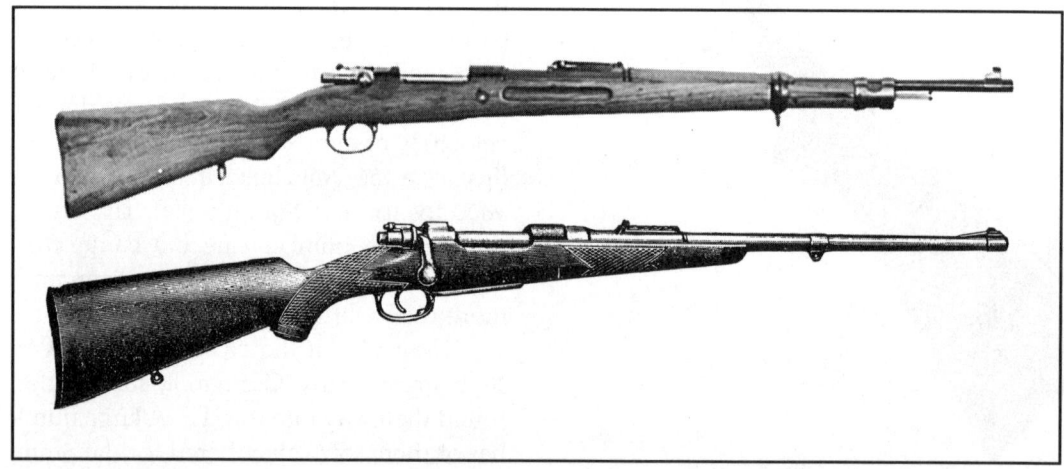

Two original German-made Mauser sporting rifles: the Mauser Standard Model (top) with straight-bolt and Model 98 military-type stock, and the Type "A" Sporting Rifle (bottom) with Circassian walnut sporting stock and checkered pistol grip and forend.

is now .323 inch with bullet weight at 154 grains for 2900 fps.

The American loading of the 8mm Mauser never credited the round for its potential. Today, the round is loaded with a 170-grain bullet at 2360 fps. A good 30-30 load projects a 170-grain bullet at 2100 to 2200 fps. To be fair about it, some problems have been reported with imported 8mm Mauser rifles. These problems stem mainly from variations in bore size, according to data, and it could be that American ammo companies wanted to load mildly to accommodate such bore size discrepancy, if indeed that did exist. Furthermore, a good many 8mm Mauser rounds found their way into rifles chambered for the 30-06 cartridge. Squeezing a 32-caliber bullet through a 30-caliber bore is never a good idea. No doubt some rifles were seriously damaged when the ammo mixup occurred. It may have been that loading "hot" 8mm Mauser ammo was considered a bad idea by American ammunition crafters. Meanwhile, European companies continued to load the 8mm Mauser more in line with its potential.

Today, the excellent firm of RWS in Germany offers the 8mm Mauser sporting cartridge in various loadings. There is a 187-grain bullet at 2625 fps and another bullet of the same weight, different design, at 2690 fps. RWS ammo generally comes out "on the button" when independently chronographed. A heavier 196-grain bullet is shown at 2620 fps and a 198-grain bullet leaves the muzzle at the same velocity. These are, in order, muzzle energies of 2862 foot-pounds, 3005 foot-pounds, 2988 foot-pounds and 3019 foot-pounds. Energy levels in the 3000 foot-pound range suffice for North American big game with proper bullet placement. Compare these 8mm Mauser figures with the American loading, which develops 2103 foot-pounds, and it's easy to see that the U.S. shooter/hunter had to handload in order to boost 8mm Mauser cartridge performance or he had to look for foreign ammo.

Mild factory 8mm ammo was a major reason for full-blown sporterizing of the Mauser Model 98 rifle. While the Springfield was fine "as is," the Mauser was not. To be sure, some Mausers were rechambered to a wildcat known as the 8mm-06 so that the original barrel could be re-

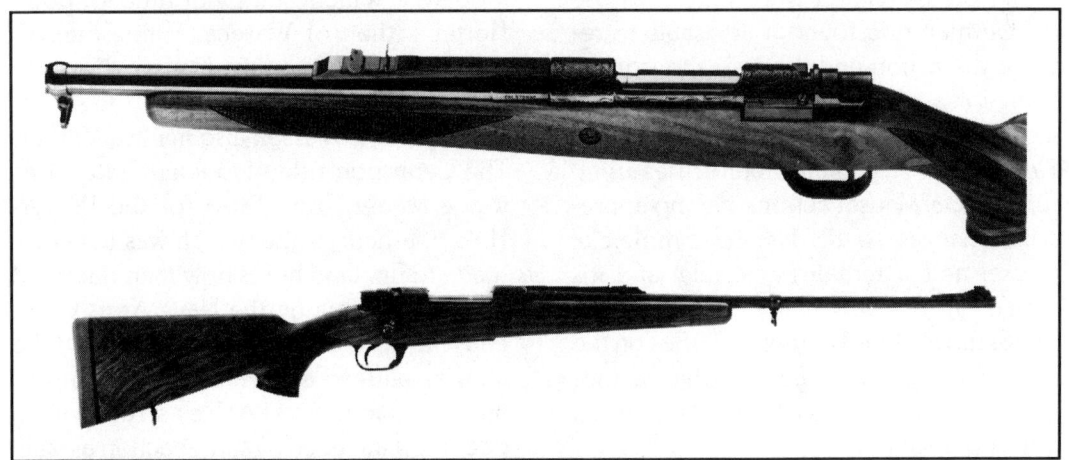

The fine Parker-Hale M81 African rifle, now made in America by the Navy Arms Company, is a fine commercial example of a modern sporting rifle built around the original Mauser 98 action.

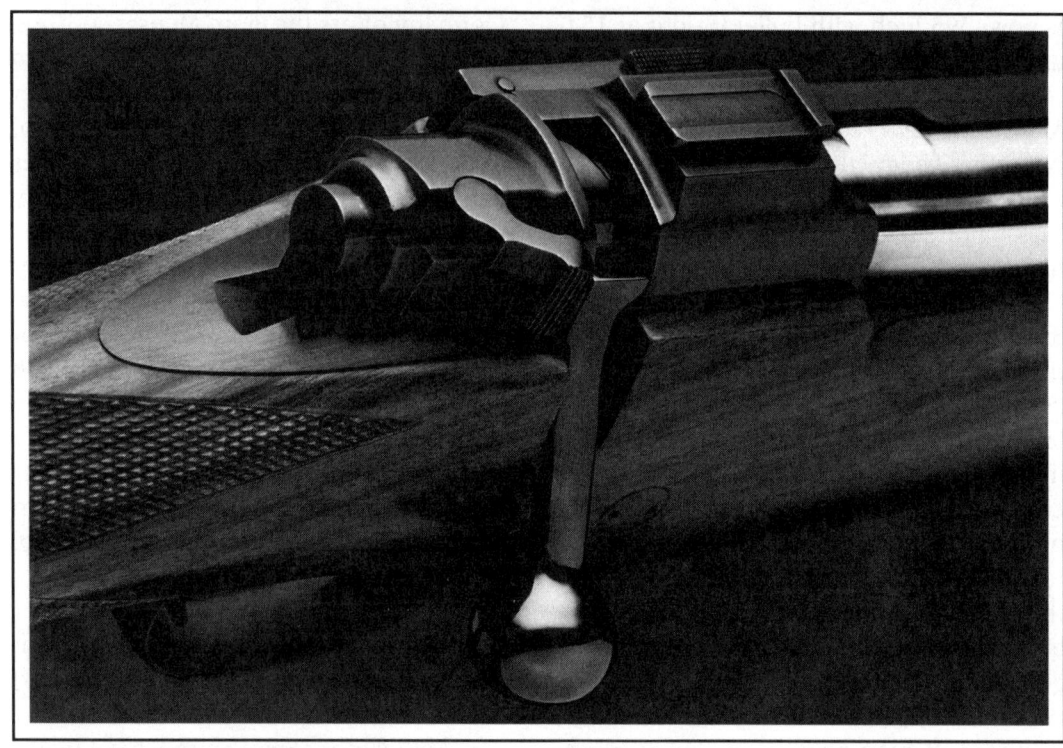

A close-up view of the Kimber Model 89 shows the Mauser-like action with the inclusion of a three-position safety and integral square-bridge scope mount bases.

tained. The 8mm-06 was simply the 30-06 case necked up to accept 8mm bullets. Properly handloaded, the 8mm-06 was a powerful cartridge. Nonetheless, many American sportsmen who wanted to use the German rifle found it advisable to remove the action and use it as the starting point for a whole new sporting arm. The success of the Mauser was so complete that a number of companies built rifles using commercial Mauser actions with no appreciable changes. To this day, the commercial Mauser action remains available, and it's difficult to say how many different companies have offered completed rifles on the Mauser design. In addition, the Mauser spawned numerous copies of itself, often with modifications.

A list of commercial Mausers past and present is a long one. One of the latest Mauser copies is the beautiful Kimber Model 89 (notice the model number, a reverse of the 98). This rifle boasts an action designed after the Mauser plus the pre-64 Model 70 Winchester, with traits of both. Herter's (then of Waseca, Minnesota) offered a rifle based on the Mauser 98 action, although not an exact copy of the 98 action. Smith & Wesson also made a Mauser. The Centurion rifle of Golden State Arms was a Mauser, too. Ditto for the Parker-Hale bolt-action rifle, which was for years made in England but is now manufactured in West Virginia by the Navy Arms Company. The Santa Barbara action carried the Mauser pattern all the way in a Spanish-made version. P.O. Ackley's riflemaking operation included a Mauser action as well. The French-made Brevex Magnum Mauser was well-liked by gunsmiths who wanted to chamber a rifle for the big ones, such as the 416 Rigby, which has become relatively popular in America of late. The Mark X Mauser remains widely available and is considered a bargain, especially in the barreled-action version. The early Husqvarna rifle of Sweden, once a popular rifle in American catalogues, is another Mauser. The Brno Czech sporting rifle is not exactly a Mauser, but neither does it depart radically from the Mauser design.

In a very real sense, the Mauser 98 is the father of most of our popular bolt-action rifles, and that certainly includes the Springfield, which relied heavily on Model 98 design. The Mauser is so important to arms history in general, as well as sporting rifle history specifically, that there is no end of literature on the subject. A book of special interest is *Mauser Bolt Rifles* by Ludwig Olson, a 1976 title that is well-read to this today. Olson is known as one of the most intelligent and resourceful of our firearms researchers. Paul Mauser (June 27, 1838–May 29, 1914) certainly deserves recognition as the father of the Mauser Model 98 as we know it, but he was not entirely responsible for every facet of Mauser rifle development. As always, many inventions preceded the Mauser 98, with a host of models that were superseded one at a time by better rifles. There were blackpowder Mausers, a Model 71/84 with a turnbolt action, a Model 87 and an 88, as well as a 91 and 93, a 95 still found as a used military arm, a 94 and so on until we reach the advent of the Model 98 Mauser, the apex of development.

The workings of the Model 98 are today considered pedestrian, because we are so used to this type of action. However, the 98 is in fact an extremely sound design that has not been vastly improved by its followers. Two big locking lugs turn to se-

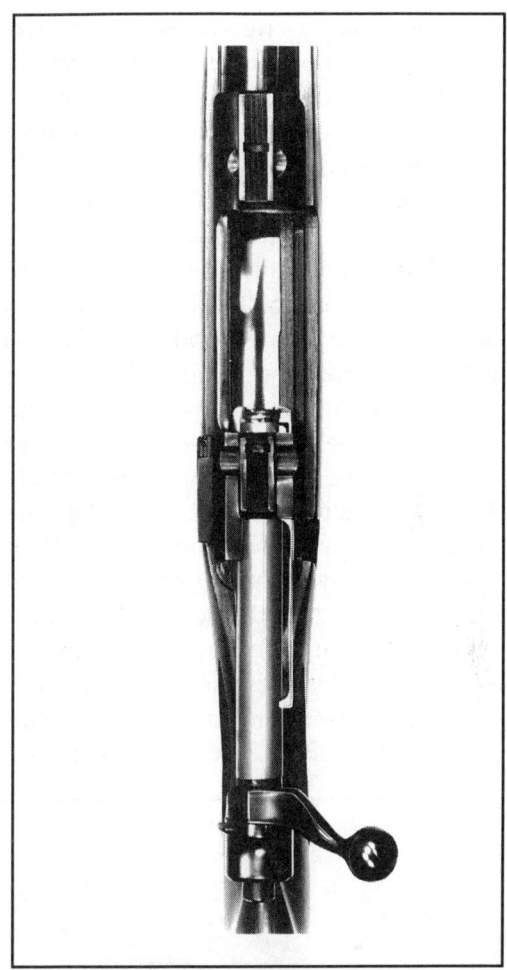

The successful Ruger Model 77 is a separate action from the Model 98, but it carries several 98 distinctions, including a claw-type extractor.

cure the bolt. A third lug appears forward of the bolt handle, which is considered a backup lug should the bolt set back for any reason. The action is cocked primarily on the opening of the bolt. Some cocking effort is applied when the locking lugs are rotated into the locked position. Some rifleman blasted the 98 because the bolt does tend to wobble around at its most withdrawn position; however, that is not a problem. The design, if anything, promotes reliability, for the 98 tends to function

SPORTING MAUSERS 245

when less than perfectly clean. Furthermore, any notion that this particular idiosyncrasy means weakness must be dispelled immediately. It's fairly well agreed that the actions which followed the 98, including the Model 70 and the Springfield, were not quite as strong as the 98.

After the Spanish-American War of 1898, American soldiers were forced to admit that the Mauser Model 98 rifle was better than the Krag. A new rifle was put on the drawing board immediately, and when the sketches turned from paper to metal, the Model 1903 Springfield emerged. There is no denying that the Springfield was bred and born of the Mauser. Both enjoyed many similar traits, including the staggered magazine box, claw-type extractor, two forward locking lugs as well as other features. Anyone who questions the family resemblance should be reminded that the U.S. Government paid Mauser a royalty for infringement.

The Mauser action lives on today only slightly modified in many sporting rifles built everywhere, and the action in both military and commercial forms is used by some of the world's greatest gunmakers in building fine, expensive firearms. On the threshold of the 21st century, in other words, a 19th-century idea clings, because it is sound. We have mentioned a number of rifles that are at present being commercially manufactured. Let's look at what can be done with the Mauser action by the custom gunmaker.

CUSTOM SPORTING MAUSERS

Gil Van Horn, custom gunmaker noted for building some of the most powerful and elegant rifles of all time, prefers Mauser actions. In one instance, he was challenged to produce a rifle "infallibly" capable of stopping the world's most dan-

The Gil Van Horn 500 Express custom rifle is a highly potent arm built around a hand-selected Mauser action. Completely reworked, with exquisite features, the rifle weighs 11½ pounds and sells in the hefty five-digit range.

gerous game. This meant the Cape buffalo of Africa, as well as lions and elephants. The rifle had to be handy and fast-working, despite its projected large size, and of course it had to have an action smoother than an oiled ball bearing.

Van Horn tamped a bowlful of data into his pipe of invention and puffed up the 500 Express cartridge for starters, a round that could be called the 510 Express, for it is 51 caliber not 50, with a bullet diameter of .510 inch. The thrust of the 500 Van Horn Express is this: the power of the fabled 505 Gibbs in a standard-length action. If it delivered power equal with its size, the 505 would drop an elephant the way a 22 varmint rifle handles a woodchuck.

The Van Horn creation came out more powerful than the Gibbs, with a 500-grain bullet at 2500 fps muzzle velocity and a 600-grain bullet departing the muzzle at close to 2300 fps. Muzzle energy was a whopping 6941 foot-pounds for the 500-grain bullet and 7050 for the 600-grain one. (The Gibbs is generally loaded with a 525-grain bullet at a muzzle velocity of around 2300 fps or a 525-grain bullet doing 2390 fps with 105 grains of HiVel #2. Van Horn wanted similar potency without the long action required for a 505 boltgun.) The Gibbs case length is 3.15 inches; the Van Horn, 2.75 inches. The head size of the Gibbs is .635 inch, while the 500 VH Express is .585 inch with a 40-degree shoulder and neck length of .375 inch. The shoulder may be slight, but it is entirely adequate for headspacing. The cartridge is prepared from B.E.L.L. 416 brass, or by turning the belts from 460 Weatherby Magnum cases, trimming to length, working through a full-length resize die, then fireforming the brass to produce final dimensions. Van Horn prefers a beltless case headspacing on the

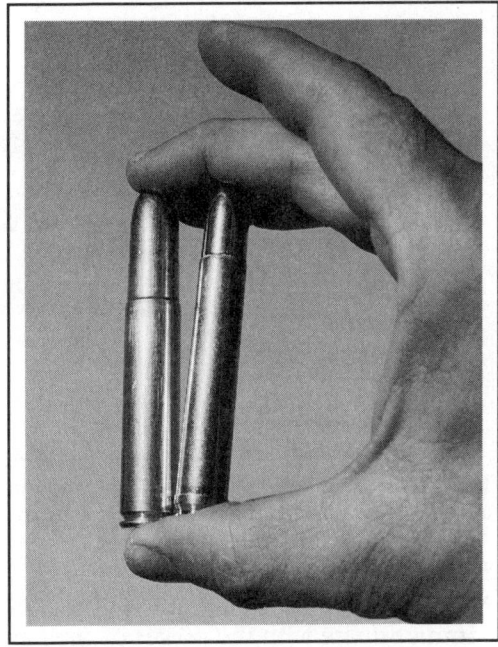

The strong Mauser 98 action has been used for chambering hundreds of different cartridges. One of the largest is the Van Horn 500 Express (left) compared here with a 458 Winchester cartridge. The VH 500 Express shoots a .510-inch, 600-grain bullet at over 2200 fps.

shoulder, rather than a belted case headspacing on the belt.

The configuration of the 500 Van Horn case conforms to the ideals of accuracy—short and squat, rather than tall and thin—with 100% loading density capability. Because cartridge design adheres to efficiency standards, the entire powder charge is put to good use. A zone of diminishing returns is not suffered with IMR-3031 or IMR-4064 powders. The major energy of the powder charge is applied to propel the projectile. In other words, this beltless magnum cartridge is not overbore capacity. While no round is 100% efficient, the 500 Van Horn's case capacity is compatible with bore size and bullet mass.

The appearance of the Van Horn rifle is nothing short of stunning. The French

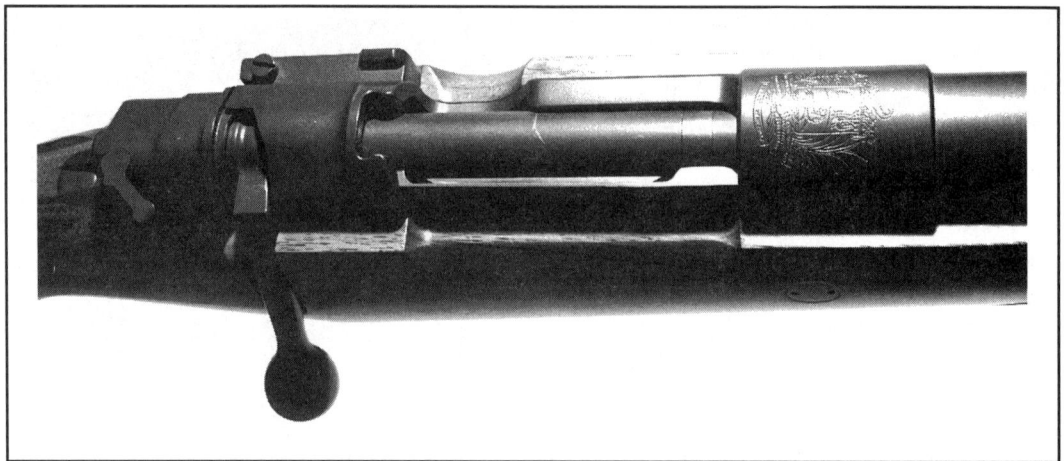

The Venezuelan "FN" Mauser action made in the 1930s serves as the basis of the marble-smooth action of Gil Van Horn's outstanding custom rifle.

walnut (also known as California English walnut) stock is big, but not bulky, and commensurate with the power of the cartridge. The choice of this type of walnut is designed to reduce the effects of "felt" recoil. The rifle was fitted to the customer who ordered it in true custom-made rifle fashion with a rubber recoil pad fitted to the buttstock. The stock finish gives the appearance of being in the wood, not on it. The stock is embellished with a forend tip and pistol-grip cap made of dry ebony. Van Horn emphasizes the word "dry," saying that this type of ebony is very difficult to locate nowadays. A nice touch of metalwork was the engraved sterling silver inlay on the cap. The rear swivel stud is from the pre-64 Model 70 Super Grade rifle—very strong.

Van Horn uses three or four methods of ensuring stock/action integrity, including a second recoil lug installed near the first lug on some of his rifles. (The Weatherby 460 uses this system, a second recoil lug close to the main lug—at least this is so on a 460 Weatherby of my investigation.) Surprisingly, this rifle does not include the second recoil lug, for the gunmaker does not believe in the small additional lug that is usually placed down-barrel. Van Horn has found that by adhering to microscopic tolerances in the action mortise and barrel channel of the stock, along with ample reinforcers, the metalwork has never broken away from the wood, even on a 500 Express rifle. But certain reinforcers are vital, he reminds. Key points are glassed in to ensure reinforcement. The gunmaker also uses reinforcing stock bolts. Furthermore, wood inserts are installed behind the magazine. Van Horn has devised a special cutter to create the mortises for these inserts. The wooden reinforcers are epoxied in place with the grain of the stock. "I've never had a stock split in my life, and I've made many big kickers," he remarks. He also uses, on some rifles, a secondary stock bolt built into the web area. He may also employ a wooden reinforcer behind the tang, the latter job accomplished in a mill with a slot cutter.

The wrist of the rifle is on the thick side. Many old-time English-made big-bore double rifles ended up with split stocks because of thin wrists, which are graceful and pleasing to the eye, but not necessarily correct on high-recoil rifles.

The action? It is a Venezuelan "FN" made in the 1930s—a Mauser all the way and reputed to carry excellent steel. Van Horn chooses only the best actions to begin with, which is part of the reason for the fluidity of his finished products. Here his goal is a marble-smooth action for safari work. For perfection of fit, the lugs are lapped into their recesses. The cocking cam is also lapped, and sometimes the opening cam in the bolt handle root as well. No compound is used on the bolt proper. Mauser bolts are inherently loose-fitted. The metal finish is also conducive to smoothness of operation: Gun Koat, which has a built-in lubricant containing molybdenum disulfide. I've yet to work a smoother bolt. The rifle handled well, even fast, considering its weight. The comparative shortness of bolt-throw also lends speed of operation in the field. The action is non-binding. No matter that the bolt handle is torqued, slick operation prevailed.

Further metalwork appointments include a handcrafted trigger guard, floorplate and magazine box after the pre-64 Model 70 style, but with an Oberndorf-type guard bow floorplate release. The follower is made from du Pont Delron, which is light, tough and dent-resistant. Furthermore, the follower does not slam forward against the front of the magazine box.

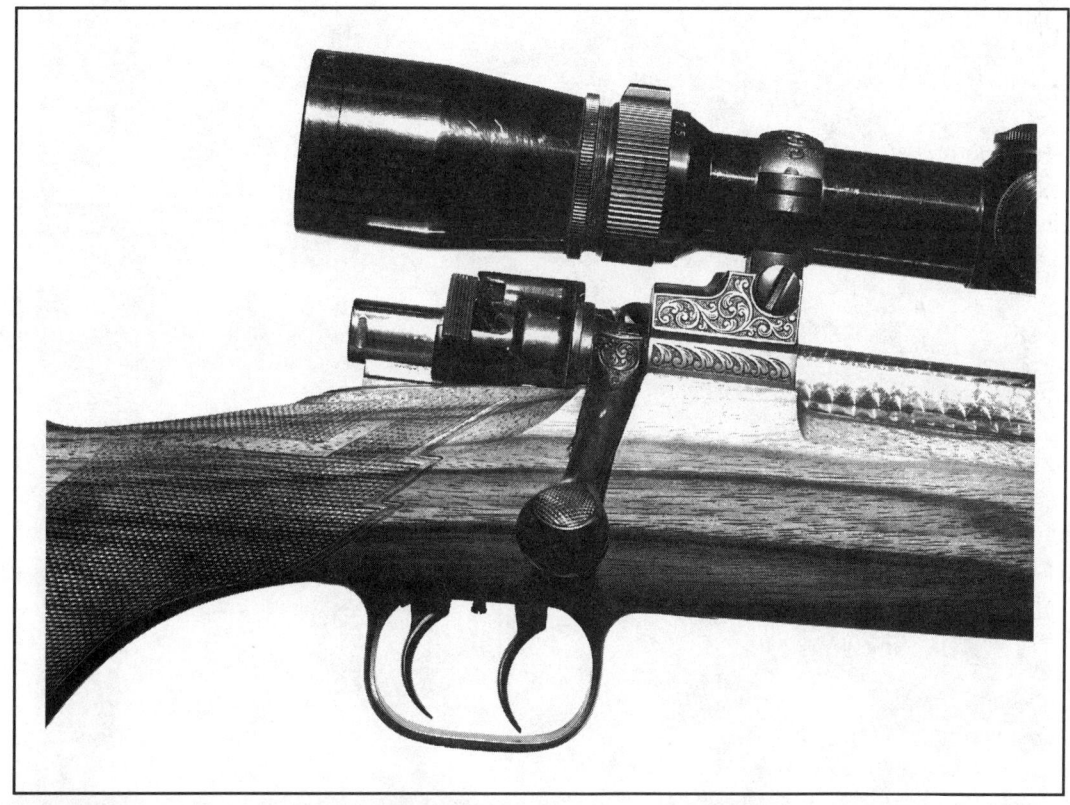

This close-up view of the Dean Zollinger custom rifle illustrates the attention to detail that distinguishes a custom rifle from the ordinary. Note the double-set triggers, engraved receiver and bolt handle and the fine checkering.

Metal followers can batter the magazine box in a high-recoil rifle. This magazine box is extra thick and made of spring steel. It is hardened in the frontal area to resist damage from heavy bullets during recoil. The barrel blank was provided by Sam May, who cut a 1:20 rate of twist in the stainless steel barrel. The barrel was turned and chambered with a Clymer reamer to Van Horn's specifications by Ryan Breeding of The Rifle Shop. The integral muzzle break is one of the highlights of the rifle. The front eye is located on the barrel. The trigger is a modified Timney, with an extended bow welded in place. The safety is a Grisel.

The sights of this custom Mauser 98 are unique. They appear somewhat bulky because they were meant to be. Van Horn witnessed sight failures on several safaris. He was determined to build his own sight style with massive construction. Van Horn calls his special sight, which he builds by hand, the "Disappearing Head." The front sight collapses into the ramp, and is returned to full battery position by depressing a button on the side of the ramp. The sight base is made of stainless steel and the rear sight V-notch is built from hardened tool steel. Considerable time and effort go into the construction of these special sights and they add a full $1000 to the cost of the finished product. Without the specialty

John Fadala prepares to shoot the Dean Zollinger 7mm Rem. Mag. custom rifle built around the Mauser 98 action.

> ### The Mauser Type "A" Sporting Rifle at a Glance
>
> **Period of Manufacture:** From the 1920s through 1930s by Mauser-Werke of Oberndorf, Germany
> **Calibers:** 30-06 (7.62×63), 7×57, 8×60, 9×57 and 9.3×6.2mm
> **Magazine Capacity:** 5-shot box magazine
> **Action:** Strong bolt-action repeater
> **Barrel:** Of steel, blued, 23½ inches, round or octagonal
> **Weight (approx.):** 7¼ pounds
> **Triggers:** Military-type single trigger or double-set triggers
> **Safety:** Shotgun-type on some
> **Sights:** Hooded ramp front, Express rear sight; optional folding peep rear, tangent curve rear or three-leaf rear variations
> **Stock:** Checkered pistol-grip sporting stock of Circassian walnut; checkered forend; with or without cheekpiece; detachable swivels
> **Variations:** Numerous options offered (see above). Mauser action used in many military and commercial models as well as custom rifles that carried extraordinary refinements and embellishments.

houses, incidentally, a Mauser sporter of this nature, or for that matter even one of less unique properties, would be fairly impossible to build.

In the bushveldt, accuracy in a hunting rifle is vital. In a well-bedded rifle, the stiff Mauser 98 action is known for its accuracy capability. To test its accuracy, the 500 Van Horn Express was shot from the bench and, as expected, it passed admirably. The test range was 50 yards in deference to the iron sights (the rifle wore no scope). Three-shot cloverleafs were the rule. Incidentally, no sandbag was used between the buttpad and the shooter's shoulder. Such tactics can result in a broken stock at the wrist.

So here is a powerhouse rifle built on a slick-working action whose design dates back almost a century. The rifle is comparatively short and supremely fine balanced. The integral muzzle brake is effective and comely. The sights are ingenious, rugged and easy to get on target with. With a four-round magazine and a round chambered in the barrel, the hunter has a cargo of five powerful blows to use against any big game. The rifle and round have been proven where it counts, in the field.

Naturally, this special Van Horn custom rifle is for the serious hunter and wallet. The test model described here runs in the five-digit range. However, this Mauser sporter is a serious lifetime investment that will still be functioning when your once-new automobile is gracing a junk yard. This account of a well-crafted Mauser sporter could be relived hundreds of times with different riflemakers' works. For the Mauser 98 remains high on the list of great actions in the building of great rifles. As with so many great sporting rifles tucked between the pages of this book, the Mauser has withstood the test of time. It did not have to be replicated, of course, because it was never deemed outdated by the shooters of the world. The 98 Mauser is guaranteed safe passage into the 21st century as one of the most widely used and copied action designs ever.

RUGER'S SINGLE-SHOT
THE NO. 1 THAT'S NO. 1

26

The year 1967 marked a special occasion for the Ruger Company. Bill Ruger took a chance on American shooters. Co-founder of Sturm, Ruger & Co. of Southport, Connecticut, Ruger bet that there were sufficient numbers of arms enthusiasts who would accept what was considered, by normal standards, an outdated but beautiful sporting arm. It was the Ruger No. 1, a single-shot rifle combining tradition with modern manufacture. A few soothsayers foretold the rifle's doom. Who would want, in a world of repeaters, a one-shot rifle for big game hunting? These doomsdayers said that in a few years at best the No. 1 would fail and that no artificial respiration from gunwriters and media advertisements would revive the out-

The beautiful Ruger No. 1B with 26-inch barrel and clean, classic lines.

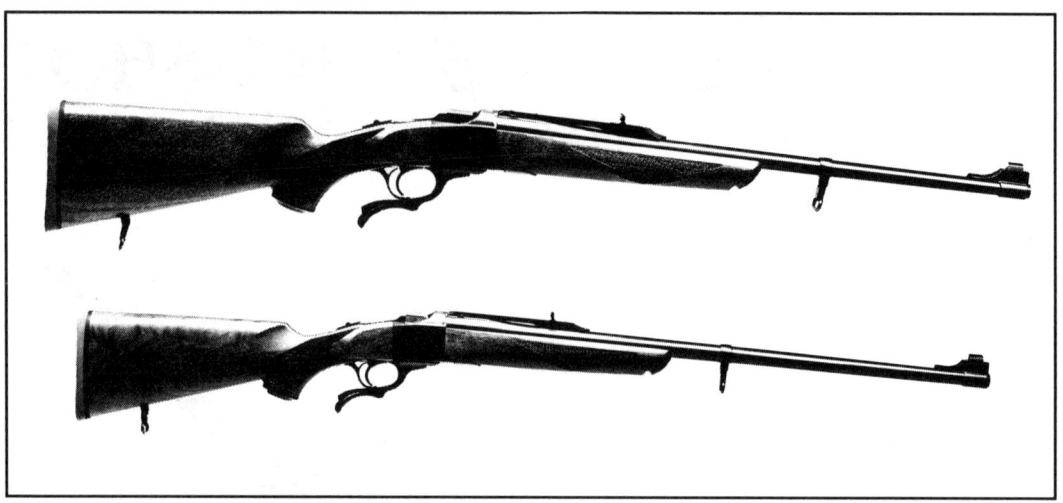

The No. 1s Medium Sporter (top) with 26-inch barrel weighs between 7¼ and 8 pounds in calibers 45-70, 7mm Rem. Mag., 300 Win. Mag. or 338 Win. Mag. The Ruger No. 1A Light Sporter (bottom) with 22-inch barrel is a little lighter in weight in calibers 243 Win., 270 Win., 30-06 Springfield and 7 × 57 Mauser. Both models have Henry-pattern forearms and front swivels attached to a barrel band.

dated rifle. They were wrong. The Ruger creation made it and keeps on making it.

The overall appearance of the No. 1 rifle is flawless. It is remindful of the great Farquharsons of the 19th century. The lines of the rifle are clean, with a stock design by renowned stockmaker Len Brownell, along with an Alexander Henry forearm style. Henry was a designer of classic 19th-century single-shot British rifles. The stock was adorned with hand-checkering by a group of New Hampshire women trained by Brownell to do the job right. That was important, because the No. 1 was predicated on the fact that today's shooters continue to appreciate the classic lines of yesteryear. If the rifle had not met with visual approval, it would have failed in the first few months of production. Of course, the No. 1 was cost-effective in its production methods or it would not have survived from that standpoint either.

The Ruger No. 1 embodied tradition from the single-shot Winchester rifle, as well as the uni-shot Sharps that dominated buffalo days. There were also the famous Remington Rolling Block and other great single-shots from the past, including the Peabody-Martini Creedmoor, Alexander Henry rifle, Sharps-Borchardt, Ballards and many varieties of Schuetzen rifles. Of course the No. 1 is a breechloader, as the rifles above are breechloaders, and used a metallic cartridge.

History played a role in promoting the Ruger No. 1, but so did the rifle's inherent excellence and the fact that its single-shot predecessors were highly reliable and efficient, even if they did fire but one round before requiring reloading. The No. 1 embodied that ancient code among hunters—make the first shot count. Not that a second shot or perhaps a third was impossible with a single-shot, but in no way could the No. 1 be compared with a lever, bolt, semi-auto or slide-action repeater. A hunter without sporting blood had no business with this rifle. The idea is that a hunter carrying a single-shot proceeds more carefully. He works to make his first opportunity a good one. He has to know his quarry, and though he need not get any closer to it than with any other big game rifle chambered for modern cartridges, he's not going to have backup ammo if he blunders.

The Ruger No. 1 is of falling breechblock design, not unlike the Sharps. But the beauty of it turned out to be a number of fine styles within the style, as well as chamberings for a multitude of excellent cartridges. It is hammerless in that there is no visible or exposed hammer. The hammer that is there is encased within the receiver of the rifle and is cocked as the underlever is lowered. The hammerless action design dates back to the 1870s.

Bill Ruger and company designed a mainspring style for the No. 1 that allowed the action to remain compact. The mainspring lies forward of the receiver and extends into the forestock. Harry Sefried and Larry Larson, two of the engineers involved in the design, wanted to ensure a slim and handsome rifle, which was Bill Ruger's goal. The mainspring idea promotes just that. Furthermore, Ruger insisted that his single-shot work well with rimless cases. The Sharps, for example, was

Loading the Ruger No. 1 couldn't be simpler. With the lever in the down position, the shooter just feeds a cartridge directly into the chamber. The scope sight fits on a special ramp that is an integral part of the rifle.

built around rimmed cases, the rims serving as a gripping place for the extractor. Some single-shots failed in extraction to a degree; in certain instances English ammo was toned down at the factory to provide less pressure to give the extractor a better chance to pull a fired case free of the breech. Ruger's requirement was for an extractor/ejector system that was capable of dealing with high-pressure ammo—rounds such as the 300 Winchester Magnum and 7mm Remington Magnum, as well as the hot smallbores like the 22-250 Remington.

The shooter does not need to pull the case from the chamber of the No. 1, since ejection is automatic. A spring, housed in the forestock (an ingenious idea), provides a kick that expels the empty case from the breech, flinging it rearward. For those who prefer non-auto ejection, the spring can be disengaged.

SUPREME ACTION STRENGTH FOR HIGH-INTENSITY ROUNDS

The supreme action strength of the Ruger No. 1 allows the rifle to be chambered for a host of high-intensity modern cartridges. While the majority of falling-block actions contain more than one pin, the Ruger has a single pin upon which the major constituents of the action pivot. There are a couple more pins, but they are inside the action. The true genius of the action lies in its simplicity of design, although the Ruger No. 1 does contain a number of interior parts. The action is wedded to a good trigger assembly along with an entirely handy shotgun-style, thumb-operated safety mounted on the upper tang. This safety is convenient and fast. The trigger is adjustable for weight of pull and for overtravel. And a small projection on the underside of the rifle for-

The Ruger No. 1 International Model has a full-length stock in the Mannlicher tradition. Equipped with sights and a 20-inch barrel, the rifle is chambered for calibers 243 Win., 270 Win., 7 × 57 Mauser and 30-06 Springfield—all popular hunting rounds.

ward of the trigger guard announces to a touch of a finger whether or not the hammer is in the cocked position and the rifle ready to go.

The final result is a rifle of simple function: lower the breechblock via the underlever; fit a round into the chamber; close the breech; shoot; drop the lever. The fired case is ejected free of the action and the process can immediately start over. It all adds up to as neat a single-shot rifle as any demanding rifleman could ask for.

From its inception, the barrel length of the Ruger No. 1 was 26 inches. Today the 26-inch length remains in the lineup in a round, tapered style along with other barrel lengths, depending upon sub-model. The button-rifled barrel is free-floated in the sense that it does not touch the forearm wood. The forearm is held separately by connection with the action and therefore the barrel and forearm are not connected. The 26-inch barrel does not result in a detrimental overall rifle length because of the short receiver, much shorter than the usual bolt design. For example, the current No. 1B Ruger is under 46 inches long. A bolt-action rifle with 26-inch barrel may measure an overall length of over 46 inches. The longer barrel was and still is offered for those shooters who wish to gain maximum velocity from a given cartridge.

This particular aspect of barrel length cannot be predicated simply on how much distance the powder can be burned in, however. For example, specific handloads with a 7mm Remington Magnum using H-1000 powder proved that after 24 inches very little velocity was gained. Nonetheless, some cartridges and given loads do pick up appreciably in velocity with a longer barrel. Tests with a 257 Weatherby Magnum proved that the 26-inch barrel gained a significant velocity increase over a 24-inch barrel.

Sights? The Ruger No. 1 has none. That is, the rifle started out without iron sights because Ruger believed, correctly,

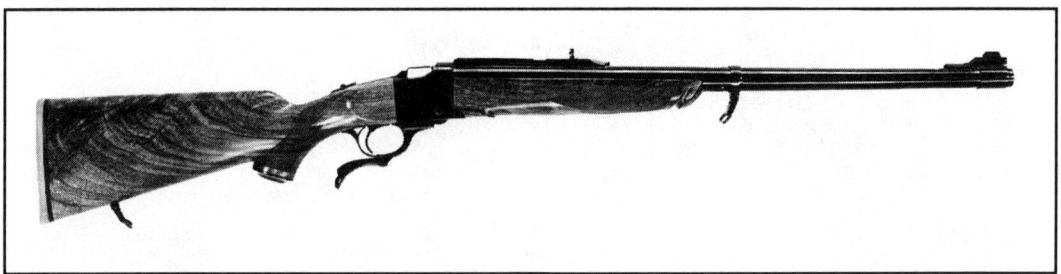

With its 24-inch heavy barrel, the No. 1H Tropical Rifle is ready for just about anything in calibers 375 H&H Mag. or 458 Win. Mag.

that his No. 1 should be scoped. An integral ramp dovetailed is ready to accept scope rings. The price tag on the first No. 1 was under $300. That was a bargain considering that it was a better rifle overall than many of the fine single-shots of yesteryear that sell for a pretty penny at gun shows, when they can be found.

If the Ruger No. 1 had a drawback, it was in the accuracy department. But let's clarify that statement. One Ruger personally tested in caliber 270 Winchester produced three-inch groups center to center for five shots at 100 yards. Consequently, the rifle was tuned via alternating pressure on the hanger via a screw for that purpose.

Jess Spencer tries his newly rebarreled No. 1, which DGS, Inc. of Casper, Wyoming, altered from 6mm Remington to 257 Ackley Improved to increase the rifle's potency on big game.

Different handloads were tried as well. The result was 1.5-inch groups center to center fired at 100 yards from the bench. That figure is more than livable for a hunting rifle. Moreover, even greater accuracy has been achieved with Ruger No. 1 rifles carefully tuned by expert gunsmiths.

A Creedmoor-style Ruger No. 1, especially made for the late gun enthusiast John Amber, provided groups without any tuning and the same rifle was later improved in accuracy with handloads. The rifle was built with a long half-octagon barrel in caliber 45-70 Springfield. Amber installed both front and rear sights from a Sharps-Borchardt rifle. The Vernier tang rear sight was initially designed for long-range target shooting with calibrations of from 600- to 1000-yard ranges.

Many hundreds of Ruger No. 1 actions have been used to build custom-made rifles. But a shooter need not seek out a custom No. 1 for the sake of variety, because the rifle has been offered in a number of variations over the years. In 1969, for example, the Ruger No. 1 (which sold for $280) was offered in a choice of standard sporter or beavertail forearm with a 22-inch (lightweight) or 26-inch (mediumweight) barrel. (The only heavy barrel offered was for the 458 Winchester Magnum chambering of the rifle.) This 1969

Ruger No. 1 was offered in a multitude of calibers, including 222 Remington, 22-250 Remington, 6mm Remington, 243 Winchester, 7mm Remington Magnum, 308 Winchester, 30-06 Springfield and 458 Winchester Magnum, plus other chamberings on special order. In 1977, a 24-inch barrel was added. The calibers listed above for 1969 remained in the lineup, except for the 222 Remington and 308 Winchester. Additional chamberings were the 25-06 Remington, 270 Winchester, 300 Winchester Magnum, 375 H&H Magnum and 45-70 Springfield. The weight remained listed as approximately 8 pounds.

Another Ruger No. 1 with a new number surfaced. This was the Ruger No. 3 Carbine chambered for the 22 Hornet, 30-40 Krag and 45-70 Springfield (Government). This single-shot with straight-grip, carbine-style stock weighed only 6 pounds. With a 22-inch barrel, its overall length was but 38.5 inches. This rifle wore iron sights, a folding leaf rear and a gold bead front.

By 1991 the Ruger No. 1 was offered in many styles and calibers, indicative of its success. These models are worth describing because they tell much about the evolution of this fine single-shot rifle:

• The No. 1A Light Sporter with 22-inch barrel and Alexander Henry-style forend weighs only 7 1/4 pounds. An adjustable folding rear sight is available on a quarter rib, which is ready to accept one-inch scope rings. A gold bead front sight is also standard. Calibers include 243 Winchester, 270 Winchester, 7×57 Mauser and 30-06 Springfield.

• No. 1B carries a 26-inch barrel, no sights, semi-beavertail forearm. It is available in calibers 223 Remington, 22-250 Remington, 220 Swift, 243 Winchester, 6mm Remington, 257 Roberts, 25-06 Remington, 270 Winchester, 280 Remington, 7mm Remington Magnum, 30-06 Springfield, 300 Winchester Magnum and 338 Winchester Magnum. Also chambered are two Weatherby cartridges, the 270 and 300, both of which gain from the longer barrel.

• No. 1H Tropical Rifle is similar to the 1B, but in calibers 375 H&H Magnum and 458 Winchester Magnum with 24-inch heavy barrel (weight 8 1/4 to 9 pounds) and open sights on ramp.

• No. 1S Medium Sporter, also similar to the 1B, has an Alexander Henry forearm, sights and calibers 7mm Remington Magnum, 300 Winchester Magnum, 338 Winchester Magnum and 45-70 Government, the latter with 22-inch barrel, the others with 26-inch barrel.

• No. 1V Special Varmint is similar to the 1B too, but with 24-inch heavy barrel in calibers 223 Remington, 22-250 Remington, 220 Swift and 25-06.

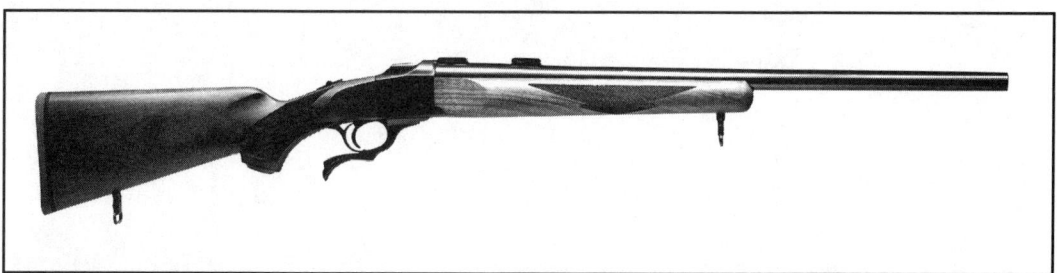

The Special Varmint rifle is ready with scope blocks for the best long-range scope sights available. In 25-06 caliber, it serves as a long-range varminter as well as a deer/antelope rifle.

> ### THE RUGER NO. 1 AT A GLANCE
>
> **Period of Manufacture:** 1967 to date
> **Calibers:** 222 Rem., 6mm Rem., 22-250 Rem., 25-06 Rem., 243 Win., 270 Win., 300 Win. Mag., 30-06 Springfield, 7mm Rem. Mag., 308 Win., 375 H&H Mag., 45-70 Springfield, 458 Win. Mag., and others
> **Action:** Single-shot falling block action with underlever and automatic ejection
> **Barrel:** 26 inches, usually, free-floating, round, tapered (standard mediumweight or heavyweight); also 22-inch lightweight, 24-inch
> **Weight (approx.):** Ranges from 6 to 9 pounds, depending on caliber and barrel length
> **Sights:** Adjustable folding leaf rear; gold bead front; some rifles with no sights, but integral ramp dovetailed for scope rings
> **Stock:** Hand-checkered pistol-grip stock of American walnut; semi-beavertail forend; QD sling swivels
> **Variations:** Several—No. 1A Light Sporter, No. 1B, No. 1S Medium Sporter, No. 1H Tropical, No. 1RSI International, No. 1V Special Varmint, No. 3 Carbine, plus many custom rifles built on the No. 1 action

- No. 1RSI International is equipped with a full-length Mannlicher-style stock with sights and a 20-inch barrel in calibers 243 Winchester, 270 Winchester, 7×57 Mauser and 30-06 Springfield.

Prices, of course, reflect the times and depend on style. Barreled actions are sold separately, which proves that making custom rifles from Ruger No. 1 actions is still popular in the 1990s.

The Ruger No. 1 is the story of a rifle that looked to the past for style, but to the present for interior design, manufacturing techniques and modern calibers. It is a success story that could have had a different ending, considering the tremendous popularity of the bolt-action big game rifle in America. A friend of mine and an accomplished hunter, Richard Reitz of Casper, Wyoming, is a single-shot fan who owns several Ruger No. 1 rifles and a No. 3. Dick is an example of the modern hunter who enjoys blending past with present and throwing in a lot of challenge. He is the kind of outdoorsman and shooter that has made the No. 1 fly—the rifle that is still soaring toward the 21st century.

WEATHERBY RIFLES
HIGH-TECH, TALL QUALITY

27

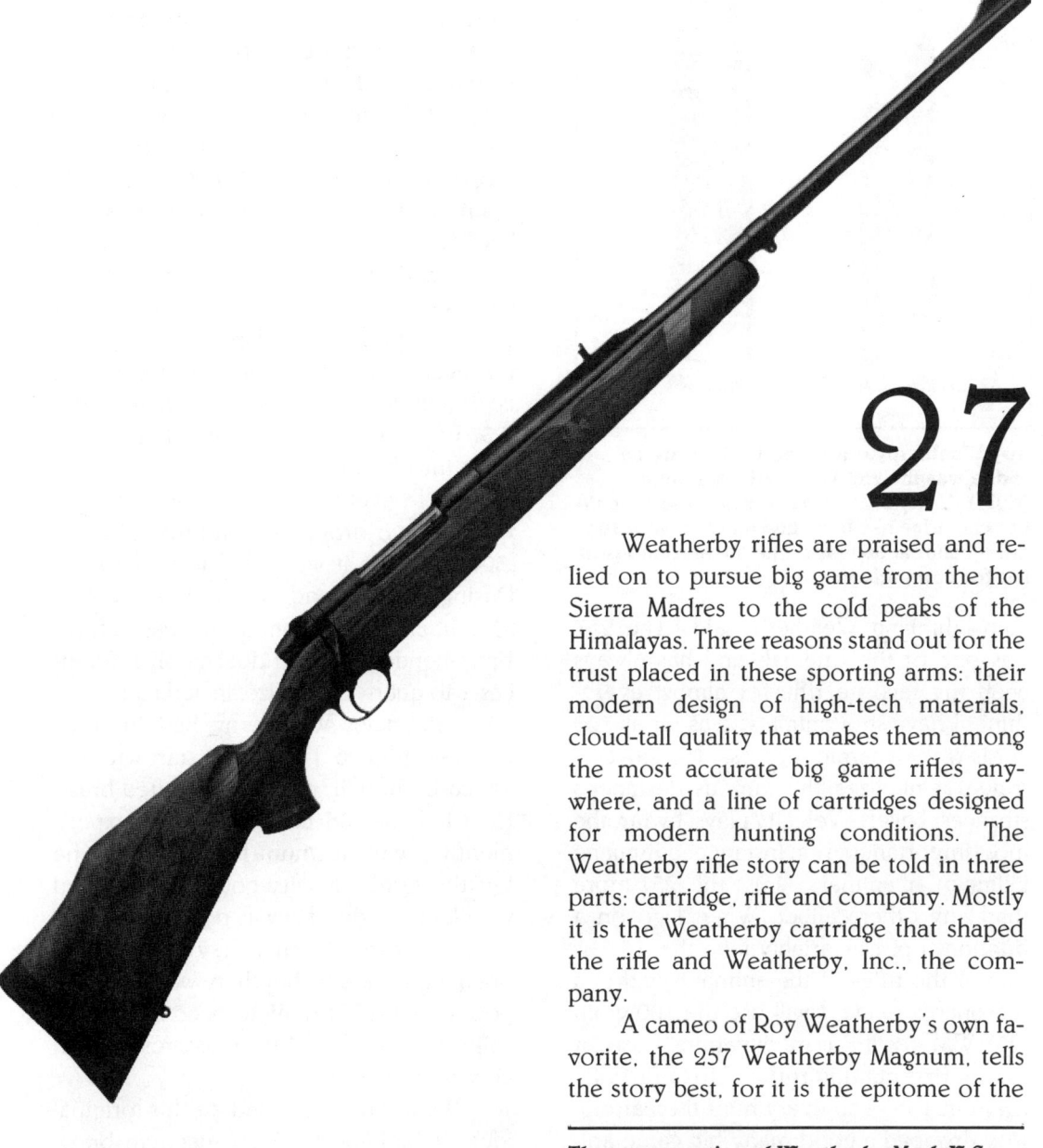

Weatherby rifles are praised and relied on to pursue big game from the hot Sierra Madres to the cold peaks of the Himalayas. Three reasons stand out for the trust placed in these sporting arms: their modern design of high-tech materials, cloud-tall quality that makes them among the most accurate big game rifles anywhere, and a line of cartridges designed for modern hunting conditions. The Weatherby rifle story can be told in three parts: cartridge, rifle and company. Mostly it is the Weatherby cartridge that shaped the rifle and Weatherby, Inc., the company.

A cameo of Roy Weatherby's own favorite, the 257 Weatherby Magnum, tells the story best, for it is the epitome of the

The strong-actioned Weatherby Mark V Safari Grade Rifle reflects outstanding quality.

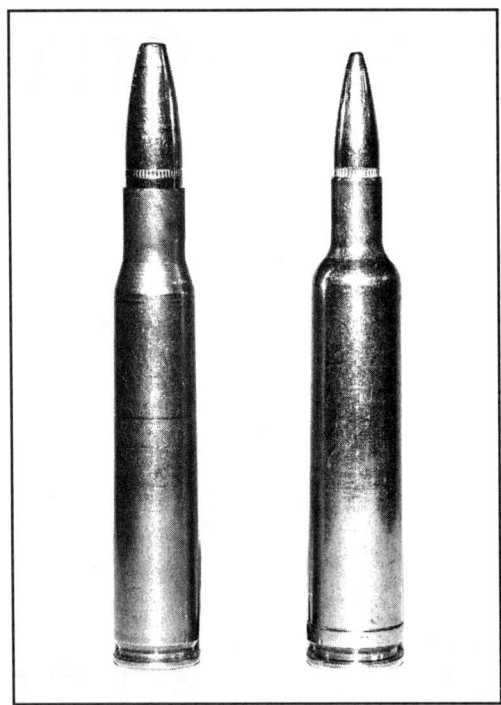

Roy Weatherby often said his favorite cartridge was the 257 Weatherby Magnum (right). Using IMR-4831 powder, this 25-caliber cartridge has been known to drive a 100-grain bullet at 3600 fps. The 30-06 round is at left for comparison.

man's thinking. Weatherby said, "The .257 was one of the originals and has always been my favorite rifle for almost everything. I have shot animals... as far as 300 yards with dynamic success." His 257 cartridge symbolizes the famous designer's strongest belief: "Velocity plays, by far, the most important part in instant and humane killing of an animal... I use the .257 more than any other caliber. When I go on a hunting trip, I invariably take the .257 as one of the rifles. If the animal is within a reasonable range, I will use the 100-grain .257 WM, for it is pure dynamite. I used it on my first hunting trip in Africa in 1948, again in 1953 and every hunt thereafter." Roy dropped a good many big game animals with his 257, including the tough zebra, and seldom was a second shot necessary. Of course, the 257 WM did not—with a single lightning blow—evaporate every game animal struck. Sometimes a second bullet was needed. Sometimes a second bullet is needed with a 300 Magnum, too, or for that matter an "elephant cartridge." Roy Weatherby wanted a bullet to enter the chest cavity of a big game animal and self-destruct, using all its energy within the game, rather than expending some of its clout in the dust beyond the target. That is why he selected the 100-grain bullet over the 117- or 120-grain in his 257.

Weatherby created several of his wildcats in the '30s, including his 270 WM in 1937. The 257 Weatherby Magnum did not become a reality until about 1944. "It is difficult to give you an exact date of the .257 beginning," Roy mused, "but when I went into business in 1945, I already had the 220 Rocket that was on the Swift case which I later dropped. I had the .270 and .300; I'm sure it was sometime in 1944." During the '30s and '40s, a great deal of 25-caliber experimentation was afoot. Brass-benders necked dozens of different cases to quarter-inch size, including the 30-06 Springfield. Weatherby had his own blown-out 25-06. He did not start with the '06 case, though, rather with belted brass. He tried the '06 case only after experimenting with magnum brass, because he felt the same velocity could be achieved with less powder. He was right. Blown-out 25-06s, for that is what they were, developed high velocity, but there was a price—poor case life. Also, high speed from a 25-caliber bullet on 30-06 brass resulted in very high pressures.

Weatherby returned to his original idea of building a 25 on magnum brass. Many great experimenters blazed the high-velocity wildcat trail; however, the amazing results they obtained in the 1940s were generated by extremely high pressure. There is no way, for example, to obtain the rocket-like velocities today that experimenters got with their 25 wildcats just before, during and after World War II, not without short brass life and excessive pressure. The 25 Sniper Magnum (or Davis Sniper), for example, was chronographed at 4011 feet per second (fps) muzzle velocity (mv) with an 87-grain bullet. That had to be a brass-melter with mid-20th century powders. Roy was a part of this high-pressure experimentation. He put a flash tube in a 25-06 case, crammed her full of fuel and drove the 100-grain bullet at 3915 fps.

Phil Sharpe, in his *Complete Guide to Reloading*, credited the 257 WM with an 87-grain bullet at 4060 fps mv and a 100-grain bullet at 3750 fps mv. Today, we do not deal in those figures because safety comes first. A tested 257 WM rifle with 26-inch barrel shooting an 87-grain pill split the airways at around 3800 fps absolute maximum. A velocity hovering around 3700–3750 fps was a more usual figure. The 100-grain missile at around 3600 fps is a maximum figure under modern rules where test devices read actual pressures. (In factory-made loads, the 257 WM's 87-grain bullet is advertised at 3825 fps, the 100-grain bullet at 3555 fps and the 120-grain projectile at 3300 fps.) Early velocity figures on the 257 WM and other high-intensity test cartridges of the era were probably quite accurate. There is no argument with the figures, only with the pressures the cartridges generated to achieve such startling results. Chronographs were crude by today's standards, but not necessarily inaccurate, as Weatherby attested: "There were no chronographs on the market in 1943 and 1944; therefore, I had to make one. It took two men and a boy to operate the damn thing and about 15 to 20 minutes to get the reading on one round. After I received my first chronograph in about 1950, I found that the loads we had chronographed with the home-built model were almost on the button, but I had no way of checking pressures."

The 257 WM went forth to slay dragons. One afternoon Weatherby was returning from a plains game shoot in the African bush. Suddenly, between Roy and his destination, stood a Cape buffalo. One shot later, the buff was down for good. A second after telling the facts of that story, Weatherby concluded that the 257 was not a Cape buffalo rifle, nor did he intend to

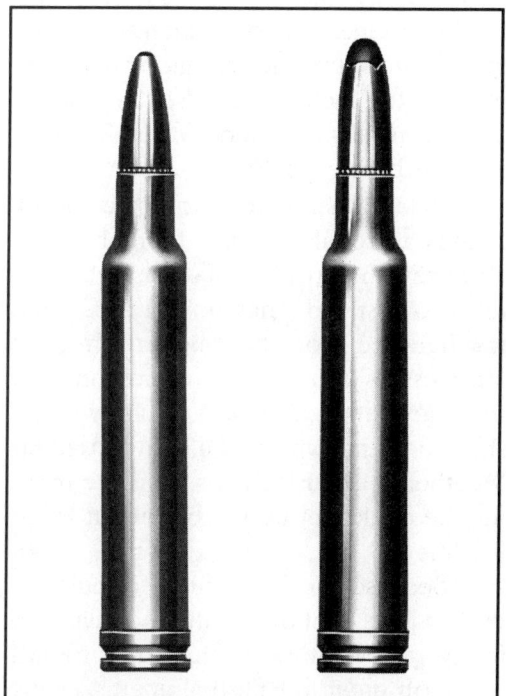

The most famous Weatherby cartridge remains the 300 Weatherby Magnum, a powerful 30-caliber capable of long-range big game harvesting. The two Remington loads shown here are the 180-grain bullet (left) and the 220-grain.

use it on another dangerous beast like that. "I just happened to have it with me. The .257 WM is no buffalo rifle." He said further, "I don't want you to get the idea that I don't use the other calibers because the .270 and 7mm WM are about the same and they are also pure dynamite. The .340 is very popular and is a good cartridge also."

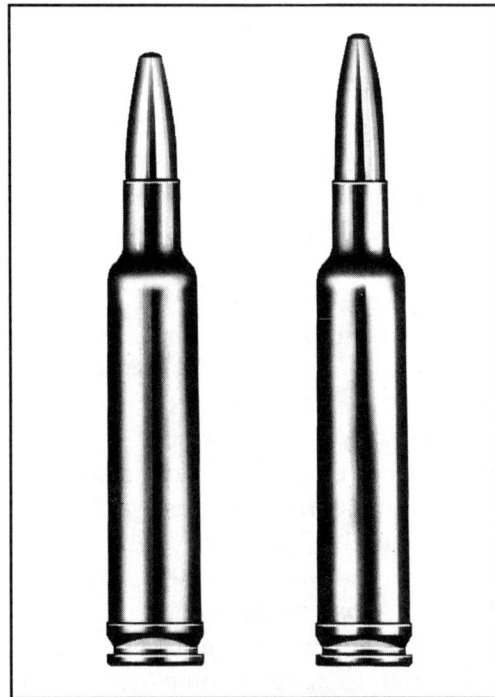

One of the finest Weatherby cartridges of all time is the 7mm Weatherby Magnum, shown here in Remington loadings with a 140-grain pointed soft-point bullet (left) and a 175-grain PSP "Core-Lokt" bullet.

Weatherby wasn't the only fan of the 257. Herb Klein loved the round and took a truck load of game with it, preferring the 117-grain bullet. Klein used the 257 for elk and grizzly as well as smaller game. Colonel Charles Askins still likes the 257 WM. The Colonel once tallied 35 Impalas with 35 shots using the cartridge. So the 257 WM is a "typical" Weatherby cartridge, a deadly long-range harvesting machine on deer and antelope and similar-size game.

All of Weatherby's rounds were patterned for the same results: high speed, and all of them were verbally attacked as "inefficient." Students of interior ballistics assured the shooting public that the 257 WM is a lousy cartridge because it is inefficient, suffering badly from overbore capacity. Indeed, these black marks are properly assigned. The 257 WM is inefficient and it is overbore capacity. A race car is also inefficient, and I suppose a correlation between cartridge overbore capacity and race car "overbore capacity" could be made. In a way, it is made when you put X into a machine and get X minus out of it. But is this sort of efficiency pertinent to the question of high ballistic energy and flat trajectory? Does it truly matter that it takes a lot of powder to get one of the flattest trajectories among big game rounds? The facts say no. Use the powder. Get the results. So much for inefficiency and overbore capacity.

Rifles chambered for Weatherby rounds were also called barrel-burners. However, the attrition of Weatherby barrels is overstated. They do not erode in a few hundred shots. Few modern shooters are blessed with so much time and cash that they can burn up a Weatherby barrel shooting game with it. If a hunter used his Weatherby exclusively for big game hunting, he could not burn a barrel out in his lifetime.

Because the Newtonian formula for energy pays a lot of attention to bullet velocity, all Weatherby big game rounds come off great in ballistic impetus, as the chart on page 266 shows. Note the retained energy of the 257 WM round. It's a pretty potent cartridge on deer-sized game to around 300 yards or so. Those who tout the 257 WM for larger-than-deer game

Three impressive examples of Weatherby's tall quality: the Mark V Lazermark (left), the Crown Custom Rifle (center), and the Varmintmaster (right). Note the rich variation in checkering and detail, including the types of scrollwork and inlays.

usually shoot their quarry much closer than 300 yards, so striking energy is quite high. Weatherby's high-velocity claim to fame holds up: terminal velocity is high with the 257 WM at the 100- to 200-yard range in which, as Roy often said, most big game is taken. Speed. Speed. Speed. If the Weatherby round weren't fast, it wouldn't be special. As the chart shows, speed generates not only energy, but also a flat trajectory that translates as follows: the Weatherby is easy to hit with at long range. Look at the 120-grain bullet skipping off to the races at over 3400 fps mv. Sighted

| A Few Selected Loads for the 257 Weatherby Magnum ||||
Bullet (Grain)	Powder	Charge (Grains)	Velocity (Feet Per Second)
75	IMR-4350	71.0	4048
87	H-4831	75.0	3876
100	IMR-4350	65.5	3600
100	IMR-7828	73.0	3650
117	H-4831	67.0	3350
117	IMR-7828	70.0	3400
120	IMR-4831	66.0	3415
120	IMR-7828	69.5	3375

Above are sanctioned loads, to be used only in the Mark V Weatherby Rifle.

| Sample Trajectory, 257 Weatherby Magnum |||||
	100 Yards	200 Yards	300 Yards	400 Yards	500 Yards
100-Grain Bullet	+2.5"	+3.0"	0	−8.0"	−22.0"
120-Grain Bullet	+2.5"	+3.5"	0	−8.5"	−23.0"

Sample trajectory for the 257 WM above was derived using the 100-grain Hornady Interlock bullet at 3600 fps mv, and the 120-grain Sierra Boat-Tail Bullet at 3400 fps muzzle velocity.

| Energy for Top Loads in the 257 Weatherby Magnum |||||
	0 Yards	100 Yards	200 Yards	300 Yards	400 Yards
100-Grain Bullet	3600 fps 2877 f-p	3287 fps 2399 f-p	2997 fps 1994 f-p	2783 fps 1646 f-p	2462 fps 1345 f-p
120-Grain Bullet	3400 fps 3082 f-p	3145 fps 2636 f-p	2832 fps 2138 f-p	2686 fps 1923 f-p	2380 fps 1510 f-p

Energy for top loads using a 100-grain bullet at 3600 fps mv derived from Sierra data; with the 120-grain bullet at 3400 fps mv, author-generated.

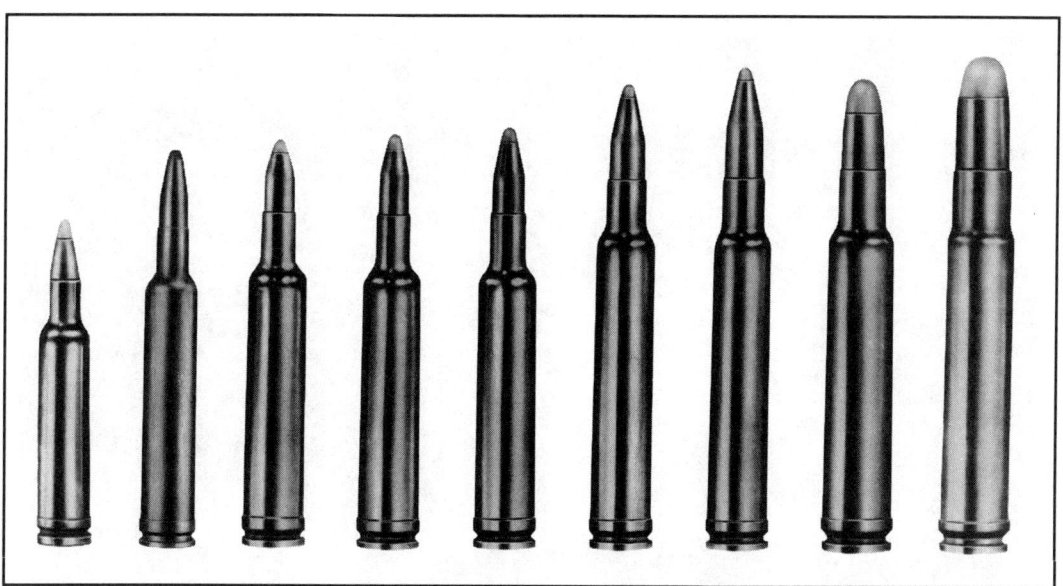

The lineup of Weatherby Magnum cartridges includes (left to right): the 224, 240, 257, 270, 7mm, 300, 340, 378 and 460. The powerful 416, not shown, was not yet invented when this photograph was taken.

approximately 2½ inches high at 100 yards, it zeroes at around 300.

This data comes from the shooting range, by the way, not charts. All three of the rifles used were sufficiently accurate to run drop tests in the field. If a rifle produces good groups at long range, drop tests are viable. The Mark V with the 26-inch barrel produced group sizes not much over a half-inch at 100 yards for three shots, and that's at full crank with the 100-grain bullet at around 3600 and the 120-grainer at around 3400. The figures speak for themselves. The 257 WM is typical of Roy Weatherby's philosophy: give me bullet speed and I'll give you results.

The Weatherby line of cartridges runs from calibers 22 through 45. There is a 224 Weatherby Magnum that shoots a 55-grain bullet at an advertised 3650 fps. It's easy to see that Weatherby wasn't trying to set the world record for centerfire 22s with this round. He already had a 22 on a blown-out 220 Swift case and dropped it. The intention of the 224 WM was to fill a niche, a gap between the 222-223 Remington and the 22-250 and 220 Swift. The 240 WM is a hot 6mm cartridge, pushing an 87-grain bullet at 3500 fps and a 100-grain bullet at close to 3400 fps. As a comparison, note that the famous 243 Winchester drives its 6mm 100-grain bullet at a bit under 3000 fps.

The 270 Weatherby Magnum is another one-of-a-kind, the only factory cartridge in caliber 270 that develops significantly higher speed than the original 270 Winchester. The 270 WM drives a 100-grain bullet at 3760 fps, a 130-grain bullet at 3375 fps and a 150-grain bullet at 3245 fps, compared with the standard 270 Winchester at 3430, 3060, and 2850 fps for factory loads with the same weight bullets.

The 7mm Weatherby Magnum is one of the finest long-range big game cartridges ever developed. It is no more or less than the popular 7mm Remington Magnum. Of course the two are not interchangeable,

WEATHERBY RIFLES 267

Weatherby's trademark is high speed, and this promise is fulfilled even in the big bores. The Weatherby 460 Magnum round can drive a 500-grain bullet at about 2700 fps with a factory loading.

because they do not share the same case shape, but ballistically they are near twins. The only difference is that Roy Weatherby had his 7mm Magnum in 1944, while the 7mm Remington Magnum did not show up until 1962. The 7mm WM drives a 140-grain bullet at 3400 fps mv, a 154-grain missile at 3260 fps and a 175-grain bullet at 3070 fps. As an all-around cartridge for big game hunting in North America, the Big 7 by Weatherby is hard to beat.

The big game cartridge that made the company famous, however, is the 300 Weatherby Magnum. Consider the fact that the 30-06 Springfield is a fine all-around big game cartridge with a 180-grain bullet at 2700 fps (factory ballistics) to around 2800 fps (special handload). Take that same 30-caliber bullet and drive it at 3200–3300 fps and it's easy to see why the 300 WM became known as a world cartridge for all but the very largest of big game animals. The 30-06 shooting a 180-grain bullet at 2800 fps earns a muzzle energy of 3134 foot-pounds. The 300 WM pushing the same bullet at 3300 fps develops a muzzle energy of 4354 foot-pounds. More than one world-traveling big game hunter has relied on the 300 WM as the bread-and-butter round for his work, along with the Weatherby rifle as his premier hunting instrument.

The 340 Weatherby Magnum is a hot cartridge in 33 caliber. This round uses 210- and 250-grain factory bullets at 3250 and 3000 fps muzzle velocities for energies of 4924 and 4995 foot-pounds. Coupling speed and bullet weight obviously provides terrific energy. While the 300 WM with its 150-grain bullet at 3600 fps gained a muzzle energy of a whopping 4316 foot-pounds, the 340 WM whips that figure by a mile.

Climbing the caliber ladder is the 375 Weatherby Magnum with a 300-grain bullet at 2700 fps and its big brother, the 378 Weatherby Magnum, another 375 actually, with a 300-grain bullet at 2929 fps. This latter factory load develops almost 5700 foot-pounds of muzzle energy, but the same 378 WM shooting a 270-grain bullet at 3180 fps produces power in the 6062 foot-pound range. That's a lot of authority.

But there is more. The 416 Weatherby Magnum drives a 400-grain bullet at 2700 fps for 6477 foot-pounds, and the 460 Weatherby Magnum pushes a 500-grain missile at the same speed for 8092 foot-pounds. Naturally, power alone is meaningless without matching the round to the game being hunted. There is no need to use a 416 WM on deer or elk, for example, and the 460 WM is strictly for the largest game in the world.

So after the pot boils, the Weatherby broth is clearly made up of the middle rounds, especially the great 300 WM, the hottest 30-caliber factory cartridge going. You can see that indeed it has been the Weatherby cartridges that have produced remarkable fame for the rifles.

The Weatherby rifles, however, are as unique as their cartridges—unique in that they are the best-distributed of their type in the world. The style is not now, nor was it ever intended to be, a copy of another rifle style. It's strictly modern, most decidedly not of the American classic design or the European style. The stock is often called the California design. It has a pronounced cheekpiece, as the photographs show, plus a Monte Carlo comb that stands right out and shouts its lines to the world. The forend is sleek and squarish, and the pistol grip is bold. It's not unusual to find a diamond-shaped inlay in that pistol grip, or the same sort of inlay adorning other parts of the Weatherby stock. Checkering is as common on a Weatherby as soles on shoes. Woods have ranged from all of the walnuts to mesquite, which is a dense, heavy wood with considerable figure. Mesquite is quite at home on a Weatherby, although it is not compatible on a rifle looking to lightness. Weatherby rifles have also gone to synthetics in answer to the trend, but they retain the lines of the orig-

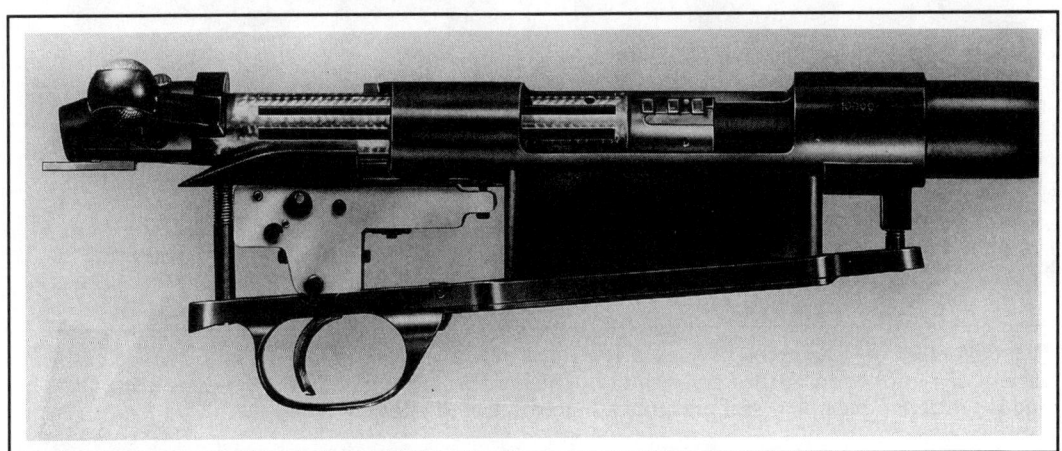

The Mark V Weatherby action, with nine locking lugs, is the heart of the high-performance Weatherby rifle. Strong and accurate, this bolt-action is as unique as the Weatherby rifle and cartridge designs.

This collection of Weatherby rifles clearly demonstrates the pattern of the stock as well as the variety of woods used. All are constructed of various walnuts, except the rifle farthest right. This one is crafted of mesquite and presents a highly marbled effect.

inal design all the same. It's easy to spot a Weatherby.

The Weatherby bolt-action design is just as unique as its stock lines. There are nine locking lugs on the current Mark V action, which is the central action of the current line. Roy and his associates developed the Mark V for super strength, and the Mark V action is more than strong. It is also different in that it requires a bolt lift of only 54 degrees instead of 90 degrees for opening. Detractors said nine locking lugs were for show as much as strength. Whether or not all nine locking lugs engage perfectly is not fabric for this discussion. Let it suffice that in tests, the Mark V held up when a bullet was installed in the barrel and shot out by another bullet from a loaded round. That sort of abuse could ruin some actions. Furthermore, the Weatherby is accurate. Having benchtested several Weatherby rifles, I have never found one that didn't shoot with fine accuracy. For example, a 257 WM provided groups of around a half-inch for three shots 100 yards from the bench. A 416 WM delivered three shots into well under an inch at the same range. Weatherby rifles are tested for accuracy before they leave the factory.

The rifles handle well. The stock design may not please everyone's eye, but it works. Weatherby rifles are comfortable to shoot and tend to recoil back smoothly. I've never had a Weatherby "bite my cheek." Weatherby scopes are also well-designed. A variable scope provided a clear image and in a recent test of optics it "read" as many lines per millimeter on a chart as the best scope previously tested. Plus, it offered an adjustable ocular so that a shooter could match the focus of the scope to his own eyesight. So it is not just the flare or the style, but the whole package of the Weatherby sporting rifle that has earned the rifle its fame. That is why so many notables have chosen a Weatherby for their most extensive hunts, including celebrities such as John Wayne, Robert Taylor, the Prince of Iran, Governor Joe Foss, the King of Nepal, Robert Stack and many others.

Cartridge, rifle, company. Couple perhaps the most advanced factory car-

Weatherby's 224 Magnum is a low-recoil, high-speed 22-caliber varminter called the Varmintmaster. Weatherby scopes—modern all the way—have always been matched to Weatherby rifles. The scopes enhance appearance as well as accuracy.

> ### THE WEATHERBY MARK V AT A GLANCE
>
> **Period of Manufacture:** 1958 to date
> **Calibers:** 22-250, 30-06; 224 Wby. Varmintmaster and Weatherby Magnum calibers 240, 257, 270, 7mm, 300, 340, 378, 416, 460
> **Magazine Capacity:** 2- to 5-shot box magazine (depending on caliber)
> **Action:** Strong bolt action with nine locking lugs
> **Barrel:** Of steel, blued, 24 or 26 inches, round
> **Weight (approx.):** 6½ to 10½ pounds
> **Sights:** Safari Grade has Express rear sight ("Safari" style); hooded ramp front; drilled and tapped for scope sights
> **Stock:** Monte-Carlo, California-style stock in various types of wood, including mesquite, with cheekpiece, pistol grip and often pistol-grip cap; various styles of checkering and extras, such as rubber recoil pad, QD swivels, satin oil finish, etc.
> **Variations:** Several variations of Mark V rifles are offered (Standard, Euromark, Lazermark, Safari, etc.) with a number of options, including non-glare matte blue barreled action, engraving, etc.

tridges of all time with highly modern rifles and success is yours. Or is it? Not without the right company to carry the product. The late Roy Weatherby was, of course, the innovator behind the cartridge line, the rifle and Weatherby, Inc. of South Gate, California. Today his son Ed Weatherby carries the reins well in hand. Roy's story is told in *Great Shooters of the World*, a Stoeger book. He was a pioneer. Of course there were many greats in early high-velocity circles, but Weatherby carried the drama one step higher than most of his contemporaries, if not all of them. The motto "Tomorrow's Firearms Today" was a promise fulfilled.

SAKO SPORTING RIFLES
PRECISION NONPAREIL

28

Sako rifles originate in Finland, home to high technology—in medicine, communications, firearms and munitions. Sako began as a gun repair business in the 1920s and has grown into a firm that today is renown for outstanding quality. The company manufactures precision rifles that are praised the world over and produces cartridges that have won numerous international competitions.

Sako traces its roots to a small rifle repair shop that was established in Helsinki after World War I. The shop was assigned to refurbish the arms of war and prepare them for the newly formed Finnish Civil Guard. As the Guard improved their expertise in military ways and marksmanship, the demand for better quality arms grew.

The Sako PPC Benchrest/Varmint model is perhaps the most accurate production rifle.

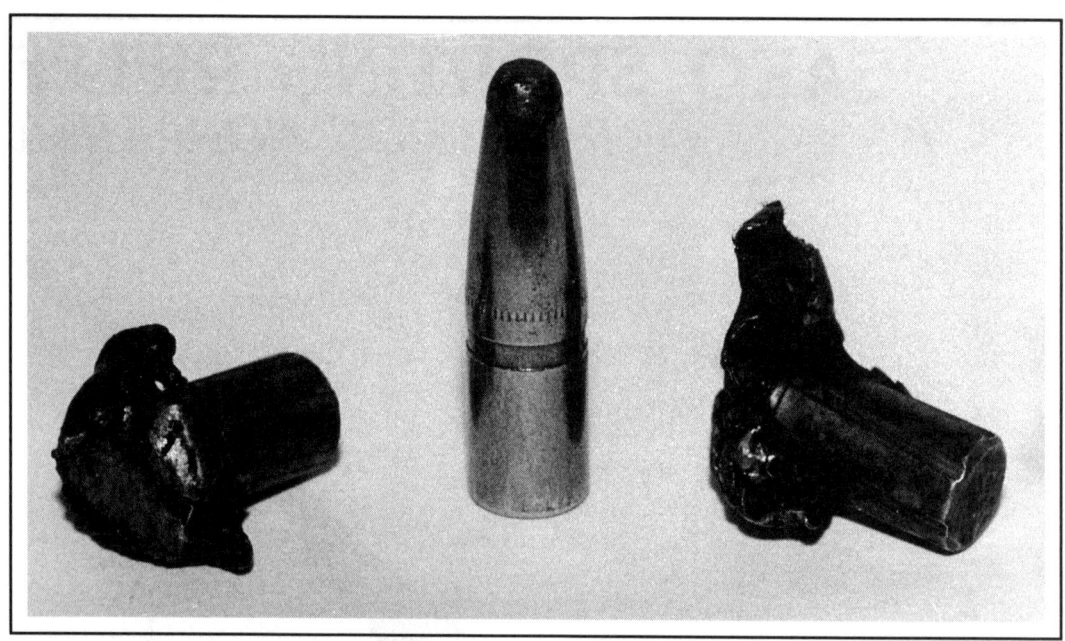

Sako is also known as a company that makes fine ammunition. In the center is an unfired 180-grain Hammerhead bullet flanked by two recovered bullets taken from moose. Note the perfect mushrooming effect without jacket loss.

Not restricting itself to repairs only, the shop became a laboratory of sorts that experimented, redesigned and refined firearms components so that the finished products were accurate and reliable. In a climate like Finland's that is often frigid and fierce, firearms had to function flawlessly.

The repair shop expanded from eight to 23, then to 100. By 1927, the operation was moved to Riihimaki, where it remains to this day. It became the "Arms and Engineering Workshop of the Civil Guard," or, as we know it, "SAKO," (pronounced *Sah-ko*) the acronym for the official title in Finnish.

Sako's reputation as a precision armsmaker received world notice in 1937 when its m/28-30 (Model 28-30) won three military events in world shooting matches held at Helsinki. The m/28-30 was a refined version of the earlier m/24, but the new rifle had a Sako-made barrel, an improved magazine and better sights. The m/28-30 was so accurate that the Swiss, who had originally supplied Sako with barrels, became interested in it. The word spread that Sako barrels were superior in accuracy. Ever striving for perfection, the Sako engineers continued to study barrelmaking and all aspects of accuracy. And Sako rifles excelled.

Despite the Depression, Sako was able to expand operations during the 1930s and began to manufacture its own bullets and ammunition. When renewed conflict with the Soviet Union flared and World War II descended, Sako was ready to assemble much-needed munitions. Asked to provide two million machine-gun cartridges every month, Sako produced—and then some. By the end of WWII, workers were turning out close to 9.5 million rounds of ammunition per month.

After the war, Sako shifted its attention to peacetime guns and ammunition. Americans had a part in it all. Sako's leaders consulted a few prominent American shooters, names familiar to arms enthusiasts to this day: General Julian Hatcher and Colonel Townsend Whelen—military men, as well as devoted sport shooters and arms writers, such as Warren Page of *Field & Stream* and Al Barr of *American Rifleman* magazine.

Sako's small bolt-action rifle made its way to America and other countries. The L 46 action (and its newer L 461 designation) remains today one of the best for rounds such as the 222 Remington and the PPC cartridges discussed later. While the L 46 was extremely successful as an action, it could not handle large cartridges. To remedy that problem, a larger bolt-action L 57 was also introduced; today's newer L 579 is made in a variety of calibers. Price tags for these export models were not low, but shooters found, for example, that with the Sako L 46 Vixen rifle, tight groups were the rule and the rifle continued to thrive. While Sako ammunition was not exported to America, some excellent companies—Remington, Winchester and Federal leading the way—provided plenty of good "fodder" for the Sako rifles.

Sako Mausers were also imported with full-length actions chambered for a multitude of cartridges. In the late 1960s when my brother was looking for a solid big game rifle for elk hunting, I found a used Sako Belgian FN Mauser in 300 H&H caliber. The rifle was rechambered to 300 Weatherby Magnum and its accuracy to this day is remarkable with full-power loads. But Sako did not stay with Mauser actions for larger calibers.

An action noted as the L 61R was born to facilitate the longer cartridges. The rifle was built in three major styles: Standard, Mannlicher and Deluxe. There was also to be a lever-action Sako with modern lines. A prototype lever-action Sako rifle was built in 1960 chambered for the popular 243 Winchester and 308 Winchester rounds. A series of refinements resulted in

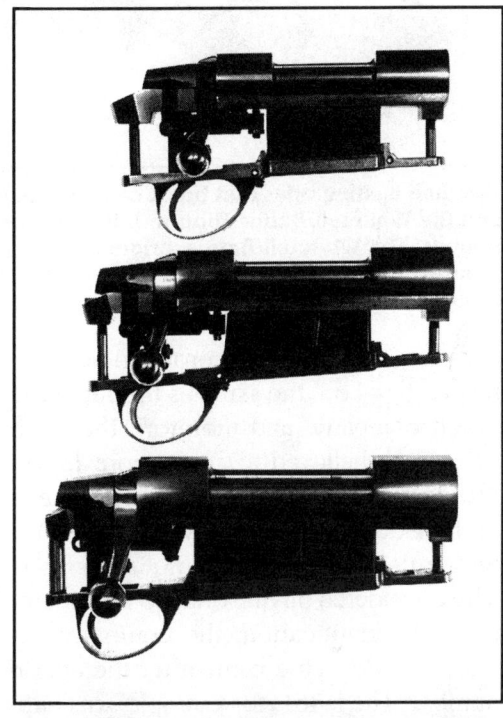

Three different Sako actions are available in various models, as well as separately for use in crafting custom rifles. The short AI action (top) covers the 222 family as well as the PPC cartridges. The medium AII action (center) accepts the 22-250 Rem., 243 Win., 308 Win. and 7mm-08. The long AV action (bottom) is offered in standard or Magnum versions to accept the powerhouse rounds.

the Sako lever-action Model VL 63, which was put into production in 1963.

Initially, Sako used its action designations to describe the different models that it offered, but this led to confusion among buyers who were unfamiliar with the system. The Finns also discovered that

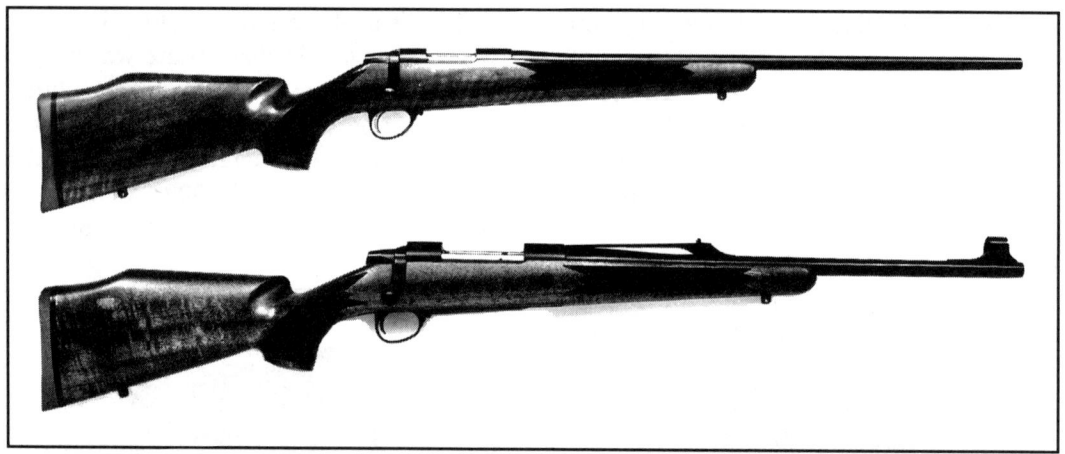

Two fine hunting rifles that boast of Sako quality and accuracy are the Hunter Lightweight (top) and the Whitetail/Battue (bottom). In the short action version, the Hunter weighs as little as 5 3/4 pounds. The Whitetail/Battue, originally designed for wild boar shooting in France, allows for "snap-shooting" when speed is required. Its special "V"-shaped sights afford the shooter a wide field of view.

Americans, for example, pronounced their name "Say-ko," the same as the Japanese watch company, and therefore the Sako rifles were believed to come from Japan. Words to the effect that Sakos were made in Finland were tastefully engraved on Sako rifles, but apparently not seen by all who considered buying one. So for greater ease of identification, the company decided to add a rifle name after the action number. The L 461, for example, was baptized the Vixen; the L 579 became the Forester; the L 61R was the Finnbear; and the VL 63 was dubbed the Finnwolf.

Today the Sako rifles imported to the U.S. bear different model names, and the actions are identified as AI (short), AII (medium) and AV (long). The three different actions are available in the various rifle models and may also be purchased separately for use in custom rifles. The short AI action is miniaturized to match the 222 family; it covers the 17 Remington, 222 Remington, 222 Remington Magnum and 223 Remington, as well as the newer PPC cartridges. The medium AII accepts the 22-250 Remington, 243 Winchester, 308 Winchester and 7mm-08. The long AV action is offered in standard or Magnum bolt face to accept the powerhouse rounds: 25-06 Remington, 270 Winchester, 280 Remington and 30-06; and the Magnum calibers 7mm Remington, 300 Winchester, 300 Weatherby, 338 Winchester, 375 H&H and 416 Remington.

The current Sako North American line includes a choice of action lengths in a variety of top-quality rifles—all meticulously crafted, test-fired and guaranteed for accuracy. The barrels, which maintain the Sako legacy, are cold-hammer forged. After each barrel blank is drilled, it is diamond-lapped and optically checked for microscopic flaws.

• The Sako Hunter Lightweight weighs under 7 pounds in the short or medium action length (8 1/4 pounds in long action) and is among the lightest of the wood stock production rifles on the market. Its hand-checkered stock is available with either matte lacquer or oil finish. (Also available

276   LEGENDARY SPORTING RIFLES

in 22 PPC and 6mm PPC calibers.)

• The Sako Deluxe model in the three action lengths features a French walnut stock with hand-cut basket-weave checkering, high-gloss lacquered finish and rosewood forend tip and grip cap. It has no sights, but rather a tapered dovetail is milled into the receiver to which scope rings are mounted. This mounting system is among the strongest in the world. The barrel length ranges from 21 1/4 to 24 inches and the magazine holds either three, five or six cartridges, depending on the action length. Weight ranges from 5 3/4 to 8 1/4 pounds. (Also available in 22 PPC and 6mm PPC calibers.)

• The Sako Super Deluxe rifle in three action lengths is a step above the Deluxe with more fine appointments, lacquer or oil finish, and is available on special order only.

• The Sako Classic possesses the grace of fine European design with its straight stock, diamond-point checkering on pistol grip and forend, matte lacquer finish and 22- or 24-inch barrel. In medium or long action.

• The chief purpose of the Whitetail/Battue rifle is for snap-shooting when speed is required. Originally designed to meet the needs of wild boar hunting in France, the shooter can get on target fast with a wide field of view because of the raised quarter-rib and wide "V"-shaped rear sight. In medium or long action.

• For sportsmen who prefer natural wood coupled with the advantages of fiberglass, there are the Laminated Stock models in medium or long action. The laminated stocks are machined from blanks composed of 36-strip 1/16-inch hardwood bonded under pressure.

• The accurate Sako Varmint rifle, in short and medium action lengths, incorporates a prone-type stock for shooting from the ground or bench and has an extra wide forend for added steadiness.

• The PPC Benchrest/Varmint model in the short-actioned 22 PPC or 6 PPC calibers could well be the most accurate factory production model in the world today. With hand-checkered Monte Carlo stock and heavy barrel, it weighs about 8 3/4 pounds and is a single-shot, bolt-action rifle.

• The Sako Carbine, with full Mannlicher-

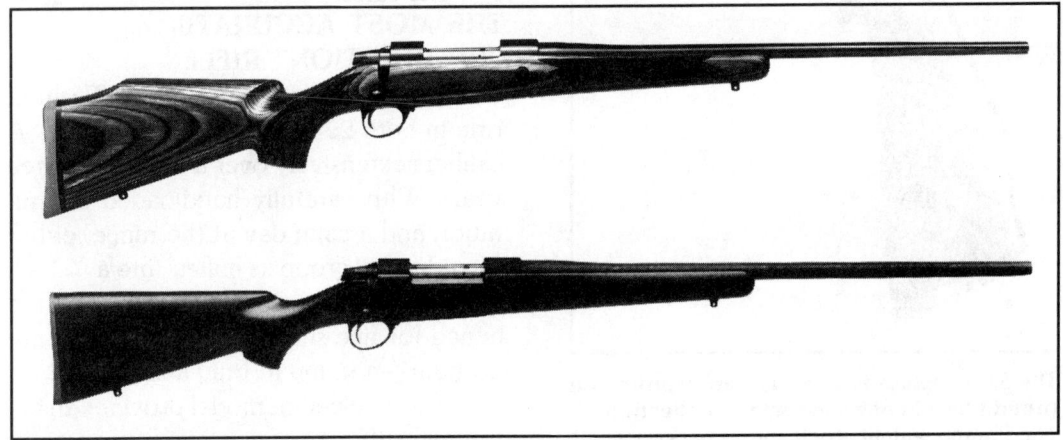

The Sako Laminated model (top) is the perfect compromise for hunters who want natural wood with the strength and resilience of synthetics. The Sako Fiberclass (bottom) is the sportsman's answer to the "all weather" rifle. With a stock made of fiberglass, the rifle is strong, lightweight and virtually impervious to all types of weather conditions.

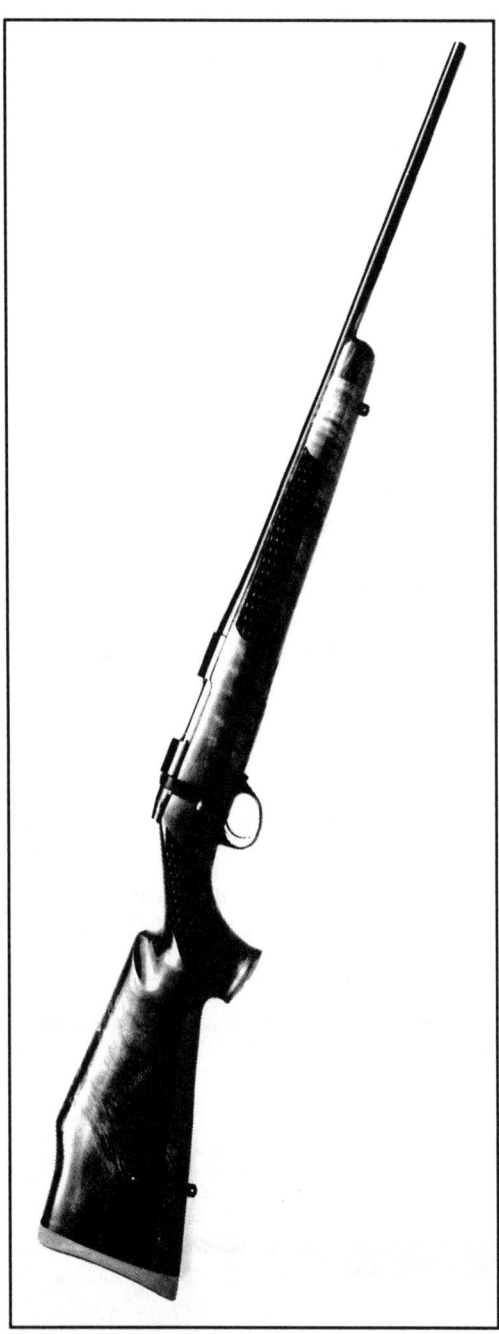

The Sako Deluxe is a work of art, worthy of a proud place in any sportsman's collection. The French walnut stock sports basket-weave checkering and a rosewood pistol-grip cap and forend. A tapered dovetail is milled into the receiver to accommodate scope ring mounts.

style stock, is available in two action lengths. A shorter 18 1/2-inch barrel makes for easy carrying and keeps the weight in the 7- to 8-pound range, depending on caliber and wood density. Overall length is 38 inches.

• The Fiberclass model has an "all weather" stock made of fiberglass—strong, lightweight and virtually impervious to temperature and moisture fluctuations in the field. In long action.

• The custom Sako Safari Grade Rifle is the "professional's" choice, designed in the tradition of the British express rifles. In calibers 338 Win. Mag., 375 H&H Mag. or 416 Rem. Mag., the magazine has been extended to allow for four belted magnums rather than three, and the barreled action is finished in a semi-matte blue. The express-style quarter rib provides a secure, non-glare base for the fixed blade rear sight, while the front blade sits on a non-glare ramp protected by a steel hood.

• The left-handed models are complete mirror images of the right-handed versions, available in the Hunter Lightweight style, the Deluxe and the Classic.

THE MOST ACCURATE "PRODUCTION" RIFLE

I have tested the Benchrest/Varmint rifle in both 22 PPC USA and 6 PPC USA calibers extensively over a period of three years. With carefully handloaded ammunition and a calm day at the range, either cartridge will group its bullets into a 1/4 inch center to center at 100 yards from the bench for five shots. Half-inch groups are ho-hum—nothing to brag about at all!

The single-shot model provides an extremely stiff action with no magazine cut-out to weaken that area of the rifle. The heart of the Sako PPC Benchrest/Varmint Rifle is the same L 461 action mentioned

The Mannlicher-style Sako Carbine with full stock (above) is chambered for high-performance cartridges. It features a shortened 18½-inch barrel for easy carrying.

earlier, and the stiff single-shot action guarantees stability. The precision heavyweight barrel, free-floated, helps to maintain uniformity shot to shot. Not a bull barrel, but with a muzzle diameter of a full .865 inch, the 22¾-inch barrel has six lands and grooves, hammer-forged rifling, with a twist of 1:14 and a concave crown.

The tight-grained walnut stock is nicely checkered and has a Monte Carlo cheekpiece with a pleasing oil finish. The semi-beavertail forend enhances the rifle's steadiness at the range and in the varmint field. A rubber buttpad is for slippage, not recoil because neither the 22 PPC nor the 6 PPC produce noticeable "kick." They are extremely mild to shoot. Rather than have sights, the receiver is dovetailed in Sako fashion to accommodate the Sako scope mount.

The rifles live up to the potential of PPC ammunition accuracy. In fact, the title "most accurate" was conferred by *American Rifleman* magazine in a quote from the NRA staff: "The 6mm PPC and .22 PPC ammunition and rifles received for testing proved capable of accuracy levels not previously encountered in shooting tests of factory ammunition/rifle combinations."

The PPCs, at least the 6 PPC has, supplanted the grand wizards of benchrest accuracy cartridges: the 222 Remington, 222½ Remington (wildcat), the 219 Donaldson Wasp, 6×47, 308 and many other fine rounds. The PPCs are now the cartridges to beat at any benchrest match, for they generally end up in the winner's circle. For a while, the 219 Wasp was tops, then the 222 Remington in its original or slightly altered form, the 222½. Now it's the PPCs, especially the 6mm version. The 22 PPC, however, also showed its winning colors by capturing the 100-yard benchrest accuracy contest at the Nationals prior to

SAKO SPORTING RIFLES 279

1975. Little notice was given. The 22 PPC produced the smallest 10-shot group fired at the Speer Match in the Unlimited Class, again in its infancy. The group was .204 inch center to center.

"PPC" stands for "Pindell-Palmisano Cartridge." At the 1974 Super Shoot, two men got together—Ferris Pindell, a die-maker/gunsmith genius, and Lou Palmisano, a vascular surgeon. They had one goal: to see a leap forward in precision shooting. The two marksmen couldn't know that they were going to invent the most accurate cartridges in the world, and that both rounds would also prove to be fine hunting cartridges—the 22 PPC for varmints and the 6 PPC for varmints and medium-sized big game, such as deer and antelope.

At the 1975 Super Shoot, Lou Palmisano won the 100-yard Heavy Varmint Class Aggregate with the 22 PPC. Five 5-

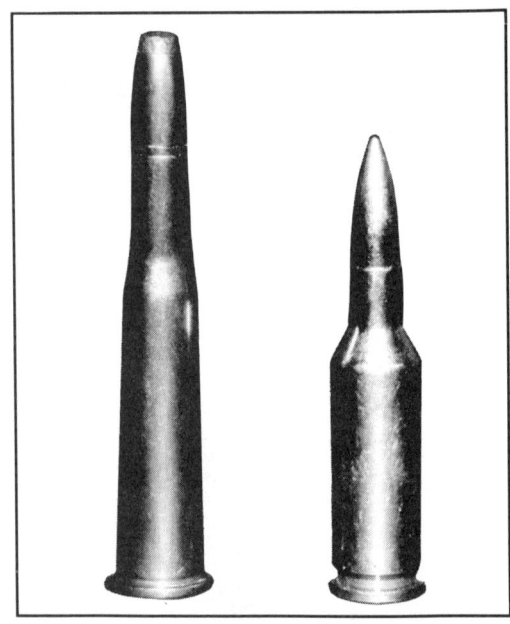

The 22 PPC (right) is shown beside a 25-35 Winchester cartridge to illustrate the old versus the new. The 22 PPC is short and rimless with good powder capacity, straight walls and a sharp shoulder.

The 6 PPC, another Sako "factory" round, is the world's most accurate cartridge according to benchrest records.

A closer look at the Sako Varmint rifle readied for an informal benchrest shoot. Its prone-type stock is designed for shooting from the ground or the bench and the extra wide forend provides added steadiness.

shot groups totaled .265 inch center to center, .050 inch better than second place that year, which in benchrest competition is significant. In 1976, a 14-year old boy emerged victorious over 80 grown men when he won a 200-yard Benchrest Shooters National Championship event for a 25-shot aggregate, firing a group measuring .3280 inch. The young shooter was David Palmisano, Lou's son, and of course he was shooting a 22 PPC. From 1981 to 1985, 116 IBS (International Benchrest Shooters) records were broken, every one by a PPC. In under a decade, 179 IBS records were bettered, 149 of them with a PPC. Although ammo factories seemed uninterested, the benchrest boys were not complacent about the PPCs. By 1981, 59 of the 60 competitors at the IBS match were using the PPC. At Super Shoot III, a 22 PPC won the Heavy Varmint Aggregate with a .264-inch group for 25 shots. At this time, the PPCs have taken several hundred first places in various competitions. When in 1987 various IBS records were set, the 6 PPC set them all. That same year, several NBRSA (National Bench Rest Shooters Association) records were set also. All but one was captured by the 6 PPC, and that one was by a 6 PPC with a shortened neck.

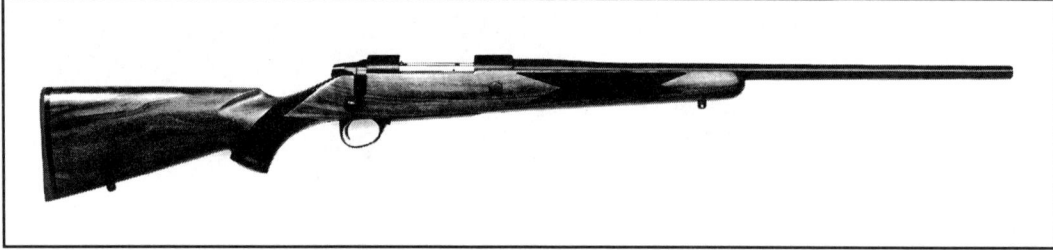

The elegant Sako Classic is another outstanding example of old-world craftsmanship combined with modern technology.

The 22 PPC and the 6 PPC were finally factory-recognized in 1988 by the experts in accuracy: Sako. They produced factory ammunition, which proved to be typical of Sako—carefully manufactured and extremely accurate. This ammo grouped steadily at a startling 3/8 inch center to center at 100 yards. A few five-shot groups were even smaller than that.

Of course, ammunition can be only as accurate as the firearm that chambers it. Sako's PPC Benchrest/Varmint rifle, imported by Stoeger Industries, proves to be matched to the ammunition, meeting all accuracy criteria. The rifle continues to delight shooters because of its accuracy. Dr. Palmisano shot an amazing witnessed target, measuring .303 inch center to center for five shots. This group was produced not at 100 yards, but at 300 yards! The PPCs spoil a shooter. He gets used to accuracy levels that were previously elusive, if not impossible, to achieve.

The Sako sporting rifle has always stood for accuracy. That, plus solid construction, has put the rifle high on the list of greats over the years. The Sako company is dedicated to improvement. A walk through the plant reveals computer operations everywhere, along with considerable handwork to refine the finished product. The byword at Sako is quality control.

SAKO'S NEW TIKKA

The Sako story will close with another rifle that embodies the points made about this riflemaking company. That rifle is the Tikka New Generation model and it exemplifies Sako tradition. The Tikka was imported into America in the 1970s, but the new completely redesigned models are quite different from the old. Tikkakoski, a

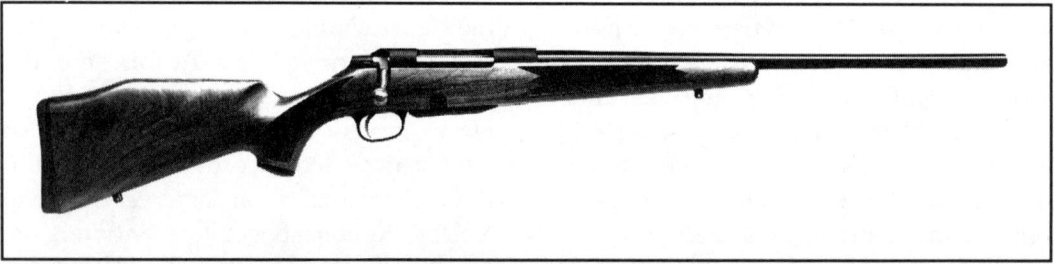

Sako's Tikka New Generation rifle is indicative of the company's far-reaching efforts to create interesting and accurate firearms. Note the spring-loaded bolt-release and the scope mount attached via an integral dovetail in the receiver.

> **THE SAKO PPC BENCHREST/VARMINT RIFLE AT A GLANCE**
>
> **Period of Manufacture:** 1987 to date
> **Calibers:** 22 PPC and 6mm PPC
> **Action:** Strong Sako L 461 short bolt action
> **Barrel:** Of steel, blued; cold-hammer forged, 23¾ inches, round
> **Weight (approx.):** 8¾ pounds
> **Triggers:** Single-stage or two-stage
>
> **Sights:** None; receiver is dovetailed for the Sako scope mount
> **Stock:** Checkered pistol-grip stock of European walnut; semi-beavertail forend; Monte Carlo cheekpiece and rubber buttpad for slippage, not recoil; dull oil finish

Finnish factory born in 1893, no longer makes the rifle. Sako does with all the latest computer-controlled machinery.

The most unique aspect of the Tikka is the bolt. It rides on a minimal-friction sleeve made of an ejection-molded poly-arylamide material. The synthetic bushing allows the bolt to almost float back and forth. The sleeve remains stationary and the round bolt alone moves in the action. The Tikka carries many other refinements traditional with Sako, including the Sako precision barrel. A test Tikka in 270 Winchester caliber produced groups that ranged from one-half to one inch at 100 yards; this was from the bench for five shots using handloads with Sierra bullets from the free-floated barrel. The test rifle, scoped and loaded, weighed a shade under 9 pounds. The New Generation rifle is offered in a range of hunting rounds.

High quality and superb accuracy epitomize Sako—and the attributes of which legendary rifles are made.

INDEX

Accouterments, Muzzleloading, *16–18, 28, 29*
Ackley, P.O., *244, 258*
Adolph, Fred, *239*
African Game Trails, 238
Amber, John, *258*
American Rifleman magazine, *125, 127, 137, 141, 146, 150, 158, 161, 163, 275, 279*
Andrews, Roy Chapman, *141*
Arrowsmith, George, *33*
Ashley, General William, *21, 24, 27, 28*
Askins, Colonel Charles, *264*

Ballard Rifles/Rifling System, *209, 254*
Balle Fusnot, *39, 40*
Barr, Al, *161, 163, 232, 275*
Bell, WDM "Karamojo,", *139*
Bennett, T.G., *56, 95*
Biesen, Alvin, *237*
Big Game Rifles and Cartridges, 100, 161
Black Powder, *9, 12–15, 26–28, 30, 33, 41, 42, 58, 245*
Black Powder Breechloading Calibers, *48, 60–64,* Chart *p. 63, 68, 69, 70–74, 77, 79–84, 87–94, 96–104, 105–114, 130, 138, 160, 205, 206, 211–215, 219, see also* Centerfire Cartridges, Henry Cartridges, Rimfire Cartridges, Sharps Cartridges, Smith & Wesson, Winchester Cartridges
Black Powder Muzzleloading Calibers, *9, 10, 11, 15, 18, 23–28, 30, 33, 34, 40, 76*
Blixen, Baron Bror von, *141*
Bolt Actions, *see* Mannlicher, Mauser, Remington, Sako, Springfield, Weatherby, Winchester Rifles
Boone, Daniel, *8*
Breechloaders, *31–38, 60, 65–74*
Brevex Magnum Mauser Rifle, *244*
Bridger, Jim, *30*
British Brown Bess Musket, *9*
British Express Rifles, *278*
Brno Czech Rifle, *245*
Brownell, Len, *254*
Browning Company, *56, 57, 59*
Browning, John Moses, *56, 64, 95, 129, 138, 168*
Browning Machine Gun, *138*
Browning Rifles
    Model 71 Replica, *165, 166*
    Model 1886 Replica, *103, 104*
    Model 1895 Replica, *131, 134*
    Model B-92 (1892 Replica), *113*
    Single Shot Rifle, *56, 57, 59, 64, 76*

Caplock, *see* Percussion System
Carmichel, Jim, *232*
Carson, Kit, *30*
Centerfire Cartridges, *62, 64, 79–84, 85, 87–94, 96–104, 105–114, 115–124, 127, 128, 131, 146, 153, 154, 155, 205, 206, 211–215, 219, 220, 232, 236, 247, 259, see also* Charts, *p. 63, 102* and specific manufacturers
Chamberlin Cartridge and Target Co., *176*
Childs, Reynolds and Risley, *195*
Cimarron Arms Co. Winchester Model 1873, *94*

Clark, Frank, *118*
Colt, 45, Cartridge, *208, 210*
Colt Lightning Sporting Rifle, *190*
Colt "Plant," *194*
Colt Revolvers, *90, 106, 110, 210*
Colter, John, *21*
Complete Guide to Reloading, 263
Conant, H., *70*
Crosman, Captain C.E., *235, 237–238*
Cunninghame, R.J., *236*
CVA Mountain Rifles, *25*

Daisy Company, *33*
DeWeese, Dall, *99*
Dixie Gun Works 1873 Winchester Replica, *94*
Dodge, Marcellus Hartley, *176*
Donaldson, Harvey, *60*
Driggs-Seabury Ordnance Company, *202*
Drum and Nipple Assembly, *15, 18, 30*
DuPont de Nemours & Company, *176, 179*

Enfield Bolt Action, *176, 177, 178, 179*

Falling Breechblock, *58, 64, 68, 70, 74, 76, 80, 81, 255, 256*
Federal Ammunition, *126, 132, 144, 208, 209, 275*
Field & Stream magazine, *189, 275*
Fisher, Homer, Company, *71*
Flintlock, *8, 13, 14, 22, 29, 30, 32*
    Conversion to Percussion, *15, 30*
Flintlock Rifles, *7–18, 22–30*
Forsyth, Rev. Alexander J., *21, 23*
Fox, A.H., Shotguns, *202*
Frankford Arsenal, *238*
Fulminate of Mercury, *21, 22*

Garand, M1, Rifles, *138, 233*
Gaston, Nelson B., *34*
Glenfield Rifles, *230*
Golden State Arms Centurion Rifle, *244*
Government, 45-70, Cartridge, *55, 61, 62, 64, 79, 80, 83, 84, 97–100, 102, 104, 116, 133, 205, 206, 211–213, 215, 219, 220, 254, 258–260*
Great Shooters of the World, 56, 100, 235, 272
Greener, W.W., Ballistics, *88, 102*
Griffin & Howe, *184, 238–239*
Griffin, Seymour, *238–239*

Harpers Ferry Rifle, *24*
Harriger, Colonel Russell, *8*
Hartley & Graham, *176*
Hartley, Marcellus, *176, 194, 195*
Hatcher, General Julian, *232, 275*
Hawken Rifles, *19–30, 31, 40, 44*
Hawken, Samuel and Jacob, *19, 23*
Hemingway, Ernest, *141*
Henry, Alexander, Rifle, *254*
Henry, Benjamin Tyler, *34, 38, 40, 41, 42, 48*

284 LEGENDARY SPORTING RIFLES

Henry Cartridges (Rimfire)
    44 Henry Flat, *35, 36, 38, 40–43, 49, 50, 53, 54, 87, 89*
    44 Henry Flat Short, *41*
    44 Henry Pointed, *41, 49, 54*
    46 Henry Carbine, *41*
Henry Repeating Rifle Company, *48*
Henry Rifle, *39–46, 47*
    At a Glance, *46*
Hepburn, L.L. (Lewis), *81, 207, 212, 219, 226*
Herter's Mauser Rifle, *244*
Hibben, Frank C., *100*
Horn, Gil Van, see Van Horn, Gil
Hornady's Third Edition Ballistics, *102, 103–104*
Howe, James V., *237, 238–239*
Hunt Rifle, *31–38*
    At a Glance, *37*
Hunt, Walter, *33, 34, 37, 39*
Hunting and Fishing magazine, *74*
Hunting Rifle, The, *160, 240*
Husqvarna Mauser Rifle, *245*

Ideal Handbook, The, *222*
Ideal Manufacturing Company, *222, 223*
International Benchrest Shooters (IBS), *281*
Ithaca's Hawken Rifle, *19*

Jaeger Rifle, *9–11, 15, 23*
Jefferson, Thomas, *20*
Jenks Carbines, *176*
Jennings, Lewis, *33, 34, 37*
Jennings Rifle, *31–38*
    At a Glance, *37*

Keith, Elmer, *100, 141, 145, 160, 161*
Kenna, Frank Jr./Sr. and Roger, *223*
Kentucky Longrifle, *7–18, 30, 40, 43, 44*
    At a Glance, *18*
    Bullet Shapes, *11*
Kimber Model 89 Rifle, *244*
King Loading Gate, *47, 48*
King, Nelson, *48*
Klein, Herb, *264*
Krag-Jorgensen Rifle, *127*
Krag, 30-40, Cartridge, *61, 82, 84, 109, 115, 119, 126, 128–134, 194, 259*
Krieghoff Autoloading Rifle, *172*

Lawrence, R.S., *70*
Lever Actions, see Hunt, Jennings, Marlin, Remington, Sako, Savage, Volcanic, Winchester Rifles
Lewis and Clark, *21, 23, 24*
Lilly, Ben, *100, 159, 220*
Linen Cartridges, *69, 70*
Longrifles of Pennsylvania, *8*
Ludlow, Major William, *42*
Lyell, Denis, *141*
Lyman's 42nd Edition Loading Manual, *89*

Madis, George, *33, 63, 90, 113, 154*
Magnum Cartridges, *74, 113, 123, 146, 151, 152, 153, 154, 155, 181, 183, 208, 209, 210, 227, 257–260, 275, 276, 278*, see also Remington, Weatherby, Winchester Cartridges

Mannlicher Collector's Association, *142, 145*
Mannlicher, Ferdinand von, *138, 146*
Mannlicher (-Schoenauer) Carbines/Rifles, *135–146, 194, 237*
    At a Glance, *146*
    Model 1903, *139, 141*
    Model 1905, *139, 141–143, 145*
    Model 1908, *139*
    Model 1910, *139, 146*
Marlin Cartridges, *200, 202, 206, 211–213, 215, 219, 220*
Marlin Firearms Company, *199, 211, 221–223*
Marlin, John Howard, *222*
Marlin, John Mahlon, *205, 206, 221*
Marlin, Mahlon Henry, *221*
Marlin Rifles
    Model 30 AS, *230*
    Model 36, *223, 226*
    Model 39, *221*
    Model 93, *223*
    Model 336, *208, 221–230*
        At a Glance, *229*
    Model 375, *228*
    Model 444, *220, 229–230*
    Model 1881, *205–206, 207, 211, 223*
    Model 1888, *207*
    Model 1889, *207, 223*
    Model 1891, *221*
    Model 1893, *203, 204, 207, 212, 221, 223*
    Model 1894, *203–210*
        At a Glance, *210*
    Model 1895, *207, 211–220*
        At a Glance, *219*
    Model of 1912, *219*
    Model 1936, *223–226*
    New Model 1895, *211, 215, 220*
    Zane Grey Commemorative, *227*
Marlin Rockwell Corporation, *223*
Martini Rifle/Action, *194, 201, 202*
Mauser Actions/Rifles, *237, 240, 241–251*
    Mark X Mauser, *245*
    Model 71/84, *245*
    Models 87 and 88, *245*
    Models 91, 93, 94, 95, *245*
    Model 98 Military, *181, 242–247, 250, 251*
    Standard Model, *242*
    Type "A" Sporting Rifle, *242*
        At a Glance, *251*
    Venezuelan "FN" Action, *248, 249*
Mauser Cartridges, *78, 82, 84, 129, 148, 149, 151, 153, 154, 155, 176, 177, 178, 182, 232, 235, 242–251, 254, 256, 259, 260*
Mauser, Paul, *138, 245*
Mauser-Werke, *242, 251*
Mayer, Frank, *72, 73*
Maynard Cartridges, *81*
Maynard, Dr. Edward, *67*
Mews, Leonard, *237*
Modena, Mario, *30*
Montana Armory, Inc., Sharps Rifles, *74*
Mountain Men, *21, 23, 28, 29*
Mulford, Dennis, *18*
Muzzleloaders, *17, 19, 20, 32, 49*, see also specific rifles of this types

INDEX   285

National Bench Rest Shooters Association (NBRSA), *281*
National Rifle Association (NRA), *123, 178, 202, 226, 279*
Navy Arms Company, *44, 84, 243, 244*
    Henry Carbine, *46*
    Henry Trapper, *45, 46*
    Iron-frame Henry Rifle, *39*
    Military Henry Rifle, *45, 46*
    Model 1873 Winchester, *85*
    Remington Creedmoor Long Range Rolling Block, *75, 84*
    Remington Buffalo Rolling Block, *84*
Ness, F.C., *150, 158*
New Haven Arms Co., *37, 38, 44*
New Sharps Cartridge Loading Manual, The, *71*
Newton, Charles, *195, 200*
Niedner, Adolph, *239*

O'Connor, Jack, *154, 160, 165, 232*
Oesterreichische Waffenfabriks-Gesellschaft (OWG), *138, 139*
Outdoor Life, *99, 100*
Outdoor Pastimes of an American Hunter, *120*
Owen, Robert, *237*
Ozark Mountain Arms Muskrat Rifle, *28*

Pachmayr, August, *237*
Page, Warren, *189, 191, 232*
Palmer, Courtlandt C., *34, 37*
Palmisano, Lou, *280, 281, 282*
Paper Cartridges, *32, 68, 69, 70*
Parker Shotgun, *139, 176*
Parker-Hale M81 African Rifle, *243, 244*
Peabody-Martini Creedmoor Rifle, *254*
Pease, Sir Alfred, *139*
Pennsylvania/Kentucky Rifle, *7, 23,* see also Kentucky Longrifle
Pepys' Diary, *21*
Percival, Blayney, *141*
Percussion Breechloaders, *65–74*
Percussion Cap, *15, 20, 21, 22, 23, 29*
Percussion System, *15, 22, 28–30*
Pet Loads, *133*
Peters Cartridge Co. Ammunition, *161, 176*
Pindell, Ferris, *280*
Pindell-Palmisano Cartridge (PPC), *273, 277, 278–283*
Plains Rifles, *19–30, 31*
    At a Glance, *30*
Pope, Harry, *60, 64*
Pope & Young Club, *126*
Powder Horns, see Accouterments
PPC, see Pindell-Palmisano Cartridge
Practical Dope on the Big Bores, *161*
Pugsley, Edwin, *128, 129*

Remington Arms Company, *194, 202, 233, 234, 240*
Remington Autoloading Rifles, *167–174*
    At a Glance, *174*
    Model 8, *167–174, 186*
    Model 81 Woodmaster, *168, 169, 171–174*
    Model 740 Woodmaster, *169, 172, 174*
    Model 742, *167, 168, 172–174*
    Model 7400, *167, 168, 173, 174*
    Model Four, *171, 173*

Remington Autoloading Shotgun Model 11-48, *189*
Remington Bolt Action Rifles, *237*
    Model 30, *176–178*
    Model 700, *143, 170, 175–184*
        At a Glance, *184*
    Model 720, *178–179*
    Model 721, *178–182*
    Model 722, *178–182*
    Model 725, *184*
Remington Cartridges, *64, 120, 153, 154, 155, 169–171, 173, 174, 176, 179, 181–184, 186–192, 222, 228–229, 256, 258–260, 275, 276, 279*
Remington Cartridges—Magnum, *64, 73, 113, 123, 148, 153–154, 155, 182–184, 209, 250, 254, 256, 257, 259, 260, 276, 278*
Remington, Eliphalet, *175, 176*
Remington Kentucky-style Flintlock, *7*
Remington Pump (Slide) Action Rifles
    At a Glance, *192*
    Model 12, *185, 188*
    Model 14, *185–188*
    Model 121, *185, 188*
    Model 141 Gamemaster, *188*
    Model 760 Gamemaster, *172, 189–192*
    Model 7600 Slide Action, *185, 191–192*
Remington Rolling Block Rifles, *54, 66, 75–84, 254,* see also Navy Arms Co.
    Baby Carbine, *78, 80*
    Military Rolling Blocks, *83, 84*
    No. 1 Rolling Block (& variations), *76, 79, 80, 84*
        At a Glance, *84*
    No. 1½ Rolling Block, *76, 81*
    No. 2 Sporting Rifle, *81*
    No. 4 (Model 4) Rolling Block, *77, 81*
    No. 5 Special High Power, *81, 82*
    No. 6 Rolling Block, *82*
    No. 7 Rolling Block, *82*
    -Rider Rolling Block, *76*
Remington-Hepburn No. 3 Rifle, *80, 81*
Rider, Joseph, *76*
Rifle Book, The, *160*
Rimfire Cartridges, *61, 62,* Chart p. *63, 64, 74, 77, 79–84, 87, 93, 94, 168, 185, 186,* see also Henry Cartridges, Smith & Wesson
Robbins and Lawrence, *34, 37, 67, 68*
Roberts, *257,* Cartridge, *74, 146, 148, 151, 153, 154, 155, 177, 178, 179, 181, 189, 192, 239*
Rock Island Arsenal, *233, 240*
Rocket Balls (Rocket Bullets), *33–37, 39*
Rocky Mountain Rifle, *23*
Rodgers, Walter, *224*
Rogers, Robert Cameron, *237*
Rolling Block Action, see Remington Rolling Block Rifles
Roosevelt, Theodore, *93, 120, 126, 231, 235, 236, 238*
Ross, Canadian, Rifle, *138*
Ross, Harry, *235*
Rotary Magazine, *135, 138, 141, 194, 196, 202*
Ruger Rifles
    Model No. 1 Single Shot, *253–260*
        At a Glance, *260*
    Model 77, *144, 245*
Ruger, William, *253, 255*
RWS Ammunition, *243*

Sako Ammunition, *274-283*
Sako Rifles, *273-283*
   Belgian FN Mauser, *275*
   Carbine (Mannlicher-style), *277, 279*
   Classic, *277, 278, 282*
   Deluxe, *277, 278*
   Fiberclass, *277, 278*
   Finnbear, *276*
   Finnwolf, *276*
   Forester, *276*
   Hunter Lightweight, *276, 278*
   Laminated Stock, *277*
   m/24, *274*
   m/28-30, *274*
   PPC Benchrest/Varmint, *273, 277, 278-283*
   Safari Grade, *278*
   Super Deluxe, *277*
   Tikka New Generation, *282-283*
   Varmint, *277, 281*
   Vixen, *275, 276*
   VL 63 Lever Action, *275*
   Whitetail/Battue, *276, 277*
Savage, Arthur W., *193, 195, 201*
Savage Cartridges, *148, 149, 151, 153, 154, 155, 171, 181, 192, 196-202*
Savage Repeating Arms Company (Savage Arms Corp.), *195, 198, 199*
Savage Rifles
   Model 1892, *195*
   Model 1895, *194-199, 201*
   Model 1899 (99), *138, 193-202*
      At a Glance, *202*
Schoenauer, Otto, *138, 139, 146*
Schoffstall, John, *71*
Schuetzen Rifles, *60, 254*
Selous, Frederick C., *139*
Sharpe, Phil, *263*
Sharps, C., Arms Company
   Model 1874 Sharps Rifle, *65, 68*
   Model 1875 Sharps Carbine, *71*
   Model 1875 Sporting Rifle, *72*
   Winchester Model 1885, *55, 56*
Sharps Cartridges, *61, 62, 68-74, 212*
Sharps, Christian, *57, 67*
Sharps Rifles, *see also* C. Sharps Arms Co. and Montana Armory
   BL Cartridge Carbine, *70*
   BL Sporting Rifle (Old Reliable), *70*
   Blackpowder Carbine, *66*
   -Borchardt Rifle, *128, 258*
   Buffalo Rifle, *54, 70-74, 214, 254, 255*
   Creedmoor Long Range, *71-72*
   Model 1863 (BL Percussion Military Rifle), *68-70*
   Model 1874 Target Rifle, *69, 71*
   Model 1875 Sporting Rifle, *71*
   Model 1878 Long Range Rifle, *71*
   Saddle Rifle, *71*
   Single-Shot, *32, 57, 65-74, 75*
      At a Glance, *74*
Shaw, Joshua, *22*
Shelhamer, Thomas, *237, 240*
Shooting and Fishing magazine, *127*
Sierra Ammunition, *266*

"Skin" (Paper) Cartridges, *69, 70*
Slide Action, *see* Remington Slide Action Rifles
Smith, Horace, *34, 37, 38*
Smith, James, *48*
Smith, L.C., -Corona, *233, 235, 240*
Smith & Wesson, *34, 35*
   22 Rimfire Short Cartridge, *35, 36*
   Mauser Rifle, *244*
Smokeless Powder, *9, 27, 40, 50, 73, 76, 77, 82, 84, 96, 107, 109, 112, 115-124, 126, 130, 132, 194, 195, 212, 213, see also* Winchester Cartridges
Sporterizing, *232-240, 241-251*
Springfield Armory, *231, 233, 240*
Springfield, 30-03, Cartridge, *126, 128, 132, 133, 235*
Springfield, 30-06, Cartridge, *11, 62, 64, 88, 125, 126, 128-134, 136, 141, 144, 146, 147-151, 153, 154, 155, 158, 162, 165, 168, 172, 173, 174, 176-179, 181, 182, 184, 189-192, 200, 233-236, 238, 240, 241-244, 251, 254, 256, 259, 260, 262*
Springfield Rifles, *127, 128, 181*
   Model 1903, *231, 233-240, 241, 246*
      At a Glance, *240*
Springfield Trap Door Service Rifle, *49*
Stent, H.V., *125, 128*
Stevens Cartridges, *81*
Stevens, J., Arms Company, *202*
Steyr-Werke, *137*
Stoeger, A.F., *112, 141, 177, 187, 189, 201, 272, 282*
Storey, Dale, *124, 163, 225, 232, 238, 239*
Sturm, Ruger & Co., *253, see also* Ruger
Sundra, John, *232*
Swiss Schmidt-Rubin Rifle, *139*

Thompson/Center Rifles
   Hawken, *24*
   Renegade, *24*
Tikka New Generation Rifle, *282-283*
Tubular Magazine, *33, 37, 187, 188, 190, 192, 206*

Union Metallic Cartridge Company (UMC), *176, 202*
United States Repeating Arms Co., *123*

Van Horn, Gil, *232, 246-251*
Van Horn 500 Express Custom Rifle, *246-251*
Villa, Pancho, *134*
Volcanic Cartridges, *35, 36, 42*
Volcanic Repeating Arms Company, *34, 37*
Volcanic Rifle, *31-38, 41, 43*
   At a Glance, *37*
Volition Repeater, *33, 37*
Voss Rocket Cartridge, *39, 40*

Walker, Merle "Mike," *179*
Waters, Ken, *133*
Weatherby Magnum Cartridges, *146, 154, 155, 183, 257, 259, 261-272, 275, 276, 278*
Weatherby Rifles, *248*
   Crown Custom Rifle, *265*
   Mark V, *261, 265, 267, 269-272*
      At a Glance, *272*
   Varmintmaster, *265, 271*
Weatherby, Roy, *261-272*

Wells, Frank, *155, 156*
Werndl, Josef, *137, 139*
Wesson, Daniel Baird, *34, 37, 38*
Wheellock, *8, 10*
Whelen, Colonel Townsend, *99, 126, 160, 184, 232, 238-240*
Whelen, 35, Cartridge, *143, 183, 184, 191, 192*
White, Stewart Edward, *126, 235-236*
Wildcat Cartridges, *74, 184, 191, 195, 234, 279*
Winans, Walter, *139*
Winchester Book, The, 63, 90
Winchester Cartridges—Centerfire, *61, 78, 81, 97-104, 121, 126, 127, 129-134, 143, 148, 153, 154, 155, 162, 165, 170, 201, 205, 211-215, 219, 224, 227-229, 236, 247. See also* specific listings below.
  25-20, *61, 106, 107, 109, 112-114, 204, 205, 207, 208, 209, 210*
  25-35 WCF, *117, 118, 122, 170, 176, 195, 200, 202, 280*
  30 WCF or 30-30, *63, 82, 89, 93, 109, 115-124, 129, 148, 150, 162, 170, 176, 188, 200, 201, 202, 204, 206, 208, 213, 221, 222, 224-230*
  32-20, *64, 81, 89-90, 92, 93, 94, 105-114, 190, 195, 201, 204, 205, 206, 207, 208, 210*
  32-40, *60, 61, 81, 118, 121, 200, 202, 206, 207, 212*
  32 Win. Special (smokeless), *81, 118-119, 122, 170, 176, 188, 225, 226, 228, 229*
  33 WCF (smokeless), *96, 99, 101, 102, 104, 157, 158, 159, 160, 162, 212, 215, 218-220*
  38 WCF or 38-40, *62, 64, 81, 88, 89, 92, 93, 94, 105-114, 190, 204, 207, 208, 209, 210*
  38-55, *60, 61, 81, 93, 118, 121, 122, 200, 202, 206, 213, 228*
  44 WCF or 44-40, *46, 61, 64, 80, 81, 87-94, 105-114, 117, 122, 190, 204, 207, 208, 210*
  243, *146, 148, 153, 155, 165, 173, 174, 182, 191, 192, 201, 202, 254, 256, 259, 260, 275, 276*
  270, *64, 146, 148, 149, 151, 153, 154, 155, 158, 165, 174, 179, 181, 182, 191, 192, 254, 256, 257, 259, 260, 276*
  308, *11, 144, 146, 153, 173, 174, 183, 191, 192, 199, 201, 202, 275, 276*
  348, *96, 143, 157-166, 212*
Winchester Cartridges—Magnum, *73, 94, 146, 152, 153, 155, 162, 182-183, 209, 210, 254, 256-260, 276*
Winchester Cartridges—Rimfire, *61-64,* Chart *p. 63, 81, 90, 93*

Winchester, Oliver, *34, 37, 38, 40, 42, 43, 48, 49*
Winchester Repeating Arms Company, *48*
Winchester Rifles, *37, see also* Browning Rifles, Cimarron Arms Co., Navy Arms Co.
  -Lee 236 Naval, *128*
  Model 53 Lever Action, *112-113*
  Model 54 Bolt Action, *144, 147-149, 150, 154, 158, 171, 237*
  Model 55 Lever Action, *122*
  Model 61 Slide Action, *168*
  Model 69 Semiautomatic, *168*
  Model 64 Lever Action, *122*
  Model 65 Lever Action, *112-113*
  Model 70, *122, 144, 147-156, 158, 165, 178, 181, 246, 248*
    At a Glance, *155*
  Model 71, *96, 100, 128, 157-166, 212*
    At a Glance, *166*
  Model 88 Lever Action, *165*
  Model 670, *149*
  Model 1866 "Yellow Boy" (Lever Action), *46, 47-54, 91*
    At a Glance, *54*
  Model 1866 Commemorative, *47, 123*
  Model 1873, *47, 54, 85-94, 96, 110*
    At a Glance, *94*
  Model 1876, *96*
  Model 1885 Single-Shot, *54, 55-64, 76, 84, 254*
    At a Glance, *64*
  Model 1886 (Golden Jubilee Rifle), *55, 95-104, 106, 128, 139, 157-162*
    At a Glance, *104*
  Model 1892 (92), *96, 105-114*
    At a Glance, *114*
  Model 1894 (94) Lever Action, *48, 53, 58, 105, 115-124, 171, 203, 223, 225, 227*
    At a Glance, *124*
  Model 1895 Lever Action, *125-134*
    At a Glance, *133*
  Schuetzen Single Shot, *63*
  Semiautomatic, *78*

Winder, Colonel Charles B., *62*
Wundhammer (Louis) Springfield Sporter, *236-237*

Zollinger, Dean Custom Rifle, *249, 250*